Für meinen Bruder
vom Be.

Weihnachten 2001

THE BOOK OF LIFE

THE BOOK OF LIFE

One Man's Search for the Wisdom of Age

Andrew Jackson

VICTOR GOLLANCZ
LONDON

First published in Great Britain in 1999
by Victor Gollancz
An imprint of Orion Books Ltd
Wellington House, 125 Strand, London WC2R 0BB

A CIP catalogue record for this book is
available from the British Library.

ISBN 0 575 06686 5

Typeset by Rowland Phototypesetting Ltd,
Bury St Edmunds, Suffolk
Printed and bound in Great Britain by
Butler & Tanner Ltd, Frome, Somerset

For Vanella

I

New Beginnings

Maybe this all began with my grandfather. I loved listening to his stories and laughing at his silly words.

'Heh heee, young 'un,' he'd go, and waggle his glass. 'Fetch me another drop o' touch.'

And on the nod from my father I'd slip out to the kitchen and mix a weaker one, but not so weak that he'd notice. Gin and water was his tipple.

I can see him now – the worsted three-piece, glass in one hand, cigarette in the other. 'I could have danced all night . . .' Arms raised, he would guide his imaginary partner across the floor, giggling half at himself, half at the fun of it. He'd been on his own since Granny Jackson died.

When he was on form, he used to tell me I had some Talbot in me, from my mother's side. Her mother was a Talbot. So then I knew what was coming. 'Red hair and curly teeth,' he'd say, chuckling again. Well, I wouldn't call it red exactly and my teeth are straight enough, but that's how I shall ever be, 'Red hair and curly teeth.'

The kitchen at Cambrai was Spartan in those days and the hallway sombre: dark panelling, brown carpet and a cold Bakelite telephone – Skelmanthorpe 2114. The sitting-room, though, was a haven, with its sunny aspect and a glowing fire lit first thing each morning. And as the door swung open I'd smell that special blend of furniture polish with stale tobacco and I couldn't be anywhere else.

Grandpa sat to the right of the hearth, his armchair scarred by one or two cigarette burns from the times he'd fallen asleep. He shook his head and tutted about that, then he'd laugh and his pale blue eyes would twinkle.

'Heee . . . Now then, young 'un, what are you going to do when you grow up?' This was a favourite question.

'Ummm . . . I don't know.' I was never sure, and a little shy.

'What about you? Are you going to teach?' he'd say, turning to my brother Edward, who that week would be thinking of becoming the man who read the news on the television. At one time I thought I might like to be an actor, or direct plays. But Grandpa would always chime in, 'You've got to work in manufacturing. You must have summat to sell.' So my dad, the protective father and watchful son, would come to the rescue by saying there was plenty of time. Grandpa would snort and lower a quivering lip to the edge of his glass. Something between a sip and a mouthful he'd swallow, making a small noise in his throat like a reptile, before exhaling with pleasure – 'Aaaaah . . .'

Textiles were his business, and his great-great-grandfather's before him. We used to weave plush cloth for teddy bears, slipper linings, imitation fur coats. Grandpa took on the mill unexpectedly, after he came back from the war in 1918. His elder brother, Donald, hadn't come home. Killed by a sniper near Ypres, he was buried by his men where he fell. Afterwards, the body was never found and his name was chiselled on the list at Passchendaele of the thirty-five thousand with no known grave. At the age of twenty-two, Selwyn returned a hero to mourn his lost companion. There had been only fifteen months between them.

As boys they grew up at Woodlands, an austere Victorian edifice set in eleven acres of grazing land. The house stood tall and square on a levelled mound at the top of a curved drive lined with beech hedges. Their father, a man in a photograph who I imagined never smiled, had bought it from a Mr Box and lived there until he died in 1941. Fourteen years later I was born in my parents' bed, early one July morning. They moved in after the war, newlyweds.

So Grandpa and I shared the same haunts: the back roof of the stables where we couldn't be seen, or under the roots of the giant beech tree, which hung dangerously over the edge of the quarry at the end of the lawn. We would kick apples across the orchard floor and dance away from bloated wasps. Wet with snow, we'd sledge down the far bank and crash into the rhododendrons again and again. We both would sit on the apex of the gable end which overlooked the kitchen garden, as the swallows dipped by in summer. We ran the full length of the high brick wall, never touching a crack along its flagstoned top, then we lowered a foot to catch the top pin, hammered in to tie the creepers. Picking our way like mountaineers, we clambered down into the shrubbery to find the spiral stone steps, dank and green, which led us out to the silence of the wood and a choice of paths.

My favourite spot was always the copper beech down in the bottom field. If Edward was glueing Airfix models too fiddly for my tender patience, I'd wander off on my own. Over the circle of iron railings that kept the cattle away, I'd swing up to the lowest bough and climb. I could have done it blindfold, every move, as far as the highest branches. There I was safe, hugged close by firm dark limbs. And when I came down I'd nip out through the front gates and venture across the lane. I'd cut up Wappy Nick and in five minutes be at Cambrai, where I'd find Grandpa sitting by the fire.

'Now then, young 'un, what brings you here?' he'd say as he looked up from his doze, a silver strand or two pushed out of place. He was a handsome man still. He'd kept the good looks and short back and sides of his youth.

'I just thought I'd come and see you.'

'Does your mum know you're here?'

I shook my head.

'Well, let's see if we've got anything for you, shall we? Would you like some pop?'

Through to the wash-kitchen, I followed his careful step and ample trouser-folds. Under the stone slab in the pantry I chose my ginger beer, a thick brown bottle from a wooden crate, then watched him pour and the fizz subside.

It wasn't just the promise of ginger beer that drew me there, though its power shouldn't be underestimated. I can still sense my innocent curiosity, which had something to do with his age and his gentle way. There was a softness, a forgiving. I'm not sure I understood how old he was, though I knew he'd lived at least twice as long as my dad, which meant he knew more, he'd done more things. But Grandpa never appeared to get any older. I knew everyone grew old, but it took so long it seemed nothing should ever change. We would always be as we were.

Not much was said. I enjoyed the moments of silence when Grandpa looked to be thinking. Then he asked about my football or how I was getting on at school. He told me again about the time he fell over among the lettuces and couldn't get up. Three-quarters of an hour he was there before George, his gardener, heard him shouting. So we laughed and he was wiping a tear from his eye.

Then he lifted himself, stood and went to the mantelpiece, a rich mahogany surround where the clock ticked lazily. Reaching above the glass of coloured splints for the fire, he took down a block of wood from the top shelf.

'Do you know what this is?' he said.

I shook my head and he fingered the wood lightly before handing it to me.

'You'd better have it now. Take good care of it, mind.'

I held what was once some small part of Bapaume cathedral, in northern France, which had been destroyed in the fighting. It was a carved detail of twisting foliage, sawn from a burnt-out choir-stall. His spoil of war, he had gouged 'BAPAUME 11/3/17 H.S.J.' on the flat side, like a schoolboy on a desk. I now use it as a book-end.

Another afternoon I went home with the gold cigarette case Granny had given him. On the inside, her handwriting was engraved just as she'd written in the shop, 'Selwyn, from Marian'. And upstairs in a box I keep the letter inviting him to play football with Huddersfield Town. He passed them all on, in good time. Then he'd see me off from the back doorstep with a hand raised and some unspoken sadness hidden behind his smile.

He hardly ever talked about the war. He was awarded a Distinguished Service Order for his gallant deeds at the battle of Cambrai. The records state that, on the morning of 20 November 1917, the 2nd 5th battalion of the Duke of Wellington's Regiment encountered intense machine-gun and sniper fire near the village of Havrincourt. Their commanding officer was killed and serious casualties sustained. Those soldiers remaining had gone to ground, taking cover where they could. Three other officers had also died; disorder and low morale were setting in. So Captain Jackson assumed command. He walked out in the open through a hail of bullets, coming back time and again to rally the men and lead them through the wire to a successful attack. The next day, a number of companies had been isolated by enemy reinforcements, so he conducted a stray tank to where the fighting was fiercest. He climbed out and, under heavy fire, issued the appropriate orders. By the time darkness fell, an entire sector of new trenches had been captured.

Once I asked him if he had been afraid, when the bullets were flying around him.

'No,' he replied, 'I was either very brave or downright stupid . . . and I think it was the latter.'

Then my curiosity got the better of me.

'Did you ever kill anyone, Grandpa?'

He paused, then nodded silently.

'What happened?'

He drew breath.

'He was a German . . . about the same age as me.'

Reluctantly he mimed how he had forced the bayonet home. Then he pulled a face and said he didn't like to think of it.

It's his expression that stays with me: the disgust at what he'd done, but without any shadow of guilt or shame. Then he shook it off. He didn't want to see that again.

'It were either him or me,' he said, with a sigh.

So I suppose I'm lucky to be here. I've often wondered about that.

~

My mother takes great pride in everything she does. You should have seen the way she used to iron our shirts – socks too. For tea that day, she'd cooked lamb's liver and bacon, glistening in the pan. When we'd been served with equal dollops of mashed potato, there was just enough juice in the bottom of the meat dish for half a slice of dippy bread each. Afterwards Dad finished off with a sweetener, the other half spread with marmalade.

I remember a dark, blustery evening, the wind buffeting the trees outside. Instead of reaching for the *Yorkshire Post* and his second cup of tea, my father cleaned his glasses with the handkerchief he kept just for that purpose, then sat ready with his hands clasped. He had something to say.

'Now then, boys . . .' He hesitated, as he did when broaching any difficult subject and glanced across at my mother. She seemed anxious. 'There's something we have to discuss,' he said. 'It's about the mill.'

I was only twelve at the time, and puzzled. I couldn't imagine what might involve the two of us.

'The thing is . . . and you may not know yet . . . but when you've finished school and university, perhaps, do you think you'll want to go into the business?'

The assumption had always been that we could, if we so wished. I looked to Edward, who went first on such occasions. By then he was keen on anything to do with the environment.

'Why do you ask?' he said.

'You don't have to answer straight away,' Mum reassured us, with a caring smile. Then she glanced at my dad. We were too young for such decisions. 'Don't worry,' she said, 'you can think about it for as long as you like.'

So he explained. They'd had an offer and were considering selling the mill. Business was steady, but they'd invested capital in a new weaving shed and competition from cheaper knitted cloth was increasing. Grandpa was against the idea, refusing to give up his birthright. But his younger brother, Uncle Garth, could foresee trouble and he was in favour. My father held the deciding vote.

Edward said no, he wasn't bothered. So all eyes turned.

The mill was somewhere I had always taken for granted, mine to explore. I was drawn into its different worlds – the steamy dyehouse down by the dam, a dim dungeon of acrid smells where the work was heavy and wet; the finishing shed, light and airy, where the machines had huge revolving drums inlaid with teazles to brush up the pile; and the stock rooms stacked high with rolls of cloth, the atmosphere dry like biscuit. I would hide there among the racks or ride the trolleys as chariots. Among the men and women, I had my friends and co-conspirators. Sam Frankland was always pulling my leg and playing the clown. Then there was Jack Kenworthy, wrapping round his apron at the stock room table, keeping a watchful eye. And Grandpa's cousin, Cedric, who organized the yarn, would take me with him to show me what he was doing. They spoke a raw language I can still conjure up, rough, hewn like stone. Off limits only was the constant thunder, the clattering roar of the looms in the weaving sheds, where I went with my dad and he had to shout at the top of his voice to be heard. With a quick tilt of the head, the weavers would wink at me and smile.

So Dad was asking if I wanted to spend my working days there. Of course I still had no idea what I wanted to do, but I didn't need to consider for long. I think if I'd said yes, maybe they wouldn't have sold. But some instinct told me that life in a textile mill wasn't for me.

~

Some twenty-two years later, Monday morning, I closed the front door to the flat with a sense of dread.

Oh, God, here we go again, I thought. Showtime.

With a surge of power here and there, the Audi quattro could beat the early traffic with ease. I cut through the park, queued at the lights, then, picking the lanes that moved fastest, threaded my way down into Soho. The hi-fi was sounding crisp and punchy, doing justice to an old Talking Heads tape, jangling rhythms that helped me focus on the day ahead.

I had ignored my grandfather's advice. In my early twenties, I had found employment in a service industry – the advertising game – and for the intervening years I'd been persuading manufacturers how to sell their wares. I hadn't done too badly. My ambition was always to reach the board before I was thirty, and I made it by the age of twenty-eight. Then I jumped agency, to the most fashionable at the time.

The names of the three founders were artily scribed on frosted glass beside the door. A wall of Sony monitors in reception played the latest music videos and a bright young face wished me a cheery good morning. I always took the stairs, something about keeping fit.

On the first floor I bumped into Ian.

'Oh hi,' he said. 'Good one?'

'Yes, thanks. You?'

'Yeah, great.' He flicked his pen nervously against the file he carried. 'You know Jane's coming in. Can I show you what we've got?'

'Sure. In about an hour? I'll come down.'

'OK.'

Charlie was in already. He had a pitch on and looked like death. They'd been working all weekend.

'Have you cracked it?'

'Think so.'

While the kettle boiled, Charlie rehearsed their strategy. 'It's all about dramatizing slender product differences,' he explained with a zealous enthusiasm. 'But we'll do it using the kind of humour folk like this appreciate.' He held up a board covered with pictures cut from magazines, showing the variety of young types in his target audience. 'That's how you unify them. Make 'em laugh.'

'How will you brand it, though, Charlie?'

He grimaced. 'Depends on the creative idea in the end, doesn't it?'

I closed my door. Bloody phone-calls. As well as running a handful of accounts, I'd also accepted the grand title of Business Development Director. This meant wooing clients to come in for a credentials presentation, so one day they might invite us to pitch. My trick was to call early, otherwise I never got past their secretaries. I did forty minutes on automatic pilot, trying not to sound how my brain felt. I sweet-talked two marketing directors. Both said, 'Not today, thank you,' and the rest I left messages.

Paul put his head round the door. I hadn't seen him since Thursday when we dined out with Fiona, a prospective client.

'What did you think, then?' he said, his grin matching the width of his bow-tie.

'I thought we were great. But I'm not sure about the politics their end.'

'She's all mouth and no trousers.'

'You bloody kissed her goodnight.'

'Only on the cheek.'

'Still a kiss.'

'So did you.'

'Only 'cause you did.'

'She loves us, though, doesn't she?'

'Who knows, Paulo? Who knows?'

Then Jerry came in, all chirpy. 'Morning, chums. Seen Nige?'

He was due back from holiday and would soon be round to find out how things were going. Jerry clenched his jaw and did his imitation of Nigel lying on the beach, checking his watch.

I left them to it. Ian's media plans were fine. He said he'd get copies of the newspapers to spread on the table and I ran upstairs to review some new work. I found the creative team looking relaxed. They'd flown back in on Friday. Another account team had sold a script that began, 'Open on sun-drenched vineyard . . .' and at this time of year that meant shooting in South Africa. Meanwhile they'd come up with two scripts to sell ice-cream across Europe. One was brilliant – sexy, witty, chic; the other didn't put across the right product message. When I said as much, I was subtly mocked for being pedantic and in the end lost the argument to the god of creativity.

Outside, Cliff was hovering to show me some artwork and a tranny. On the light-box he pointed out how they'd changed the colour of the hayfield around the farmer and his tractor.

'Great. It works well. How much did that cost?'

'It's OK. We'll squeeze it in.'

'How much, Cliff?'

'Well, the last lot was about three grand.'

'Urrgh . . . We've got to come in under budget.'

Cliff grinned and told me not to worry.

Back in my office, Cindy and Phil were waiting to take me through a presentation about how to advertise a new kind of petrol. The trouble was that your car's engine performed better, but not in a way you'd really notice. So we kicked around some ideas about how to convey a benefit, then degenerated into discussing the client's foibles and his dress sense.

My phone rang – it was the client. I signalled for hush. He said they'd had a chance to discuss the latest work we'd presented, and while the ads satisfied their corporate objectives, the guys in Retail suddenly weren't sure. I reminded him that the objectives we'd agreed for the advertising were deliberately limited, but this seemed to have been forgotten. Then came the matter of the typeface on the press ads. The managing director had expressed grave concerns, which were now rumbling around the organization. It may be modern, but it looked like some kind of printing error. I did my best to fend off their complaints, then before I knew it he was wanting to brief a completely new approach.

'What?'

'That's what's been agreed here.'

'But the agency hasn't even been involved,' I said, digging in. 'Could we possibly talk through some of the issues first? We wouldn't want to throw out a whole campaign just like that. I'd welcome a proper debrief and a chance to respond.'

'I don't know where it'll get you, but sure. I can do four o'clock here.'

'I'm afraid the earliest I can make is first thing tomorrow.'

Down went the phone.

'Bastards!'

It was still only half past nine.

A little after seven-thirty, I climbed back into the quattro and fired the engine. The controls lit up sweetly and the tape-machine clicked back into Talking Heads. I pushed Eject and joined the queue of traffic. I was feeling wiped out.

The rest of the day had gone much as expected: more meetings, a dull hour discussing fee proposals, half an hour returning phone calls, a client lunch – starched white napkins, a bottle of fine wine and the inside story on the latest budget cut. Back by taxi, I sat through a pre-production meeting on two commercials costing nearly half a million pounds, a full thirty minutes being spent by a room of twelve people debating if the lead actor was old enough and whether he should wear purple or green. Then I did a credentials meeting with a man who owned a chicken factory and I smiled through our reel of commercials for the umpteenth time. Finally, up to the boardroom, I swiftly downed two glasses of champagne to celebrate the arrival of our latest account. The tribe was there in force: earnest young men with sharp haircuts, smart young ladies. They were having a great time, but I'd soon had enough. I slipped away and headed for the door.

Vanella was already home. We stood in the kitchen sharing a large bottle of Czech beer, still togged up in our expensive suits. She was running her own business, strategic planning and research.

'You look tired,' she said. 'How was your day?'

'Oh, nothing special. Onwards and upwards. What about you?'

'I don't know,' she sighed.

'What don't you know?'

'I don't know why we do all this.'

'I can give you a few reasons. The mortgage, the lifestyle . . .'

'You know what I mean.'

'I know, I know. I was thinking on the way back, I don't suppose anything I've done today will actually make a difference. And all that money. For what?'

'So people eat more chocolate.'

'The energy that gets expended, it's crazy.'

'I sometimes wonder if I shouldn't be doing something else.'

'Me too, but what?'

Vanella shook her head. 'It never lets up, does it? I'm just not sure. It doesn't feel right any more.'

The job did have its moments. I enjoyed the cut and thrust, and the camaraderie. But the older I got the more it seemed a shallow existence. I worried that reality, wherever it was going on, was probably going on without me. I was always forcing myself to be someone else, someone I was expected to be. And the trouble was I didn't like him very much.

'How did I ever end up like this?' I wondered. 'You know, it scares me how narrow-minded I've become. There's no time, no space in our lives. I mean, the last book I finished reading was over two months ago.'

'I'm not happy,' said Vanella, looking decidedly miserable.

'Come on, cheer up.' I put my arms around her.

'What are we going to do?'

'I don't know. I'm hungry.'

'I'm tired.'

'I don't fancy cooking. Shall we go up the road for a Japanese?'

Opposites attract, they say. Well, Vanella and I are diametrically opposed. Even our astrological signs are as far apart as they could be.

She swims, I run. She's impulsive, I'm considered. She paints, I take photos. She creates mess, I clear it up. I need things buttoned down, she wants more ideas. I can't dance, she can't sing. She can be outrageous, I can be quiet and withdrawn. When I'm pessimistic, she's the optimist. If I'm confident, she's full of self-doubt. And so it goes.

It seemed to work, somehow. I fell for her coltish vulnerability, and eyes which are the colour of seaweed. She fell for my walking boots, which she spied in the back of the quattro. We had met at work, become friends and then lovers. We'd been married a year and just when we should have been settling down to keep an eye on the pension plan, our conversations were sounding dangerous.

We lay there one Saturday morning, staring at the ceiling.

'So if you chuck it in, what would you do?' She's always questions, questions.

'I'm not sure. But I don't want to be doing this when I'm forty-odd and going grey. I want to be more in control, I want to do something worthwhile with my time. And I don't want to have to answer to anyone any more.'

'That means working for yourself. Doing what?'

'I don't know, I don't know . . . We could just go off and buy a cottage in the country.'

'That's not the answer. Anyway, how would we afford to live?'

I pulled a face and got up for a shower. We were going to have to think this through.

A week or so later, I found myself on a train. Four of us were on our way to see a client: me, Jerry, Paul and Charlie. We spent the journey having a good gossip, vying with each other through our stories. There was much hilarity and lively conversation. Then, as we alighted at Swindon, a perfectly ordinary-looking businessman approached. He was grey-haired, maybe sixty.

'Excuse me,' he said. 'I couldn't help overhearing. I'd like to give you my card.' This he pressed into Charlie's hand, then turned and disappeared into the crowd. We all gathered round to look.

Jerry made a dismissive tut and pulled away.

'Blimey!' gasped Charlie, as Paul expelled a high-pitched laugh.

Who he was doesn't matter. On the back he had written four bullet-points:

- WHAT INTELLIGENCE
- WHAT WIT
- WHAT VITALITY
- WHAT A WASTE

I make no claims about the first three. But as for the last, it rang so true. I finally knew I had to make a change.

~

Then Hilary died.

I'd met her a couple of times, but I didn't feel properly introduced until we called round one evening. Vanella's father opened the wine and I seem to remember everyone drank a little too much. It was all very confusing.

'I was born within the sound of Bow Bells,' Hilary told me. We'd been talking about Yorkshire and she'd gone, 'Eee by gum.'

'You don't sound like a cockney.'

'I'm not,' she said, laughing. 'I don't know what I am. English, I suppose.'

Her accent was refined, maybe even put on at times for effect. In fact, Hilary's mother came from Lancashire. I eventually worked out that her father had been in the Army and that she'd grown up in Malaya, Germany and Wales. She went away to boarding-school but didn't conform and was always being sent to another one.

Certain images keep coming back: big brown eyes, her toenails painted bright red.

'What do you think?' Hilary asked, as she caught me looking.

'The shoes?' I pretended. They were lurid green platforms.

Vanella came to help me out. 'Mum, you're so embarrassing. She used to pick me up at school wearing much worse than those. And do you remember your black and white drainpipes? You only did it to wind up those frumpy tweed ladies, didn't you?'

Hilary laughed again, her broad mouth splitting an attractive face in two.

'Fancy having a mother who's never cooked chips?' said Vanella.

'What, no chips?'

'Never baked a cake either,' Hilary said with some pride.

Nothing ordinary, ever. I heard how she'd sent her daughters on a school outing with *coq au vin* for lunch, the remains of the previous night's dinner-party, and a dog had stolen their chicken. And when Vanella's friends came round one time Hilary served dandelion leaves in the salad, picked fresh from the lawn.

They rocked against each other as they laughed, the pair of them, and I joined in as best I could. Hilary wore rings on her fingers and several also on her thumbs, I noticed.

The mood was quite different if ever we were alone together. I actually found her rather daunting. I was inclined to be serious, a little wary, and never gave much away. I've loosened up a bit since, but it used to be safer like that. So we were awkward, but mainly on my part. I didn't know what to say. There was never a time I was around when she wasn't ill, although you wouldn't have known because Hilary didn't give much away either. She never let on how bad it was.

We used go round to see her. She had her own business and kept on working, running the office from the front room as she lay on the sofa. One day, the hairstyle had changed, but there was always something new so I didn't say anything. Then, while Vanella was in the kitchen making tea, Hilary slipped off her wig.

'Never seen anyone bald before?' she said, noticing my reaction. Then she smiled.

'How are you feeling?' I asked.

'Oh, I'm all right.'

Hilary had fought breast cancer for more than ten years. She'd defied all the odds, they reckoned, but then they never really know. She protected everyone around her by simply carrying on being Hilary. I'm guessing now . . . we say 'larger than life'. In Hilary's case, it was because she faced off death every single day. Vanella says, in truth, Hilary used to get really frightened. She once found some pills hidden under the pillow and had to break her mother's fingers open to wrest them away. Then, of course, she worried whether she'd done the right thing. At times they were partners in crime, so alike they could have been sisters. They'd fight and scream. Or they gossiped and shared secrets and Vanella called her Pooh. The only medicine for Hilary was to keep living life to the full.

When she left home for the last time, Vanella had secretly packed her bag. Hilary thought she was only going in to see the consultant. A few days later, he came to say there was nothing else they could do. The words were well rehearsed.

'When people get to this stage, they can decide that the time has come. You should prepare yourself now, Hilary.' He was telling her to stop struggling.

'What do you think, girls?' Hilary said to her two daughters. 'Is it time? Shall I give in?'

'That's up to you, Mum.'

She took both their hands and squeezed. 'I've always been a fighter,' she said.

The vigils continued. We'd sleep in her room at the hospital and Hilary would wake in the night from the pain. Vanella would get up to soothe her, and as she held her hand and wiped her brow, she'd show her own fear. So Hilary would comfort her baby and say, 'Come on, now, don't worry. You need to get some sleep.'

When she slipped into coma it was only a matter of time. Knowing what was going to happen didn't make the moment any easier, holding a warm hand, kissing a warm forehead when the life had gone. Vanella said it hurt like the cut of a knife, the very sharpest pain. I'd already gone home, I had an early start. But I was called straight back, into a room that an hour ago had been subdued and peaceful. Someone had switched on the strip-lights, and Vanella, Colette and their father were standing around being brave. I was useless. I didn't know what to say.

At the funeral, the priest said he'd never seen so many people. She was the most generous person. We would have been good friends one day, I'm sure.

And for the next year or more, whenever Vanella's grief welled up and overflowed, all I could do was hold her and hug her close.

~

In my case, I was still coming to terms with a different kind of loss. I can see now how deceptive it all was, how we wanted and tried to carry on as usual. Of course, it happens all the time, but for me and my brother it was the ultimate surprise. One day, my parents announced that, after thirty years of marriage, they were going to separate. There hadn't even been an inkling.

It transpired that selling the mill had sparked a series of events. Grandpa had retired, disgruntled – all his hard work had come to nothing. Uncle Garth lasted five months before being asked to leave, Dad walked out after six. With no job, he worked all day in the garden. I used to watch him from an upstairs window, with his cloth cap on and that grubby old blue anorak done up against the cold. He'd dig and make good, talking to himself, trying to figure things out. Then he took Mum on holiday around the world and came home having decided to set up his own business, exporting to Australia. He threw his energy into starting afresh. They built a new house, and we left Woodlands. Dad went to Australia every year or so, and every other time took Mum along. I went to university, kicked around, found myself a job and everything trundled along much as usual . . . until that morning.

We'd been home for Christmas. Dad put his head round my bedroom door and asked me to come to the office, where he worked from home. It was a small, plain room with a gas fire and a picture window.

We all sat waiting, my dad behind his desk. He didn't know where to start and looked at my mother.

'I'm not saying anything,' she said. 'You're the one with the talking to do.'

It must have been the hardest thing he ever did.

'We've got a bit of a problem,' he said.

'What's that?'

'Your mum and I are going to split up . . . I don't know what we're going to do. I shall probably leave home. Not immediately, but in due course.'

I tried to catch up on what was happening and noticed Mum was looking desperate. I began to go numb.

'Why?' Edward asked bluntly.

'A number of reasons. It's complicated.' Dad looked at Mum again and she looked away, her eyes brimming with tears.

That was about all. Edward and I went to our rooms, without even speaking.

Five minutes later Dad came in. 'I've made a bugger of it, haven't I?' he said sheepishly. He smiled, but I couldn't smile back. He'd been playing around and had gone too far. 'Your mum found me out . . .'

'What are you going to do?'

'I don't know. We'll have to see.'

Totally incapable of dealing with what was going on, any of us, we then sat down around the kitchen table and had lunch. Mum had made soup.

Eventually he moved into a rented house a few miles away. Over the following weeks and months I'd visit and find he was living like me, learning to manage on his own. Sometimes I tried asking what went wrong, but he was never comfortable. He half told me what had happened, but he wouldn't or couldn't say why. I found that hard to understand. Why wasn't he prepared to do something to put things back together again? It couldn't have been that bad, surely. Life had been so normal. But I didn't realize they'd been protecting us, as the situation had become something neither of them was able to fix.

I missed him being around. Even years later it could catch me unawares, like the time my brother commissioned a painting for his birthday. Dad flew Beaufighters during his war, out in Burma. He loves flying and given half the chance he'd be telling us some tale about landing in the jungle. The painting was a replica of the machine he flew, up above the clouds with the rest of his squadron. The week before we were going to present it to him, I had it at the flat. Dad's old flying jacket always hung there on the coat-stand in the hall. Even though it was too small for me now, it was still in perfect condition. Suddenly the two things connected and I found myself in tears, sitting on the floor. And Vanella came to hug me and hold me tight.

My grandfather died on my birthday, in his eighty-ninth year. The receptionist called me out of a client meeting to the phone. It wasn't my father, strangely, but a business colleague of his who gave me the news. Dad had gone to Cambrai. Grandpa had been ailing, so it wasn't such a shock. In fact, I felt nothing, other than remote. I said I'd go home in a day or two and returned to the debate over some poster layouts.

'Everything OK?' someone said.

'Yes, don't worry. My grandfather's just died.'

I accepted their commiserations and carried on. I can't think how. I should have walked out into the street and cried to the sky.

The service was held at Skelmanthorpe Methodist Chapel. Dad

called by to pick us up and the four of us went together in a long black car. We travelled in silence. It was more awkward being a family than being at a funeral. Down through the village towards the mill, little had changed, except cars were parked now where there used to be only one or two. The old weavers stood waiting along the wall and took off their caps as we rolled past.

Later, back at Cambrai, everyone rallied. 'Bury 'em with ham,' he always used to say. And all the great-aunts, with their handbags and their powder-puffs, said, 'Come on, let's have a drink. Dear Senny. He wouldn't want us to stand around being glum, would he?'

But I couldn't help feeling sad. We'd lost him, the mischief in his laugh, his view on the world. I always wished we had him on tape, just for the sound of him. Then the older I got, the more I thought I'd like to talk to him still.

Once, when I mentioned to my father the time Grandpa killed a man, he said, 'Funny. He never told me that.'

And I wondered how many things there are which we never tell each other.

~

A journey became inevitable. Vanella and I both needed to walk away, to look for some answers. Then we'd come home to make a new beginning.

The defining moment came one Sunday evening as we stood at the corner of a ploughed field. We'd been visiting my brother in the country and were bracing ourselves to return through the traffic to London. The air was warm and still, the strongest stars beginning to show through in the twilight. We stopped to listen to an owl shrieking in the wood. Arms round each other, we went through it all one more time.

'We are going to do this, aren't we?'

'What have we got to lose?'

'Nothing. What do we have to gain?'

'Everything.'

'Except I still don't know what I want to do.'

'That doesn't matter. Wait till we get back. Where shall we go?'

'Everywhere.'

'We can't go everywhere.'

'OK, nearly everywhere.'

'And what will we do?'

'We'll have to think. We can't just travel. We'll go mad, skimming from place to place.'

'I want to learn.'

'Mmmm . . . Why don't we give it a purpose?'

Somehow things then started falling into place. The more we thought about it, the more it seemed right. We decided to go and talk to the oldest people in the world – the elders of the human race.

For a few more months we made plans. Then I resigned, Vanella closed her business and we let the flat. It felt scary, like jumping off a cliff. And yet it was the easiest thing we ever did.

My mother wasn't at all happy, but in her protective way. We might get hurt or killed. My father seemed surprised at first, then was curious, then supportive. He knew that if I had my mind set on something . . . By then he had remarried and was soon to emigrate to Australia. Vanella's father went silent. Perhaps I wasn't the son-in-law I'd seemed, after all. And our friends? I don't know, they could have felt betrayed or envious, or that we were just crazy bastards.

Packing our old life away in boxes turned into a military operation. I drew up lists, where everything went. There was so much of it – furniture, kitchenware, mountains of clothes, wedding presents we'd never unwrapped, books, records, files, old tennis rackets, all manner of junk. Everything had to be labelled, delicates and paintings protected in bubble-wrap; in went the two-foot-long African crocodile from the hall at Cambrai. We borrowed loft space and filled a lock-up garage to bursting. It all had to be stowed away, until we were left with only what we could carry.

My mother took a last photo as we said goodbye. Vanella and I are sitting on the wall outside her cottage, wearing our outdoor gear. It is a strange effect. Although we are in our thirties, we somehow look like children, pudgy-faced and innocent.

~

It seems such an auspicious beginning. As we pass through the ticket barrier, I can't help but laugh. It's the train. The red name-plate on the engine about to shunt us on our way, it says: *Planet*. I point and we grin as we make it our omen, and stagger on down the platform.

Vanella's cheeks are flushed and I can feel the sweat breaking out on my chest as I strain unused muscles. We're overloaded. Even with one of everything I could possibly need for two years, I'm in big trouble. I pray I won't get bumped by some harassed commuter, because over I'll go and there I'll stay, kicking like an upturned beetle.

Leaving *Planet* and England behind, we strike out across a flat, grey North Sea to Denmark; Esbjerg, which the following morning smells of fish and engine-oil. By the afternoon we are crossing Jutland, experiencing a strange mixture of emotions. We're on our way at last, but all our insecurities are bubbling under. There's no going back now. We have willingly cut ourselves adrift and my only certainty is that I have to start to look at life anew.

I gaze out at the red-brick houses with corrugated roofs, farms where manure would be a dirty word. The Danes have perfected the art of just so, I decide, and wonder what could ever happen here in this orderly land. Then I have a stretch and realize it's years since I felt so good. It seems I've already begun to shake out the dross of my previous existence. I feel like I did as a boy, eight years old, free-wheeling downhill with the wind in my face. No one can touch me now.

2

~

Travelling Light

Our accommodation is advertised as a chalet, but turns out to be a weatherboard shack in an empty campground surrounded by tower-blocks. We're living in some kind of dog kennel with imitation lace curtains I daren't touch, strung on wire between rusty eye-hooks. We have two gas rings, one light-bulb, and the floor is sticky underfoot. We sleep in our bags on a hard, draughty platform in the roof above. As I climb the ladder on the first night, Vanella shivers pointedly as she rummages around in search of warmth. 'What the hell are we doing here?' she groans.

If only our friends could see us now, is what I'm thinking. But I don't answer and simply grunt. We're here because it's cheap and we'll probably find a lot worse than this. Carefully I fold my sweatshirt for a pillow and adjust the torch strapped to my head like a miner's lamp. It isn't even nine o'clock. At least there's plenty of time to read in bed.

In the grey chill of morning, we spot our neighbours, two doors down at number eighteen – an Alsatian dog and a grossly overweight woman. Both know how to give a mean stare, so we keep ourselves to ourselves. The shower block gives me the creeps, but no hot water. Then over a cup of tea, I'm thumbing through a have-a-wonderful-time-in-Copenhagen magazine we picked up at the station and I see it describes the area as 'our very own switch-blade society'. We peer out at the tower-blocks and wonder if it isn't time to find new digs nearer the centre of town.

Vanella's pack amazes me. Normally she's all over the place, a total mess; but the prospect of not being able to find anything for two whole years has brought about a sudden transformation. Apart from her boots, polar fleece and jacket, everything has now been methodically filed. I'd come home one day with some sturdy colour-coded, see-through plastic bags with zips and she immediately commandeered the lot.

She has a hot-weather bag (two T-shirts, one dress, a sarong and a pair of shorts); the cold-weather bag (thermals, long sleeves, thick socks); an underwear bag; the medical bag (needles, pills, sun-block and more needles, just in case); her girlie bag (one lipstick, one eye-lining pencil, face cream and toothbrush); a things-to-make-and-do bag (her watercolours, a miniature magnetic Scrabble set, writing paper); then the essential odds-and-ends bag (a plug for all basins, the elastic washing-line and gaffer tape – someone said we should never be without gaffer tape). So all Vanella ever has to do is lob in seven plastic bags and sit on them to squeeze out the air. Then she folds her arms and taunts me, the tidy one, as I roll T-shirts, look for my comb and put everything back in its rightful place.

'Come on, Boot!'

That's a nickname. Actually, it's an abbreviation – Jackboot is the official version. An old friend used to send me letters, each addressed in turn: Dear Jackpot . . . My dear Jackdaw . . . Dearest Jackboot. Thank God she never tried Jackass.

It's funny how things stick. Looking back, it seems I had almost no control over what happened. Vanella and I had been going out for a year or more when we reached a watershed and both of us began to have doubts. It was make or break. We split up – on my initiative, but she says it was hers – then, after a few days of pain and contrary advice, we were back together again. She'd looked so hurt I could hardly bear it, so I found myself phoning to see how she was, and before I knew it I'd told her I loved her. That was a first. I'd always been a little wary with my affections, maybe because of Mum and Dad. Actually, I think that was the first time I ever said it to anyone. So how did I know? I said I loved her, when probably I would have been a lot more comfortable saying I was really very fond of her. But that wouldn't have been enough.

We were reunited, and resumed where we left off. But something had changed. I remember being more aware of her affection for me. There was a tenderness I hadn't seen before, which made me feel warm and secure. Then, some time later, I remember thinking I didn't want to be without her. It just felt right, the two of us, together. But I couldn't say anything – that might involve commitment.

Then came the night of the shepherd's pie contest. We both claimed to make the finest shepherd's pie in the world, so we invited everyone round and our pies were judged against various agreed criteria. Inevitably, what we each served up was completely different. Hers was enormous, made with beef and had sweetcorn and peanuts in it. Mine was perfect. No, I did cock up the potato, but I still won. Even now she maintains it was a fix. I scored better on 'Close to your idea of shepherd's pie'. And I got full marks for 'Creativity' by garnishing each plate with a plastic farmyard sheep.

By the time they'd all gone home it was well past two in the morning. I was lying on my back, on the floor, drunk. Miles Davis was blowing some enigmatic cool and the idea just popped into my head, a whim. Then it popped straight out of my mouth.

'Do you think we should get married?'

She was crashed on the sofa.

'No.'

'Did you hear what I just said?'

'Yes . . . No.' She sat up, looking uncertain then surprised and smiling, all in quick succession.

I crawled over.

'Please!' I was on my knees.

'Do you mean it?'

'Yes. Why not?'

'Oh, all right. Yes.'

She always says she knew. I may have been dour, difficult and undemonstrative, but something inside told her we were soul mates. And so, a year later, we said, 'I will,' in front of everyone who mattered. And there we were, together for the rest of our lives.

Of course, I wasn't to know that would mean twenty-four hours a day, as we are now. We keep joking about it and pulling scared faces. Because we have left behind many of the things that maybe used to keep us together. And I'm beginning to realize that everything, each move we make, has to be negotiated and agreed – what we do next, which way we turn.

We spend our days mostly out on the street. We walk miles, just looking. We don't *have* to do anything. It feels like we're playing truant, as though somehow we might get found out. But it's delicious. We can afford to admire Danish ingenuity in bicycle design: some upright with a leather seat like a hammock, some with boxes built out front for the kids, tandems, bespoke designs of all sorts. We note how the traffic-lights beep in a more continental way and we're surprised how no one jaywalks, ever.

In the end, though, we turn up more similarities than differences. Copenhagen has its own trendy area of cafés and bars, not unlike Soho. The shops we browse in sell the same familiar brands. The Tivoli Gardens appear to have been turned into a theme park. We take in the squares, the statues and a few old buildings, and we end up weary and restless. Most afternoons we retire to the cinema for a warm, taking comfort as the characters talk to us in our own language. Then we go foraging for food and sometimes treat ourselves to undeniably the most expensive lager in the world. By half past seven we have the night ahead and only ourselves for company. So we drift idly, eyeing the designer bars and candlelit restaurants with a twinge of jealousy, then agree to return to someone else's spare room and the security of our padlocked gear.

Then, one wet Saturday afternoon, we climb an echoey stone stairway with a faint whiff of carbolic in its lifeless air. A few floors up, we stand and check we're presentable. Vanella's looking nervous.

'What are we doing?' she says softly, then gives me a playful push.

I take a deep breath, knock boldly and we are greeted by the grumpiest maid ever to unbolt a front door. She comes complete with black dress and pinafore, but neither a smile nor a hello. Letting us into a cramped hallway, she watches as we struggle with our jackets. Then a voice calls out to the rescue, 'Come in. Come on in.' All we know is it belongs to a lawyer who is somehow associated with Russia.

The place looks like a museum. There are antiques everywhere. On the walls hang some exceptional paintings, and two gleaming samovars stand guard at either end of the dining-room. Hermod Lannung remains seated at the table. He greets us, in perfect English, and we settle ourselves on the far side of a white linen tablecloth.

I was worried he might be a bit too . . . well, decrepit, but he looks pretty good, considering he's the oldest person either of us has ever met. Very formal in a grey three-piece suit, he holds himself upright and sports a neat wave of silver hair, though the skin on the side of his neck is creased and leathery. I can't help thinking it reminds me of a tortoise.

We don't really know where to begin, but soon we're talking about Russia. Lannung first went there in 1917, when he was twenty-one.

He'd been given the job of protecting the rights of Austro-Hungarian prisoners of war. Denmark, being neutral, was looking after the diplomatic interests of the Habsburg Empire in Russia. He had worked in their embassy in what was then Petrograd.

'They were crucial times,' he tells us. 'Earlier that year the rule of the Tsars had ended and Kerensky was in power. Then Lenin returned from exile to Petrograd, with the help of the Germans. They wanted him to stir up trouble and tip the political balance in their favour.'

As he speaks, I'm reminded of my history lessons. When I used to imagine the turn of events leading up to the revolution, they seemed to have taken place in another time, another world altogether. But this feels different somehow. History is alive, here, talking to us. And the fact that we are soon about to venture into Russia doesn't rate as quite so intrepid after all.

'In those days,' says Lannung, 'it was a dream for everyone. They were free.'

Vanella is jotting notes in her lap, while pretending not to. She's gone quiet, letting me lead. She gets a little tongue-tied sometimes. Lannung rests his hands on the table and his head is up. He's away.

He says the October Revolution was a mild affair. Everything was at a standstill. There was war and famine, no fuel for the fire. People were ready for change. Kerensky couldn't make peace, because he had an obligation to the Allies to stand against the Germans. But Lenin proposed peace straight away. You couldn't have a Great War and revolution at the same time in a country like Russia. So it was an easy victory for the Communists.

'What they plucked that November was a ripe fruit,' Lannung says, then tilts his head to one side. 'Do you say pluck in English?'

'Pluck or pick.'

'Mmm . . . Well. It was a ripe fruit.'

Lannung taps his perfectly manicured fingers on the tablecloth, then fiddles absently with a small flat china dish. And I'm wondering what sort of treasure we've stumbled upon. I realize I covet his mind's eye. I do sometimes yearn to have lived at some other time, when life was simpler, less frantic, more elemental, perhaps. I wish I could see the streets of Petrograd as he does and sense the mood of the people. But then I'd probably be shocked by the poverty and injustice, or the precariousness of human existence. Maybe what we are doing is best, a more comfortable form of time travel.

I press Lannung and he tells how he used to negotiate with the Communist secret police for the release of foreign prisoners. He'd been transferred to the Danish Red Cross in Moscow.

'It was interesting work,' he says, nodding. 'I had to deal with Dzerzhinsky and Peters, the leaders of the Cheka. Do you know these names?'

We shake our heads and he assesses us.

'You ought to, yes. Dzerzhinsky, he was a very bad fellow. He was in charge of the Cheka. They were very brutal. These are things everybody should know. I beg your pardon for being impolite, but most Britishers would know this.'

I'm already feeling inadequate. I had forgotten all about the Cheka and, of course, I was once taught about Peters. I now remember it wasn't his real name. Then, Lannung takes us on a journey.

In November 1918 he was sent to Kiev to have talks about some prisoners of war. Still under German occupation, Kiev was of strategic importance, so the Communists gave him his own railway carriage for transport, together with two guards. When he crossed the front at Borísov, he thought he'd arrived in heaven. Suddenly they could get fried duck, even a bottle of wine. There was so little to eat in Russia.

With his business in Kiev concluded, he happened to discover an abundance of sugar there. They had none whatsoever in Moscow, so Lannung decided to buy a large quantity and take it back in his carriage. Everyone said he was completely mad.

'How much sugar?' I ask.

Lannung pulls at an ear lobe and grins. 'Oh, as much as you can get in a railway carriage. I don't know, it was rather a big wagon. There were several compartments. I had one for myself, one for my help. The rest were full of sugar.'

They headed back, but the going wasn't easy. Events and armies were converging, the dog-end of war and revolution. The Communists were coming to rout the Germans and the railroads were being broken up, so they had to make grand detours, often waiting for days at some remote station for an engine. Finally they reached the river that formed the frontier between the Ukraine and Russia.

Lannung recalls what greeted him with a faint smile. The night before, they had blown up the bridge.

'I am old now and afraid of everything,' he says, 'but then I was a young man and afraid of nothing. I asked the station master to bring our carriage to the river. Then we found eighteen peasant sledges. They went down over the frozen water and up the other side with the sugar.'

His eyes sparkle at the sight of it.

On the far bank, he was promptly arrested by Communist soldiers and very nearly shot, but his life was saved by a member of the Russian Red Cross. They then set off again in a freight wagon, the three men sleeping on top of the cargo. In Minsk they found food, but, while they were eating, their wagon left without them. Only by walking along the railroad all night in the freezing cold did they catch up with it. And so, eventually, they found their way back to Moscow.

'There,' says Lannung, 'the sugar was gold. We gave it to the Red Cross and the hospitals.'

Now that, I think, is giving your travel some purpose.

Lannung reaches up and presses a bell-push hanging from the ceiling. After a lengthy pause the housekeeper appears, looking as if she resents the interruption. He requests tea. She gives a gruff acknowledgement and stomps off to clatter noisily in the kitchen.

It isn't long before, unwittingly, he has me again. After Kiev, he came home to study for his law exams, but instead worked on an idea he had to bring together those who recently had fought each other in the trenches. In August 1921, a conference took place at the castle of Christiansborg, where young Germans, Austrians, French and British shared their experiences and views. Lannung received telegrams of congratulation from prime ministers all around Europe. It is the one achievement he's most proud of – and this, from a man who became leader of the Social Liberal Party, who represented Denmark at the Council of Europe and, for many years, at the United Nations.

As for my own youthful ambition, I may have eaten in all the best restaurants but I now can't help feeling it didn't get me very far. This old gentleman makes me want to jump up, go out into the world and do great things.

Lannung was soon back in Russia. He was invited to work for the High Commissioner of the League of Nations, Arctic explorer Fridtjof Nansen. He travelled to Samara, Sarátov and the corners of the old empire, inspecting Nansen field representatives.

He slips a hand into his jacket pocket to feel the chemicals they were told to leave in their overcoats to keep away the lice. Then he touches his shirt.

'. . . Yes, and if you had silk shirts, then these barbarian lice, they didn't like it. It was an idea, I don't know.'

He's still chuckling when the maid comes to serve the tea. She lays the delicate yellow china as if she's in a dockers' caff. Pencils land on the floor. Down come more plates and then an exquisite teapot, with a thud. Lannung speaks tersely to her in Danish and she retreats, grumbling. For all her social skills, she does make extremely fine biscuits, and as we munch we hear his Lenin story.

When Lenin died in January 1924, his body was returned to Moscow. Lannung was waiting at the station, now a high-ranking Nansen official.

'I was there with Stalin and all those other bad fellows behind the coffin,' he recalls. 'When we came out it was very, very cold. The procession moved through the frozen, snow-clad streets to the Trade Union house. There were soldiers on guard, of course. I should never have been allowed in, but I was a young foreigner wearing a good Western fur coat. I got my chance and they allowed me to go to where Lenin was lying in state. His wife and sister were preparing him and they placed his hands more or less like this.'

Lannung pats his chest, hands crossed, elbows bent, to show us the Orthodox way.

'I said to myself, "That can't be done. That is so anti-Communistic. It will be interesting to see the pictures tomorrow."'

In the press, there were no hands. So, one time, in Moscow, when he was president of the Danish organization for co-operation with the Soviet Union, Lannung had been visiting the museum. He asked to see the very first pictures of Lenin after his death.

'They showed me, and I was right,' he says. 'It's only a funny little thing, but it's nice because everyone said I was wrong.'

I receive his stolen glimpse like a gift. To him it's just another story, but I feel one step removed from something precious.

Vanella is admiring his antiques.

'I have collected things my whole life,' he says. 'These all have their own history, a special story in every case. When you are an old fellow, everything has a story.'

Looking around the room, I point to the samovars. One in particular is a monster.

'That one,' he says, 'I bought that from Countess Alexandra Tolstoy, the daughter of Leo Tolstoy. It came from his estate at Yásnaya Polyána. When Russians see it, they have tears in their eyes.'

I make a mental note to touch the three feet of polished brass as we leave, for luck. It's not every day I find myself in the company of the kettle that made the tea that helped sustain the writing of *War and Peace*.

The silverware is stunning, mostly Russian, much of it sixteenth century. Dozens of goblets stand in rows, large ones for wine, smaller ones for slugs of vodka. The paintings he acquired in the 1920s.

'One third of my pictures are already in a museum. All the silver and the rest of the paintings will go there when I am dead. Some are very important.'

'You have many beautiful things,' Vanella says.

'Ah, well well well,' he mumbles.

'But you can't take them with you when you go,' I say, then regret it immediately.

'When I am sitting in hell and looking on, at least I will know where they are,' he says.

'In hell? Or in heaven?'

'Oh, in hell. Not in heaven, with all those angels singing all the time. Not good. Too noisy.' And he laughs more than he has all afternoon. 'I am an old fool now,' he says. 'Very soon I will be lying in the Western Churchyard. I would like to continue, because life is always interesting. Until a few years ago I was very active, but now my legs are bad. I still work morning to night for several causes. I have been working hard for a global security system. Do you know the CSCE?'

We don't, but we ought to: the Conference of Security and Co-operation in Europe.

And then I wonder if time travels more quickly for him now.

Lannung gives a little grunt and nods. 'If you are as old as I am, time goes . . . oh, a year is a very short time. But I never get tired. That's only when I am dead. My legs have never been so bad as they are today.'

He had tried to have them build a lift up to the third floor, so he could at least get out. He'd even offered to contribute to the cost, but it was physically impossible.

'It can't be done,' he says. 'Anyhow I have all my things here, so I couldn't dream of moving.'

Only then do I see him, a bird with broken wings.

As we stumble out into a heavy drizzle, the failing light reminds me of hot cups of tea and football results on the radio. We find a café nearby where we can collect our thoughts.

'What will you be like when you're that age?' Vanella asks, toying with the froth on her coffee.

'Same grumpy old fart, I imagine. What about you?'

I see her as mildly eccentric, busy, wearing thick woolly socks loose and rumpled at the ankles – a granny her granddaughters love to visit because there's always some new scheme. She'll be painting vases or up a ladder somewhere.

'I don't really expect to live that long,' she says morosely.

'What do you mean? You can't go around thinking like that.'

'Oh, I don't know . . .'

She slurps some more chocolate topping. It's her mum. She could have the genes.

'Come on, you don't know that.'

'Well, I've a pretty good chance, haven't I?'

'Not necessarily.'

'It's either that or my stomach.'

In fact, it isn't her stomach, it's her small intestine – the part where food gets digested. As a baby, Vanella suffered from a condition called intussusception, which causes an obstruction. She had to have a section of her small bowel removed; the priest was called to baptize her before they operated. The scar tissue around the area still gives her problems and she gets obstructed sometimes. It's really painful. Once or twice she's needed to go back into hospital. They have to pump her stomach and wait for everything to clear. But by experimenting, we've found that I can often work the problem away with a little careful massage.

'It just worries me, you know,' she says.

I take her hand and give her a smile of encouragement.

'Don't worry. You'll be all right.'

We decide to cross over to Helsingborg. I have our route planned out, but nothing is too fixed. I like the way we can pick up and move. If things don't work, we can simply walk on and leave it all behind.

We journey to the small town of Bålsta, an 'S' train ride out of Stockholm to the end of the line, and then a bus beyond. From a distance, it looks like the scale model they made before they built the real thing. Situated beside a lake and surrounded by tall pine trees, Bålsta is a town planner's fantasy: a modern creation with the supermarket as its centre of gravity. As we step off the bus, a bitter wind cuts through us and I have a sudden sense of being a long way far to the north.

Bo's house is only a short walk away. His seventy square metres, he calls it, a small unit in a drab housing estate. He used to live in a beautiful half-timbered house on the south coast, but the family thought it best he move nearby so one day they loaded up his things. All Bo had to do was walk out with the papers he was working on at the time.

We are sitting, each with a stack of books on our knees. Bo has shuffled off to find yet another title.

I glance across at Vanella. The look she gives me says, 'What's going on?' So I shrug and smile. I have no idea either.

Bookshelves line every wall. Apart from small spaces reserved for family portraits, a painting or a crucifix, the place seems entirely devoted to books. I leaf through something called *The Mirror Mind*, where the pages are alive with underlinings. 'Be attentive' has been scribbled in the margin of page 106.

Bo is back, showing me a typed document: *On the overcoming of Disunity between People* . . . 'You might like to read this,' he says. 'Please take it with you.'

I hesitate. He seems to want to give us these books and we already have plenty to keep us busy. Bo hands me the paper and moves across to his chair. Slowly he sits down.

There appears to be little remarkable about him. He is a frail old man. He wears grey trousers and black shoes, a plain blue shirt with a thick navy sweater that zips at the collar. His furniture is utilitarian, upright armchairs with rectangular seat cushions. But Bo seems to know more about what we are doing than we do.

The document he's given me is something he penned himself. It remains unfinished, a section on quality of life marked in the list of contents 'To be written'.

'You will get it better from me when I have written it,' he says meaningfully.

He speaks ever so slowly, halting between words and taking time to clear his throat.

'I am writing my experience of life, as you are also going to write,' he says, with a look in my direction. 'As I grow older, so I understand more and more what really happened. It becomes clearer and clearer.'

He is telling us, I presume, about his attainment of that advanced state – the wisdom of hindsight.

Then he's up on his feet again, concerned we should eat after our long journey. Leading me to the fridge, he starts pulling out frost-coated packets, even though I plead that we really aren't hungry. I spot a carton of yoghurt with a picture on the label of a sufficiently wrinkly but equally healthy-looking old man, wearing a Cossack hat.

'Is this the secret of your longevity?' I ask, smartly, pulling the tub from its shelf.

'What is that?' He turns to look at me through thick-rimmed glasses, which sit heavy on a learned face.

'Yoghurt. Isn't that how they live for ever in the southern parts of Russia?'

Bo's brilliant blue eyes sparkle with humour. 'No, I don't think so,' he replies, his voice husky and accented. We are close. I can feel the presence of his age and I see he has some difficulty now shaving his neck.

He puts a hand on my arm as I coax him away and we sit down again. There is a moment of silence which, as it lengthens, becomes increasingly uncomfortable. I'm about to speak, but Vanella cracks first. She almost blurts it out. 'Could we talk a little about your work?' she says.

We're behaving like detectives, looking for clues. We have to see the full picture before its meaning can be considered. Problem, solution – years of training.

Bo raises his eyes. 'You must slow down,' he says softly. 'You are speaking too fast. I can understand you well enough, but it is important that we talk more slowly.'

I'm beginning to think we'll never get anywhere, but this turns out to be a small revelation. Bo makes us change pace. Suddenly, there is time – for him to think, and for us to listen and reflect. He seems to use time almost like a power supply. He'll pause to consider some remark; the pause might drag on into minutes; he responds, 'Yes . . . and no,' then pauses again before giving a lucid answer, which fully justifies his ambiguity.

Searching out a piece of paper, he shows us a map of his life with his age span drawn across the page, calibrated like a ruler. Above are the posts he held managing sugar refineries; below, boxed titles read: 'Research and Explorations', 'Industrial Level' and 'Spiritual Level'. In later years, Bo recognized that his life wasn't sufficiently enriching, in a spiritual sense. So he decided to do something about it.

'My life is a development line,' he explains, 'first on a material level, then gradually more spiritual until, now, that way is all. As an engineer, my interest in things that are exact was able to be developed. But I found out that most things I worked on had no value in the long run. When I got older, I found that much was on the scrap pile.'

I think I know what he means. Most things I ever worked on were so transitory they hit the scrap pile after a couple of months. And my life was conducted in a conspicuously material fashion, all those things we packed away, once prized for being new and shiny. As for the spiritual, that was something I'd conveniently pigeon-holed, so I could deal with it later. I always had trouble being convinced I believed in God. Dad used to take us to church and I'd be more interested in the colours of the sunlight piercing the stained-glass windows than in some tedious sermon. In divinity lessons I learnt the Bible stories, but when I asked if prayers really worked, I didn't find 'Sometimes' a particularly satisfactory answer. As a teenager, away at school, anything I was made to do was immediately rejected out of hand. So I had no faith, nothing to be confirmed. Jesus may have talked some sense, but a bloke with a long beard somewhere in the clouds moving the pieces about?

One of my school reports once said: 'He is thoughtful, in that he thinks a lot.' I remember going through a phase of moping around with a furrowed brow, hands deep in my pockets. My housemaster even called me in one day to boom at me, 'Come on, Andrew, what *do* you think about all the time?' If I knew, I wasn't going to tell him. Apart from some anguished grappling with my own identity, I was often just wondering what life was supposed to mean. Why me? Here. What's it all for? Eventually I decided it couldn't be put down to mere chance. Time and space were far too big for that. And then, later on, as I began to enjoy walking, climbing hills, on my own, I experienced something – call it . . . the awesome power of Nature. A gentle majesty. I got as far as describing it as a life force, then put it in a box marked 'belief', so I could say when necessary, 'Yes, I believe in something, I'm not sure what, some kind of life force.'

Bo runs a finger across the page as he peers down at his own life laid out before him on the table.

'Listening to what I am saying,' he says, 'it would seem as if there were only two lines, material and spiritual. But, of course, there are many ways to the ancient road.'

He smiles and watches us both. I feel he's leading us to something.

He begins to talk about his family. His grandfather died young, so his father had been educated by Bo's grandmother. She was of the old Lutheran type. In those days, everyone went to church and they found a serenity in their religion.

'They respected Matthew's fifth chapter very much,' says Bo. 'The Sermon on the Mount. The Beatitudes . . .'

'Yes. "Blessed are the pure in heart . . ."'

'As rules they are very strict. One by one they are very clear, but they overlap. When you steal from your neighbour, you break more than one. You can't have eight or nine rules in your mind all the time. Christ was himself tested, if you remember, by the Pharisee who asked which was the most important. He gave the answer: to love God and your neighbour as yourself. But even there, one can object and say, "How shall I play these rules in any situation, day and night?"'

'Mmmm . . .' Vanella is keeping close to his logic.

'So find something that includes this, but is simpler,' Bo continues. 'That can easily be done. Two words have been an enormous help to me. One is "honesty" . . . You are either honest or you are not honest. You are nothing between. Then instead of "love" you can take the word "harmony". We have been quarrelling too much about love – what it is, how much it should include or not. Shall I love now and then, or when? It is difficult, but the word "harmony" doesn't raise such difficulties.'

I blow a little air through my nose in surprise, at the sheer neatness of it. Honesty and harmony.

Bo sees my smile. 'Well, I'm going to write some more about this and I'll clear it up. But I have a job, I'm very busy.'

For Bo, the most important thing in life is to work and work and work. Not for the sake of sweat, just for the pleasure of it.

'Sleep, eat and work,' he says, 'and by sleep, I mean stillness, meditation and prayer – all three are one.'

Through his bedroom door I can see a reclining contraption rather like a dentist's chair, where he practises his meditation. St John of the Cross was his teacher. It is said that the Spanish Carmelite friar often slept for only two hours and spent the rest of his nights in rapt contemplation.

Bo is scanning the shelves again. The titles range from Christian to Buddhist and Hindu. So I ask about his religion.

'Originally I was a Lutheran,' he says. 'And I am still a Lutheran but, in truth, I am ecumenical. In Greek, this means "of the whole world". Oh, yes. I am a researcher, full-blooded.'

'You research all forms of religion?'

'I leave nothing behind.'

He pauses. It is growing dark outside. Vanella looks thoughtful. Bo is gazing into space.

'Would you like some tea?' he asks.

We help him prepare Earl Grey in a fine old teapot and lay out apples, cheese and biscuits. Bo crunches his apple, licking his lips and swallowing each mouthful carefully before continuing.

He explains how he observed that creativity and change were constant in the secular world. Man's material advancement has been rapid and extensive, whereas our spiritual progress over the millennia has been painfully slow. So he wondered what might happen if the same principles of experimental research were applied to the spiritual. Like any experiment, for it to be valid there had to be practical results. And, of course, he himself was the guinea-pig.

He strives to make progress every single day. He rises at five and reads, anything that might help: copies of the Pope's latest speeches, *The Ecumenical Review*, books such as *The Big Bang Never Happened*, *The Special Nature of Women*, *The Inner Eye of Love*. Everything is put to the test. His desk is buried beneath scattered papers; four grey filing cabinets are bursting with rarefied stuff. Some books he hasn't time to read. He begins with the first chapter, skips to the last so he has the gist of the argument, then trawls the index for anything worthwhile. If he comes across an important work, one that adds vital data, he reads it twice, diligently.

'I am curious,' he says, 'interested in everything that is creative and positive. I am looking for new ideas and I have changed many, many times. I have no patience with theoretical speculation. You can keep on for as long as you like, but don't try to waste my time.'

'What about all these books? Aren't they full of theories?'

'Yes. You cannot imagine how much I discard.'

'What practical proof do you have?'

'The proof is really very simple. I am back to the word "harmony", creative harmony. I put things to the test, but in a practical way. If it develops me, if it gives me a higher position in the art of living, then I keep on. When it does not, I try to redefine it so it can take me further. The simple idea is to be, always, a leading model in your living. Try every theory that improves you. My life is made up of a set of practices which are developing me in the right direction and nothing else. The rest . . . off, I haven't time.'

'So even today you are still developing?'

'Yes, steadily, steadily, steadily. I have Christ as an ideal.'

Bo has no doubt – plenty of questions, yes, looking to be answered, but he possesses such a serene confidence. He firmly believes that God is in charge of whatever it is we are all doing here and that He works through us, if we are disposed to let Him. He wants us to learn, all our lives. Bo believes in the power of healing, and in life after death.

'Oh, I never die,' he says. 'Nor do you.' And he looks me straight in the eyes.

Bo hugs us both tight on the doorstep. He slaps my back so hard it hurts. He has taken me completely by surprise. I wasn't expecting, this wintry afternoon, to be handed some kind of template for life itself.

Next morning, we call to see him again before we catch our bus. Bo seems overjoyed and holds both hands outstretched.

'We are very fine today,' he says emphatically. We are old friends now.

His room looks more cluttered by day. The files and papers stacked on the floor catch the light slanting low through the window. We resume our seats and Bo again offers us one or two books. Then he hands me another document.

'Last night I was thinking . . . You might like to read this. I belong to the Travellers' Club, in Malmö.'

He has been a member for forty-eight years. It's a copy of the letter he sent on the fiftieth anniversary of the club's foundation, addressed to the chairman, his old friend Sune. Bo writes:

> In old age it becomes more and more difficult to undertake voyages of discovery into unknown parts of the world. It is therefore desirable to open up and find new possibilities. If inner and spiritual worlds exist . . . then the demand for physical mobility is eliminated. Instead, spiritual courage and persistence are required to venture on voyages of discovery into inner worlds, with adventures and difficulties of a different kind.

He offers no actual proof that this spiritual world exists for would-be travellers. But he cites the experience, over the millennia, of seekers, both learned and unlearned, of prophets, saints and martyrs. They provide a weighty foundation for a hypothesis that a creative force exists. They are the living proof, but are valid only for themselves, one by one.

Bo laughs as he remembers his companions from the old travelling days. 'Our most important rule was to spread the joy,' he recalls. 'No traveller was allowed to be a pleasure killer. If so, then we killed him!'

He sits patiently for me by the window as I take his photograph. Vanella is leafing through yet more pages.

'My natural self is sometimes smiling,' he says softly, 'but not always. I am a rather serious man. Sometimes I am trying to think.'

'Thinking of what?'

'Whatever I have the inclination to. Flexibility. Just trying to penetrate some darkness.'

'Where is this darkness?'

'In here.' Bo taps the side of his head and we laugh.

'Can I come close to you now?' I want his face to fill the frame.

'Mmm. *Ja*.' I am inadvertently on my knees in front of him. His voice is quieter still.

'You know, whatever you have started with your travels, you will end up as ecumenics. You will have seen so much, understood so much and discovered knowledge which has been hidden. And you will pick it up and see if there is a way it can take you.'

He pauses. I am waiting.

'And then that moment when the stars come out, remember you are not alone. There is always somebody watching you, sometimes with lights . . .'

3

The Struggle

I experience an involuntary tightening of the gut as we pass the barbed wire. An observation tower stands threatening and two parallel high-security fences curl up over the hill. Vanella turns to me and I nod to show I've seen. We're in, and it's silly but it feels like we're entering the unknown.

The morning sun cuts shafts through the forest, where the trees grow straight and evenly spaced. A hundred yards from the track, we spy a weatherboard house painted sky blue. It looks Russian, suddenly, no longer Scandinavian. For a moment, it becomes our focus through the pines as those closest flick by with the speed of the train, while near the house they merely slip away. We see the bent figure of a woman in an apron, feeding her geese. I guess she must be old, but she's wearing a headscarf and doesn't look up to watch as the train goes by.

Next day we're out on the streets of St Petersburg. Through the rain, we can see in the strained faces that their struggle has been for ever. A tramcar is so full that all light has been squeezed from the inside. It makes a gallery of glum expressions framed in dirty windows. The roads are pitted with potholes, pavements cracked, awash with water. Once grand buildings suffer the same helpless decay. Grey is the prevailing colour – only a broken umbrella in flowery blue or a vivid splash of baby-doll lipstick stands out among the crowds. For those who bother to glance up, our outdoor gear makes us look as alien as we feel. Our walking boots hold their fascination for ages: they're so unattainable, from the planet West.

But the people are free and the free-market economy is in full swing. Everyone can sell, if only someone will buy. We pass a man displaying just four bottles of the local beer, a woman with only a few cigarettes.

Another hopeful has three pathetic cans of fish arranged on her fruit box. Spotting our boots from afar, young men are suddenly walking with us and Vanella's grip on my arm tightens. They do a sideways 'Pliz, change money?' then disappear into the throng as quickly as they come. Sometimes it's a plastic bag containing an Army belt, medals or a captain's hat.

'Military watches, caviare, Gorby doll?'

We decline with smiles. The more desperate plead, 'Pliz, we just want your money.'

We advance on Moscow, where we've been booked into the Hotel Rossia, at a fixed price and with no other option. The Rossia is supposedly the biggest hotel in the world, with some six thousand beds. A massive square block, it covers the area where a second Kremlin used to stand, before they demolished it for this monstrosity.

The taxi man dumps us at what looks like the main door and we hitch up our packs, only to find a heavy-looking gentleman barring the way. We try explaining but he shows us back outside. His English is none too good, though better than our Russian. It seems we're at the wrong door. We have to go to Reception. We plod around the exterior of the hotel for ten minutes, then ask. People point and we dutifully follow, but no Reception. We return to our friend the heavy, working up a sweat from the exercise. This time he takes us upstairs to a desk guarded by two stern women who reply in unison, 'You must go to Reception.' It's definitely outside somewhere. Another ten minutes and we find a small doorway that looks like a back entrance to nothing. We enter a huge blank room with glass-fronted counters down either side. We enquire at a window and the man says we have to go to Reception. We can't take much more of this. Then he points to where two men are standing in line. On a scrap of paper stuck to the glass we see, scrawled in biro, the magic word.

Inside, the Rossia is a warren, a bizarre underworld populated by shady businessmen, hookers, traders and anonymous men in grey suits. On every one of a thousand corridors sits a concierge beside a steaming samovar. When at last we locate ours, she tries a discreet 'Pliz, you can change money,' then shows us to our room. For something costing serious dollars, it is a shabby affair, skilfully decorated to avoid all possible taste but with impressive views of the city. The wallpaper peels in the corners and the telephone is a lurid green, fresh from a sixties spy movie. Once we are settled in, we discover we share our new home with a mouse, who pops out to inspect us at quiet moments.

It takes an extensive recce for me to establish that at all four corners of the building, on every floor, there is a buffet bar. They sell a limited selection of food, but each appears to buy in different stock: number twenty-three might be big in smoked fish, while thirty-seven could be the bread king. We queue for ages to put together some semblance of breakfast, often hopping between bars up and down the back stairs to get the pick of what's on offer. So does the rest of Moscow, it seems. One morning our local bar on the eighth floor is especially busy, full of burly men with greasy hair, dandruff and the most astonishing halitosis. A trolley-load of roast chickens rolls in, they each buy as many as they can carry and scuttle away unseen.

In the middle of the night, the phone rings and I haul myself from sleep to hear someone babbling at me in Russian. Vanella groans and asks who it is. I quickly lose patience and hang up. Then the next night the same thing happens, and the next . . .

The strain begins to tell.

One afternoon, we are resting in the room. I'm reading my John Updike and Vanella is writing a letter. Her first question seems casual enough.

'How much do we have in the bank?'

'Um . . . I don't know.'

Like most aspects of the expedition, I have assumed control of the finances. I can't help it, I have to do things my own way. But something strange has happened. The eye for detail I used to employ in business appears to have forsaken me entirely.

'Will the rent have come in yet?' she asks.

'Probably.'

'But how much longer are we going to be here? It's costing us a fortune.'

'That depends.'

'We're going to end up broke, you know. They'll be charging us interest and you don't even seem to care. I thought you had everything under control.'

I'm caught off guard. We don't often argue, but when we do things can get out of hand. I always get defensive, so then she comes back at me. Sometimes I just walk away, not wanting to fight. That really annoys her.

'I have got it under control,' I claim.

'You haven't,' she shouts. 'God, you're frustrating. You want to do everything, keep it all to yourself, but then you don't bother.'

So I shout back, 'Well, maybe it would be a damned sight better if you handled the money yourself . . .' And at that moment the phone rings.

'Hello,' I say curtly.

All I hear is an admonishing whistle. So I whistle back. Someone out there is listening to us. But who?

Later we ask a fellow Englishman who works in Moscow what's happened to the KGB, now that Soviet ways are a thing of the past.

'Still up to the same old tricks, I should think,' he replies. And I begin to wonder who is keeping our mouse in cheese.

We are escorted to Spartak headquarters by Masha, our interpreter, an attractive young woman with a sophisticated taste for things Western.

'I think we will learn something about old times from Mr Starostin,' Masha says ominously, as we pass through the front gates. Nikolai Starostin is chairman of Spartak Moscow football club.

We wait in his freezing cold office, a very brown place. Only the carpet isn't brown and that is grey. Team charts, flags and photographs cover the walls and a collection of ancient electrical equipment – the unplugged radiator, a fan and a red telephone – suggests that little has changed around here for about forty years. On the desk a plastic hedgehog looks mournful, speared by cheap biros.

The boss arrives, smartly turned out in matching grey and brown. I can hardly believe he's ninety, he looks so fit. He carries himself with the air of a man on a busy schedule. As he pulls off stiff leather gloves and a heavy overcoat, there is little doubt about who's in charge. A flurry of activity surrounded his coming and my ear can decipher a great deal of 'Yes, boss. No, boss.' A man in a black leather jacket, perhaps the team coach, takes orders, pretending to be more in control than he really is. Finally the door is closed.

Mr Starostin seems a serious man. A ruddy nose and a pair of bushy eyebrows complement his steely blue eyes. We are both across the other side of the desk, but he looks at me rather than Vanella. He draws breath. I'm half expecting a history of the club, but it's a different kind of story he tells.

They were once four brothers: Nikolai, Alexander, Andrew and young Peter. All played football for Spartak Moscow and all represented the USSR national team. Nikolai was captain of the USSR, 1928–34, then Alexander, then Andrew, 1939–42. The boys did well. Spartak won the Cup of the Union in '36, '38 and '39.

In 1937, a special match was organized in honour of Stalin and played in Red Square: Spartak versus Moscow Dynamo, the great rivals. Dynamo and Spartak were sports societies with different teams in cities around the Soviet Union. After the game, a reception was held where Nikolai met Stalin.

So the hand I've just shaken once shook hands with Josef Stalin. I ask Starostin what his impression was and he narrows his eyes. He sees me probing.

'You can't say bad things about those who've died. Either you say good or you say nothing at all,' he warns, but then continues. 'In fact I was amazed, because Stalin looked nothing like his public portraits. He had red hair. His face was very pale and badly scarred with pock-marks.' Starostin allows himself a stony laugh and I catch the glint from a gold tooth. 'He didn't look like a great man to me,' he says.

A week later the players received their medals and to everyone's surprise, even Nikolai's, he was awarded the highest Lenin medal given to any sportsman. He didn't know why he'd been singled out. The captain of the Dynamo team took home a lesser medal, the Red Flag. And so the needle between the two clubs grew worse.

Nikolai clenches his hands together and the sound of the Russian tongue, familiar but impenetrable, lends atmosphere to his tale.

The next year, Spartak won the Cup of the Union. They beat Tbilisi Dynamo, 1–0, in the semi-finals. Then they defeated Leningrad in the final. A week later, when the celebrations had died down, the Dynamo organization protested that the winning goal in the semi-final should have been disallowed. The issue was whether the goalkeeper had carried the ball over the line.

Stalin, of course, came from Georgia, of which Tbilisi is the capital. So did his evil henchman, Lavrenti Beria, head of the secret police. Starostin first encountered Beria in a football match back in 1922, when Spartak played away against Tbilisi Dynamo. Starostin used to wear the number seven shirt; Beria played at left back, and so marked him. I expect Nikolai ran one too many rings around the Georgian that afternoon.

By 1938, Beria had become a powerful figure in Dynamo's central organization. He joined in the dispute, supporting the claims of his team. He told Stalin that the referee had been wrong and that Tbilisi had been robbed of victory. So Stalin ordered a replay of the semi-final.

'The mood was terrible,' Nikolai says, shaking his head. 'All the fans were against the decision, as were other members of the Party leadership, but everyone kept their silence. We received strong advice it would be better if we lost this time.'

But the Starostin brothers played their hearts out and Spartak won again, 3–0. When the third goal went in, Beria stood up in his special box. He was a big fat man with round glasses. He simply turned and left the stadium.

Nikolai taps the desk with the fingertips of both hands. 'That was the cause of it,' he says. 'From then on life became more difficult. We were always under pressure from the authorities.'

Beria bided his time. Then, in 1942, he was able to implicate Starostin in a plot to kill Stalin. He was supposedly the ring-leader, planning to shoot Stalin during a sports parade. All four brothers were arrested, thrown out of the Party and spent two years in prison, while their lawyers did whatever they could. In the end, they were deemed innocent of the charge of terrorism, but found guilty of anti-Soviet propaganda. They had apparently been singing the praises of capitalist sport. For this imaginary crime, they were sent to separate forced labour camps, the *gulags*, for another ten years.

Suddenly I find myself wondering how on earth we got here. What did they do to him? What horrors has this man seen?

Nikolai didn't return home until 1954. He was only released after Stalin's death, when Beria had finally been arrested.

I ask if he'll tell us about the prison camps, but he can't.

'I don't know what to say,' he says grimly.

He blinks and turns his head away.

Late that afternoon, Vanella and I take another look at Red Square. We decide they must always have used a wide-angle lens when those armies of tanks paraded past a pale-faced Brezhnev because, oddly enough, it's only about the size of a decent football pitch. St Basil's Cathedral, with its gloriously coloured onion tops, makes a splendid grandstand. I imagine Nikolai speeding down the right wing and chipping in an immaculate cross.

'He was sad, wasn't he?' says Vanella.

'Nikolai?'

'Mmm . . . There must be hundreds like him.'

'Thousands.'

'So how did he survive?'

'He wouldn't let them beat him.'

'And now?'

'Football. His passion. It's all he knows. You don't see many men his age, ordering around twenty-year-olds in track suits.'

'Maybe it helps him forget.'

Along the touchline, we reach the black marble mausoleum wherein Lenin's body lies, arms resting straight now. Behind, the imposing walls of the Kremlin fly the white, blue and red colours of the Russian flag, a symbol of new identity and hope. But we're not so sure. Moscow feels like the Wild West. Everyone's out to make a buck; guns and violence are on the increase. There's an uneasy tension in the air and we are told to keep off the streets at night.

We stroll on towards Revolution Square. Near a soap-box corner, an elderly man wearing a blue peaked cap and Solzhenitsyn beard attaches himself to us. He has plenty to say on the subject of Communists and decides we make an ideal audience. 'Look at that man's face, he could only be a bloody Communist.' He points at one of the speakers, who shouts and spits angrily, florid with exertion. No one is listening.

'A good Communist is a dead Communist,' urges our man. 'But a better Communist is a *killed* Communist.'

We rumble to Kiev overnight by train in the company of Petr, a microbiologist in his forties who enjoys practising his English.

'Sorry, mmm, pliz, your Pink Floyd, it is very good. I very much like your English Webber and Lloyd, your *Jesus Christ Superstar*.'

But economics and politics are mostly on his mind. Petr wants to know how much everything costs in the West – TVs, hi-fi, cars – and then, even when we underplay, he can't believe it. We share our packet of chocolate-chip cookies, a luxury acquired in a hard-currency shop. The biscuits he offers in return are plain and stale. Every way we turn we can't help feeling like fat capitalists. Petr sips his tea and speaks about the changes with some concern.

'What good is it if my grandmother cannot buy bread?' he says. 'Once it cost only a few roubles, but now she has no money. Before there was food but no freedom. Now there is freedom but no food.'

* * *

Dr Bezrukov is expecting us.

We bounce across Kiev in a clapped-out taxi, risking more than one head-on collision. The month is May and the horse chestnut trees lining every street hang heavy with blossom, in resplendent contrast to the rest of town, one rectangular grey monolith after another.

The Institute of Gerontology seems little different, though perhaps grander than the average block. The reception area comprises a dark marble hall with an enormous mural of a genealogical tree in coloured cements. Beyond that, nothing is predictable. Somewhere off-stage a workman hammers away at some concrete. Someone calls out in frustration but gets no response. Phones ring. Young women in white coats parade up and down the central stairway, dolled up as if this is the Institute of Beauticians. The receptionist wears a white coat and headscarf and is at least seventy-five. She's shouting down a telephone, deliberately ignoring a small queue of visitors. Another phone rings and she picks it up. With one earpiece to each ear, two mouthpieces to her lips, she carries on shouting. Then she slams both phones down as one and looks up at us. She snaps what I guess is Ukrainian for, 'Can I help you?' The name Bezrukov works wonders.

Dr Bezrukov's assistant, a kindly lady called Maya, takes us upstairs to his office. He is nothing like I expect. Around fifty, square-jawed, silver-haired and good-looking, he has more than a passing resemblance to Steve Martin, the American film comedian. I suspect his girls probably find him a bit dishy, especially in his white coat, but I have to keep reminding myself that Dr Bezrukov is a leading gerontologist. His staff assist by speaking English and calling him 'chief'. We are honoured guests. A programme of meetings has been laid on, but first we have to visit the museum.

This turns out to be a room bristling with gerontological memorabilia. We also discover it suffers from unbelievably creaky floorboards, so bad it's impossible to walk and talk at the same time. If I alter my body weight only slightly, the creaks somehow suggest I'm not paying attention. So as we all stand stock-still, Bezrukov talks us through the heroes of Soviet gerontology, men with names like Mechnikov, Nagorny and Bogomolets. He points to their photos on the wall with a long Perspex wand. Then the museum door swings open, letting in sounds of youthful exuberance from the staff in the corridor. Maya creaks over to close it. Bezrukov keeps on, waving his teaching stick so enthusiastically that a balsa-wood parapet goes flying from his scale model of the Institute. Mysteriously, the door opens once more and we hear laughter. Maya creaks again. When it opens a third time, Bezrukov himself deals with the problem. A short sharp 'Shhht' and there is silence. The chief turns to us and grins.

Our lecture continues with records of gerontological conferences, stamp collections and a scarf from the 'I want to be 100' club of Japan. Then we learn a new Russian word. In these parts, people are not old, aged or even elderly. With appropriate respect, they are *dolgozhiteli*, the long-lived. The glass cabinets are stocked with products to help us join them, everything from low-fat yoghurt to ginseng. For years, Dr Bezrukov has studied the people of Abkasia, Georgia and other regions of the Caucasus, but he remains matter-of-fact.

'The effect of such things is only ever part of the story,' he says.

'So how do you explain the longevity of some of the world's oldest inhabitants?' I ask.

'It is not simple,' he replies, nudging his glasses back up the bridge of his nose. 'There are many contributory factors, but no single answer.'

So much for all the research, I think. But, then, if you have studied anthropology, demography, ethnopsychology, genealogy, neurology, odontology and socio-cultural parameters, you probably aren't destined to come up with too clear a picture.

In truth, there doesn't appear to be one secret ingredient that guarantees long life, although diet, exercise and a stress-free environment seem to play an important part. The air and water in the Caucasus are pure; the common diet is high in beneficial anti-oxidants; physical labour is still a way of life; and, until the recent civil wars, there hasn't been too much to get wound up about.

Most interesting is the status of the *dolgozhiteli*: essentially, the older you are, the more you are revered. Abkasian proverbs say 'The elder is a shield' and 'He who is without an elder is without a God'. The old are the mainstay of the social group. They lead the community; without them life would simply be intolerable. There is even a pecking order over food. The younger men cook and the eldest eat first, slowly and calmly, small, choice portions. Above all, it seems perfectly normal, there in the mountains, to lead a long and useful life. Naturally, people fulfil that expectation and live happily to ages of a hundred or more.

An old Caucasian tale tells of a woman renowned for her curses being asked to deliver her worst. She gave her answer: "That you may live in a house where there are no old people to give wise advice and no young people to listen."

Maya takes us for a walk in the botanical gardens behind the Institute. Our pace is a gentle stroll, but she appears eager to explain, as if telling us will somehow make a difference to the way things are. People often seem to want to open up to us. We are outsiders, and the fact that we're a couple must be less daunting. They can always confide in one or the other.

Maya addresses Vanella mostly.

'We believe it is more important to watch the blossoms change here in the garden than it is to wait for the fruits of *perestroika*,' she says. 'That change will be much slower.'

'This is a beautiful place to pass the time.'

'Time is all we have.'

Maya reveals her sadness as she talks about Chernobyl, which isn't far from Kiev. Everyone still talks about Chernobyl. They remain bitter because they weren't told by the authorities until two weeks after the accident at the nuclear reactor. They can't go to the forests any more; the theory is that the pine needles still hold radioactivity. And so they grieve. They know one day history will take its toll.

'It is like a kiss of death placed on our lips,' says Maya, with a sigh. Then she smiles. 'Come, we need inspiration. I will take you to see Grigorii Artemovych.'

She knocks on his door and Grigorii Artemovych Dobrenko looks up. It's extraordinary – he's an absolute double for George Bernard Shaw. He gets to his feet, beaming through his bushy white beard, quite unable to contain his excitement. With great care he arranges his bedside chair for Vanella, then perches himself on the edge of the old iron bed, chuckling. He wears pyjamas made of a coarse cloth: the top half pink, the bottoms from another pair, patched and stitched down one leg.

Grigorii is a priest. A prominent figure in the Baptist community, he spent many years avoiding repression by the Communists. It's hard to imagine how much courage that must have taken, when the entire system was preaching atheism against him. For all that time, there was no freedom for those who had faith. They were watched. Children were never allowed to go to the meeting-house. Open gatherings were prohibited and the houses closed from time to time.

Grigorii remains surprisingly unmoved. It became second nature.

'Many of my brothers were sent to prison for no reason,' he says. 'You could make a mistake, any kind of mistake, and it was used as evidence against you.'

A resolution was once passed to arrest him. But a KGB colonel learnt about the order and warned him to be careful. He liked Grigorii very much and said it was better that he himself should sit in prison rather than a priest.

'I ask you not to mention his name,' Grigorii half whispers. 'There are people alive who I still meet, they should not know this.'

He prefers to stay silent about the bad times. He can remember everything, but he doesn't wish to say any more. The past still keeps its hold. Only under Gorbachev was he able to practise his religion openly, but his caution, now inured in him, will never let him be free. A devout man, living strictly according to the teachings of his Bible, he is nevertheless able to forgive those who repressed him.

'There is only love,' he says. 'When Christ was on the Cross, he forgave those who persecuted him.'

Then he grows agitated and Maya looks concerned. She is so dedicated to her work; she loves the old people and they love and respect her in return. But Grigorii only wants to read to us, a passage from St John's gospel.

'I follow the principles of the Bible to the word,' he says. 'I do not worship idols or ikons. An ikon is not a true expression of your inner soul. God is spirit. The power of God makes us strong.'

He explains the differences between the Baptist religion and the Orthodox Church. Baptists work for spiritual resurrection.

'It is a spiritual rebirth,' he says. 'Water is the symbol of Christ's teaching and the spirit is God's strength.'

Lines are etched deep across his forehead, but his eyes shine with certainty beneath bristling white eyebrows. He fumbles for a pair of well-thumbed glasses and reads to us again. His voice is rasping, lively and enthused. I imagine the moment as a tableau – Grigorii bent over his book, Vanella and I listening, Maya, in white, silhouetted against the open window where a gentle breeze is blowing the curtains.

Maya paraphrases from time to time. It is the story of Paul's conversion on the road to Damascus, his blinding and, after three days, the scales falling from his eyes.

It dawns on me that Grigorii is still working. He automatically sees us as potential converts to his faith. He doesn't seek to persuade. He simply tells the story and leaves us to judge.

He is convinced his long life is the direct result of abstinence. He has always avoided smoking and drinking. He fasts for as many days as he can and, in fasting, gives deep submission to God.

'If a man thinks good thoughts,' he declares, 'then good juices are released into the body. If he thinks evil, so the opposite will happen.'

He tells us in earnest that he trusts in moderation in all things, even sex. But then he confesses to having fathered ten children. And he looks surprised when we all laugh.

He is now in his nineties, so we ask if he wants to live to be a hundred. Grigorii chuckles to himself before replying.

'When I was young, I had many wishes,' he says. 'Now I want nothing. I give prayers at the meeting-house; that is enough at my age. My children tell me I have to last out till I'm a hundred, but I prayed to the Lord, saying, "If you need me to continue working on earth, let me live here." And I understood at that moment that I am still needed, because we have few priests who can teach the younger generations. As soon as God wants me, He will take me.'

I find myself hesitating. It's as if my question is too sensitive to ask someone who is so much closer to death. I've really no idea what happens to us when we die. Ashes, dust. Are we simply switched off? The screen goes black. Or do we get the white shining light? Bo said we never die. I wonder what Grigorii thinks.

He fingers his long beard and lets go a wheezy laugh. 'God takes care of believers,' he says, with an air of finality. It all comes down to faith.

Soon Maya gives us a sign and, as we prepare to leave, Grigorii stands and shuffles about nervously. He tries to give Vanella the flowers from his table, five tulips a little past their prime. She refuses – they are for him to enjoy. Then he turns and catches me unawares. He grasps me by the shoulders and plants a full kiss on my lips.

'I kiss you like a brother,' he says.

It is a prickly but poignant moment. I find I am moved by his affection towards me, a complete stranger. There he stands in his funny old pyjamas, radiating joy. He takes Vanella's hand and makes a performance out of kissing it with much courtesy.

We are brothers now, sisters too.

* * *

The phone still rings in the middle of the night. Tired and undernourished, we agree it's time to buy some train tickets.

The first challenge is to identify the correct window to queue in front of. Everyone professes to know, but actually no one has any idea because windows open and close for no apparent reason. But the longer we wait, the more we appreciate the ancient Soviet art of queuing. We book our seats at one window, then pay at two others – part roubles, part dollars – then go back to the first to claim the tickets. Eventually, we realize the locals are standing in at least three queues at the same time. They turn up, hang around a while, then say, 'I'm here, OK?' Then they move on to stake their place in another queue. So we never know how many people are ahead of us until we've reached the scrum at the window. We calculate that six people we can see means sixteen we can't. It also means an agonizing relationship between time and the length of queue ahead. Then there are the lunch hours and frequent tea breaks when everything shuts down.

When at last we've fought to the very front, when the locals we've spent the previous four hours with are still trying to push in, the price originally quoted goes up. They won't say why. We find we don't have enough dollars and they won't take our emergency fifty-pound note. We are completely stitched up.

This is all too much for Vanella. She finally flips. Pushing the fifty pounds back under the glass, she shouts, 'You've got to take it. There's nothing wrong with it. It's perfectly good money.'

The two granite-faced women behind the desk impassively push the money towards her. Vanella shoves it back. Their stubby fingers force it through again.

'No. Look. Here. English. Sterling. Fifty pounds.' Her fingers flash, but the women look beyond us for the next in line.

'You can't do this,' she screams, but it makes no difference. I shepherd her away and make reassuring noises.

We spend the next hour back at the hotel, where the cashier also refuses to accept sterling. The 'Change money?' boys look at me in blank disbelief as I try to swap a huge roll of useless spare roubles for hard dollars. So I resort to pleading desperately with the receptionist, telling her we can't leave the country unless someone changes our money.

'Wait, pliz,' she finally says, takes the fifty-pound note and disappears behind the scenes. Some minutes later she slyly hands over a few precious greenbacks.

After more queuing, we work out it's taken six and a half hours to secure two tickets.

It's so obvious we're still being watched. One minute before the train pulls out of Kiev, a couple run hand in hand down the platform and kiss ostentatiously in front of our compartment. The woman joins us, offering only a flicker of a smile, then unrolls her bedding on the bench seat opposite. Throughout the day, from behind her paperback, she watches Vanella update the expenses and reorganize her plastic bags. She sees me making notes, then wrestle with a can of sardines I have great difficulty prising open. We eat them mid-afternoon with a stale roll, a block of cheese and the last of the dried apricots that have been with us since Helsinki. She then witnesses the panic when Vanella realizes she's lost her customs' declaration form and thinks she'll never be allowed out of the country. At the border, in the early hours, our companion suddenly packs up and vanishes.

A customs' official appears, a thin young woman with a deathly pallor, and after frantic sign language she supervises the filling-out of new documents. She checks my papers and gives me an icy stare.

'Roubles?'

I still have a large wad in my trouser pocket, the ones I couldn't swap. We're not supposed to take any out with us. Fearing a search, I own up.

'Pliz. Come.'

Obedient, I follow. Leaving Vanella, I climb down from the carriage and stumble in pitch darkness beside the track, tripping now and then, banging my shins on the sleepers. Amid clanks of iron, the train begins to move off in the opposite direction.

We reach a deserted platform and I'm led behind the station building to what I guess is a bank. A sign by the door says, '24 hours'. I'm impressed. It's two-fifteen in the morning.

The customs' official knocks. No reply. She tries again and a guard opens up, showing us into a dark, wood-panelled room. There are four windows for conducting business, but no sign of life. Tat-tat-tat, the girl raps on one glass, then another. Tat-tat-tat. I hear a groan, deep down. Then a dishevelled head slowly raises itself above one of the counters and an enormous woman wearing an apron looms into view.

She yawns grossly as she looks at my currency exchange slips. She turns them upside down and scrutinizes them closer still. She switches on a huge calculator and then announces she can't possibly change my roubles. I have Russian exchange slips; this is the Ukraine. The calculator is switched off with feeling and she slumps back below decks.

I can't work out if the next building is a bank or not. My roubles are taken from me and counted. I'm handed a chitty, carefully cut out with scissors along the calibrations to show the exact amount in tens, hundreds and thousands. I can claim back the cash when I choose to return to the country.

'You must be joking,' I say, and they look at me, uncomprehending.

Her task complete, the customs' girl points me towards the ticket barrier. I left my ticket on the train, I remember.

'*Kassa*, *kassa*,' I claim, and for once I'm waved through.

I wait in a cold marble hall, wondering if I've been left behind. Panic has already set in when a train rolls up to the platform and I'm reunited with a greatly relieved Vanella. She thought she was never going to see me again.

We watch the officious Ukrainian guards make their final sweep through the train. We lurch two hundred yards. Then a line of swarthy Magyars in scruffy uniforms shambles along the corridor and we know we are safe.

I pull out the quarter-bottle of whisky, reserved for special occasions and bona fide travellers.

Freedom!

4

Born Again

I hang on the motion, as I watch the dawn creep over the eastern plain. It's a trundling motion – with an occasional roll and a clack-ata-clack – the perfect speed: slow enough to see the dormant world go by, quick enough to feel that we're getting there. Fields of poppies, more than I've ever seen, raise their heads to greet the day. Another man stands near me, watching; he wears a vest and smokes an acrid cigarette. We've nodded. It's too early to speak. And when the light comes, it is silver.

We pull into Budapest over an hour late. But a little lady is still waiting, down along the platform. She wears the expectant look of someone who doesn't know whom she's meeting, until she sees us.

'Room. You want room?' she asks. 'Very nice. No family.'

Vanella hates arriving with nowhere to stay, so we've worked out a routine whereby the primary needs get sorted: local currency, then base camp and a securely locked door. She is also naturally suspicious of anyone offering us goods or services. I'm the other way – if anything, I'm too trusting.

'Very nice. Is near,' says the lady. With a finger she sketches a map on her hand, drawing in the river, the station and a few streets in between. I suggest we take a look and soon we're following her waddling figure out of the station.

'Are you sure this is all right?' whispers Vanella. 'She could be taking us anywhere.'

She says her name is Julie, so we christen her Mrs Julie. Silver-haired and dumpy, she wears a top coat with an apron underneath. Climbing aboard a bus, the three of us are watched by rows of curious Hungarians on their way to work. We smile and, to our amazement, they all smile back.

Mrs Julie smiles too as she brings us through the side-streets to her flagstoned courtyard, four floors of iron railings and window-boxes in pink. Up the stone steps, she points out where she lives, one below, then opens our front door. The place feels recently vacated. We have one room and a simple bathroom; to the right of the hallway, a door leads to another room. Vanella rattles the handle as Mrs Julie is leaving.

'Is lock, is lock,' she says sweetly.

When she's gone, we rearrange the furniture and push the beds together. Another system now operates whereby my bed (or my side of the bed) is always on the right, Vanella's on the left. It's one less decision. Then I inspect a small stuffed mammal in a glass case and a saint with a long face amateurishly painted on wood. What we need now, we agree, is a hearty breakfast.

We sit upstairs in a nearby coffee bar, all alone. The toasted open sandwiches arrive soggy, the coffee comes frothy and weak, but everything tastes just delicious. We guzzle stale poppy-seed rolls, order more coffee and greasy sausages for seconds. Back at the room, I spend a whole hour lolling in the bath, topping up the hot with my toes, while Vanella takes a nap. Then, out on the street again, we're lured by the sophistication of a burger bar where we consume more coffee and fries. We stroll. We gaze in shop windows; even stationery is interesting. We romance the Danube and slurp ice-cream. We drink more beer than we should, and overeat comprehensively at a local restaurant – goulash soup, followed by a dish of veal and goose liver with onions and peas. Then dessert.

We decide that the river Danube is like a hinge. On one side, there's the old city of Buda, old Europe; opposite lies Pest. The one is formal and reserved; the other outgoing and businesslike. Here we see the might of the Habsburg Empire in the grand architecture; there we feel the stolid presence of forty years of Communism. These days, the promise of a thousand cola signs spreads insidiously through the streets. Remembering each turn, we make our way, and climb the flights of dark stone stairs.

Within minutes, Vanella free-falls to sleep. For some reason, I'm wide awake. My sheets are cool, the religious paintings black shapes now in a ghostly light. I've lost the motion at last. Lying perfectly still, I try to work out if the sensation I can feel is the blood circulating in my legs. I close my eyes and my limbs are blanked out, support systems only. I feel like I'm floating.

I think about our new life. It's like we're learning to live with each other all over again. Five weeks in the world we are, and it could be five months. Five weeks in the office used to go by in a flash. This new relationship we have with time is an unexpected treat. We've stepped outside ourselves and all the old rules are blown away. Nothing is predictable. And I can't believe how good I feel as a result. It wouldn't surprise me if the very act of travelling has some beneficial effect on the ageing process.

Across the room, I hear the fridge click off with a shudder. Then the sound of a key in a lock. A shuffle of footsteps. Breathing. Someone is in the bathroom.

Vanella jerks awake.

'What's that?' she hisses.

'Someone's running the bath.'

The fact sinks in.

'What do you think we should do?'

'Go back to sleep.'

I lie perfectly still, listening to whoever it is humming Hungarian folk songs.

For all the bravado of leaving and the joys of being abroad, the same question keeps haunting me. What am I going to do? I've tried to shed my skin. But it isn't as easy as just walking away – so much of my past stays with me. I feel curiously exposed, my new skin as yet unformed. What am I going to do with my time? No false starts now, no getting it wrong. Because what I do with my time will undoubtedly say who I am.

But I don't know, I really don't know. I hear my grandfather still calling, 'Now then, young 'un, what are you going to do when you grow up?'

Vanella is being very patient with me. 'I thought you said you wanted to write?'

'Yes, maybe. But what if it doesn't work out? What will I do then?'

'You really don't have to decide anything now.'

She's right, of course. But I worry still, so we decide to take a break for a few days. We opt for Lake Balaton, Europe's largest stretch of inland water.

'Very good. Balaton. Very good. Many pictures,' Mrs Julie says as we leave, promising to return.

Naturally, we envisage a tranquil spa town with a couple of quaint inns. So we're quite put out when we see the hordes of German tourists.

And we have to rent a flat with a squeaky fold-down bed, plumbing that makes a fearful knocking noise and a resident infestation of ants. We are lodged in a characterless block down the far end of what we call Grockle's Way, a broad concrete strip flanked by pizza houses and al fresco drinking pens.

By day, Vanella sunbathes or sneaks into one of the hotel pools for a swim, and I sit at a makeshift desk with a pad of paper and a view of some trees. A pair of woodpeckers has nested, keeping me occupied when my attention wanders.

It seems fitting. Starting again.

I'm thinking about the General, who we met in the Parliament building in Budapest. We climbed its marble stairways, gazed up at the vaulted roofs. Every edge was gilded. Miles of red carpet ran along fifty-foot-high corridors and stony-faced statues peered down as if they knew better.

The General emerged from a panelled ante-room. Formally introducing himself, he took an immediate shine to Vanella and gave her a kiss on each cheek, leaving her a little embarrassed. He was between meetings and concerned that our arrival shouldn't endanger his lunch. So food was promptly ordered, and I remember thinking it just a touch bizarre that there we were outside the National Assembly, of a Wednesday lunch-time, munching open sandwiches with a member of Hungary's Defence Committee.

Kálmán Kéri was his name. Small and dapper, with boyish features, his uniform shone with bright gold buttons and two thick red stripes ran up each trouser leg. When his colleagues passed by, he would smile and wave like a jovial old uncle. They would respond by saluting or with a quick click of the heels and a nod in acknowledgement. The General was a happy man, now he had his egg and salami.

All his life a military man, Kéri had risen through the ranks until, in 1944, as commander-in-chief of the Carpathian Regiments, his troops were obliterated by the Russians on the eastern front. Then the Nazis invaded and immediately appointed him commander-in-chief of the 1st Hungarian Army. That November, he was sent to Moscow to negotiate a truce and while he was away, the Russians liberated Budapest. Come December, Kéri was handed back by the Russians to a new Communist-controlled Hungarian government. He was ordered to organize a new defence ministry and rebuild the army. Then he was charged with sabotage and thrown into prison.

He was released, became a civilian and studied medical chemistry. He was imprisoned again for the crime of having Western relations, released after a few months, then imprisoned again. In February 1949 he was imprisoned once more, without sentence, and placed in a cell where, for a whole year, he never saw the sun. Next he was sent to the concentration camp at Recsk, an extermination camp. Cold and hungry, he toiled in the quarry. Four years later he was released and found work as the manager of a department store. He retired in 1963, studied some military history and gave language lessons.

Then, with the fall of Communism in 1989, Kálmán Kéri found new employment as a member of the new Parliament. At the age of ninety, he was learning to sound like a politician.

'I would like to see an era of co-operation between all parties of the world when tensions could be settled without wars,' he said gravely, as if the words had been carefully rehearsed. 'We must learn to live within a new community and be unselfish in the interests of something bigger.'

Then he looked at his watch and apologized. He had to rush to another meeting. Inviting us back any time, he stole another kiss and bounded off down the corridor.

What a funny man. He ran in mock slow motion, forearms halfway to a salute, springing on his toes like an athlete in baggy shorts. What an extraordinary man. It was as if his spirit had been set free.

My woodpeckers have gone, I realize. In the kitchen I find a scrap of bread and drop some crumbs out on the balcony. For twenty absorbing minutes I watch a battalion of ants send messages, regroup and carry on.

Maybe I shouldn't think so much about what I'm going to do. Perhaps it's the doing that is important.

On our return to Budapest, one evening we meet Andrea, a local girl our own age. Standing together behind the old castle district, we watch the day settle over the Buda hills beyond. Dogs are barking in the distance, then the whine of a motor-scooter intrudes until we're still once more.

'Isn't it loofely?' Andrea says. She must have learnt her English from someone with a northern accent. 'Sometimes I still don't believe we are free. We can talk and discuss. We have our own culture back. You know, there are folk dances people haven't danced for years. We are learning them again.'

Andrea sounds like she's recovering from amnesia. She is rediscovering her identity and proud of her country once more.

She's keen to show us the ruins of an old church, where only the tower remains standing.

'This is where the Resistance used to meet,' she says, as we form a small group inside. 'My sister was a member, working underground. She was always artistic, very musical. She fought the system and took many risks. My father was a Communist. Of course, everything is different now, but he is still a Communist. He cannot change. It is sad.'

Andrea leads us to a quiet garden on the hill just outside the old city wall. The twilight is closing in, blackbirds ticking out the last song of the day.

On a stone bench, we see the figure of an old man. He is reclining, legs crossed at the ankles.

'Who is he?' whispers Vanella.

He is a perfect statue, a blackened bronze.

'Zoltán Kodály, the composer,' says Andrea, laying a warm hand on his shoulder. 'At the beginning of the century, he travelled around Hungary collecting folk songs, so that our music would be preserved.'

The old man looks downcast. From the corner of his eye, a raindrop hangs masquerading as a tear.

The next morning, a bus heaves us towards the top of one of the Buda hills. The women with their shopping smile as we jump off and climb the rest of the way to the square. We are expecting to find a small retirement flat, but counting along, checking the numbers, we work out that the address can only be the impressive yellow mansion down one end. A line of taxis stands waiting outside. I peep through the iron gates at a perfectly striped lawn. The security system buzzes, we skirt its moody Alsatian and a maid takes us upstairs to an open reception area. Vanella and I catch each other's eye. We're in shock. We've been getting used to finding ourselves in some strange places, but this one is decorated like a wedding cake.

Béla Varga looks comfortable in his black suit and priest's collar. He is clean-shaven, his head mostly bald and a little freckled. With him waits a well-known television announcer, a striking woman called Julia Kudlik. She's come to help things along. They've been told we are American. He seems delighted to learn that we're English.

'I love England,' he says immediately, the voice husky, his English spoken with only a faint accent. I see his hands shake a little. He apologizes, he has Parkinson's disease. From time to time, his words falter and Julia speaks with him in Hungarian.

Béla Varga was born into a poor peasant family. His father had sailed to America to earn some money, in order that young Béla could go to secondary school, and so fulfil his vocation.

'I always wanted to be a priest, ever since I was a small boy, an altar boy.'

He must have been angelic. His face looks innocent still. His watery blue eyes show only kindness.

'Hitler hated me,' he says hurriedly. 'I worked with the Polish people who escaped from Poland.'

As a young man, he had taken the post of priest at Balatonboglar, across the lake from where we stayed. He understood the ordinary peasant folk who lived there and soon established a good reputation. When war came, he pitied how the Poles suffered under the Nazi invasion and took it upon himself to organize the Polish refugees who were escaping into Hungary.

'Hitler *hated* me,' says Béla. 'He *hated* me personally, hated me as much as he hated the Polish. He condemned me to death because I helped them.'

He speaks of one man's hatred with a gentle humour. He can afford to now, but I guess such threats to his life were always treated this way.

Because Hitler prohibited all schools in Poland, Béla opened one for the refugees at Balaton. For a time it was the only Polish school in the world. It was the centre of his war against Hitler and later against Stalin also. So when Germany invaded Hungary, Béla was imprisoned and would have been executed, had he not escaped and fled the country.

He is eager to show us his decorations. The maid is dispatched and returns with an armful of red and blue boxes. There's some fussing because the British one isn't among them.

Béla fingers a gold medal in a trembling hand, the highest and oldest honour that can be granted by the Polish nation.

'They accepted me as a brother,' he says, still touched by the emotion. 'My whole life was sacrificed for the Poles. I helped over two hundred thousand Polish people escape through Hungary.'

'The Poles called Hungary their paradise,' says Julia, opening another box. 'It was their only hope of escaping the pogroms. Ah, look. This one is Hungarian.'

'That's amazing,' says Vanella.

I take my turn to cradle an enormous weighty cross.

'You'd fall over if you wore this,' I say, and Béla smiles.

After the liberation of Budapest, he returned home. In January 1945, he was arrested by the Russians and sentenced to death. But they set him free. As a member of Parliament, he then served as president of the National Assembly, until Rákosi and the Communists took over the government in 1947. Béla was forced to flee again, first to Switzerland, then to England and finally he sought exile in the United States.

'Forty-six years, my friend, forty-six years wandering in the world without a country.'

'That's half a lifetime.'

'I was in London many times. I have friends there still. We have much to thank the English for. I was with Churchill when he made his first speech against the Cold War. He said the Iron Curtain had come down. I liked Winston Churchill very much. A strong man, a man of courage.'

'You are also a man of courage.'

'I was condemned to death in my life many times,' he boasts playfully.

'But you are still here.'

'Still here.'

I wonder where he found such courage, half expecting his faith, or God, to be the answer. But he's not sure. He simply did what he believed was right and refused to be deflected.

'I didn't know fear,' he confesses. 'To die for one's country is the greatest glory. I am not proud of this. It is natural, to love my own country. I was happy, really happy to sacrifice my life.'

This is his greatest happiness – the love of his country. He hopes that younger generations will now be able to love their country better. After forty-six years it had come as wonderful news, the day when Communist rule was brought to an end by the will of the people.

Of course, we want to know how he felt. Béla smiles. He says he remembered standing before the American senators, as he had many times. 'Tell us, what are your feelings?' they said. 'But don't play politics with us, tell us the truth.'

'I am perfectly sure Communism will fall,' he had replied.

'Don't be ridiculous,' they told him. 'The Russians occupy half the world.'

'They may,' said Béla, 'but they do not occupy human nature. The future of the world lies with human nature and human nature is stronger than anything, stronger than any government.'

Still they didn't believe him, the old senators. Somehow Béla always knew he would return. He never resigned his position as speaker of the National Assembly. And so, in June 1990, still the legal president, he was asked to open the first session of the new Parliament. He came home for the last time. He was made provost of the Roman Catholic Church and given a house to live in for the remainder of his days. He has no further ambition.

'I don't want to be anything. I am a happy man.'

'Do you like old age?'

'I love life,' he answers quickly, with a tender smile.

He makes no complaints about his illness, shows no sign of regret or sadness. He is at peace.

I lean forward to touch the only dot of colour he wears, a tiny red badge in his buttonhole. It is an automatic gesture, an expression of the familiarity I now feel.

'What's this?'

'It is French. I fought together with the French. The French didn't like Hitler.'

'Who did like Hitler?' says Julia and we all laugh at the Führer's expense.

'The greatest honour of my life was that Hitler and Stalin both hated me personally.'

I imagine this is the closest Béla Varga can ever get to pride.

He apologizes for his failing voice.

'If you ever come back to Hungary, please visit me. If I am healthy, I would be happy to see you. I love England. If I go to England, I will find you. Where will I find you?'

'We are wandering the world for two years.'

'I will find you.'

He shakes his fist with determination. Then, as we stand, Béla kisses me affectionately on both cheeks.

'I will never forget you,' he says.

And I'm beginning to wonder what's going on. For the second time in my new life, I have been kissed by a priest.

5

OLDO

Our journey east from Bratislava takes the best part of a long hot June day and is spent in the company of a ragged, grizzled old gentleman. Standing over us, he first makes a brief speech, doubly incomprehensible because he not only slurs, he slurs in Slovakian. Then, apparently satisfied, he slumps by the door, his breath alternately rattling and wheezing. From time to time along the way he wakes, rolls a bloodshot eye and informs us, with some considerable pride, 'Me Slovak!'

Miloš Ruppeldt had been convinced the Tatras region was the place. He showed me some grainy old photos of wooden churches and villagers in folk dress. On the map he'd pointed to the mountains of eastern Slovakia, and somewhere called Liptovský Mikuláš. Miloš worked at the embassy in London and was generous with his help. He ended up inviting us to a memorial for Jan Palach, the Czech student who, in January 1969, burnt himself to death in protest against the Russian invasion. So Vanella and I had rushed from work to stand in the chill of a dark winter evening, feeling conspicuously out of place. Prayers were said and anthems sung. Afterwards in the meeting-house, we were welcomed by everyone from the consul to Miloš' cousin, Ilya. There had been much nodding about the Tatras. 'Go to Liptovský,' they said. 'You will have no problem. They will help you there.'

By the time we arrive, the small town of Liptovský Mikuláš doesn't seem quite so forthcoming. Apparently there is a man who rents out a car, but he can't be traced. The charming Mrs Chovanova at the language school can offer us a couple of hours in the mornings, but no more. Then at the office of Liptour, the local travel company, we learn that our only chance of transport comes with chauffeur attached. We don't like the sound of that much, but reluctantly agree to enter discussions. Fifteen minutes later a young man appears, in jeans and a T-shirt, with a bum-bag pouch slung across his stomach. The first impression is of a wheeler-dealer.

'Hallo, hallo. My name is Oldo.' He pronounces his first O short. 'Where you stay? Hotel?'

'Hotel Jánošik.'

'You stay with me. Is better.'

We mumble to cover our confusion. It would be great to leave the Jánošik, another uninspiring concrete block, but we're not sure. Undeterred, he takes us off for coffee and listens to our story.

'Is no problem. You are the boss.' Oldo says he can take care of everything.

'Don't you think this is weird?' I say.

'Is weird? What is it . . . weird?' he asks innocently.

Vanella can't help laughing.

'It's strange, odd. Your name.'

'My name? My name is Oldo.'

'Your name is Oldo. And we are looking for old people.'

'Ha ha. Oldo will find old people, yes?'

But I wonder if he isn't some kind of angel, sent to help us on our way. On his round, friendly face he wears silver-framed glasses with lenses like pennies and springy hooks for the ears. The back of his head has a squarish look, dark hair shaved close with a hint of grey at the temples. He tells us he used to be an actor, but he gave up films and stardom for military service. He became the guy in surveillance who eavesdropped on NATO security codes and warning signals for the West's nuclear weapons. If anything changed from the norm, it was Oldo who sent the alert back to Moscow. I see him in a secret, darkened room, wearing headphones, his glasses glinting in the red and white of the dials. In the winter months he is now a ski instructor and he's also developing his entrepreneurial skills.

And so Oldo becomes our guide, our driver, detective, interpreter, chef and very fine host. Next morning, he picks us up at the Jánošik and we return to Liptour, where we drink a glass or two of the local wine while he makes phone calls to various *matrikas*, the village council offices.

'We have ideas now,' he announces, waving a piece of paper and, switching to chauffeur, leads us to his faithful white Škoda. As we drive off, people wave. He deliberately aims at someone crossing the street and blows the horn. The man jumps back startled, then grins when he realizes it's only Oldo.

He takes us to his modest house in Liptovský Trnovec, a village not far from the town. We unload, and then pay a visit to the campsite Oldo used to manage. There, we drink a cold beer while he attends to some business, and we're off again.

Away on open roads, we can appreciate the countryside for the first time. We are surrounded by big-dipper hills and mountains with jagged teeth, blue in the faraway haze. On the lower slopes, villages nestle in lush farming land, all called Liptovský Something-or-other. Workers busy themselves in the fields, cutting the ripe hay and stacking it wigwam-style to dry. The dam, Liptovska Mara, built in the 1970s, had once submerged thirteen other little Liptovskýs under twenty-two square kilometres of water. Oldo says their needs for electricity have been far exceeded. The best land was down there too.

We're headed for Partizan Lupča, up on the south side. Before assuming the name of the partisans, the place was known as Nemecka Lupča, meaning German Lupča. During the Second World War, the eastern front had moved constantly back and forth across the area – so much so it was said the Nazis and the Russians were really only battling it out for the distillery on the edge of town.

The village of Partizan Lupča stands frozen in time. A rough, unkempt patch of grass forms its centre, around which the houses crowd close, with red roofs and paintwork the pale pinks and greens of ice-cream. Narrow alleyways run in between, where scruffy children play and the flagstones were once laid with specially carved ruts for cartwheels.

Cyril Murva is waiting for us. In fact, he's been waiting all morning, ever since they ran to tell him about Oldo's call to the *matrika*. He hasn't been able to contain himself any longer and he's been at the *borovička*, the local juniper-flavoured gin. He's having a lie-down now, they say.

We are ushered through a small opening in a barn door and into the house within, a maze of rooms with beds everywhere. Painted ikons adorn the walls, lit with twinkling fairy lights. In a cramped sitting-room, Cyril's granddaughter and great-granddaughter have the best china ready for coffee that tastes like mud and biscuits they never offer.

Suddenly, a door to the right opens and there stands Cyril, a little shaky on his pins. Spying us, he points a finger then bursts out with a 'Hey hey hey . . .' before making his way over. Short and bow-legged, he wears a tweedy blue jacket, a brown shirt with huge round collars and a cap, which his head seems to have shrunk beneath. Unshaven patches show on his weathered, impish face. Tottering unsteadily, he holds between thumb and forefinger an untipped cigarette dangerously heavy with ash. Deliberately he flicks it on to the floor and an ever-patient granddaughter holds out an ashtray. Cyril lurches towards a chair. 'Hey hey hey . . .' he rattles, revealing some lonely old gums.

In due course, Oldo manages to ask him why he thinks he's lived so long.

'Hey hey hey . . .' he cries. 'I've lived through two wars . . . Not too much to eat, only one cup of porridge a week . . .' He speaks out of the side of his mouth, his lips pressed together at the front.

Oldo tries again.

'I was a herdsman for seventy years, until I was eighty, working in the mountains with the cows . . .'

So we wonder what the skills of a good herdsman might be, but Cyril keeps leaping from subject to subject.

'My sons didn't like to go fighting in the war . . . It's a new age for us now, we should be happy . . . hey hey hey . . . I was tending the cattle in the mountains for the last time and two heifers were stolen. I had to pay forty-five thousand crowns for them . . . You must come, on the twenty-fifth of July I'll be ninety-five . . . ha ha . . . I'm a Catholic. I keep going to church because I don't know when I'll be finished . . . hey hey hey.'

Oldo looks helpless and I shrug, resigned to never knowing the secret art of the herdsman.

'Wait, wait, I try something else,' Oldo says as he adopts some new tack.

'I had two sons and a helper,' replies Cyril, 'three hundred and fifty head of cattle, bullocks and heifers, nine cows and only one dog. We lived up there in a wood cabin all summer, fencing staked out for the herd. But someone killed my dog . . . They knew I'd be no good without it . . . Have you heard the one about the young shepherd?'

'No,' we answer hesitantly.

'Well,' says Cyril, 'this shepherd was up in the hills for the first time and he asked the other shepherds what they did for sex.

'"We make love to the sheep, of course," they said.

'"No, you don't, I don't believe you," said the young lad. Well, the days passed and he couldn't stand it any longer, so he chose himself a sheep. He was just beginning to enjoy himself when he looked round and saw them all laughing. "What's wrong?" he said.

'"But it's such an ugly one!" they roared.

'Hey hey hey . . .' Cyril likes his story so much he wheezes himself to a standstill.

Then we all watch as he tries to light another cigarette. He smokes forty a day. His tough old hands look deformed. On his left, the third and little fingers once suffered frostbite in the mountains and are rolled over into his palm. The other little finger is hooked at right angles through arthritis, bent like a claw. The rest are thin and curved from a lifetime of milking. There's his head too. He fell badly when very young and nearly died. Removing his cap, Cyril shows us a knobbly yellowish wound, still scabby, on the flat of a bald white pate. He must have fallen head first. He was lucky.

'I've had my share of bad luck. That'll be why I've lived so long,' he says. 'Hey hey hey . . . God takes good care of me.'

He doesn't need persuading to have a photo taken outside. As we're getting our things together he's up and staggering to the door. Seeing him list perilously, I lunge and just manage to catch him in a full body hold before he crashes to the floor. Cyril smells of hay, tobacco and *borovička*.

In front of the barn door, Vanella sits with him, laughing and encouraging him to pose. But Cyril has a different idea. All he wants to do is put his tongue in her mouth. He takes her so much by surprise at the first attempt that he even succeeds. I see her recoil, horrified but somehow still smiling. She says his tongue was all hot and slimy.

Back home in the kitchen, Oldo the chef prepares dinner as we admire his impressive collection of finger-dolls in Slovak costume.

'Are you angry?' he says.

'Angry? No, we're not angry,' says Vanella, surprised.

'Are you angry, hangry . . . er, hungry?'

It's a good thing we are. Oldo serves up homemade goulash soup, spicy sausages in a piquant sauce and a main course of pork with lemon and walnuts, all washed down with a foaming jug of beer. Then we sit and talk into the night, realizing we are about the same age and that we've grown up either side of the Iron Curtain.

Oldo says they used to trust the socialist system. 'You are told to believe. You don't question. You think this is how it will be for ever. But now this is gone, it is like part of your body is ripped out. So for many people it is difficult. They are told not to believe any more. For me it is easier, perhaps, because I have been travelling.'

In some ways, the changes have been deceptive. Slovakia has to stand on its own now. But the Communist politicians have merely switched colours, the old factory managers have become the new entrepreneurs. There had been a bigger change for Oldo when he gave up his career. His father was a famous film star and Oldo had been a child actor, following in his father's footsteps. In the end, Oldo decided he wanted to live a normal life. But still this wasn't easy.

'My face is well known here,' he says, 'so people judge by what they think is the exterior. Because they see me as different, they are not interested to know me. Is bit difficult.' Oldo shrugs and pours more beer. 'We are all the same inside,' he says.

The three of us look one to another and raise our glasses yet again.

Tired and happy we retire to bed, only to be woken, viciously, by the bells. Oldo's house stands opposite the Catholic church, which plays alarm clock to the village at six o'clock. The Lutherans, a short distance away, don't impose so cruel a penance. There is no possible escape from the din, no chance of sleeping through. The bells pummel away for ten hellish minutes each morning.

At the *matrika* in Liptovský Hrádok, they show us a beautifully fluent signature in the record book – Maria Zemanova. In what used to be called Lenin Street we find a run-down three-storey block of flats and the same name on a label by a door.

There are two of them, two little old ladies set in motion by our arrival. One is still in her dressing-gown and slippers, Maria's daughter. She's seventy-three. Maria herself is tiny and hunched, and going to be ninety-nine this year. She welcomes us in a frail, squeaky voice, fussing around in confusion and asking for her best headscarf – the cream one with the red and green flowers.

'Do you want a big cup of coffee or small?' they ask. Oldo says we don't mind, so big ones are ordered and the pan put on the stove. Then we are made comfortable on stools with squares of crochet as cushions.

Maria arranges her scarf. Everything in their cramped flat appears to match in blue floral patterns: her dress, the wallpaper, her pinafore and the plastic tablecloth.

She's looking worried. 'I am very old, you know,' she warns. 'I am soft in the head now. It's gone, all gone.'

Hard work and little else has kept her alive and healthy for so long, she tells us. She grew up in Orava, a region to the north. Her father was a rafter who transported logs down-river to Zilina and she'd been his number two from the age of thirteen. It would take a whole day to ride the logs down and they would walk back, at least until the railway was built.

'Sugar?'

'No thanks.'

'No, you must have sugar,' she says.

'It is not possible to drink without sugar,' whispers Oldo, having tasted the coffee. 'It needs lot of sugar.'

I take a quick sip. It's so thick, gritty and unbearably strong, sugar will make little difference.

Maria smiles warmly, and she positively twinkles at Vanella. 'I have been happy all my life,' she says. 'I was very poor, but I always tried to be fair and good.'

When she married her husband, Slovakia was under the rule of the Habsburgs and thousands of young men had been recruited to fight Russia in the First World War. Granted four days' leave, he came to ask for her hand. She wanted to marry him, but was afraid of what might happen when he returned to the front. In those days a girl had to do as her father said. Maria's suitor asked hers about the dowry and that was that. They were married on the morning of his last day; in the afternoon he had to go back to the war. If he hadn't, he would have been shot as a deserter.

Oldo is grinning again and Maria looking concerned.

'She says you must drink your coffee before it goes cold. Even without sugar.' Oldo has already finished his, so while we struggle valiantly, he does the talking.

'When her husband went back to the fighting, one time it happened he was shot from behind, here.' Oldo points at his groin. 'And the left egg was shot . . .'

'Left leg?'

'Egg, egg. You have two eggs. The left one was shot. She said it was problem. Normally people had twelve children. They had only two daughters.' We hear that her second daughter died when only three weeks old.

Vanella looks sad for Maria as she sighs away the memory. She has grown very fond of Vanella and they're already holding hands. Vanella looks like she does when she's with her own granny, focusing her love. Maria shows her a ring on her finger.

'I want to give you this, from my heart. It has been blessed by the priest.'

'No, you must keep it, it's yours.'

'Are you married? Are you happy? Is he good?' Maria points a wrinkled finger at me.

'Yes, he's good.'

Maria wants to know how long we've been married and if we have children.

'All right. If anything happens, you can be happy if you forgive. You must always forgive.'

She wrinkles her nose and points at me again. 'The most important thing is that you must be good.'

I promise. I will.

'Josef Zeman was a very good husband. When he made me cross, I wouldn't speak to him and we would be in silence. When he wanted to say sorry, he'd come over and say something like, "Now, where did I put my glasses?" and I knew he wanted to start again. Then I would have to forgive him.'

'They were hungry, er, hangry, angry with love,' says Oldo, winking.

'You two must be the same,' says Maria. She gives me a stern little look and I know I have to be good, or else.

Then she shows us a picture frame where two separate photos have been cut out and spliced together as one, her precious family. Josef had gone to the United States to find work when their daughter was four and was away eight years. He stands proud in some American studio, in his best suit and oiled haircut; back home, Maria is in black and her daughter wears a pretty bonnet and clutches a spray of flowers.

'You make do with what you have and you have only what you can make for yourself,' says Maria. 'It was a poor life, but it was just.'

Maria and Vanella are now firm friends. They chatter away, without understanding each other much, and she keeps stroking Vanella's cheek affectionately. They've been counting.

'How old are you?' Maria asks. 'Thirty-one? But that's so young.'

In return, she counts out her own age on her fingers, 'Ten, twenty, thirty, forty, fifty, sixty, seventy, eighty, ninety—'

'Stop, stop,' we cry.

'What are you going to do on your hundredth birthday?'

'If I am still alive, I will celebrate,' she says emphatically. 'And you must come. I would like to show you how I can dance.'

We say we'll try, but that it might be difficult.

'Then you must write and I will write back.'

She copies out her address for us in the same steady, graceful hand we saw earlier. And so we kiss goodbye. Maria squeezes our hands and sends a prayer with us on our journey.

As we drive away down Lenin Street, two tiny figures at the first-floor window are waving furiously. The little lady in the flat below waves back too, blissfully unaware that our waves aren't really for her. In her free hand Vanella clutches a charm of the Virgin Mary, which Maria finally persuaded her to accept.

Behind the wheel, Oldo is looking thoughtful.

'You crazy English,' he says. 'You give something to the old people. It is something . . . how do you say it? . . . not physical . . . spirit. Yes. You keep them going another year, I think.'

But I'm beginning to understand that it is the old people who are giving to us, each in their own way. I'm glad that my assumptions are being challenged, and I already know that nothing can ever be the same. Then I wonder what they are doing for Oldo.

'I love these people,' he says. 'Slovak people.'

Oldo looks funny when he's being polite. He becomes all awkward and boyish. I always feel I want to snigger as he's introducing us. He rattles off some Slovak then stands blinking, waiting for a response.

'Jesus Christ,' is the immediate reaction he gets from Martin Brezina's granddaughter. She rushes back inside, panicking, and we're left standing by the steps. The house, built from solid, natural timbers, is situated on the main road through Východná, a village a little further to the east.

A huge roar comes from within and the shouting grows louder until Martin stands framed in the door. He is very excited to see us. His granddaughter bellows back, trying to calm him down.

Martin shouts out that he's ninety-three. He used to work on the railways.

Oldo helps to coax him indoors and, after some minutes of chaos, we're settled. A tiny square of window lights the side of Martin's face, picking out his silvery stubble. His blockish head is half bald, half cropped short. Suddenly he rolls up his sleeve to show Vanella his arm, badly scarred at the elbow. He'd been shot, fighting for the Emperor Franz Josef, against the Italians.

'I was only eighteen,' he says. 'I was so scared, I cried every day.'

There was such a stalemate on the front line at the river Piave, the two sides used to fight during the day then drink together in the same bars at night. Martin was hit by shrapnel while crossing the river. A plane came over shooting at them, his iron helmet was struck with a deafening clang and then he felt the pain. He was taken prisoner and at the military hospital they operated to save his arm. He sat out the next year in Milan.

'I liked the Italian girls,' he confides to us quietly. The granddaughter is away in the kitchen. 'And the Italian girls liked Slovak boys. "You are a white boy," they would say, "not dark, like our boys." We would walk the streets, sing and wave at them. We all had our Italian girls. We would meet in the evenings and stay together. The Italian boys were very angry.'

Oldo laughs and encourages Martin some more.

'*Piccolo*, *piccolo*,' he whispers behind his hand. 'There were a lot of children, new members of the Slovak nation.' Roused by the memory, he gives us a short snatch of song: '"What can happen to me, if I say that I love you . . ."' Then he cheers himself enthusiastically, both arms held high in triumph. His eyes bulge, his face grows red and his blue checked workshirt falls out of his trousers.

Oldo gives us a helpless look. There's nothing we can do to keep Martin away from his Italian girls.

'You had an Italian girlfriend?'

'Oh, yes, yes,' he says, with much bravado.

'What was her name?'

He can't remember. But she was very beautiful. '*Bella*, *bella*.' Martin cheers himself, and cries, 'I am ninety-three and still alive.'

'I think this is a very happy man,' observes Oldo drily.

The three of us can only watch as Martin stands and paces the room, gabbling wildly, his eyes alight and his chest heaving. Then he sits and tells aspects of his stories over again.

There was the time he spirited five insurgents into the house as they were being marched past by the Nazis. Then, as the Germans were retreating, some soldiers came to him and said, 'You are Protestant. We are Lutherans too, we can drink together. We will sleep at your house tonight.' So Martin served them food and *palenka*, his home-made moonshine. The Nazi officers tried to get him drunk, so he'd tell them where the partisans were. In fact, they were watching what was going on nearby and Martin slipped out to speak to them.

'We must kill the Fascists in your house,' they urged.

'No, no, go away,' said Martin. 'If we do that, more will come to kill us all. They will destroy everything. Leave it to me.'

So it was Martin who got the Germans drunk. They fell into a deep sleep and the peace was kept until morning.

Of course, a few weeks later, he couldn't resist entertaining the Russians in similar style when they passed by, going the other way.

For once, Martin falls quiet, and Oldo mistakenly asks if he's tired.

'*NOOOOOOO!*' he bawls. 'I'm not tired, I like my old age. I see my friends. We have a drink. I sing my songs.' He raises his head with military pride. 'Long live Slovakia! Rise up, you Slovak people!' he half sings, half shouts. 'We Slovaks have been repressed for too long . . . by the Hungarians, the Czechs, the Russians.' Now his hands are held together in prayer. 'May God grant freedom to the Slovak people.' Then his fists are punching the air as he roars, 'O SLOVAKIA!'

We cruise home in high spirits. Oldo has a habit of letting the Škoda build up speed then, shifting into neutral, he turns off the ignition to save petrol.

'You want to be as strong as Martin when you are old man?' Oldo asks.

'What a nutter!'

'Nutter? What is nutter?'

We explain.

'Nutter, yes. He is big nutter.'

We find Oldo's friend waiting for us at home. A quiet man in his seventies, with a slight build and a kindly look, Janko Chalúpka is his name. Oldo seems to have taken him under his wing and he's been invited for supper. Oldo's pocket dictionary tells us that Chalúpka means cottage, hut or cabin. In the end, we settle for Johnnie Smallhouse.

Janko weaves baskets. When he was at school, every child in the village used to choose their own exclusive craft to learn. In the early summer he's still to be seen in the fields, bent down searching out his special grasses. They have to be cut at just the right time.

'All you can see above the high grass is this cap, moving along,' says Oldo, with a grin.

Janko adjusts his green cap and has a scratch. Then he shows us two beautiful baskets. He asks Vanella which she prefers and immediately makes it a present.

'Soon, such things will be lost for ever,' says Oldo. 'His skill is not passed on to anyone. It is sad, I think. But these are the times.'

Oldo has served a chilled dessert wine with a touch of vermouth, which he claims is another ancient Slovak custom. Janko is not impressed.

'Where's the *borovička* then?' he teases. 'No self-respecting Slovak can get drunk on this stuff!'

The following morning we drive north through country lanes. With the engine switched off, the Škoda flies along with a whoosh of air through the open windows. Skylarks ascend, invisible in the clear blue. The meadows brim with the colour of wild flowers. Sunlight flicks off the scythes being swung to cut the hay. On we speed through quiet villages – a white-walled church, houses with red roofs, some with green.

In the tiny hamlet of Kvačany, they direct us to a house set back from the road with a dark wooden gable-end and strawberry pink walls. Oldo calls out at the open kitchen door, but there's no reply. So we look around, as hens cluck and peck by our feet. We follow him through the old barn and out the other side, where to our right stands a small hut with its door leaning open. Suddenly Oldo is dodging back towards us, giggling. Instinctively, we run behind him to the house, without knowing why. Then he explains. We just interrupted Irena Púčikova's morning constitutional on the lavatory.

But neither she nor we mention it. The old lady emerges from the barn and invites us into her sparsely furnished living-room, which contains not one speck of dust. There is a double bed with a thick eiderdown, a table and an old sewing-machine. The floorboards and roofbeams are bare, the walls painted a rich green. At each casement, one set of windows opens outwards and another inwards, leaving a ledge in between for pots of geraniums in bloom.

With her breath regained, Irena chatters away happily. Her early life has a familiar pattern. Born in 1901, here in Kvačany, the family had left to find work in Canada when she was six. They returned three years later, leaving her father behind. Her grandmother had written saying she was going to sell up if they didn't come home. Her father stayed on for another eighteen years, during which time he sent back not one dollar. As the eldest, Irena had to work as a farm labourer to support the family. One day her father did return, penniless. The story went that he'd been drunk, had fallen off a train, broken some bones and been deported as unfit for work. He soon became ill and died within the year. Such was the fate of Andrei Kuran.

Outside, a hay lorry clatters by along the road as the clock on the mantelpiece chimes ten o'clock.

When Irena talks about her husband, I'm reminded of a story in some foreign film. All the boys had been after Irena.

'I had ten of them round my little finger, all at once,' she says, laughing quietly. 'They all wanted to marry me. I had some fun with those boys.'

Behind the wrinkles I can still see an attractive young girl – firm, high cheekbones, neatly plaited hair, lovely challenging eyes and a smile that is nearly naughty. She knows how to look her best. Her pink shirt, short-sleeved dress and bright pink and blue apron are set off perfectly by a pretty headscarf.

Out in the sunshine a yellowhammer trills, as the breeze stirs the geraniums.

Matej came from another village, but she knew him. He was an Evangelist Protestant; she, a devout Catholic. When he declared his love for her, she said she could only love him like a brother, because she must love God first. So Matej left; he travelled in France for a time. He stayed with Catholics and studied the religion. When he returned, he had become a man and had the pick of all the girls. But he visited Irena and read the Bible with her, correcting her if she said anything wrong.

'Maybe he was pretending,' she says, with a little shrug. 'I didn't know. But from that moment I was crazy about him.' She laughs brightly, resting her head on her hand.

Matej used to invite the Catholic priest to her house while he was learning his catechism. So Irena asked the priest what he thought. 'Will Matej be good?' she said. 'If I had another one like him,' answered the priest, 'I should be very happy.' So Irena was happy too and married him in the name of God.

She had two children, but her boy lived only five hours. The labour lasted three days and three nights. She had no help and he died. Then, while her daughter grew like an angel, Matej became violent, wild like a tiger. But after each rage, he would always pray. It was like watching two people, one bad and one good. He hit everything all the time. He struck the chickens so hard they died. One time a cow wouldn't give milk, so he beat it till it bled.

Irena screws up her eyes at the memory. Oldo whispers he thinks Matej probably beat her too.

One time, he was here alone in the house while Irena was working a few miles away, planting trees. Matej was boiling the *slivovice* and chopping cabbage. They used to make their own plum brandy and the cabbage, fresh from the garden, was for a sauerkraut to keep through the winter. Matej had been drinking, and while he was putting the cabbage in the mechanical shredder, he caught his fingers. Then his whole hand became trapped. As he tried to free it, his shirt caught as well, then his other hand. He had to shout out to the neighbours to turn off the machine. At the hospital they amputated one hand and operated on the other.

Irena shakes her head disparagingly. Outside, one of her geese honks out a warning.

'He taught himself some work,' she says. 'He had a barrow which he strapped to his stump. He just about managed to lift it.'

Such was the fate of Matej Púčik. He died some twenty years ago. Irena now lives on her own. Her daughter has married for the third time.

'I have three grandsons, all from different fathers. My daughter had her first son before she married, the second by an alcoholic whom she divorced, the third by another she hadn't yet married.'

'All the men were living with her just for the hole,' says Oldo, in all seriousness.

'The what?'

'The hole, the hole. It is not possible to show you now.'

I'm laughing at the subtlety of his translation when suddenly Irena pipes up, 'Father, Son and Holy Ghost. Amen.' She still has smatterings of English from her short stay in Canada. She can count up to fourteen before getting stuck.

'Hundred!' she says, and we applaud. Then she chuckles. 'Son of a bitch . . . Go to Hell.'

Rolling back to Oldo's, we're on good form. Vanella leans forward, elbows up on the front seats, and Oldo is smirking. 'You know I thought she said, "Sun on the beach",' he says.

We hit a stretch of new tarmac with fresh white lines. Oldo suddenly pulls out into the path of an oncoming truck to celebrate. Our eyes fix on the truck as its mass looms towards us.

'We are alive, we are alive, we are alive,' cries Oldo, and we smile, unconcerned, exhilarated. Just in time, he steers back, slips into neutral and we sail down the next hill.

That evening, we eat a huge last supper and talk again into the small hours. We sleep briefly until the bells, then we gulp some coffee and Oldo takes us to catch our train. At the station he says, 'Come, we have time,' and leads the way to the café opposite, well patronized at such an early hour. He orders three huge shots of *borovička* and a glass of beer each.

'Watch.'

Oldo holds his shot glass against his cheek with the back of his hand. He rolls it round to his mouth and, without using any fingers, flips the glass and downs it in one. After a quaff of lager, he announces proudly, with watering eyes, 'Slovak breakfast!'

Then it's our turn.

On the platform, as the train rumbles in, Oldo zips open his bum-bag and shyly holds up one of his finger-dolls from the kitchen. She wears a green dress, a white shirt with tiny red flowers and a blue headscarf. He gives her to Vanella and she gives him a hug.

'*Dovidena*,' I say. Till we meet again, my friend.

6

Paradise Gained

How many travellers down the years have passed through the gates of Istanbul as they journeyed east? I can see the crowded bazaars where beguiling traders are haggling over silver, sweetmeats or myrrh. I touch soft embroidered cloth and feel the deathly cool of alabaster. I walk narrow cobbled streets worn smooth by the traffic of horse and cart, then turn to hear the wailing chant inviting the faithful Muslim to prayer. And in a corner there, we'll find an old Levantine with a crooked nose who tells us how he fished with nets by the Golden Horn and once sold his entire catch to a Frenchman whose daughter was to be wed that day.

I can always dream, but I would never have imagined Istanbul to exude such an unholy stink. The city's garbage men have chosen their moment to strike and they've been out long enough for the rot to take hold. Summer is high and the mountains of rubbish lie festering in the streets. We happen to have one growing on the pavement opposite our hotel, ensuring that our windows stay firmly closed at night. Without the blessing of air-conditioning, we perspire and boil in our beds. We've been going through a phase of sleeping late, soaking up the rest we haven't noticed we've been missing all these years. So when we wake, the sun has been up for hours and our stuffy little room is strangled by the heat. We lie there, unable to move, fearing the advance of the evil stench outside.

God, it's awful. We're forced to go out and return at a run, with hands clasped over our faces.

'Hello! Robert Redford!' the man at the desk shouts. He's been letting me make free calls on his phone and this is his way of developing our rapport. Needless to say, I don't look much like Robert Redford and he doesn't know too many old Turks.

We scour the bazaars and instead find a thousand carpet salesmen eager to show us their kilims.

'Hello, we have a nice carpet here. Hello, friends, what you are looking for? Excuse me. Welcome to our crazy country, welcome. How are you, madam? I hope everything is OK.' His accent sounds American, a young Turk wearing blue jeans.

'We're very well, thank you.'

'You from 'Stralia? New Zealand?'

'England.'

'Whereabout?'

'London.'

'I know it. Middlesex, Hounslow ... Yes, please, we have a nice carpet here.'

It's not his fault he sees us as a walking bankroll. They come in their coachloads to see the Blue Mosque and the Sultan's Palace. They arrive by aeroplane these days and the ancient ways of the city are choked with motor cars.

Mrs Duran hasn't even sat down before she tells us, proudly, that she is one of the few remaining relics of the Ottoman Empire.

'Yes, when I came we still had the Ottomans,' she says. 'It was Constantinople then.'

She had arrived by accident. It all began with a brief encounter, a very long time ago. Call it fate. Her life was to be utterly changed and, at the fine age of one hundred and three, she is still enjoying the consequences.

Corinna Duran is English. She hails from Brighton and remembers the seafront as it was in the reign of Queen Victoria, with its two piers and the military bands you could go to hear for tuppence every afternoon. It was London by the sea, Brighton. The morning train took them up and they came back down in the evening, the early commuters. And in summer, adventurous holiday-makers would come to promenade and take the air.

Funnily enough, we were in Brighton only recently. Vanella's grandmother lives there. We went to see her before we left and she sang her songs for us. 'Cockles and mussels alive, alive-o ...' That's always the clear favourite. Vanella held her hand as we all joined in. Dear Pat. She's getting on, well into her eighties. Vanella worries she might not be around when we get back.

Anyhow, so of course we swap addresses. Mrs Duran had lived in Rock Gardens and Vanella's gran in Dyke Road.

'Oh, yes,' Mrs Duran remembers with surprise, 'we always used to go to the dyke.'

She is looking something like a jockey today, I think. It's probably the chequerboard blouse, fastened at the neck with a silver brooch. Knees pressed together in a tight skirt, her white cotton socks are pulled as far they'll go up her shins.

That fateful encounter had taken place in a teashop. Corinna had arranged to meet her sister on the front and they ended up sharing his table. The young man was visiting from Paris, where he studied at the Sorbonne. Corinna had learnt some French, so they spoke a little together. The following year he returned to Brighton with a proposition of marriage. But her mother had a different view on the matter. 'I'll have no foreigners in my house,' she said. So Corinna eloped to France, whereupon he informed her that he wasn't French at all, but Turkish. Faik Sabri was his name.

Mrs Duran shakes her head, lips pursed. 'I haven't told anyone what I'm telling you now,' she says, with a little conspiratorial look. 'England wouldn't marry me. France wouldn't marry me. Because he was Turkish. Polygamy, you see. They were all supposed to have four wives in those days. "Well," I said, "what are we going to do now?"'

It was the Turkish consul in Paris who married them in the end. The year was 1911.

'What made you fall in love?' asks Vanella. She's always one for the romance.

'Oh, it wasn't a love marriage,' Mrs Duran whispers. 'It was convenience. I wanted to see the world and he said he would take me.'

So the romance of travel had won a young girl's heart. She adored Paris, but was captivated by the thought of Constantinople. What she found there was a cosmopolitan melting-pot of nationalities: Greek, French, Italian, Armenian and even a community of Spanish Jews. These were the last days of the sultans. Everyone spoke French. Everything was so exotic, invigorating, far from the demure pretensions of Brighton. Although Muslim codes were strict, Corinna enjoyed the freedom of being a foreign wife. Rather than don the veil she simply wore a hat, and she could go to the theatre if she wished, unlike the Turkish ladies.

Then, one day, there came a knock at the door. An officer saluted and said, 'You have an English woman here. I have to take her to be interned.' The First World War had been declared and Corinna was now the enemy. Her husband asked for a week's grace; she had to get her things ready. When the officer returned, he was able to say, 'There's nobody English here.' In the meantime, Corinna had given up her British nationality and become a Turk.

I'm suddenly finding this rather disconcerting. Our lady is now Turkish, but all the same she remains as English as they come. Here we are in the cosy sitting-room of the flat she shares with her daughter, Loulou, a sprightly seventy-year-old. On the side-table lie copies of English newspapers. We take tea, eating sponge cake with a fork. And if I wandered over to the window I'd expect to see the placid grey of the English Channel and a drab wintry sky to match. It's her voice – as she describes the old streets of Constantinople: how they went everywhere by horse and carriage; the dazzling, bright fabrics, the noise and scents of the bazaar – those flat middle-class tones, they sound so English. For me, they evoke only Brighton, antique shops and fish 'n' chips on cold, wet afternoons. Then I hear the crackle of the microphone and the call of the *muezzin* begins to ring out across the neighbourhood, inviting the brethren to prayer in the mosque. And I am transported. His singing is masterful: long notes held in perfect control, quavering, stepping up and then down. But throughout his performance the English ladies keep talking as if he doesn't exist. When he's finished, Mrs Duran pipes up, on cue, 'Let's have a drink, shall we? What would you like?'

'The wine isn't cold,' Loulou calls out from the kitchen. 'It'll have to be gin and tonic or champagne.'

Charged with clinking gins, we move upstairs to the roof terrace. Mrs Duran shuffles her way there, more or less under her own steam, and we sit looking out over the Bosphorus, where sirens blow as the ships ply their trade.

'Cheers. Good health,' we concur. My, that's a strong gin.

Although her husband died young, in 1942, he did keep his promise. He became a professor of geography and a writer of books. He wrote about the lives of animals, about travel and the stars. Every two years they would go on tour around Europe and the Mediterranean. They travelled by train or merchant ship, visiting Egypt, Greece, Albania, Italy. They travelled through Bulgaria and as far north as Sweden. Her husband produced an atlas, which they say is still published under his name to this day. When Mustafa Kemal, the Atatürk, had decreed in

1935 that all Turks should now adopt a surname, Faik Sabri chose Duran, meaning 'he who stays'. A strange choice for a travelling man, but then I wonder if it also might mean '*she* who stays', for Mrs Duran has lived here ever since.

The world has turned around her. Constantinople isn't what it was. English people aren't English any more.

'No, there's nothing left that's British,' she says. 'I was born with Queen Victoria. I go by her.'

That's like people who grow old with the same hairstyle they had as teenagers. It would be like finding me living in some remote Indian village in the year 2060, white-haired and frail, saying, 'It's only rock 'n' roll, man.' That's the thing. We have to keep moving on somehow.

Mrs Duran says she's had enough. 'Now it's dull. Life's dull,' she says. 'I want to die.'

She grimaces, her powdered face looking more deeply lined in the early-evening light. To be precise, she wants to die in ten days' time. '*Je veux vivre jusqu'à vendredi prochain*,' she declares. A week on Thursday, her English gentleman friend has promised to take her out for a drive. If the weather's nice, they'll stop off somewhere for lunch.

'But I do love the Bosphorus,' she enthuses, extending a hand out across the water. 'It's so pretty. Across the other side, it's all villas and gardens. It changes all the time. The sun comes and then the moon and the stars. Oh, and you can breathe . . .'

They have a fine view. Away in the distance, the old city smoulders in a smoky haze, a jumble of rooftops camped among the many splendid domes and pointy minarets.

Gazing across, I ask her what she thinks of Istanbul today.

'Babyish,' she replies.

'I'm sorry?'

'Babyish.'

'What do you mean by that?'

'They don't know what to do or say,' says Mrs Duran. 'All the real old Turks, they've died.'

Some men have arrived to deal with the rubbish, but it has already begun to suppurate. They come at it with broad shovels and folds of yellow ooze spill out on to the pavement.

'Hello! Harrison Ford!' calls my friend on the desk, as we steel ourselves for a dash. We have a few hours to kill before we catch the night bus south, so we think we'll freshen up. Vanella and I head for the corner and disappear through separate doorways.

The Door Man shows me down the steps into a reception area, quaintly fifties in style. There are slatted wooden seats, a cash desk and a burbling fountain circled by lazy carp. The bar is fashioned in chrome and, in a steamy ante-room beyond, I can see half-naked fat Turks standing around smoking cigarettes. I wonder if I'll be in with them. The Door Man introduces me to the Lobby Man, who speaks in pidgin monosyllables. He points at my dusty loafers, then to a row of leather sandals on the floor.

'Chenge,' he says.

I consider how many sweaty Turkish feet have stepped before me, but quickly decide this isn't in the true spirit of the exercise. Best to carry on. The Lobby Man points to the gallery above.

'Chenge.'

I wave my toiletries, as if to say, 'Do I need these?'

'Yus, yus, chenge.'

Upstairs, I'm intercepted by Cubicle Man, who pushes me into a strip of a room, containing a narrow bed, a mirror, a filthy metal ashtray and three clothes hooks. It smells used.

'Chenge,' says Cubicle Man, handing me a cotton wrap, which smells even more used.

I emerge feeling conspicuously English, the wrap tucked around my waist, toiletries in hand. Cubicle Man shows me back to the stairs and the Lobby Man points to a new row of cloggie sandals. I switch footwear before he can even say. I think I'm getting the hang of this.

I clop towards the door he opens for me and enter a steam-room, showers on one side, giant washstands on the other. A half-naked Turk emerges from the mist, wearing a wrap like mine but girding six times the stomach. He is completely bald.

'Mussidge?' he asks.

I presume he's staff – the Lobby Man is no longer around to help. I don't see why not, a massage would be very pleasant. So I nod. The Half-naked Turk Man picks a fresh wrap and leads me on through the next door.

Once I've recovered from being whacked full-frontal by the heat, I'm able to take things in. This is the bath-house, a square space with a giant dome and octagonal skylights through which shafts of white light shine dimly down. The heat is emanating from a raised marble plinth, where I'm supposed to recline on a foam-rubber mat. The Half-naked Turk Man arranges the wrap, says, 'Wait,' and I am left alone. I clop about admiring this temple of steam. Outsize washstands with brass taps line the tiled walls, each full to the brim with deliciously cold water. At the four corners, a doorway leads to identical smaller chambers, with more rows of basins.

I stretch out on the slab. Although my foam headrest smells of unwashed towels, I relax and seep for a while in peaceful meditation. Gazing at the paint peeling damply from the roof, I wonder if they're ever busy. Then I wonder how Vanella's getting on. She's in her own temple somewhere nearby.

I smile to myself. This morning I found a message, scribbled in biro, upside down in the top corner of my notebook. I only ever use pencil for my notes, so I couldn't miss it. The frisson of annoyance I felt because my space had been defiled soon vanished when I turned it round to read, 'I love you so much, Jackboot! I do, I do really!'

'Do you love me? Do you love me?' she then goes, when I reveal I've seen it. Do I? Yes. I do too.

A new half-naked Turk crashes in and slouches across to a corner chamber, dragging his wooden feet. He splashes around for some time and I can't decide if he's staff or not, but then he comes and stands over me.

'Fife minit,' he says, and disappears.

I reckon he must be My Man. At least twenty minutes pass before he returns, picks up my toiletries and shows me to the massage table. A muscular fellow with a protruding nose and bristling black moustache, he makes me lie on my back and unpeels the cotton wrap, exposing me totally. He gives my willie a curious look, making me check to see if I should be embarrassed. I bet he does that to everyone.

My Man doesn't use oil, but soap. Expertly, he gives every muscle in my body, and the bits in between, a thorough work-out. He applies a force that's on the vicious side of vigorous, treading a thin line between pleasure and pain. Finally, he rounds off with a few tricks. He cracks all my joints. He puts me on my front, grasps a fold of skin at the base of my spine, lifts me off the table and drops me. Then he moves higher up the spine, picks me up and winds me yet again.

He leads me back into the main chamber for my bath. This involves sitting on the floor beside a washstand, being alternately soaped and doused with basinfuls of icy water. He washes my hair and douses me;

he scrubs me with a rough glove foaming with suds and douses me; he slaps a floppy white brush and douses me. Each basin is a leaden torrent that cleanses me through to my inner being.

Suddenly, he's shaking me firmly by the hand, telling me what an exceptional bath I've had. At least, I imagine that's what he says. I'm in no state to disagree. I feel beaten up and brilliant at the same time.

My Man shows me out. My friend, the Half-naked Turk Man, serves me a mineral water and I'm passed back through the ranks. I dress, then find Cubicle Man hovering between me and the stairs. I've been warned that tipping is very much the order in these joints, so I'm ready with some small notes and loose change. I give him 5,000 lire. Not enough, he says. So I give him a few more coins. The Lobby Man stands with his hand out and is awarded 5,000 too. I get away with 3,000 to the Half-naked Turk Man; My Man himself receives 20,000 and looks despondent. Then a new character, the Cash Desk Man, relieves me of 110,000 lire for the massage and bath, though I escape tipping him for the pleasure of taking it from me. I'm nearly through, but the Door Man bars my way. I risk 3,000 and stumble out into the blinding light.

Vanella sits waiting in the shade.

'How was it for you?' I enquire.

'Great. What about you?'

'I feel like I've just been mugged.'

~

Only a few years ago Marmaris was a quiet fishing village, tucked away down the Aegean coast. Today it is a seaside town swarming with tourists, a destination. They can't build the hotels fast enough. From all over Europe the punters come to lie out on the gravel beach, grill themselves and swim around in engine-oil. They eat, drink and party; they buy leather gear in the street bazaars and fly home bronzed and happy.

Along the quay pleasure-boats line up to tempt them, fifty-footers with names like *Neptun* and *Kleopatra*, white rails a-shining.

''Allo, where you from?' the boys in T-shirts call. Their job is to tout and hustle.

''Allo, you from England? Manchester United! You like boat trip? We take you to Paradise. Today. Tomorrow? Here, I show you.' He points to a map.

There's a place along the peninsula called Paradise – a quiet beach with a restaurant, a swim in deep, clear water.

'Tonight it is disco on the boat. You wanna dance?'

Every night the disco drifts, pulsating, against the black backdrop of the bay. But we're only pretending to be on holiday. We've checked into a modest family-run hotel, where we eat omelettes for breakfast and make friends with the waiters. We join everyone on the beach for a few hours one afternoon, but we don't share their dedication. We aren't expected back at our desks a week on Monday. Instead, we go exploring and bump into Hüseyin, who works in the tiny office of a travel company round the corner. He's an amiable sort, in his early forties, not at all interested in hustling. Hüseyin's favourite pastime is sitting out drinking mint-flavoured *chai* in small glasses with whoever will join him. He introduces us to his friend Mustafa, a relaxed young man with a black brush moustache who smokes his Marlboro with a passion. Over the fifth glass of tea they reveal they know of a very old lady. She has quite a reputation, they say.

Next day, Hüseyin leads us along one of the roads out of town. We move slowly, conserving our energy in the crushing heat. The lady lives in a block of flats behind a filling-station, where the vapour shimmers dangerously around the pumps.

Indoors we find welcome relief. Removing our shoes, we pad into the corner room of a ground-floor flat shuttered in a half-light of reflected sun. The walls are pink, the woodwork pale green. The cool tiles soothe the soles of my feet as we exchange greetings with the family. Smiling, they invite us to sit on the floor where a gentle breeze blows and they offer us refreshing water melon, which soon dissolves away to slippery pips.

Fatma Toksoy sits cross-legged on a raised divan, surrounded by bolsters and cushions. It is as if she is enthroned and we have come to listen at her feet. She quickly tidies her hair and arranges a cotton shawl to cover her head, a tight motif of hearts that drapes around the shoulders and folds across her breast. To her right, a wooden chair supports her needs: a plastic jug of water, towels, talcum powder and a family-size aerosol of fly-spray.

Her lovely old face is wrinkled like a walnut. They say she is a hundred and two. She has outlived all but one of her six children.

'Thanks be to Allah,' she murmurs, peering down through thick-lensed glasses, one eye magnified considerably.

'Are you husband and wife?' she asks.

We say we are.

'He is your master,' she reminds Vanella, who nods but I can see she's not convinced.

The old lady tells us about her first husband. He died fifteen days after returning from the war at Gallipoli.

'Was he wounded?'

'It was the evil eye,' she says.

'The evil eye is what we call *nazar*,' explains Hüseyin. 'You have seen the eyes in the bazaars?'

We have indeed – round flat talismans of blue glass, dark pupils and pale irises, basketloads of them staring from every corner. Used as ornaments or jewellery, they protect against the advances of the dreaded *nazar*. Its power is so strong they have been known to shatter into tiny pieces.

'The doctors could do nothing,' says Hüseyin. 'Her husband came from the war, saw the evil eye and he died.'

She was forced to marry again, against her wishes. Her mother had cried all the while until finally she wed the man who had been chosen for her. To him, she gave three sons. 'I still have my youngest,' she says. 'God left him to take care of me in this world. You also will have children and they will take care of you.'

We haven't given that idea too much thought – children. If we had, I don't suppose we'd be here now. I imagine one day we'll get round to it. I wouldn't want to be too old to be a grandfather. Of course, it is customary in a country like Turkey for children to look after their parents in their dotage. This always strikes me as a fair deal. Parents take care of their children until they can fend for themselves, then the children return the favour later on. Our Western society seems to have done away with such ancient tradition. We think our old people have so little to offer and, anyway, we really haven't the time. We put them in homes so we don't have to worry. I might regret this one day but, frankly, I'd rather die. Watch out, kids. Maybe I'll escape. I'll take up my stick and go travelling instead.

Fatma Toksoy is shaking her head. 'If I didn't have my son to look after me, I would be in a bad way,' she admits. 'So my heart is always like a child's.'

When she was a girl, she was blessed with such a beautiful voice. She attended the Koran school, and when she read, everyone came to listen.

Before we have time to notice, her words are sliding into a rhythmic chant. She is speaking Arabic and sounds as if she has a marble bobbling in her mouth. We listen, and as the words cascade on and on, she seems to enter a kind of trance. A car horn blows out by the petrol pumps. A voice calls up the stairwell in the hall. At last she slows to catch her breath.

'She was saying a prayer from the Koran,' Hüseyin whispers. 'It is all she has to remember, the Koran.'

She can still recite the entire work by heart – all 114 chapters, 6,236 verses. Even now, each year she reads it aloud ten times from start to finish. This is what keeps her alive. The Koran contains only part of a book, believed to reside in heaven, which is a record of all that has ever happened and all that will happen. Koran means 'the word of God'.

Fatma Toksoy drifts back into prayer, her fingers flickering upwards. She slows again, points at me and asks Hüseyin to write something down.

'*Bismillahirrahmanirrahim*,' he copies out.

'*Bismillahirrahmanirrahim*,' she repeats, so fast the syllables disappear. Then slowly, and with emphasis, she pronounces, '*Ya baki, entel baki, huvel baki, Allahim, sensim baki*.'

The first is the prayer she says before carrying out even the most ordinary of actions. The second translates as, 'My God, You are before, You are after, You are for ever.'

I look up from my notebook to find she is watching us. She gives me a little nod. 'It was a different world when I was young,' she says and, collecting her shawl around her, she tells the story of one Hajji Fazil, who came to the region many years ago.

'This Hajji was a holy man,' she begins. 'He could fly like a bird, by praying the prayer I have told you. And so people wanted to see whether this was true. They went to his house, half of them deliberately unwashed and the rest clean. If he was indeed holy, he should be able to tell the difference. In our religion, we wash before we pray. The body must be clean before we can be spiritually clean. And so this Hajji Fazil, he took the clean ones inside and to the rest he said, "You should be clean before you enter my house." So they cleansed themselves and returned. "O Hajji, teach us that prayer so that we too can fly," they said. So the holy man taught them the prayer, but none could fly. Only the Hajji did fly, for he was a prophet.'

'Did he literally fly?' I ask.

'He was a prophet, from an older generation,' says the old lady, nodding. 'That was a former time.'

From her side, she lifts the heavy volume bound in red leather. She turns the stiff vellum to find her place.

'Young people should always remember the fact of death in our lives. I will die and you will die,' she says, pointing a crooked finger. 'You may live a short life, but still you should live in the way of the righteous. And after reading the prayers I have given you, you will be able to enter paradise. So it is written.'

I still don't know if I believe in the idea of heaven. It could just be wishful thinking on our part. One day, for sure, my body will wither and die. My bones will crumble. But what will happen to me, this invisible strand of quicksilver here inside which I know is me? It's a comfort to know there will be an after-life, another level in the game. But what if there isn't?

The old lady begins to read again.

'She prays all the time,' whispers Hüseyin, 'so that she, her family and everyone else will enter paradise.'

'What will she find there?' I ask.

Fatma Toksoy closes her eyes and rocks back and forth a little. 'God will give you the heavens of paradise,' she says. 'Everything will be ready, food will be brought and you will eat. God will give you life again. You will not need to work. There is no death in paradise. In hell, everything will be boiling. There, the evil ones will burn.'

And so she prays, 'Allah is the only God, Muhammad is the only prophet.' She reads again, working a finger back across the flowing Arabic script, her very lifeline. Rocking to and fro, she appeals to the heavens, on and on, as before, but longer, much longer. Out pour her prayers until finally she promises us our place in paradise.

'Say Amen.'

'Amen.'

'Love God and He will not let you go to hell.'

Her hands are working upwards, fingers flickering, rings flashing.

'Bubulubulubulubu,' she wails as she describes the bubbling fires below. 'Frrrrrrrr,' goes her tongue and she raises her eyes in reverence. 'All is well,' she says. 'You will be with us in paradise.'

7

Loaves and Fishes

Vanella isn't happy. She gets that look sometimes. I know it's only because she's tired, but it shows as grim determination – she won't let go till we have a bed for the night.

It's late, we just arrived in Cairo and we've nowhere to stay. We phoned ahead too. But when we roll up at the hotel the man says he's given our room away. Tomorrow is no problem, but right now the place is full. At least he apologizes. We suggest he finds us a room somewhere else for the night and he makes a call. He'll send his boy with us and even offers to pay for the taxi.

So we're OK. We plunge back out into the night, where the air is thick and heavy, the hottest so far. Our taxi dodges traffic for two minutes, then stops in a side-street.

'Here we are . . .' I try to sound reassuring as I search for any sign of a hotel. The boy leads us to some metal lift doors that give straight on to the pavement. There is graffiti scrawled everywhere and Vanella still has the look. The lift arrives, the boy presses six and up we go.

The doors open and we find ourselves in some kind of bar with subdued boudoir lighting. Men are drinking at secluded tables on tawdry, red velvet seating. Round the corner we find a reception desk, some faded plastic flowers and a fat man with a moustache who says he has our room ready. He checks our passports and hands them back. I'm filling in a registration slip when I sense someone at my elbow.

'Ah, British,' says a voice. 'New arrivals.'

I turn to find a man who is maybe forty, wearing the local dress, a long cotton *galabeya* and sandals. It's odd, because he looks European and sounds like he could be German.

'We're only here for the one night,' I say, and try to ignore him. This doesn't work.

'See, you can sit out and enjoy.' The man seems oblivious of Vanella's presence beside me as she signs her form, and he draws my attention to a roof terrace where more customers are drinking. To humour him, I move towards the door and take a look.

'Very nice.'

'Anything you want. Everything is easy,' he tells me knowingly. I can't work this out. There's something very dodgy going on here.

'Jackson!' Vanella calls, with some urgency.

A man in a red jacket, worn grey and greasy at the elbows, shows us to our door. First, we have a sitting-room, furnished with tatty vinyl armchairs and a large wardrobe. My eyes are immediately drawn to the carpet, which is, in every sense, quite awful – brown, threadbare, filthy. It's the cigarette ends that really get me. A smell of stale sweat hangs in the air and I can't see any evidence of air-conditioning.

Vanella is already through in the bedroom, which is painted pale green and all but taken up by a large double bed. It sags in the middle and looks conspicuously unmade.

'Yurrgh . . .'

I check out the bathroom, the largest of the three rooms. We have no toilet seat, no paper, only dripping condensation and a thick layer of brownish grime. I wouldn't even wash my hands in there.

'Jackson!' Vanella calls from the sitting-room. 'There's someone outside. I can hear voices.'

I take a look. No one there.

'What are we going to do?'

'I don't think we've got much option.'

I'm trying hard to play down how disgusting the place is. Someone's even gobbed on the carpet, for Christ's sake.

'We can't sleep in this,' she says, as we inspect the bedroom again. She's right, we can't. I suggest we open up a sleeping-bag, then lay our cotton ones on top. We have these handy sheet sleeping-bags, which are proving invaluable.

We hear a knock at the door. I open it and there stands the German.

'Yes, hello. You can change money if you want,' he says, rubbing his fingers.

'No, thank you,' I tell him, and close the door.

Vanella screams. She's found a cockroach in the bathroom. It ran back into a hole by the door, at waist height.

'Oh, God. Oh, no. I hate them, I hate them,' she shouts. 'Will you get rid of it, please?'

I fish out the torch to take a closer look. He's huge. For a moment I'm fascinated by his evil little eyes and the sensuousness of his movement as he waves his antennae at me.

'Gregor,' I taunt him. All cockroaches are called Gregor ever since I saw the film of Kafka's *Metamorphosis*.

There's another knock. It's the German again; he has a boy with him this time.

'Hello. I am sorry. He wants your passports at reception, please.'

'I'm sorry too. No way. Good-night.' And I firmly shut the door in his face.

'I don't like this,' says Vanella.

'We'll be OK. Don't worry. Come on, let's try and get some kip.'

Reluctantly we lay out protection on the bed. I'm playing at being practical and reassuringly casual, but I'm definitely not touching anything in this room with any part of my body. It's so hot it looks like there's sweat coming through the walls.

We are cleaning our teeth, using the remains in my water-bottle, when this time I actually hear the door open.

'What's going on?'

I reach the sitting-room in time to challenge whoever has just let himself in with a key. He's an Egyptian, sporting a waxed moustache and oiled, foppish curls.

'Can I help you?' I'm less than polite.

He pretends to be surprised.

'Oh! Good evening. I was just looking for some soap.'

Soap! In that bathroom?

'No, we don't have any soap and we don't want any either. Thank you. Goodbye.'

I push him out of the room.

I can feel it coming. Vanella starts moving furniture.

'I am not sleeping here with people walking in, as and when they fancy. Come on, get the wardrobe.'

'What?'

'The wardrobe. Against the door.'

She means it. It's tacky with grime, but I heave it round, then add both armchairs as a second line of defence. On these I balance the coffee-table, so it'll fall first and give us some warning.

I don't remember sleeping. I just remember us lying huddled next to each other in a pool of perspiration, waiting for the dawn.

~

I strain to catch what the man who gives his name as Hamdi is saying. The incessant din of Cairo street life comes crowding through our window – a blast of music, shouts, whistles, the clash-clash of the liquorice-juice man's cymbals and the constant parp parp, beep, pip parp of the traffic. Only the joker with the *Dr Zhivago* theme tune for a horn provides any respite.

The phone line crackles with interference.

'I'm sorry, I can't hear you.'

'I have one name,' repeats the man called Hamdi, 'Sir Saba Habachy Pasha, a well-known figure.'

'And do you know where I will find him?' I ask, scribbling furiously.

'I am sorry, sir, I have no idea. I cannot be of any assistance to you there.'

I thank him and begin to wrestle at some greater length with the Egyptian telephone system. My end is a sticky, cracked heap of buff-coloured plastic, with a dial that has to be gently nursed clockwise, then watched as it rotates back in agonizing slow motion. Getting an outside line takes at least three goes. Then I patiently dial the number, to be greeted by nothing but an eerie silence. In the end, the only way is to apply the Zen approach to telephonic communication: a belief gradually instilled in my soul that time is of no consequence and that the machinery will work only when it so desires.

A voice answers at the offices of *Al Ahram*, the local newspaper, and I describe my quest for whoever Sir Saba Habachy Pasha might be.

'Moment,' says the voice.

'Hello, yes,' says a second voice, a full minute later.

I explain again.

'Moment.'

The long silence is finally broken by a scruffling sound.

'Hello . . . hello?'

'Hello. Moment,' says another voice. Then the line goes dead.

I abandon the Zen and Vanella suggests we visit *Al Ahram* in person. It's only a few blocks away. There, from the phone in Reception, we speak to a more helpful voice, who gives us the name of a lawyer who should know how to find Saba Habachy. We need to look for a man called Adil Kamel in the same building as Kasallian, a jeweller, in a particular street somewhere across the city. So Vanella sensibly elects to return to the hotel, while I set out on foot.

The afternoon sun presses its heat like a weight against my face as I walk the cross-currents of people and traffic. The air swirls blue with fumes and the road tar feels spongy underfoot. Down the backstreets, I am watched by the curious eyes of men who sit beside their bubbling hookah pipes. I pass spice mountains smelling of red, green and golden flavours, in canvas bags the shape of chimney-pots. 'You are welcome to Egypt,' calls out the smiling man in a long *galabeya* and white skull-cap, making a half-salute.

The busy street where Kasallian is supposed to trade is home to every other jeweller in town, it seems. I look blankly at the name-plates beside a large doorway, rows of plastic strips covered in squiggly Arabic. I ask the doorman who sits on the broad stone steps if he knows of Kasallian and he points along the street. I ask in a shop and they direct me around the corner. I ask again, and an Armenian jeweller sends me around another corner to a building site where three thoughtful-looking goats stand tethered. One more attempt and I end up back where I started, in front of the doorman. So instead I ask for Adil Kamel himself. His office has been upstairs all the time.

But he's not in. The bemused lady who lives next door kindly gives me his phone number.

Back at base, I diligently practise more telecom Zen and a whole day later succeed in speaking to Adil Kamel. He promises to enquire with Saba on our behalf and the next day he reports back. He gives me Saba's number, which I call on three occasions but each time the phone just rings and rings. More Zen, another day, and I find myself speaking to the great man's wife. An appointment is fixed.

The taxi we hail is a black and white Peugeot, dented and scuffed like an old cardboard box.

'How much to El Dukki?' I ask the driver.

'Twenty,' comes the reply in sign language, twenty Egyptian pounds.

'Twenty? No, no, no.'

'OK, ten.'

'No. Ten too high. Five.'

'OK, five,' say his fingers.

We jump inside, where the seats are covered with carpet, furry beads hang from the rear-view mirror and the driver's ID on the dashboard bears no resemblance to the face grinning back at us.

'Where to?' he signals.

'El Dukki!' we repeat in astonished unison.

He doesn't even know where he is. So a journey which should have taken a quarter of an hour takes three-quarters, with me shouting out directions from an inadequate map of the city. Meanwhile, we are entertained by our man rocking at the wheel to local hit sounds at full volume on the radio as he blasts the horn at anything that blocks our way. Once we've crossed the Nile, we have to ask to find the street. Then we have to ask again to locate the house. 'You are welcome to Egypt,' says the pizza-delivery boy, then sends us in completely the wrong direction. Hot, exasperated and very late, we climb the front steps and, with a sense of considerable triumph, I press the Habachys' doorbell.

It turns out that Saba is a wise old owl. In his time, he has served as a lawyer, a tribunal judge and a government minister. He's been professor of Islamic Law at Columbia State University and once acquired two doctorates from the Sorbonne in the same year.

Saba claims he is now ninety-six.

'No, he's not,' calls out Lady Beatrice Habachy, as she comes in with a tray. 'In November he'll be ninety-five.'

'So you are ninety-four?'

Saba chuckles. 'Perhaps that is more correct. I don't want to cheat God by one year, or even two.' He speaks softly, his pronunciation precise. 'My beard, of course, now that is only three months old,' he says, with a glint of mischief, which dares me to ask why, after all these years, he has decided to grow it. 'Why not?' he can then reply, with an enforced shrug of the shoulders, eyes wide in feigned surprise.

Saba looks a little like an owl too. The eyebrows arch, olive cheeks are puffed up to pinch. His silver hair is brushed back, distinguished, and the dark blue dressing-gown he wears is soft in its silken sheen.

Meanwhile, Lady Habachy is handing out glasses of chilled mango juice so fibrous it comes with a spoon and ends up lodged mostly between our teeth. She settles herself in one of the many chairs that populate their spacious sitting-room and casually leafs through the pages of a magazine. If Saba errs on any detail, she leans over to scold him affectionately. 'Now, Saba, what did you just say? When did we get married? . . . Don't try to be old, Saba.'

And he replies, with a twinkle, 'The lady knows better than I do. I am learning about myself, I think,' his shoulders bobbing up and down with mirth.

First, we have to hear all about their children, from both previous marriages, and then there are the grandchildren. Photo frames are displayed at every turn. Once in a while, a power cut puts out the lights, but neither of them appears to notice. Outside, the traffic pips and parps, and someone next door practises tunelessly on a *mizmar*. And as I'm wondering what we have to learn from this genial Egyptian gentleman, he begins to talk in a roundabout way, with a certain befuddled charm, about the things that matter to him most.

As minister of industry, commerce and supply he had fed the hungry mouths of Egypt and the British Army, as Rommel advanced across the Western Desert towards Alexandria. He made himself very unpopular with the wealthy landowners of the Nile delta, who wielded great influence in those days. Their valuable cotton crop had to be substituted with wheat and rice. But the policy had proved correct. According to Saba, there had been no shortages.

He had, of course, resisted any temptation for personal gain. The minister of supply enjoyed tremendous power and wheat had become a premium commodity. A colleague once whispered to him, 'You control the fixing of the price, Saba, why not buy the wheat yourself and sell when the price is high? Any bank will lend you the money.' But Saba had no desire to enrich himself. His duty was to his country. It had been a very difficult time, the war.

For his good work, he was made a Knight of the British Empire, an honour bestowed on him by King George VI. As Lady Habachy is quick to remind us, he is now the last remaining Egyptian knight. The government of Egypt also awarded him the title of pasha.

'This pasha is a pompous thing,' he says, 'a left-over from the Turkish Empire. I can be pompous, but it is no use for myself or my own. I don't believe in all these titles. I never used any of them.'

'He was known by his friends as the Minister of Shyness and Humility, you know,' Lady Habachy adds, peering over her spectacles.

And Saba simply pulls a face, eyebrows raised and eyes popping. 'You are welcome to Egypt, of course,' he says, deflecting all admiration.

Not everyone was so generous. Saba is a Copt, that minority race of ancient Egyptians, and so a Christian. He had always been hard-working and ambitious. His legal practice grew successful by taking on the most difficult cases involving foreigners. There used to be many Greeks and Italians, especially in Alexandria. And although his business associates and some close friends were Muslim, he found himself persecuted by his Arab countrymen. They ridiculed him in the newspapers and around the university, calling him the Minister of Commerce, Supply . . . and the Seven Fishes.

'The seven fishes?'

Saba throws out his hands in dismay. 'Yes, because I was a Christian, because Christ had fed the multitudes . . . I didn't understand the joke myself at first. Of course, I had no religious bias one way or the other. But there was some feeling of jealousy. My policies had worked. Why should I, a Copt, succeed? Then also, I had a great uncle, a man named Boutros, who belonged to the wealthy upper class. I did not. I always remained middle class, but even so people invented stories about me.'

After the revolution, when Nasser came to power, Saba decided it best to leave the country. It was a tough decision, but he had friends overseas and a good reputation as a lawyer and economist. He taught in Ethiopia, travelled and worked abroad, then took up residence in the United States. He had been away nearly thirty years, when Professor Saba of Columbia State University came home one time on a cultural visit and decided to stay. He preferred life at home, now that times were more tolerant. Another reason to remain was Beatrice, whom he met on his return. She, too, was a university professor and, says Saba, '*une dame de société*'.

He points to a portrait of his first wife across the room. In another painting, Christ carries His cross. A third depicts an idyllic, pastoral scene beside the Nile with a pyramid in the background – a lush, fertile land where wheat once grew – the Egypt close to Saba's heart. I imagine this painting used to hang somewhere nearby throughout the time he was away.

Of all his achievements, Saba claims he is most proud of his teaching, but Lady Habachy swiftly takes issue. 'No, Saba, there are more important things.'

'What? But that's my job.'

'No, that's my job, Saba, not yours.'

'All right, we'll share it.'

'Because it is my only job. You have had many more. Can I tell you about his achievements?'

Saba chuckles. 'Go ahead. I am listening,' he says.

'He was a top lawyer with Aramco, the oil company, in the States. He was one of the arbitrators in a famous case between Saudi Arabia and Onassis.'

'Oh, I am discovering myself,' he says.

'He was always the youngest. Youngest minister, youngest lawyer ... Now, of course, he is the oldest. As the minister of industry and commerce, he started our textile industry. But with the revolution, the factories were nationalized and because the Army had no ability in administration, they were ruined. They were mostly Jewish. He helped them start again, based in Geneva. They built textile plants all over Africa and Latin America. Ethiopia, Somalia, Eritrea ... they spread all over the world. You should see the map covered in red dots.'

Saba is still chuckling.

'Saba is trying to be modest,' says his wife.

'I hope I am not trying. I hope I am succeeding,' says Saba.

At that moment, the phone rings. But neither Saba nor Lady Habachy flinches, suggesting either a mild deafness or possibly the attainment of some higher level of telecom Zen. It rings and rings before whoever is calling gives up in frustration.

Saba is, if anything, his own man – something we all should be. He is self-made, for sure. When he was young, he was astute enough to give himself a broad and varied education. He read widely in various languages. Young people should do whatever they can to be enlightened, he believes. They should then be humble with it. He has retired only recently, in order to catch up on some reading. He knows French, English and Arabic, of course. He is currently working on his German and always keeps himself abreast of current affairs. He can quote population figures in some detail. This is a matter of grave concern, for Egypt and the whole world. The trends are potentially catastrophic and, at the same time, some of us consume far too much.

I wonder how significant it is that the values Saba champions, embodies even – diligence, perseverence, thrift – seem quirky and old-fashioned, somehow at odds with the world today. Saba had worked out his own philosophy for himself. Gradually, over the years, it became his way of life. He was a Christian, but no fanatic, and he'd never been able to find a satisfactory answer as to why humanity exists here on earth. Although he'd read astronomy and learnt about the formation of the world, he still found himself asking the same questions. How come? Why are we here?

'So how do you describe your philosophy?' I ask. 'Moderation?'

He has led a simple, unpretentious life. He eats sparingly and believes that we don't drink nearly enough water.

'Moderation, yes. But also the sentiment of service, the idea of trying to help others, regardless of race or creed.'

He goes to bed early and wakes at daybreak. Until recently, he used to skip one hundred and twenty skips of his skipping-rope each and every morning, out on the verandah. People would stop by to watch.

Lady Habachy looks up and smiles. 'Early to bed, early to rise, makes you healthy, wealthy and wise,' she says. 'That applies to him literally.'

So Saba turns to pull his funny face, eyes wide in innocence.

And it occurs to me that a little homespun philosophy should probably come of all this, one day.

~

From the rooftop, I gaze out over the Nile at Aswan and watch feluccas tacking their course hard against the wind. I close my eyes and feel the heat. For the first time I really know we're in Africa. The people move a fraction more slowly, their skins are darker and every evening the sun sinks, a molten disc of fire, into the mountainous ridge of sand that forms the edge of the Western Desert.

Vanella seems engrossed, catching up on her diary. She writes about four words to each line, an erratic, rounded hand with a backward slope. She's right-handed; I'm left. My pages are smaller and I still get nine or ten to the line. We're not allowed to see what each other writes. It's one small way we can be on our own sometimes.

It has taken me this long to understand that she finds travelling harder than I do. I've learnt I have to compromise. She gets tired before I do, so it's best if we go at her pace. I'm often keen to do too much anyway. Today I wanted to explore, but she wanted to relax. I always have to go out exploring. It's best when I'm alone though, I can cover more ground. The trouble is, Vanella can't really go on her own. She gets such hassle from the men; they ogle her all the time. I have to become all butch and protective, performing exaggerated body language supposed to signal 'THIS IS MY WOMAN. KEEP OFF, YOU LECHEROUS BASTARDS.'

Vanella looks up from her exercise book and smiles. The sun has turned her skin the colour of honey.

I'm trying to knock out some postcards, but I might give up on them. I hate postcards. They're designed to suppress communication. 'We're here, we're well, it's hot, the food's extremely average and we're going to meet an old Nubian tomorrow.' No, it's worse than that. They encourage deception. I'm forced to say something that means very little, other than 'I'm here, you're back there and I've taken the trouble to think about you and spend twenty-five minutes queuing for stamps in the post office.' How can I possibly tell them about the patterns the feluccas are weaving as they zigzag their trails up river, mesmerizing me like some work of kinetic art, or the very fierceness of the sun I can feel beating down on my hat, or the fact that we've done nothing for two whole days and it's absolutely bloody wonderful?

Ibrahim arrives eight-thirty for eight – Egyptian time. We're waiting for him at the Shesha Café, drinking hot black coffee from glasses that were last washed when Moses was a lad.

Ibrahim is the tall but hopelessly laid-back boatman who has agreed to take us to a Nubian village on the west bank. He beckons to a boy who runs to fetch him tea, then he introduces his man, Ibrahim. So before us we have two Ibrahims, both dark-skinned and crinkly haired, both wearing moustaches and long flowing *galabeyas*. Thankfully Ibrahim II reaches only two thirds the height of his boss and is positively brisk in nature. He goes off to prepare the boat, leaving Ibrahim I to take tea and idly bubble a little smoke through a hookah.

'We meet good people,' he says. 'Very old man.'

We had hoped for a felucca, but transport for the day turns out to be a small, oily craft with a canopy. When at last we cast off across the blue-black waters of the Nile, Ibrahim II steers with the outboard while Ibrahim I reclines in the prow, trailing a hand over the side. He doesn't say much and it occurs to me we have yet to see him smile.

Life on the far bank moves with the steady flow of the river. There are no cars to go parp, no fumes, no hustling from vendors, no crazy cyclists heading the wrong way up the street. Instead, a pair of camels ambles by, ridden by two boys; women in black carry baskets on their heads and young children dig in the sand. Along the shore, pied kingfishers zip by like skimming-stones on automatic, while gawky white egrets poke about furtively among bright green shoots.

As Ibrahim II guides us in, we see an old man with a staff and a white beard hopping about at the water's edge. Grabbing the rope thrown to him, he pulls as best he can, then helps us step down a shaky gangplank. The old man seems friendly enough and looks a good age but, with the boat secured, the Ibrahims barely acknowledge his presence, turn and lead us away on a meandering path beside the river.

They take us to the ancient village of Qopa, where what passes for streets is merely sand, deserted except for one man plodding by on a donkey. The houses are painted bright pink or powder-blue. Bricks made of mud have been left to dry in the quiet permanence of the heat. A blind boy finds us, shakes all our hands then runs off, sent by Ibrahim I on some mission. Further on, by the mosque, we enter a small courtyard enclosed by thick whitewashed walls. A chubby-faced woman dressed in a long black *galabeya* greets us with a glassy eye. She wears flat hoops as earrings, which stick out at right-angles.

'The man, he come,' promises Ibrahim I, and we are left to explore. In the corner of the yard there is a domed structure we can almost stand inside, where we find an old oven. Vanella picks up one of a stack of round clay platters on which the dough must sit when being baked. She rubs it with the palm of her hand, then holds it to her nose.

'Try this. It's wonderful.'

I choose one for myself. It looks ancient and has a wholesome aroma, but not like bread. I can smell the full richness of the earth.

The lady of the house soon beckons us and we go through an arched doorway into an intimate, darkened room cooled by a huge whirring fan. Ibrahim I has already ingratiated himself and is sucking on the end of another hookah. We are shown to a well-worn sofa with lively springs and while tea is prepared, we gaze at our surroundings. The place is both spotlessly clean and a riot of colour: a confusion of pink and blue pastel, with splashes of orange and fuchsia. There is a table, a bench, an armchair and a stretch of yellow plastic sheeting pinned to the wall below a charcoal drawing of someone's grandmother.

We smile and our hostess smiles back, showing us the gap in her front teeth. I love this sort of moment. We're so far removed from anything familiar, sitting in yet another living-room. Today it happens to be Nubian. I feel as if my senses are attached to the end of some giant funnel. We absorb like sponges. Everything is taken at face value, no effort required. We just keep moving, and the world keeps coming towards us.

Ibrahim I looks up through a cloud of smoke as a figure appears, framed in the doorway. I see a flowing white robe and what looks like a red tea-towel wrapped around the old man's head. We shake hands and he immediately lights a white-filtered cigarette. But no business can commence until we have taken mint tea, served from a brass teapot into small glass tumblers, each heaped with four spoonfuls of sugar.

Saad Imam Muhammad is his name and Ibrahim says he's ninety-two. His skin shines dark; his nose, a fine and noble structure, almost reaches his top lip. Listening attentively to Ibrahim, he strokes the stubble that lies like new snow along his jaw.

We hear the word 'English' and Saad begins to nod, if not subservient then with a noticeable respect. We have stumbled, by chance, upon the vestiges of Empire. Egypt was a British protectorate for a time after the First World War and our two countries were linked by Ottoman history, cotton and the Canal. Although the British presence was far from popular, Saad appears to have fond memories and can still speak the language, in broken fashion.

'Cairo, Alexandria, Port Said . . . I worked with English people,' he says. 'First, I was kitchen boy. After two months, second waiter. Twenty months, big waiter. Then after, I was number one cook . . .'

He made them Irish stew, Indian curries, roast chicken and pigeon. He remembers with affection a certain Brigadier Howse, someone he calls 'Lazlie' and Brigadier Mansell, who was always a very fair man.

Saad lights himself another cigarette. He sits with one leg crossed and jiggles his foot incessantly. Again he lowers his head and nods. 'English good,' he says, 'not high collar, not high talk. We talk gentlemen, man to man.'

He recalls the ways of the British were somewhat particular. There were always too many reports, too much typing. 'All the time, typin', typin',' says Saad.

In ones and twos, more of the women now join us. Inquisitive, they rustle into the shadows, dressed in black, except for one who is resplendent in yellow.

Ibrahim II has crouched in a corner to take a nap, while Ibrahim I draws on his pipe till he needs to call for a new block of molasses-flavoured tobacco. The fan rattles on the ceiling as Saad chatters away. He describes Cairo when the streets used to be full of camels and donkeys. Nowadays, it takes too long to get anywhere, he says, because of all the cars. And, inevitably, life has become much more expensive.

'Now everything, price come up. One loaf bread, one piastre,' he says, demonstrating its length, from the point of his elbow to the tip of his fingers. 'Now chicken seven pounds. Before was five, six piastres. And all the time, children wantin', wantin' . . .'

He lets his head drop and gives us a doleful look. With his dark brown eyes, sunk deep in a network of folds and creases, he reminds me of a faithful old dog.

'Now is a different life,' he says. 'Aswan was once beautiful. I want history back again.'

I double take. What was that? Like me, Saad wants to go back in time. And he's been there before.

If we go back, together, what will we find? The waters of the river Nile will run clean and clear. We will make our way down, cup hands and quench our thirst straight from the bank. We will see shoals of fish, which we can catch for food. We'll sit and pass an hour or two watching the feluccas work their course up-river, some carrying well-heeled visitors from foreign parts. From time to time, the river will flood and leave its silt behind to enrich the land. Our wheat will grow tall. We will spend our days in peace, living beside the water; and the mighty desert will reach as far as our eye can ever see.

Saad says there are too many boats these days and too much disease in the water, the bilharzia. The dam now blocks the horizon like a mountain range. No silt can get through to fertilize the crops any more and all the fish are gone.

'The Nile, it is our blood,' he tells us. 'Irrigation, it make life good. But High Dam no good.'

His own great-grandfather had come to Qopa in 1882, from a village that now lies submerged beneath Lake Nasser. Many thousands of Nubian people had been relocated in the 1960s when the High Dam was being built. They were forced to leave the fine old houses of their forefathers, made of dried mud and palm leaf. At times of drought, when the water level in the lake was seen to be lowering, Saad's cousins would camp in the desert waiting for their homes to reappear.

'We want time back,' he says. 'Nubian people not like Egyptian people. Everything about us is different. Egyptian people are crafty, stealing. Nubian people have white heart inside. When a man is sick, everyone want to help him. When the old die, we go to the house and comfort. Friendly people, easy life.'

His wishes for the future are simple. He wants to be remembered as a good man. In all his life, he has never done anything bad. But still he hopes his children and those who come after will live better than he.

'Do not kill, be well liked. Help others and make everything good,' is what he told them. If they didn't behave, they soon found themselves beaten with a stick and shut in a room all day without food.

'Nubian people happy people. All the time Nubian people smiling,' says Saad emphatically.

On some foolish whim, I'm curious to find out if there is such a thing as a Nubian joke. I see Vanella looking askance as I try to explain.

'A joke. A story invented to make people laugh.'

'Invited?' Saad queries, perplexed. 'Story to laugh?'

'Story . . . Ha ha . . .' I try a clownish grin and notice Ibrahim I staring at me in blank amazement. 'Story. Funny. Ha ha ha . . .'

'Ha haaa,' goes Saad. 'Jokin', jokin'.'

The women join in, tittering nervously.

Then Ibrahim II wakes with a start, to find the Englishman pulling faces and everyone dissolving into fits of giggles. He looks to Ibrahim I, who simply takes a long pull on his hookah and winds his hand in languid despair.

8

The Old Country

On we head into the gloom, following a thin strip of bitumen that divides the rich russet red of the earth. It looks like rain. Shades of grey are brooding ominously. Far away to the west, where the bush recedes to a washed-out watercolour horizon, silvery showers are drawing their veils across the land. Here and there an acacia tree stands its ground, a flat-topped silhouette sculpted by the winds of time.

By the roadside, a bow-legged old Masai wearing a tweedy coat he's picked up somewhere is tending his cattle. He stares for a moment as we go by, elbows crooked over the long knobbly stick yoked across his shoulder-blades. Then, just as I'm beginning to think I might be Robert Redford after all, in one of those scenes from *Out of Africa*, a *matutu* minibus veers towards us, crab-like and lopsided, bags, boxes and furniture piled on top. I try to give it a wide berth, but still feel the tug on the Jeep's steering as it passes. Inside we glimpse a mass of black faces, all eyes meeting ours.

I remember the Muthaiga Club – Friday lunch-time, gin and tonics all round. Walking into the bar, it was the noise that had sounded so familiar, like a Home Counties' cocktail party in full swing. Their clipped vowels formed such a wall of ebullient conversation that they all had to raise their voices to be heard. The entire room was very nearly shouting, in the nicest possible way. Old and young, everyone knew everyone – they were a cheery, self-assured tribe. And although we stood there among our own, we didn't feel the slightest sense of belonging. How could we? We were migrants passing through an idea of England that was preserved long ago and is still defended to the hilt.

'Whatever you do, don't give anyone a lift,' they said. 'If you come across a man lying in the road, drive on. Don't stop to help . . . We've had a lot of trouble, you know.'

They told us their stories, about the robbings and the murders. They don't walk out in Nairobi at night. They don't drive in the bush after dark. Not any more. There are gangs who'll shoot them for their car. They won't even let their arm hang out of the window in a traffic jam, because a man with a machete might chop it off, keep the nice watch and throw their arm away.

Splash! The first drop of rain explodes on the windscreen like a waterbomb. An inky black cloud towers over us, higher than the sky where I guess Mount Kenya should be. Within a minute, we can barely see through the deluge hammering down on the glass, even with the wipers on double speed.

We pass a young man walking along by the side of the road. His ragged shirt and torn trousers are drenched, but he doesn't care. He walks happy. And the red earth darkens as it drinks.

The next day, we're only a few miles away and yet we could be visiting some leafy English suburb. The house makes the shape of a T, red-brick, two-storey, the only modification to the design being a cedar shingle roof, which extends low to provide shelter from the elements.

We are standing around inspecting Ron Nelson's front lawn.

'We were in a bad way until yesterday,' he says. 'No rain since April, so I started up the pump – does about five hundred gallons an hour – threw water everywhere and then it poured with rain. Ha ha!' He laughs lightly, alto in pitch. 'At least I'll be able to get the mower out for a change.'

The lawn does look a bit patchy, more of a dull brown than green. It slopes gently down to the river Naro Moru, which flows along the edge of the garden. Naro Moru itself, half a mile away, had been little more than a collection of colourfully painted shacks and the ubiquitous Coca-Cola sign. But we found the old railway line nearby and the bumpy track that runs beside it then curls away out of sight to emerge in this delightful wooded dell. You'd never know you were out in the middle of the bush.

We sit round the verandah table in camping chairs, discussing the weather as only the English can. Zoë and Dinky, Ron's Jack Russells, are still absorbed by the exciting smells we've brought with us. Over in the corner, a jigsaw lies half completed, a quaint scene entitled 'The Duck Pond'. Ron tells us he's keen on jigsaws, but they have to be the old wooden ones. He can't seem to get them much any more. Down the far end, two hanging bird-tables are a-flutter with tiny sunbirds. Vanella watches enchanted as they flash scarlet on invisible wings, darting and hovering, nervously sipping sugared water with their long curved beaks. Then the big bad mousebird comes and bullies them all away.

'Shame the mountain's not out,' says Ron, pointing through the gap in the trees to where Mount Kenya ought to be. 'When there's no cloud, the mountain's just there. Always a different view. Sometimes I get the light picking up red dust on the glacier.'

With a firm hand he smoothes his bald pate, nut-brown like an acorn. His eyes are clear and blue, the eyes of an innocent. I would have confidently guessed him to be a fit seventy-year-old, and I would have been twenty years out.

'Never been up,' he clips. 'Don't like sleeping cold. I'll sleep hard or in the desert, but up there, three in the morning . . . oh, no, I don't see any fun in that,' and he gives us another of his boyish laughs.

Son of a Warwick gelatine manufacturer, young Master Nelson had been packed off to school at Rugby, which he hated. He wasn't the gregarious type and would rather be away bird-nesting. So he was always in trouble. The faster he could get out of the place the better. At eighteen, he sailed to Australia, to work the back-blocks of New South Wales and western Queensland for Sidney Kidman, the cattle king. For five formative years he mustered cattle, moved sheep and mended windpumps.

'Never saw a house,' he says brightly. 'We lived out. If it rained, you got wet. If it didn't, it was all right.'

Home on leave one time, an uncle offered him a free passage out to Kenya to take a look-see at his coffee plantation, a plot awarded by lottery to officers of the First World War. But it had already gone bust by the time Ron arrived. He reckoned the manager had run the place down because then he bought it for nothing. Ron wasn't staying there – dreadful spot, too hot and too much malaria. Instead, he came and found work here in cattle country. Australia stood him well, for those were still the pioneering days and he was a useful chap to have around. He repaired fences and fixed the boreholes.

Kenya was like the promised land, back then. There were no roads. The nearest shop was a day there and a day back in the ox cart. No more than twenty so-called neighbours lived within riding distance.

He would go for miles and see no one, only green grass, rivers and endless, endless game. There weren't even any Africans roundabouts, so labour was hard to come by. And for an African to be employed, his whole family had to be provided for with a piece of land.

Ron bought himself a place out towards the Aberdare mountains and set up as a dairy farmer. He started a creamery, supplying butter and cheese to the civil servants in Nyeri. There were about seventy of them with their families who needed feeding. His man would carry a load on his back all the way there, about fifteen miles across country.

'It was a terrific life,' Ron admits, 'at least until 1929, when the world went bust. Then we were in the soup.'

Those were the days when he could only get sixpence for a gallon of milk and the big fat bullocks he raised went to the butcher's for just five pounds. But if ever the larder was bare, all he had to do was walk out of the door and shoot the next buck that happened to saunter past. And so he kept his labour in meat and his dog happy chewing the bones.

Vanella gets there first, as she often does. It's an interesting thought. What does a young Englishman, living in the middle of nowhere, do for female company – especially one so gentle and unassuming as Ron? Once or twice a year there might be a get-together for polo or a race meeting. Occasionally he'd be invited to a dance, best bib and tucker. But these were local gatherings at Nanyuki and Nyeri, hardly the wild parties of legend. There can't have been too many eligible young ladies about.

'Did you marry?' Vanella suddenly asks.

There's a nervous pause, then he nods. 'She was my first cousin,' he says, a little bashful. 'We were both pretty ancient.'

I feel for Ron. I know how excruciating it is to be a shy boy. No amount of cajoling can persuade you to face whatever has to be faced – not when you feel that wretched. You'd rather be somewhere else, preferably on your own. For some reason, though, I didn't mind going out on stage. I quite enjoyed the spotlight, as long as I was sure of my lines. But only when I reached my twenties did I finally force myself to stop blushing at awkward moments.

I did a strange thing once. I would have been ten or maybe eleven, old enough to know that boys were supposed to have girlfriends. Some of my pals at school used to brag about theirs. But in the holidays, life at Woodlands tended to be rather solitary. Even now I can't work it out. One day, I took a blank sheet of paper and, with a black felt-tip, wrote in large letters: I WANT SOMEONE TO LOVE. Carefully folding my message, I went down to the bottom field by the lane, where I posted it in a nook in the dry-stone wall. I've no idea who I expected to find it. Next time I came home I went back to have a look and it had gone. Not a trace. But I didn't worry. I felt that somehow the message had been received. The other thing I sometimes did was try to imagine the name of the girl I'd eventually marry. I would close my eyes to see what would rise to the surface. That was a fruitless exercise too. Never in a million years would I have come up with Vanella.

Ron's bride was called Rachel. They returned to the new farm he bought near Naro Moru and together lived the good life. But it wasn't long before they were paid a visit by the Mau Mau.

Ron even had the Lancashire Fusiliers camped on his property. They were supposed to be fighting the Mau Mau, but they made such a noise and smoked so much that everyone knew precisely when they were coming or going. They slept so well in their tents that night that the whole of Ron's milk herd of eighty head of cattle was driven off. He had his own guards there too, but they were told, 'Keep quiet, and we'll leave you alone. Make a noise, and we'll kill your whole family.'

So Ron's livelihood was spirited away into the night.

'What did you do?' we ask.

'I bred ducks,' he says, with a smirk.

Then one day, a few years later, the minister of agriculture paid him a call:

'Good morning, Mr Nelson,' he said, 'I'm taking over your farm.'

'I don't think so,' said Ron.

'You will co-operate, Mr Nelson . . . or else.'

And that was the end of that. At least they had somewhere to go. Ron had already bought this house from the local vet, who saw his own business disappearing overnight too.

He still thinks independence was a good thing, however. Had to be. But he's not so sure about what came after it.

'Now we have these politicians, who fill their pockets with money,' Ron remarks, with eyebrows raised. 'It's such a shame. These people have so much potential.'

We ourselves came across the President only yesterday, as we left Nairobi. We were puzzled at first by the armed policemen standing guard at fifty-yard intervals all through the outskirts of town. Then we hit the roadblocks, one every ten minutes, each causing a five-lane jam. Out in the country, it was worse. The dust clouds rose, and delighted fruit-sellers took advantage of some static trade for a change. Then we saw a banner stretched high above the road. 'We wish a safe journey to His Excellency President Moi', it read, a message from the hundreds of schoolchildren in bright blue and green uniforms who were turning back to class after parading to wave His Excellency's cavalcade past.

Ron is quickly to his feet. 'Now, I'll set the table, shall I?' He goes indoors, leaving us to pull surprised faces. It seems we're invited for lunch.

We go in through the sitting-room, with its old writing desk and faded floral sofa, into a tidy, low-ceilinged dining-room with spindle-backed chairs. And we're home. We're back in England, only instead of the South Downs or the Lake District, a painting of what Mount Kenya really looks like hangs on the wall. It's the view they had from the farm.

Lunch is laid out on the dresser: new potatoes and bully beef, peeled tomatoes, shredded lettuce and beetroot relish, which we spoon on to plain green plates like Vanella's grandmother once had. Everything is home-grown. Ron pours out the lemonade, pressed from the fruit outside on the tree.

It's as if we're visiting an old relation we don't get to see too often. Ron wants to know about our travels, what we've been doing in Nairobi. We compliment him on the relish. And then that reserve peculiar to the English highlights the clacking of our knives and forks. He's being shy again and so are we. He says we're to help ourselves to some more and Vanella commends him for the life he's made.

'Never stopped farming, really,' he says. 'I've got eight acres, two cows, some hens and the ducks. I feed them and I feed myself, so it's, you know . . .' He trails off, not needing to explain that he's almost entirely self-sufficient.

The kitchen garden, a large area beyond the lawn, caged to keep the wildlife out, provides all his needs. He has some help from his gardener of twenty-five years, a man we met earlier wielding a large machete.

Ron lives on his own now. He passes the time pottering. He tends the garden and takes care of the cows, keeping a close eye on his personal food chain. It's not a bad way to spend the rest of your days.

'Now, who's for strawberries?' he says, looking up at three clean plates.

They're fresh, of course, with cream straight from the churn. Then comes the cheese, which I can't resist christening Double Nelson. For his finale, Ron brings in a battered tin, his own brand of dog biscuits, which Zoë and Dinky are allowed to scamper in and scoff.

We take strong dark coffee back out on the verandah and nibble chunks of Cadbury's Dairy Milk, as the thunder rumbles somewhere away in the distance.

'Is it going to rain again?'

'Shouldn't think so,' he says. 'Been doing that for weeks. Would you like to see the garden?'

We admire the long rows of vegetables and some mighty spring onions. Ron shows off his sweet peas and tells us about the time a herd of elephant came through. Then we wander down to take a look at the river. Once a celebrated trout stream, it is his water supply and comes straight off the mountain. Some chap once came to analyse it and told him he shouldn't touch it. He said it was more like Epsom salts than water.

'Never did me any harm,' says Ron.

I breathe in a lungful of heavy sweet air. What a place to live, or die.

'Are you a religious man?' I ask.

'I'm not a member of any Church,' he replies. 'In fact, I believe we were all part of some flying-saucer outfit. We were brought and put here, I think.'

For someone who has spent the best part of his life in the Rift Valley, believed to be the cradle of humanity, this is a mildly contentious view, I observe.

'Well, they found human bones mixed up with *homo habilis*, so we can't be descended from them. And after all, this world can't be the only one, not with a hundred million suns around the place. There must be plenty of others started before we did.'

I can't tell if he's being playful, or what.

'Do you believe in God?' asks Vanella.

'I don't know how to answer that. We all have God in us and what we do about it is our affair,' he says.

We're strolling back up the lawn, when a grasshopper loops in and comes to rest right in front of us.

'Oh, look at him!' I say, pointing. He's a fantastic luminous green.

Then as we watch, to our horror, Ron scrunches downward with a sharp twist of his shoe.

'Don't want him around,' he says, unperturbed, proving once and for all the soundness of the theory: survival of the fittest.

We wave goodbye to Ron and head for Nanyuki, a few miles up the road and around the mountain. It is a small town with a quaint row of shops and a Barclays Bank, outside which a gang of young Masai are loitering, red in hair and wardrobe. Without too much difficulty, we find the cottage hospital and, as we're being shown round, we bump into Peter, the resident doctor. He has to rush, but surprises us with an invitation to dinner that same evening.

A little after seven o'clock, we present ourselves at the Nanyuki Sports Club, an old settlers' watering-hole that nowadays smells musty like a potting-shed. Peter is waiting for us by the roaring log fire in a high-ceilinged, wood-panelled room. He must be in his late forties, a wiry, mousy-haired Englishman with an intelligent look. Although he's an attentive host, I detect some air of melancholy about him.

Over drinks, he quizzes us about what we're up to and gives us the standard warning. We say we're going to Thompson's Falls the next day, so Peter tells the story of the time his son was ambushed. One night, he'd swerved to avoid a rock in the road and ended up in the ditch. Faces emerged from the dark. Although the axle was bent he managed to get back on the road, but only scraped along a short distance before having to stop. Three more faces surrounded him. They stole everything. He didn't have much money so they took all his clothes, even his shoes. He had to keep himself warm with newspaper until someone came by in the morning.

'He knew his way around too,' Peter says. 'You must be careful. It's best not to go out after dark.'

Dinner is served. It seems we're the only white people in tonight. Tables have been set in the other half of the room where an African gentleman in a suit is eating with his wife, their voices muted. At another table, an Indian couple are looking at the menu. To start, a thin vegetable soup, which comes bolstered by soft floury rolls; then we have a leathery peppered steak, carrots and long white chips, the institutional flavour of which I find I quite enjoy.

Peter is good company. Our paths will probably cross just this once, but we have enough in common and plenty to learn from each other to make a very pleasant evening.

He's been at the cottage hospital a few years. He runs the place with the help of Matron, the bubbly, businesslike lady who'd given us our tour. We were sent there because it's where they take care of the old people when they're no longer able to fend for themselves – white folk, those who can afford it. Matron said we could speak to Mrs Amy but it would need to be through her ear-trumpet. But when we reached her room we found her asleep. So we went and said hello to everyone downstairs. We followed Matron along the corridor through into the sun-room and suddenly we were confronted with the old age we all secretly fear.

The shades had been drawn around five old ladies who sat or slumped in their neatly cushioned chairs. To a greater or lesser degree, all were suffering from some kind of dementia. One lady was lolling, head and mouth slack; another jabbered nonsense as she nodded sagely; another looked to be asleep. The other two seemed confused.

'We look after them in here, so they don't disturb the others too much,' Matron whispered.

I wasn't ready for this. I desperately wanted to leave immediately but froze, rooted to the spot, as my eyes scanned their anguished faces.

Matron was wonderful. She talked to one lady in a loud but reassuring voice to check she was all right. People like her make the world go round. Vanella noticed my distress and went into overdrive, asking Matron questions, and soon I was back in the corridor with the door closed. Please, don't let me end up like that.

'Did you see the new Aids wing?' Peter asks us, as we're finishing off with tinned fruit salad and ice-cream.

We did, a clinically clean room with a single iron bed and sharp white linen. The bed was empty.

'Trouble is, the Africans won't admit they've got it,' he says, 'for fear of being ostracized by the village.'

'How widespread is it?'

'We know that eight out of ten Africans whose blood we test here are HIV positive.'

'What?'

'Eighty per cent?'

'It's rife. It's probably going to wipe out the best part of a generation.'

The disease has spread down the backbone of Africa. The truckers on the highways have had their girl at every stop. African males always pride themselves on their virility and they're not especially renowned for being monogamous.

'It's going to need education and time,' Peter says. 'A lot of them think it's some scourge the white man has invented.'

He admits he's finally decided the risk is too great. If anyone comes to the hospital needing surgery, it is he who has to stitch them up. And his facilities aren't exactly the most advanced. One slip and that would be that. So he's leaving, to take up a post as ship's doctor on a cruise liner touring the Indian Ocean.

Of course that's no reason to be sad. Peter is lonely, we discover, because his wife's just left him. That's what he really wanted to tell us.

The old colonials we meet up and down the country are a sorry lot – Army officers, civil servants, ladies who once came on holiday and never left; even the man who set up as Nairobi's first optician. Oh, they're cheerful enough, and very sweet and hospitable and frightfully English. They tell us about their ox-wagon journeys; living in a tent, then a house made of mud and wattle, the old boxes they used for furniture. They remember how they were nearly killed by lions or the natives or the malaria. One old boy recounts how he once shot four lion . . .

'Two in the evening, two in the morning. Didn't have to look for lion. If you shot a zebra, then lion looked for you.'

It had been a great adventure. What went on at the Muthaiga Club was nobody's business, those wonderful parties. Things had only gone awry as the sun finally set on the Empire. Now all they have is their health and each other. Most of their friends have died. Their families still live back in England; their children, more often as not, grew up, looked around and left.

'It was empty, it was clean,' says one old lady. 'It was a lovely, lovely country. Like living in a great big zoo.'

'Kenya is so desperately attractive,' says another. 'You arrive and you never want to leave.'

So they won't be going anywhere. Why should they? This is home. They've had their land taken away. Their once charmed life has gone. Nairobi, their beautiful town, which used to have flowers growing down every street and where you rarely saw a black face, is so changed they hardly know it. The old PC's office on the corner has been left to crumble. It's a disgrace. It ought to be made a national monument.

No matter. They'll be sticking it out to the bitter end, behind their high walls and security fences. For they have nowhere to go and there is nowhere else they'd rather be.

9

Ancient Wonders

Something happens when you set foot on Zanzibar.

First, take the air. The small port has room for only a few dhows to moor, thirty- and forty-footers, weather-beaten, slung with canvas and matting. Strong-armed young Swahili men are loading, the ropes and rigging they tug coarse and fibrous. Others wait for work by the warehouse sheds. '*Jambo*,' they call out, with broad smiles, everywhere '*Jambo*' and the rattle of conversation. Some wear the local hat, a soft, embroidered white pillbox; others go bare and shiny-skinned, save for an oily wrap around the thighs. And the air, the air is full to the brim; not just fragrant, more the all-out assault of an industry in cloves. We stand for a moment, inhaling the spice deep into our lungs, and soon we feel our heads begin to clear.

Then on, past the ornate splendour of the House of Wonders, we enter the narrow alleys that thread through to the heart of the old town. Here it is cool and dark, the way wide enough only for a cart or a bicycle to brush by. The dark green double doors of the shop-fronts open on to the steep step that forms a strip of high pavement on either side. Within, we see different faces selling their wares: African, Indian and sometimes Arab. We pass heavy wooden doorways carved with intricate swirling patterns of leaf and fruit and flower. The buildings rise three and four storeys, windows arched and shuttered, canopies edged with wrought-iron frills, balconies overhanging. Today, these glories are forgotten, though, left untended, and the sultans of Oman, who once made this the centre of their world, remain but a memory. Whitewash flakes off the moulding walls, paint peels in faded blues and greens, and rusting metal drains away to a stain. So it is that the Stone Town of Zanzibar crumbles in majestic decay.

Wandering, half lost, we come to a quiet junction of alleyways where we notice an Arab sitting on the corner. Wrapped in a white robe and head-dress, he has a long, ragged beard and looks very old indeed. We hesitate, but then decide to approach. He doesn't seem to understand English, so we appeal to a young African shopkeeper across the way. He asks in Swahili how old the man is, but with no greater success. The Arab utters not a word. He simply stares at us vacantly from behind thick, black-framed spectacles.

Mr Joshi brings us better luck.

We happen to eat in his restaurant one evening, on the first-floor balcony of a house overlooking the harbour. An Indian, originally from Gujerat, Mr Joshi is without doubt one of life's great enthusiasts. He has jet black hair and goofy teeth, but he's a handsome man nevertheless. He keeps stopping by every now and then to tell us some new snippet about the slave trade or the spices that grow in abundance all over the island. By the end of the meal he's pulled himself up a chair. He says he divides his time between Zanzibar, where he runs a number of businesses, and his house in Dar es Salaam. He also owns, I notice, the hairiest ears ever seen on a man.

We tell him about our quest. His eyes gleam as we explain we're looking for the oldest people on the island. Then he grins and reveals that the house where he rents a room in the Stone Town is owned by a merchant, well into his nineties. His name is Mansang Velji Shah.

But it doesn't end there, the luck. Mr Joshi is telling us how Zanzibar's Indian population has always prospered, ever since the days of the British, when suddenly he pauses. 'Have you seen our temple?'

We shake our heads, not even knowing where he means.

'Then you must go there, to the Hindu temple. Shall we go now? Yes? Come, I will take you.'

We follow the vague form of Mr Joshi's white shirt into the labyrinth of pitch black alleyways. Every night the power supply gets shut down for an hour or two and the town is plunged into darkness. An unseen shoulder brushes mine. Swahili voices call out to one another from the houses close by on either side. Vanella walks behind me, tightly gripping the hand I hold back for her. We have absolutely no idea where we are.

'You will need to be careful here,' Mr Joshi calls, and we're stumbling over a threshold when the electricity comes back on.

A single bare light-bulb dangles awkwardly from the roof to illuminate this spiritual home from home. As our eyes grow accustomed, we admire the simple grace of the architecture, once exported from the shores of India, which with the neglect of the years has acquired a rare beauty. We climb the stone steps and pass through a fine, pointed archway. Inside, the raised marble platform is balustraded, open to the air. The ceiling and pillars are decorated with worn tiles or washed-out, peeling patches of pink and lime-green paint. To the rear, the gods reside each in a dimly lit chamber. And so Mr Joshi introduces us to the Lord Rama and Ganesh, the elephant god.

He lets us gaze and wonder. I find I am drawn to Ganesh. I find his animal form more approachable than the other figures, whose stories always seem so complex. According to Mr Joshi, Ganesh is a remover of obstacles.

'You know, I have been thinking about this old man from my house,' he says, coming to stand beside me. 'I hope you can meet with him. It would be very good for him, I think. I look at him and I am happy. He takes his age well. Sometimes he can be difficult. He becomes cross if his tea is cold and he complains about feeling weak. But this age is a natural thing. You cannot fight with time.'

'That's very true.'

'Yes, you cannot escape it.'

'If only there were some way of running alongside, of keeping pace with time. Perhaps there is some magic formula which can reduce its effect?'

'This you will find out from your journey,' says Mr Joshi, giving me a toothy smile.

I become aware of the stillness and realize I feel quite at peace, as happy as I could ever be. A man we have known for barely two hours has drawn us into this, his secret world.

Vanella strolls back, looking thoughtful.

'You know, I feel it is destiny that brought you here,' says Mr Joshi. 'I am sure it is significant that we have met.'

Footsteps announce the arrival of another visitor. Fearing the spell has been broken, I turn to see a man in his late forties, Indian also. He wears a baseball cap and seems to be looking around as if for the first time. He exchanges a few words of greeting with Mr Joshi, then comes to introduce himself.

'My name is Kandli,' he says, shaking us by the hand. 'I come from Bombay. Are you travellers?'

'Yes, we are travelling,' I say, with a smile.

'Ah, good,' says Kandli. 'I travel also. It is the best thing anyone can do, don't you think? Isn't this a beautiful place?'

We agree it is, and Mr Joshi speaks again in Hindi. Kandli is a short, handsome man with a thin, greying moustache. His brown eyes keep examining our faces as he listens.

'I cannot believe this. What are you doing? Looking for the old people of the world? Are you coming to India?'

'Of course. Next year.'

'Then you must come to stay in my house. And you must go to see Morarji Desai. I will take you.'

It's my turn to disbelieve. I know all about India's former prime minister, but haven't even considered how we might reach him. He is now nearly a hundred years old.

'When you come, we will go to find him,' Kandli promises. 'He lives in Bombay. My father spent time in prison with him.'

And so, there and then, we exchange details and agree to make contact. In my notebook, he writes his name: H. P. Upadhyaya, then his address, and signs himself simply – Kandli.

Two days later, we chance our way up a derelict side alley and find the temple again. Mr Joshi has invited us to join their celebration of Diwali. It is a few minutes past eight in the morning.

Inside, all is calm, the space deserted except for the caretaker who shuffles around barefoot, making preparations. We sit and watch him as he visits the various shrines. By day, the faded colours and the dilapidation are all the more exquisite. Lengths of old frayed bunting have been brought out and strung from pillar to pillar. A bell is rung and at last they begin to file in, the wives in beautiful saris, their long dark hair tied or plaited, their daughters pretty in pale blue dresses. The young boys look uncomfortable in their best suits and oversized collars. They shake hands like the grown-ups, then immediately try to poke each other in the stomach. Gradually everyone gathers as one large family, saying prayers and ringing the bells suspended from the ceiling on the end of long black cords. They greet one another, then go to anoint the gods, standing before the figures of Lord Rama, with his brother Lakshmana and wife Sita; and the head of Shiva, a garishly hand-painted likeness strewn around with glistening yellow petals.

Mr Joshi arrives with his wife Hemlata, steadying the arm of the old gentleman, Mansang Velji Shah. We shake hands and the Joshis go to make their observances. Then Mr Joshi introduces us to all their friends and, even though the month is October and the climate equatorial, we find ourselves saying, 'Happy New Year,' to one and all.

Mansang sits cross-legged on the temple steps. He smiles at everyone who approaches to pay their respects, his slender hands pressed together in greeting. He has come barefoot, dressed in simple white *khadi*, a dark jacket and a Nehru hat. And, with his skinny hooked nose, his pointed chin, close-cropped silver hair and glasses, he looks not unlike Gandhi.

Mansang Velji has never had a birthday. He was born in a remote village near Rajkot in the west of India, some time in 1901 – he doesn't know the precise date.

He was but a lad of fifteen when he first came to Zanzibar, travelling with his brother-in-law and a group of Gujerati men who set out in search of fortune. Loaded up with cloth and dry foods to sell, they were carried by the same trade winds that had brought foreigners to these shores for centuries. It was the Sumerians, they say, who first ventured down the east coast of Africa in boats. Then came the Assyrians, the Persians and others from Asia Minor; then the Arabs and the word of Islam – the first Omanis landed here as early as the seventh century AD. And so people came from India, China and further east.

Mansang and his friends had set up store in the Stone Town and Mansang helped out in the shop, selling groceries. After three years, he went home to India, bought more stock, and returned with new cloth to trade. This time he settled on Pemba, another spice island some thirty miles away. He opened his own shop in a small village and began supplying the Africans with groceries and colourful *kangas* for them to wear. A barter system was soon set up with his brother-in-law on Zanzibar. Mansang would buy cloves locally at five rupees per thirty-five pounds, or dried coconut at two rupees and send it across the water in a dhow. His brother-in-law would then send back rice, sugar and salt.

It was the enterprising sultan, Seyyid Majid bin Said, who first introduced the mighty clove when he moved his capital to Zanzibar in the 1840s. By Mansang's day, the plantations were thriving, owned by wealthy Arab families. Each year, when the clove harvest was complete, the boats would come across from Dar es Salaam, first to Zanzibar, then on to Pemba, but because there was no harbour there, the merchants had to get down into smaller boats before they could carry off their precious commodity.

The life on Pemba had been primitive: there were no roads, only donkey tracks, and the drinking water was brackish. Mansang and his fellow Indians built their houses and made roads to their doors, wide enough for a bullock cart. Then they dug wells, which yielded purer water.

Every three years he would return to India. Any rupees earned from the shop he would save and use to buy golden guineas and jewellery from ships that came up the coast from South Africa. He then sailed home, where he traded the gold for rupees again, at a profit – for there was no exchange control in those days. He would buy more cloth to sell back in Pemba and come south on the winds once more. Thus the wheel of commerce turned and Mansang's business grew.

'Every three years they were going and coming, going and coming,' prattles Mr Joshi, rocking his head from side to side. 'The flow was very big, very big, because people in India came to know there is an easy life here.'

We are listening to Mansang's story in Mr Joshi's simply furnished room, on the second floor of the house where they live. A small clattering fan is providing no relief whatsoever from the humidity, as the sing-song cries of children playing in the street drift in through the open window. Both men are in talkative mood, Mr Joshi translating and commenting, Mansang forever interrupting and offering us another memory. They could almost be father and son.

'If you had any paper coming from India,' Mansang tells us, 'the British immigration officer in the House of Wonders would stamp it. He never asked how much time you wanted to stay.'

The old merchant is now wearing a loose white singlet and what look like cotton pyjama bottoms. His arms are thin and scrawny, and he sits with one leg tucked under him, his collar-bones sticking out like a coat-hanger.

Zanzibar had been a British protectorate in those days. The sultans ruled still, but under British control. There were no restrictions because they wanted to build the railway, the so-called Lunatic Line, up through

Kenya to Kampala. Many Indian people came: to Mombasa, where they found work on the railway, or to Zanzibar and Pemba.

Mansang had married the first time he went home, but he left his new bride behind. At that time the women were afraid; they were single men only who came to the islands. He went back to collect his wife after another three years.

Mr Joshi can't resist. 'The Sultan of Zanzibar, Seyyid Khalifa, you see, he was watching,' he explains with relish. '"Why are you Indians coming alone? Why are your wives not with you?" he asked himself. So he passed a decree that Indians were allowed to bring their wives, because these bachelors somehow were starting . . .' He hesitates, points at Mansang, then half whispers, 'Maybe he is afraid to say, but I know it – they were wronging it at night with the Arab ladies.'

Mansang doesn't seem the type to be wronging it with anyone, so Vanella tactfully ignores the gossip with her own line of questioning. She wants to know how they got on with the Africans.

'There were no problems, no thieves,' Mansang says. 'Everyone left their doors open. I used to walk out at night, because I supplied other villages with materials. I would come back with money, alone, but they didn't touch me.'

'And the Arab people?'

'We were like brothers. When I was sick, they were coming and watching; when they were sick, I was going. In that time people were believing in mankind. There were no problems. Everything was available and it was running very nicely.'

'How did it compare to India?'

'It was like heaven, for a merchant, because there was no competition. I spent forty-five happy years on Pemba, until the revolution . . .'

The revolution took place in 1964. After Britain had granted Tanganyika and Zanzibar independence, it withdrew its protection and left the Arabs and Indians to fend for themselves in the new United Republic of Tanzania.

Mansang shakes his head. 'Hired soldiers came . . . mercenaries,' he says. 'It was wicked. They came with a lorry, these people, and said, "Now leave! This is not your country, or your business." My shop was looted, so I came here to Zanzibar. I used to have nine acres of land and many clove trees. I had carts and bullocks. I left everything there . . . Then they started abusing us. "Indians are thieves," they said, so we began sending our wives and girlfriends home from Zanzibar. But

I said, "I am an old man, if they want to put me in jail, I don't mind. I am too old to go."'

'Who were they, these people?'

'Karume's men,' says Mr Joshi. 'The first president of Zanzibar. We Indians were abused very badly.'

But the Arabs suffered the worst. Only this morning, Mr Joshi showed us the stretch of beach, just outside the town, where he himself saw the Arab bodies lined out along the sand. Thousands had been killed in a single night.

Mansang never returned to Pemba.

'Why should I go back there?' he says, caressing his unshaven chin gloomily. 'After the revolution, some Chinese came and cut down two hundred thousand clove trees, a hundred thousand palm trees also. Everything was made barren. They didn't know the price of cloves. They thought they would plant rice farms. It was a wrong thing, but who could tell them?'

Still, Mansang has few worries. He enjoys life. He doesn't have to work; his food is brought to him; and every day he prays to God.

'The secret of my health is the food I eat,' he says. 'Pure food, ghee, plenty of milk and the pure water of India when I was young.'

He believed always in eating only at home or at a relative's house, where he could trust that everything was pure. No hotels, he has never in his entire life eaten in a restaurant. No vices, he has never drunk liquor and never taken medicine, except for a local herb sometimes to prevent malaria.

He is pure in word and deed. He won't say anything bad about anyone.

'When I say this life was good and people are good, then I am happy,' he explains. 'But if I claim that this is bad, this man is like this, he is abusing me, then there will be no balancing. There are bad people, I admit, but I want to go my way. I have seen good days. I know I'm going to die and when I do, I want to take good things with me. I want to die happy.'

With this, he begins to recite an old Gujerati poem by the sixteenth-century poet, Narasimha Mehta. It describes the hardships suffered by the gods, kings and queens of Hindu mythology:

Why bring happiness and sorrows to mind, when
  our bodies are imbued with them;

Even if you try to avoid this you will not be able
to do so, because it is God's will.

Mansang hurries through the verses, as if he might yet forget the words he once learnt by heart as a boy.

Mr Joshi is transfixed. He has never heard the poem before.

'Nobody can escape from happiness or sorrow. So what is the use in worrying?' he concludes, with a waggle of his head.

~

If anyone can find us an Arab elder it will be Mr Choma, we are told. Mr Choma belongs to a prominent Arab family and lives somewhere within the maze of the Stone Town. A boy leads us to his house and leaves us to consider his imposing front door with its substantial brass knocker. The resounding thud is still dying away when a startled and somewhat dishevelled head shoots out of a first-floor window to stare down at us through bottle-bottom spectacles. A bizarre moment then ensues while I shout up an explanation for our intrusion, followed by a more difficult one as it dawns on us both that we have already spoken on the telephone. I had first been told to contact a Mr *Juma*, who hadn't been much help. It seems unlikely that his double, Mr Choma, will be any different.

The head disappears and we wait while footsteps slap all the way down to the hall and the door swings open. We've woken him up. He's still groggy and wisps of grey hair stick out at all angles, but with good grace he invites us in. Upstairs in the family sitting-room, we admire the old framed photographs of his grandfathers and various uncles who stand alongside turbaned sultans with small eyes and thick underbeards. There were once sixty thousand Arabs on the island, he says, but large numbers were killed after the revolution. His family had owned many clove plantations. It was the lucky few who got away with only having their property confiscated by the government.

Mr Choma is perfectly charming, particularly as we're being such a pest. He urges us to sit and for a few minutes entertains us in conversation, while we wrestle with his disconcerting squint. He seems to stare past me, so I don't know where to look and instead shuffle along the divan into his line of sight to try another request for help. He is immediately reticent.

'Old people, you say? Well, there was one very old man, but he died

Bo, our spiritual guide, sees us on our way. His research has reduced life to two essential words.

The glorious onion tops of St Basil's cathedral, Moscow.

Cyril Murva still smokes forty a day: Partizan Lupča, Slovakia.

Maria Zemanova gives us some marriage guidance: Liptovský Hrádok, Slovakia.

Grigorii does his impersonation of George Bernard Shaw: Kiev, Ukraine.

Martin Brezina's enthusiasm is unbridled: Východná, Slovakia.
All the boys fell in love with Irena: Kvačany, Slovakia.

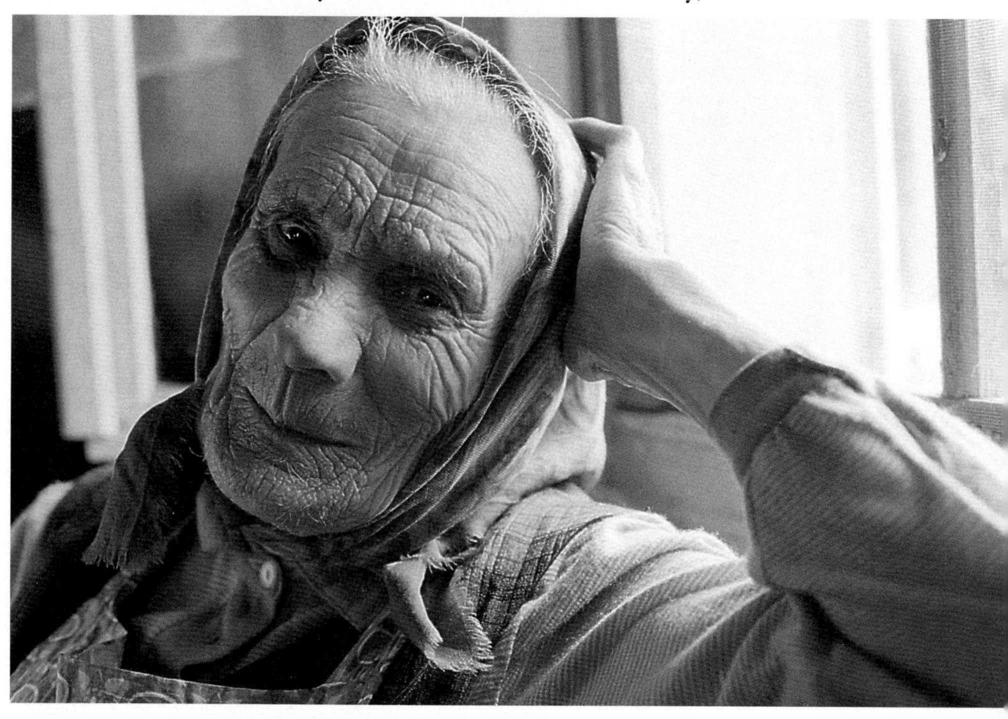

Fatma Toksoy reads the Koran aloud ten times a year: Marmaris, Turkey.

Main street of the Nubian village of Qopa.

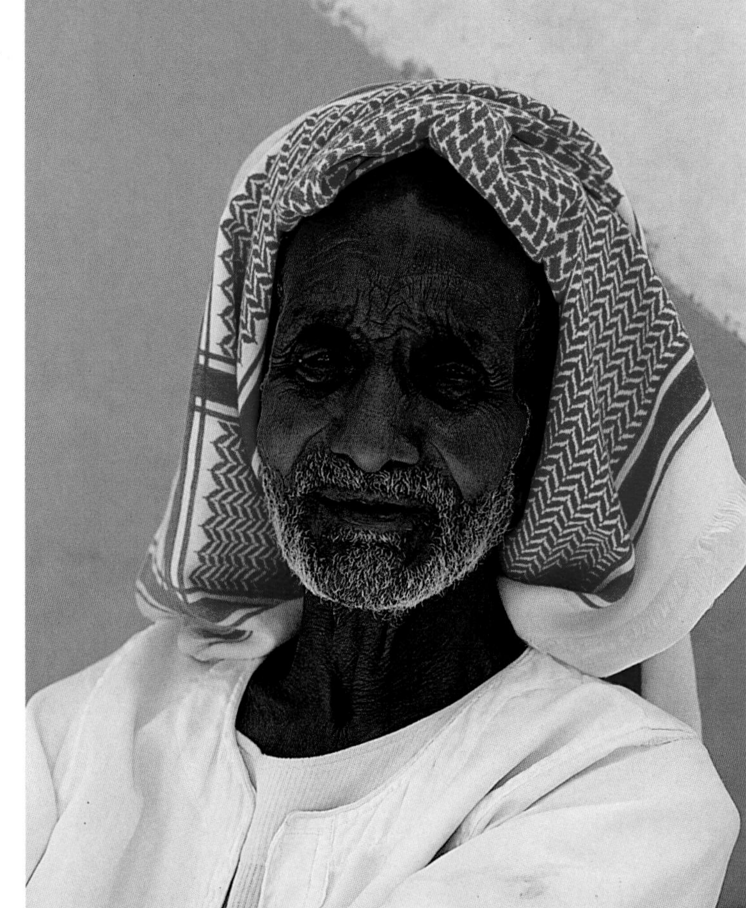

Saad Imam Muhammad wants to go back in time: Qopa, Egypt.

Saba is a wise old owl: Cairo, Egypt.

The boyish and self-sufficient Ron Nelson: Naro Moru, Kenya.

Zanzibar's Stone Town crumbles in majestic decay.

Mansang Velji, Indian merchant, in the Hindu temple, Zanzibar.

recently, and there is another I know, but he is not well. I am so sorry, but I really cannot be of help to you.'

So, in due course, we bid him good morning and take our leave.

Chance, however, decides to bring us together one more time. Another day, as we're strolling along on the edge of the town we bump into Mr Choma again. He is sitting with eight or so of his Omani friends along the wall by the old laundry, a motley array of noses, missing teeth and embroidered Zanzibari hats. And there, at the far end, is none other than the old Arab gentleman we tried to speak to on our first day.

Mr Choma hails us and orders coffee, which comes poured from a battered kettle into tiny cups decorated with a moon and star motif. The men all shift along and we join them in the shade to watch the world go by.

The old man's name is Gharib Salim and he is nearly a hundred, the oldest Omani on the island. But before we can get too excited, Mr Choma is quick to make his excuses:

'Alas, it is not possible to speak to him. He really cannot remember anything.'

And so, as Gharib Salim continues to stare out from behind his well-thumbed spectacles, the rest of that story will, perhaps wisely, remain untold.

~

When the tide is up, there's a distant roar, like a jet plane somewhere in the sky. I keep imagining it should soon pass overhead, but it never does. Then if I screw my eyes against the light, I can just make out a hazy white line dividing the purest of blues, two halves: one turquoise, the other azure. The roar of the jet plane is the sound of the Indian Ocean pounding the reef, one, maybe two miles out. The lagoon is turquoise. It can rise high and swollen, waves crashing and foaming up the palm-fringed bank, or it can ebb away to reflective, paddling flats.

It is at low tide that the lagoon comes to life. When the morning sun turns the sands to mercury, we look out eastwards into the light and see a population of tiny silhouettes, local Swahili women and children, digging for clams, planting seaweed or looking for shipwrecked octopus. Or if the tide is out for the afternoon, the day will cool and the dozen or so species of waders and heron, who prod for food around the shallows, will stand with an eye cocked, looking twice their height on mirrored stilts. We need to tread carefully: under slippery feet, razor-sharp mussel shells wait among the sandy weed to slice a casual step. At the water's edge, hermit crabs hobble about in their borrowed homes. If I pick one up and hold still, when he's bold enough he'll uncoil cautiously to show me his soft armour, in lagoon colours of turquoise and orange.

I have fallen in love with the boats. They seem to have been handed down from an ancient time, wood simply spliced and held together with rope. A trunk is hollowed out, made thin and sleek, its line rising with a sweep at the prow. Two cross-beams are lashed to the hull, fore and aft, with extensions bound on, like two pairs of arms dipping down to the water. Then, at the arms' length, a stabilizer stretches fingertip to fingertip along the length of both sides. In full sail, with a holey patchwork of greasy grey canvas and a stripped branch for a mast, a prototype trimaran glides across the water, only one wing ever touching the surface. When the tide is out, they lie forlorn, one wing resting on the sand, like flying-boats grounded on a desert airfield.

We soon pass the test the women throw at us. They approach along the beach, wrapped in their bright *kangas*, and shout, '*Jambo*,' as they go by. It takes a few turns until they've shown us the ropes.

'*Jambo*,' we reply. Hello.

'*Habari?*' they sing. How are you?

'*Msouri sana*.' Very well, thank you.

'*Karibu*.' You are welcome.

We are welcome indeed. The boys show us how to play *bao*, their high-speed board game – beans dropped into holes carved in a flat piece of wood. A game of football is played with a bundle of rags tied with twine. Vanella has the young ones painting with watercolours and they go crazy listening to their voices on the Walkman through headphones. There is laughter and shouting. The palm fronds crackle in the breeze and, for once, the colour of our skin matters not a jot.

We live in a hut, with sand on the floor. When there is water, we pour it over our heads from an old paint can. We eat papaya and coconut and fish from the sea. The rhythm of the days is told by the sun and the moon. And we want to stay for ever.

James spends hours teaching us *bao*. He is a boy no more, but not yet a man and has the longest, sexiest eyelashes I've ever seen. Each morning he turns up and patiently takes us through the finer points of strategy. It makes little difference though, of course, because he beats us every time. His fingers move so fast, picking up, flicking and dropping, and he always plans at least sixteen moves ahead. And when it looks really bad for us and the game is almost certainly up, James claps his hands and smiles.

'Pau . . . fraysh,' he reminds us, drawling out the words. 'Pau . . . fraysh.'

He maintains that the best chance of a winning run comes from such an apparently hopeless position.

Poor. Fresh.

Like an old man of the sea, with two days' stubble on a face of polished mahogany, Omari sits with his back to the wall, untying what looks like a tangle of fishing net. The faded crew-neck sweater he wears has lost most of its shape and nearly all of the stitching to two brown shoulder patches. His trousers are in tatters, knees showing through dark as coffee beans. Maintaining the dignity of his years, he looks on with mild amusement at the sudden invasion of the shade in front of his house. Gathered around is an expectant group of young men and, in and among, the two of us. At the back, those who can't find room to sit are loitering in the sun, feigning disinterest or shooing away overexcited children. The women watch everything from a distance, where they sit tying bundles of twigs.

The entire village is alive with chatter. A new-found friend, a man by the name of Hilal Suleiman, led us along the beach to Mfumbui, which is little more than a cluster of dwellings with a main street of sand overlooked by waving palm trees. The houses are roughly built in stone, held together with a coarse lime cement; some have tin roofs and battered wooden doors with numbers chalked on them. The older ones, like Omari's, are covered with a thatch and have front doors made from finely woven palm.

'Omari Jecha Kichachu,' Hilal spells out in my notebook, painstakingly joining each letter. He is performing his volunteered role very seriously. Jecha was the name of Omari's father, Kichachu his grandfather. We give our names and the old man repeats them softly in his gravelly voice till he has them correct. Then, with a smile, which reveals more gaps than brown teeth, he returns to the mess of twine around him.

I wonder what he must think. When he was a boy he would have run away into the forest, afraid, if an Englishman had chanced by.

Then we turn up specially to see him, talking of books and faraway lands, when he's lived all his life in Mfumbui and only ever been as far as the Stone Town, a three-day journey on foot once upon a time.

I presume Omari is a fisherman, but Hilal tells us otherwise.

'You know, he had four works,' he confirms, after a brief exchange in Swahili. They are confused by my use of the word 'job'. The concept of a job, as such, seems inappropriate. 'They lived like animals in that time. They were thinking about eating and sleeping, no more.'

For his first work, Omari had been a farmer. He grew maize and a little cassava. In his younger days, he'd also been a coconut-tree climber, shinning up the bark with a piece of rope between his feet to knock down the ripest nuts. Then he became a tamer of animals.

'I would take cows into the forest and leave them somewhere with plenty of grass for the day,' Omari says, his Swahili gruff yet lyrical. 'The next day I would lead them to a different place, so that the animals came to trust me. They knew that I was their lord.'

His fourth work proves me right. He was indeed a fisherman. He recalls an ancient time when the harvest was plenty. 'I used to fill the boat with fish. In the shallows you could see them everywhere. In those days, we were afraid to go outside the reef, because there were so many big fish and we only had a poor line to catch them with. Nowadays, a fisherman can go and return with only two or three fish, even though he uses a trap of nets.'

Omari rubs his furrowed brow. His fingertips are pink, as if the pigmentation has been worn away with use. From where I sit I can smell his warm, earthy odour, all yeasty, as he leans forward to pick up some strips of cloth, which he then begins to tie to the netting.

'What is he doing here?' Vanella asks Hilal. 'Repairing his nets?'

'He is repairing, yes, but not for fishing. This is for seaweed.'

'Seaweed?' I look closer. The tangle of net is a bizarre arrangement of nylon line, cloth ties and coloured twine.

Hilal shows us. 'He cuts these and ties them in the fishing line here.'

'And seaweed grows around it?'

'Yes.'

'Ah!'

'And the net is tied from this stick to another and the seaweed is tied here and it hangs in the water. The seaweed grows and within two weeks you go back to harvest. It is sold to the Koreans.'

So we are witnessing work number five. And when I ask what he has learnt in his old age, Omari says that as well as knowing how to find seaweed, he now has acquired the wisdom of buying rope from the women and selling it in the town. They make their rope by stacking mounds of coconuts in the shallows of the lagoon for at least a year, then winding the fibre from the inside of the shell. Omari the rope merchant makes six works.

He is certainly adaptable, and usefully so because the village of Mfumbui and this whole stretch of eastern coastline is about to experience one of the most fundamental changes of the century: the coming of the electric cable. Before long, they will have light-bulbs, air-conditioning and soap operas, like everyone else.

A thought occurs to me and I ask Omari whether he ever looks at the stars at night.

'Yes,' replies the old man quizzically.

'And do you look at the moon?'

'Yes, I do.'

'And did you know that men have flown to the moon?'

'Now that I do not believe,' he says, with a reproachful look, as if I am pulling his leg.

That night, Vanella and I walk out along the beach. Though the land lies under a cloak of darkness, the heavens are open, a black basin of sky sprinkled with a zillion glorious pin-holes of light. A furtive moon is rising behind the palm trees and every so often we see a shooting star silently fizz and die.

The tide is out, a stiff breeze blowing down from the north and, near the edge of the lagoon, there is a boat on fire. Sometimes they build a fire around the hull to burn off the weed and algae.

We draw near to watch. The roar of the surf is up. Across the sands, away beyond the piping of the wader birds, we can see more boats alight.

A tall Swahili figure holds a blazing firebrand of dry palm leaves. He raises it high and a trail of embers blows away into the dark. He swings the firebrand down and lights more fronds lying along the far side of the boat. In seconds, the fire has caught and sparks whip away in a lively display.

The man stands straight and takes breath, his muscular brown torso lit by the glow. He looks our way and bows his head a fraction in the most imperceptible of greetings. All three of us hold quite still. Then he turns to feel the cool of the wind, and a plume of smoke, like the wake of the boat, disappears horizontally into the night.

Footnote

Three weeks later, elsewhere in Africa, Vanella calls out from the bath.

'Jackson, have we got a needle? I think there's something living in my foot.'

'Uh-huh.'

'No, honestly. Come and have a look.'

The wet foot I'm offered has a blister on the fleshy bit of the second toe, up by the nail.

'Hang on. I've got one of those.' I'd assumed it to be a blood blister, but couldn't think how it got there.

We compare symptoms: a slightly swollen, squidgy bump with a blackish centre and if you look carefully and prod, the black bit moves . . . by itself.

It doesn't take me long to find the needle. I gallantly offer it to Vanella, who prepares to prick the surface of her squidgy bump. We are transfixed. The point slips in easily, the pressure releases and with a gentle squeeze . . .

'Oh, my God,' we say in unison.

We watch in horror as her toe becomes Vesuvius in miniature. Eggs!

I grab the needle. Emergency. I have to operate. The more I squeeze, the more tiny white eggs appear and the more revulsion gives way to pleasure. Whatever it is, it's better out than in. After the eggs comes blood and the worst is probably over – except that the black bit is still in there.

Vanella calls for all available surgical apparatus. She's having no more of this alien invasion and cuts out a large chunk of flesh, leaving a gaping sore. I opt for a more natural remedy: once nothing more will squeeze out, I apply a dab of antiseptic and I leave well alone.

A week later, after much scraping and picking, I am able to extract the dried carcass of a jigger flea. The female of the species lays her eggs in anything warm and fleshy she can find in the sand.

10

MOTHER AFRICA

The old Toyota rattles along a straight, empty road under clear blue skies. In the back we have Nessie and Alice, who are quiet at first but the further we drive out into the country, the more they relax. Nessie and Alice work for white families in Harare. They are city girls going home.

Nessie has a lovely round face and tightly curled hair. Alice, her younger sister, has inherited some cheekbones. Both wear lipstick and earrings for the occasion. Nessie is looking prim in a green and blue patterned dress, while Alice aims for a touch more glamour. It's odd. Vanella and I are kitted out for the bush; they've come dressed for dinner.

As the day hots up, conversation becomes easier and we begin to quiz each other. Nearly everything we say surprises them.

'How much does it cost?' asks Nessie, leaning forward, hands resting in her lap.

We are talking about education.

'There are some private schools, but most children in England go to school for free.'

'The schools are free?'

'Yes.'

'Oh . . .' There's a pause, and then, 'We always have to pay for the schooling.'

Vanella says that in England the government will give you money every week if you have no job.

'Oh,' they both go.

'Do you have a swimming-pool?' Alice timidly asks.

We smile.

'It's pretty cold there much of the time. Anyway, we only live in a flat. It's not really big enough for a pool.'

More silence in the back. Then Nessie wants to know if we have servants.

I shake my head. I don't really count Bridie, the lady who used to iron my shirts.

'It's not like it is here,' says Vanella. 'Not many people do.'

'Oh. But there are black people living in England, aren't there?' says Nessie.

'Yes. Quite a few.'

Another pause. Then Alice leans forward. 'So there are black people living in England and they aren't servants?' she says.

They retreat and chatter to each other in Shona, marvelling perhaps at that faraway paradise called England. Meanwhile we eavesdrop, enjoying the cadence and rhythm of their language as if it were music.

Soon, we cross another dried-up riverbed. It hasn't rained here for eighteen months; the last rainy season passed without a single drop. The land is parched, drained of colour. The rivers have shrunk into the sand or reduced to little more than a trickle of mud, still nevertheless attracting the women with their pots. People are hungry. Another dry wet season will probably mean disaster. But there's still hope. Last night we heard thunder rumbling around Harare. The rains are due any time.

Only a week ago we watched ships unloading grain at the port of Beira, in ragged, war-weary Mozambique. Armed convoys of trucks then hauled up over the mountains into Zimbabwe, where we've witnessed the other end of the supply line: Shona villagers swinging triumphantly down the road with a weighty sack of grain on their heads, safe for now at least.

We are loaded up with mealie-meal ourselves, bags of ground maize from which they make *sadza*. *Sadza* is a stiff yellow porridge, a staple of the Shona diet. Before maize was introduced they used to make it from a small grain called *rapoko*. Nessie has shown us how they cook *sadza* and we've eaten it with pumpkin leaves and tomato. It's good stuff.

Off the tarmac and on to the dirt, we find our way to Zimunya, the area named after their tribal chief. A few more miles and Nessie says we're to go left at the bus stop, which turns out to be a gnarled old tree with a man sitting beneath it. We turn up a narrow track, but it's crazy. Deep chasms have been carved by the floodwater at some time and the Toyota only just holds out as we scrape over at absurd angles. Nessie and Alice don't seem the least bothered. This is obviously quite normal. We've noticed the healthy relationship Africans enjoy with the motor car. They'll always take a lift as far as it'll take them. If the car stops or gets stuck or breaks down, it's very simple. They walk.

Their brother Simon has heard us coming. A tall, gangly young man, he's put on suit trousers and a clean white shirt. We park under a tree and shake hands. Simon nods and smiles, then they lead us on a narrow footpath across two ploughed fields, up the slope to their father's house. At first, I'm distracted by the sight of Alice picking her way in high heels. But then I notice dark green shoots pushing tentatively through the soil. I blink and look again. They have maize growing. I ask Simon what's going on.

'Rain will come, we thought,' he answers. 'We plough and sow. It rains.' His voice is soft and easy.

Only a little rain has fallen. Now they need more or the seed and all their effort will be wasted. They are lucky, they still have cattle to pull the ploughshare. Their father once owned eight but, because of the drought, only four remain. He's half the man he used to be, literally. Cattle mean everything to the Shona. They have ceremonial uses at every step between birth and death. They're a source and a sign of wealth; they're used for trade and as dowries. They provide milk and food. And when the rains do come, a family with no cattle will be digging the earth by hand.

We reach the house, a rough construction of exposed timber and concrete with a tin roof, comprising a main room and two bedrooms. They say their father is out visiting; their mother died some ten years ago. Our boots resound on the spotlessly clean floorboards of a living space with a familiar style of home comfort. Nessie shows us to two old armchairs facing a well-worn sofa across a makeshift coffee-table. A low wooden sideboard is decorated with petrol brand stickers and a shaky, glass-fronted corner-cupboard contains the best crockery, a fantastic assortment of one of every piece. The girls then busy themselves preparing lunch in the kitchen corner, where the cupboards are of a post-war design, still painted post-war pale green.

Simon sits on the sofa, hands on his knees. He looks at us with questioning brown eyes, then smiles coyly. He doesn't know what to say and neither do we. It's our turn to be shy, and for an awkward moment I suppress a dreadful urge to talk about the weather. In the end, the silence is so embarrassing we all just burst out laughing.

Then Nessie brings the plates, one for us and one for them, each piled high with soft white sliced bread. Alice pours the tea and while we slurp its earthy flavour and eat the finest bread and marge in the world, I make a fool of myself doing regional English accents – Yorkshire first, then Cockney, West Country, Birmingham. Then I have a go at Welsh, Irish, Scottish . . .

Do they laugh? There's no stopping them.

After lunch, we set out on foot to look for Ruth, their grandmother. Simon says she is staying with their uncle.

Zimunya is a land of hills. Cone-shaped, they stand seven or eight hundred feet high, the tops rounded and sides covered with scrub. Here and there on the flat sandy ground in between, huts are grouped together in kraals. Each has a mango tree laden with fruit to tide them over, in a normal year, while the maize ripens.

The mealie-meal we are carrying is a gift for Ruth and her family. I've already tried a bag on my head, African-style, but it fell off and I now have it slung over my shoulder as I chat with Simon. I like climbing mountains, so I ask him how long it takes to get to the top of one of the hills. Simon gives me a very strange look. It transpires he's never been up.

We trudge along in the heat, our path skirting untilled fields until we reach a gaping hole where the entire corner of one plot has collapsed.

'Over agriculture. Washed it away. Big rain,' Simon explains in his jumbly way.

I look up into a deep blue sky and spot a solitary buzzard, hanging on the wind watching us. There's still no sign of rain.

We find their uncle sitting cross-legged under a tree, preparing a hand-plough. He's binding a sturdy length of wood to an old iron blade. Instead of his workman's hand, he offers us a forearm to shake and we grip the sinewy muscle under his dark dry skin. A toddler runs out of a hut, stares at our whiteness and bursts into tears. Then a young girl lays out matting and positions two rickety wooden chairs. I offer my seat to Nessie or Alice but they insist, and we've just sat down when the uncle announces that Ruth isn't there at all. She's at her daughter Margaret's place, over by Tindindi.

It's so perfectly African. We have to walk all the way back to the car, load up the mealie-meal, rock down the crazy track to the ancient tree by the bus stop. Then we drive another mile or more, giving a lift to everyone we meet along the way. And when finally we reach Margaret's, they tell us Ruth is having a bath.

A kraal isn't quite a village, more a collection of huts. Here, four are the typical rondavel type, with a conical thatch and two-tone ochre and mud-grey walls. One of these is the food store, raised on bricks to keep the creepy-crawlies out. Two others boast a more convenient kind of architecture: concrete, rectangular and topped with a hard corrugated roof. The bathroom, though, remains a shambolic arrangement of planks and odd bits of wood, which somehow manage to support each other.

We ask them to tell Ruth not to hurry and everyone gathers in what seems to be the family hut. For all the intense sunlight in the doorway, it is dark inside. The furniture consists of an old bed, two wooden chairs and a table. The bare walls are painted green; the floor gleams like gun-metal, mud layered on mud and worn with use. And although there's no fire burning, I still catch the primal taste of woodsmoke at the back of my throat.

So we have Margaret, Ruth's daughter – she is blind. Gracie, Ruth and Samuel are more of Ruth's grandchildren, cousins to Nessie, Alice and Simon. Then come Manyara and Hanzvinei, two great-granddaughters, and little Leon, a great-grandson. And with the three neighbours who've turned up to see what's going on, plus Vanella and me, we make fifteen altogether in the one small space.

Introductions and explanations are exchanged. When it comes to Samuel, I shake him by the hand and say, 'So you'll be Sam Marizani then.'

There's a silence while they look at each other in surprise; no one has mentioned the name Marizani. Then I point at a roof beam, where some time has been chalked: 'Sam Marizani, last born'. Well, they just fall about, helpless with guffaws of carefree laughter. They laugh a lot, these people, these deeply happy people. Their faces merge with the shadows and for a moment all we can see are flashes of bright white teeth.

Half an hour later, a small figure emerges from the bathroom. Leaning on her stick, she makes her way over and the volume of noise from the women rises as she enters the hut. She smiles all around, says hello and sits on a crocheted blanket in the middle of the floor. Her cheeks shine like well-polished apples, her skin is translucent, a shade lighter than the rest of the family. Only her chin and forehead show any sign of wrinkles.

Ruth looks at Vanella, then at me, and she smiles again. Her eyes are liquid, dark brown.

'You are welcome here,' she says, speaking softly, her voice a little hoarse. She wears a bright blue dress reminiscent of a nurse's uniform and clearly lives in her grey woolly hat.

Stretching out her legs, she makes herself comfortable and we learn the Shona greeting. The women gently clap their palms two or three times; the men lightly touch their fingertips together, hands parallel and pointing upwards. They do this whenever they meet or, in this case, to say, 'Right, now we're all here.'

I soon realize that Simon, Samuel and I are outnumbered in every sense. This is women's work; they are all here because of Ruth. Beyond the gossip about who's been the latest to decide to plant some seed, I can tell the respect they have for their elder. The way they laugh with her, their easy-going chatter – she is their friend, their sister. And how naturally Vanella has joined in. She sits among them, surrounded by small children who stare or smile shyly as she tries to play. She has grown her hair longer now and the mildly puppyish look she first set out with has gone. In fact, I don't think I've ever seen her looking so well, so relaxed and happy.

Little Leon's nose needs a good wipe. He crawls over to his great-grandmother, who hardly appears to notice as he begins playing with her toes. Then a cockerel crows right in the doorway and makes me jump, which makes them all laugh again.

We learn that Ruth began life with the name Masabva Muteera. When she was still young, her parents were persuaded to move to the Methodist mission at Old Mutare, where she was christened Ruth. She later married a man whose new biblical name was Paul and whose surname was Muranda, meaning 'like a slave'. Ruth had no formal education, but she helped out in teaching the toddlers where their eyes and ears were, and how many fingers they had. She also worked as a midwife.

'How did you learn what to do?' Vanella asks her.

'I had my own babies, so I have the experience,' says Ruth.

'And what's the most important thing about being a midwife?'

'Not hesitating,' she replies, with a smile.

She worked by instinct and was happy to let nature take its course.

'So how many children have you brought into the world?'

Ruth points around the room. 'You, you, you, him, her . . .'

They laugh and cheer. She was there every time.

'*Maningi, maningi*,' she says, beaming with matriarchal pride. Many, many hundreds. Ruth is mother to them all.

We try to figure out how old she is. More cynical colonial types have warned us that the natives most likely won't know their age. And at first it looks like they might be right.

'Now, how old am I?' Ruth asks Margaret.

'How should I know?' her daughter replies, to everyone's great amusement.

They are keen to debate the question, but eventually we do it by working backwards. Nessie is forty. Her mother, Rebecca, Ruth's seventh child, was born in 1933. And Ruth knows that she got married in 1918. So we reckon it's likely that she was born some time at the end of the nineteenth century. She says in those days they used to marry in their mid-twenties, which means she must now be well into her nineties, a fine age for the bush. She's had ten children of her own. The first two, twin girls, died young but, of the rest, five are still living. We've met only a fraction of the family so far.

Ruth says they used to delay in getting married so that they would stay with their husbands.

'Nowadays, some girls have three husbands in three years,' she says. 'We try to tell them to be in a good way, but they don't do it. They're the boss. They think what they're doing is right. We try our best to tell them, but they don't listen. "That is the old background," they say. "We don't want that."'

Education seems to be at the heart of the problem. The older generations never went to school, so the young ones think they know everything.

How times have changed. To begin with, there used to be plenty more to eat, even in periods of drought. In the old days they used to hunt their food: impala, jackal, warthog. The men would go off into the bush for a week or maybe two. They would trap the game, cook and dry the meat before carrying it home. But now all the animals have been wiped out and anyway hunting isn't allowed any more. Today, if you want meat you have to go to the butcher with money in your pocket. So mostly they eat *sadza* and vegetables.

The look of the land is different too. Ruth tells us that once upon a time all around here was bush proper. The trees have been cut down for firewood or building material. The population has expanded and used up the space, so the villages and kraals now sit closer together. They used to walk two, maybe three miles without seeing a single hut. Now they complain they're living on top of each other. All this has happened, we hear, only in the last thirty or forty years – during my short lifetime, in other words. And I can remember a time when the kitchen at Woodlands was still painted that post-war pale green.

Ruth's earliest memory is playing mummies and daddies. When she was five or six, they would make toy houses out of mud. At harvest-time, they'd go to the fields and pick up the leftovers to store in their tiny huts. They made pots and plates out of the skin of small fruits and cooked make-believe *sadza*.

When she grew older, she carried wood and fetched water. She ground *rapoko* on the stone and made *sadza* for real, serving it in wooden bowls carved for vegetables and relishes. Ruth shows us the ones they still use. They are dark and smoky.

Then she has the girls giggling again. She tells us how they made small loincloths from the fibres of tree bark. Nessie calls them rugs.

'We used to tie one at the front and one at the back and not worry about our breasts,' Ruth says, to much sniggering. 'We wore jewellery too. We would grind some *rapoko* and my father would go off to trade it. I don't know where he went, but he came back with coloured beads which we'd wear strung around our necks and waists.'

'Why don't you dress like this any more?' asks Vanella.

'*Ngunguzani*,' they murmur, looking sheepishly one to another. The white men.

These ways stopped when the white men came to civilize them. This was in the time before Ruth was married.

Her memory is surprisingly good. She can recall, as a child, hearing the adults talk of a war, the one fought by Lobengula, head of the Ndebele tribe.

'They were fighting for who was going to be chief,' she says. It was the white settlers who had won that war.

She can remember the droughts too. Apparently there was a big trouble drought in 1933, when they had to leave home and go hunting for water. That time, when they ran out of *rapoko*, they would climb Tindindi, the hill nearby, to find a particular root. Ruth says they dug up the root, ground it and dried it in the sun so they could make a *sadza*.

So they do climb the hills. But when they do, they have to be careful.

'If you go up Tindindi to collect wood,' Ruth explains, 'you need to behave yourself. You mustn't say bad things because there is a big spirit. If you say something bad, you will disappear and no one will see you ever again.'

We can tell from their faces that this is true. The atmosphere in the hut grows quiet as they run out of nervous laughter. Tindindi commands respect. It is a powerful spirit which lives there, watching over them. The mountain must be a spooky place to go on your own.

They have to visit Tindindi to bring rain, too. When the rains are due, the elders will spend three days making a beer called *makonzo*. The spirit won't allow the young people to do this. The chief of Zimunya then comes to oversee small pots being hidden in caves around the hill. At night, when all is quiet, the spirit will appear and drink the brew. The next day, it is the turn of the people. They go in search of the pots the spirit has drunk from and the celebrations last until midday. Some time later, right on cue, the rains will come.

So something has been going wrong.

Ruth thinks they haven't been doing things in the right order, or perhaps they've forgotten some vital part of the ritual.

'Or maybe it's the pythons,' she says. 'A long time ago, we never killed snakes. It was said that if we did, the rains would not begin. Nowadays people are killing pythons. They don't follow the old traditions. So we have no rain.'

Ruth shrugs and holds up her hands in despair. There's nothing she can do with youngsters these days.

Down in the village we are heroes. Simon insists we drive along to have a look, whereas in truth it's the other way round. He wants the village to take a look at us, his new friends.

The buildings are scattered across a dusty expanse dotted with a few spindly *musasa* trees. Across the way, half a dozen men sit in the shade of the bottle store. The butcher's shop looks closed.

Loaded up with more hitch-hikers, we roll to a halt in front of the general store, which is packed with noisy schoolkids clamouring for sweets. Young men Simon's age loiter on the steps and we pose with them for an obligatory photograph. We all shake hands and grin wildly.

Then as we drink a quenching lemonade, I examine the posters pinned on the walls. New Brilliant Household Soap looks like a section of blue girder, but still it promises a whiter wash. A cigarette claims to be the coolest taste in smoking. Some brand of toothpaste offers extra protection for those teeth. There's still no escape, it seems, from the relentless march of the *ngunguzani*.

We take Simon, Nessie, Alice and a couple of others back to the ancient bus stop. Nessie and Alice have decided to stay over.

'You remember message,' Simon says solemnly, as we shake hands under the old tree.

'Yes, I remember. I'll try,' I promise.

As we were saying goodbye to Ruth earlier, Simon had tugged my arm excitedly. 'Listen,' he said, 'she wants to say something to you.'

Ruth was holding Vanella's hand and mine.

'Go carefully now,' she told us. 'God be with you. And when you get back home, make sure you say hello to the Queen Mother for me.'

11

THE LONG LIFE MEN

The new year begins in China.

Thousands of miles out, a whole year still to go and a place called home seems far, far away. Although no longer bound by its trappings, our life on the road has nevertheless acquired its own inevitability – another country, a new exchange rate, the usual search for a decent breakfast. And we have been travelling for so long now we appear to have developed a strange condition. We both feel permanently displaced, as if we don't belong anywhere. I do get homesick occasionally, I admit, but that tends only to be a hankering for autumn leaves or a decent cup of tea. This is more subtle, a kind of emptiness. It isn't always with me. Only when I stop sometimes, I see the rest of the world going about its daily life and I know I can never be included. Not really. If only I had the gift of tongues, to be able to speak to every man in his own language.

There's also the yawning distance we sense between us and everyone back home. We manage snatched phone conversations now and then to let them know we are alive. Those letters that reach us are few and far between, and of course the friends we hope might write never do. We take comfort imagining them doing the same old things in the same old way, like we used to. Whereas novelty has become fundamental to our way of life. Each day bombards us with any amount of new stimulus. Familiarity with our surroundings is only ever temporary. We can stay a few days, even a couple of weeks, but then we're hitching up and moving on again, to another place which has to be touched and tasted. Our survival skills are now so well honed that routines for preservation have become second nature. Out on the street, our two pairs of eyes are a match for any lurking danger. All this time, we are outsiders, and although good for the objectivity, we would still rather go anywhere but another dingy hotel room.

I suppose I'm to blame. I seem incapable of controlling my desire to go absolutely everywhere. I want to do Burma, Vietnam, Korea. But Vanella found she was growing tired of waking up with a different view each morning. So now we travel, then hang out for a while longer. Even then I feel the need to go wandering, and still walk out on my own exploring the back ways, just so I know where I am.

Something seems to be compelling me to keep moving – not simply to see the world, or because there might never be another chance, but because the very act of moving gives me a sense of security. I've found a direction and a purpose at last and no longer feel I'm walking away. Rather, I am walking to. I'm on some kind of mission. When we started out, we didn't really know what crazy idea we'd dreamt up. Now, I've become a little obsessive about meeting old people. I love it, every minute, every aspect. But Vanella doesn't feel quite the same.

We are shut in our scruffy room in the Hotel Dong Fang one afternoon when she complains that she doesn't have much of a role to play. Although we spend each hour of every day together, I haven't even realized. Maybe that's half the problem – there's just no escape.

'It's your project, isn't it? It's your book, not mine,' she says.

'No. We're doing this together.'

'But you're the one who's writing it.'

'That doesn't mean you can't contribute.'

'Yes, but everything always has to be done your way. You're like some sergeant-major, everything in order, always ticking your lists.'

'No, it doesn't . . . And I've always made lists. You know I can't help it.'

'You don't understand, do you?'

'I'm not sure I do, no.'

'You're so frustrating. You just want answers all the time. And if any idea I have doesn't fit with what you're thinking, it gets dismissed.'

'No, it doesn't.' What is all this? I always want to hear what she has to say.

'It's like you sit there in judgement. I'm under the hammer all the time. Something is either right or wrong. Or it's "I'll just think about that one." '

'And what's wrong with that?' Now I'm the one who's getting frustrated. I'm raising my voice.

'You just absorb everything so you can work it through later. Our conversations are never a springboard. You never want to give anything back.'

'Maybe that's just the way I do things.'

'It is, I'm telling you it is. Everything I say is either knocked down because it's irrelevant or, if I'm very lucky, it gets squirrelled away.'

'But I'm only trying to work things out. When it clicks, it clicks.'

'Precisely. But it's all going on inside your head. I don't get a look in. You never say, "Tell me why you feel like that," or "Is there another reason?" That's what I find interesting. This isn't a one-way street, you know. Sometimes I wonder if you really value my contribution.'

'I do. Of course I do.'

'You're at it again, see. You won't hear me. Please try to understand. Oh, I don't know what I'm doing here. Look at this place . . .'

She huffs out a painful sigh and seems close to tears. Then she utters the awful, immortal words: 'I want to go home.'

'Oh, God, no.'

'What?' Now she sounds annoyed.

I stand for a moment with hands on hips. 'But we still have a long way to go,' I plead. 'We've *got* to keep going. Think what's in store. Who knows what'll happen?'

'I know. But I'm finding it really hard. I just want you to understand.'

'OK. OK.'

I reassure her as best I can. I'll try. I don't know how, but I'll try. For her, there's always another question to be asked. Me, I just want to get everything sorted. We'll do the travel in bursts. And I'll forget about Burma. The plan is to visit Japan next, then make our way back across to Pakistan. We have to wait for the weather to improve before heading up into the Karakoram mountains.

It scares me, all this. Suddenly I think the whole thing could fall apart. If she goes, I go too. Something inside me froze when she said it – I just dread the idea of giving up and going home. Because the trouble is I don't expect home will mean what it used to mean any more.

I think we need a change of scene. Anyway I could do with some air.

I hold out my hand. 'Come on. Let's go for a walk.'

Outside we can smell gunpowder. The Year of the Rooster is still two days away but the fun has already started. The pavements and back alleys are littered with fragments of spent firecrackers, like confetti at a thousand miniature street weddings. They play the full orchestra for us: from squibs to rattling cracks to big bang booms, to two dozen deafening explosions from some fire-monster hung over a road sign.

This isn't the only reason I'm jumpy. We were promised help by a government department and I've heard nothing. So we set out in the hope of finding the office of the Chinese People's Association for Friendship with Foreign Countries.

Oh, it's cold – minus temperatures, six layers of clothing required just to put your nose past the door. The midwinter sun can barely lift itself above the horizon, flooding the streets with a low, silvery light that bleaches out all colour. Only to the north is there a hint of blue in the sky. A thick layer of grey dust covers the city, fallout from the coal fires and factories. Plumes of smoke curl into the still air above the shambles of brick dwellings that sprawl one against another. Down the alleyways in between, bicycles and tricycle carts crowd together in a jumble of old metal. In the tiny shops where paper lanterns and fireworks are for sale, a patchwork of diminutive brands presses tight against the glass. And everywhere we hear the loud, elongated 'hoick', then a spit, a split second before a ball of phlegm hits the pavement, soon there to freeze.

They all turn to stare at the freaks. We're tall as giants and we don't have black hair or chubby, grubby faces. We grin back and say hello, so they think we're a bit loopy too, probably, but at least it breaks the ice and smiles are returned. Sometimes the schoolchildren shout to us in English, waving furiously across a bustling street.

This is Boomtown. Market stalls, shops, restaurants: the place is humming. Boys call out, hawking mountains of fresh fruit and vegetables; clouds of steam billow around the street dumpling man; a cheery lady chops ginger root and spring onions expertly on a wooden block; and the owner of a roadside roast-chicken factory shows off his entire production line, start to finish. Calculators, cosmetics, leather jackets – the free-market economy has cut its teeth and everyone is buying or selling, or going to or from buying or selling. There are some eight million bicycles in the city of Beijing.

Along the way, we happen to notice a figure standing in a herbalist's window. He is an old man with a huge bulbous bald head and a white beard that hangs long and straight. In one hand he holds a wooden staff with a gourd tied to its end, while in the other he carries what looks like a large onion, but Vanella peers through the glass and assures me it's a peach. Dressed in a fine yellow robe, the old man stands against the painted background of a forest scene. He is accompanied on either side by a young deer and a tall bird known as a crane. Jars of ginseng root and a display of tiny dried sea horses have been arranged at his feet.

Naturally, we wonder who he can be, so we enquire within. Young men in white coats are serving at polished counters, mixing potions into paper packets from a hundred wooden drawers around the walls.

There are embarrassed laughs when I ask. Then one of them replies, in English, 'Long . . . Life . . . Man.'

'Ah ha!' we say.

Early the following morning, a little blue taxi bounces and squeaks through the flow of bicycles along one of Beijing's broader avenues. The Chinese People's Association for Friendship with Foreign Countries had been trying to get hold of us and we are already in the company of Zhang Jinghua, our friendly guide. He is probably about my age and seems very willing. We turn along by the expanse of Tiananmen Square, flanked by impassive government buildings and Chairman Mao's portrait hung large for all to see. Suddenly I feel like I'm in a movie. A scene has to be acted out. I bend my head to the side window and gaze across an empty plain. It all happened, just there. In the distance a line of red flags is silhouetted black against the light. I feel the need to say something to Zhang Jingua, but I don't. A silence has fallen, charged with meaning for us all. My urge to speak is cancelled out by an equal pressure not to say anything and I'm left wondering why.

Soon the taxi pulls up in a side-street lined with stalls and immediately causes a traffic jam as we disembark. Horns blow, bicycle bells tring. Two men, smeared with blood, are unloading pigs' carcasses from a van. In through a red door and along a passageway, we quickly withdraw to a peaceful courtyard where the sun's weak rays slant in. A little snow lies frozen on the ground and a set of bookshelves, stacked with paperbacks, stands by the front door.

We are expected. A smiling lady shows us into a modest living space with a tiled floor. Most of the furniture is arranged against the panelled walls, like a waiting room. Shelves are piled with brown-paper parcels tied with string, presumably books or manuscripts. The television has been draped with a cloth, as if it's a parrot in a cage, and a clump of narcissus bulbs floats in water, the small yellow flowers sweetening the air.

As Mr Xia emerges unsteadily from his room, I can see over his shoulder a vast collection of musty books and yellowing pamphlets, a lifetime's work. He doesn't look too well, I must admit. His front teeth are broken and his cheeks so hollow I actually wonder if he isn't ill. One leg appears to be shorter than the other. The shoe has been specially built up to compensate and his shoelaces are only loosely tied. Settling his walking stick against the armchair, Mr Xia sits down carefully, then straightens his blue, collarless jacket with long, delicate fingers. They are feminine, his hands, the nails buffed and manicured to perfection.

Jasmine tea is served and Mr Xia begins to speak through pursed lips.

'You are a writer?' he asks me.

I nod, but know I am a sham. In his company, I am nothing.

'If only I had the time,' he says wistfully, 'it could be very thick, this book of yours. I have myself written a whole book on just my first fifty years.'

Mr Xia turns his head and stares at me obliquely through thick spectacle lenses. Those eyes have seen it all.

Xia Yan was a pen name. He was born Shen Duanxian in 1900, in Hangzhou, Zhejiang Province, southern China. He was first published when he began producing articles for the newspapers, while still a middle-school student. The warlords were squabbling at the time and he had called for an end to the disorder. But he didn't finally decide to become a writer until after the May the Fourth Movement. Towards the end of the First World War, Germany had occupied two cities in Shandong Province, but was driven out by the Japanese. During the Versailles peace conference news filtered back that the Chinese delegation was about to concede Shandong to Japan, so on 4 May 1919, the students in Beijing initiated a massive street demonstration. Their protest was quelled, peacefully, but the seeds of a nationalistic fervour had been sown and Shen Duanxian was converted to Marxism.

He soon became involved with the Party and worked as a journalist in Shanghai where he was instrumental in founding the Shanghai Arts and Drama Society. This promoted the idea of proletarian drama and began staging progressive works. By that time, the uneasy alliance between the Communists and Chiang Kai-shek's Nationalist Party was over. Chiang had seized power and his Kuomintang government was suppressing pro-Communist activity. It wasn't long before the police came to close down their theatre.

So Shen Duanxian changed his name to Xia Yan and his art became political. He wrote in protest, against Kuomintang repression and the threat of a Japanese invasion. He founded, together with other leading figures, the influential League of Left-wing Writers.

Xia Yan speaks quickly and succinctly. His mind is still sharp.

'I was an ordinary person,' he says, 'but my time was not ordinary.' He delivers his words to the room in general, but I become aware that now and then his eyes are watching, assessing me.

I'm wondering what made him want to be a writer, what his ambitions had been.

'My inspiration came from my time,' he says. 'I experienced many things. All the social inequalities meant that I could not stay calm inside. I had to write. I wrote for the people, in the interest of the people, and for the independence of the people. I wrote to awaken them. All writers should be so driven.'

My response is involuntary, crass even. 'Of course,' I say.

Xia turns to me, but says nothing. He then resumes. 'They were times of turmoil. I knew the people would eventually win the struggle. I did not know how. So I wrote plays and screenplays. I wrote about a wide range of subjects, but most of my characters are ordinary citizens. In one screenplay, called *Under the Eaves of Shanghai*, I described the lives of ordinary people in the 1930s. I was dealing with the period before the Anti-Japanese War, when people couldn't see the future. So at the beginning of the piece, I wrote about the continuous drizzle in March. They couldn't see beyond it . . . Then I wrote another called *The Fascist Bacteria*, all about the Japanese invader.'

Xia translated Gorky into Chinese; he adapted several novels for the screen. He wrote plays, edited newspapers and became one of the leading literary figures of his time.

So I ask him how the left-wing writer had felt when Mao's vision had come true, on 1 October 1949. By then, Xia had been appointed deputy director of the propaganda department in the East China Bureau of the Communist Party's Central Committee.

'On that day,' he replies, 'I was on the rostrum in Tiananmen Square with Chairman Mao Tse-tung. I was standing alongside him as he declared the independence of the People's Republic of China.'

Xia stretches out his left arm, pointing a slender finger upwards to the platform. He laughs when he sees the expression of surprise on my face as I gaze up at the imaginary figures.

'My happiest day was August the fifteenth, 1945, the day Japan surrendered at the end of the war. So October the first, 1949, would be my second happiest.'

Xia had been an important Party official. He knew Mao well. He also encountered Chiang Kai-shek, who he says was a very bad man, politically. But Chairman Mao was a great man. Xia delivers his eulogy with ease.

'Mao was a great thinker,' he says. 'He was clever, because he understood Chinese history and the growth of our culture. He could also see the social realities, so he combined these two aspects together to create a new role for the Chinese revolution.' Xia pauses, checks himself, then goes on. 'He was a great leader, even though he made mistakes in his later years. We had the good years, the time of enlightened reform in the countryside. We had the years of anti-right-wing activity, then afterwards the years of anti-left-wing activity.'

It is hard to tell, but I think I notice the nearest thing to a twinkle in his watery eye. And when I ask if his plays were ever repressed, he will only admit that most of his work was prohibited by Chiang Kai-shek and the Kuomintang.

But I should remember that, in China, the truth is more often contained in what is not said.

Xia forgot to add that he was singled out at the onset of the Cultural Revolution. In 1958, he adapted for cinema a famous novel from the thirties called *The Lin Family Shop*. Some seven years later, its central character, a small-time merchant, was deemed too bourgeois. Workers, soldiers and peasants were the true heroes of the revolution. So Xia Yan was officially discredited, publicly criticized by his old friend Mao. His art no longer served politics and, cruelly, he fell from grace. He disappeared from public life until after Mao's death. Only then would he return to his representative posts in literary circles. But, after ten years in prison, he had grown old and he could hardly walk because of the treatment he had received.

He displays no outward sign of bitterness. His haunted face bears witness to his tenacity.

'I am still a man of the revolution,' he says. 'Younger people may think I am too conservative, but I don't feel that way.'

'Does the older man write better than a younger man?' I wonder.

'I don't write much these days,' he concedes. 'But we old men do know history and we have the advantage of experience. Experience is the key. You must always write from experience. Your basis has to be reality.'

With this, Xia turns and gives me a look that is almost affectionate. The eyes are dulled now, his expression grim, but it is the knowing look of a comrade.

He smiles weakly and says, 'Finish.' Then, raising himself from his chair, slowly he struggles back to the sanctuary of his room full of books.

The Chinese People's Association for Friendship with Foreign Countries invites us for lunch, back at the office, a handsome building that was once the Italian embassy. Seated around a large circular table, we are served by attentive waiters. Our party is joined by Zhang Jinghua's boss, Mr Wang, and two other members of their department. We are guests of honour and the conversation is polite as we pick our way through the many dishes that keep arriving. But the longer the meal goes on, the more I know we have to say something. That same pressure is there again. I don't want to be rude, but it can't be left unspoken for ever.

In the end, Vanella does it. We are chatting about China's economic progress, of which they are suitably proud, and how most young people support the government. That's when she says it – the T word. Not Tibet, the other T word.

'But what about Tiananmen Square?' she bravely asks.

The silence doesn't last long, but it's there – a crack in time when we all think whatever we think.

'Much has changed since the events of Tiananmen Square,' says Zhang Jinghua, with a good-natured smile. 'The economy is growing well. Everyone can see that people can do better for themselves.'

Then Mr Wang speaks. 'What happened there was unfortunate. But it could not be helped. The government knows that change must come, political change. At the time of the Tiananmen Square demonstration, the change would have been too fast, too soon. It would not have led to stability. Look at the example of the Soviet Union.'

'But that can't be a justification for what happened, surely?' says Vanella. We're getting in deep.

'No, of course,' says Zhang Jinghua. 'Bloodshed is never a good thing. But the government had no choice. They had to make a show of strength. What happened was in the interest of the people. There is a plan. Economic reform will come first, then in time political reform will follow.'

'So are you saying that China will be prepared to consider democracy one day?' I ask.

'There will be political reform that suits the needs of the Chinese people.'

It's so hard to tell. They seem to have no problem talking about what we feel is a sensitive issue, even if we are being spun the Party line. They have a point, though. Deng Xiaoping's idea of putting economic change first does make sense in a country as huge and complex as China. And, of course, the government will want to control any political restructuring. But do our friends really believe this is a good enough excuse to massacre students in the town square, for their bodies to be left in a heap for all to see?

If they don't, it is something we are never going to find out. The greater good of the people will always prevail. And what is not said will be more telling than what is.

We see him here, we see him there – in jade, in porcelain, on paper-cuts and wall-hangings. We catch a glimpse of a china statuette on the top shelf of an old display cabinet. There he is inside an antique glass egg. Next he's promoting a brand of tea. We even eat a packet of his biscuits.

On the street outside one of Beijing's department stores, the colourful figure of the Long Life Man stands twice my height. His deer is alongside as usual and today the crane appears to have a mushroom in its beak. People stop to look and smile; the children point at his funny bulbous forehead. As Vanella and I draw near, we notice that the old man is grinning.

Lao Shou Xing they call him. He is the god of longevity, a legendary character whose origins lie back in the mists of time. Often he is to be found teamed up with two younger colleagues, the gods of wealth and happiness. The god of happiness is the one generally seen carrying a baby.

But Lao Shou Xing is our man. Some say it is the peach of immortality he holds in his hand. His gourd and the crane are symbols of long life. The deer represents happiness, as does the bat, which is often seen flying above his head.

A few hundred yards further down the street, we witness history in the making, a direct consequence of China's new Open Policy. We watch as a young Chinese couple take what is obviously their first ever tentative mouthful of hamburger. They look uncomfortable at first, chewing thoughtfully as they check each other's reaction.

We wonder what our friend Lao Shou Xing would make of this.

'Which would you choose?' I ask Vanella. 'A double cheeseburger with fries or the peach of immortality?'

'No contest,' she says.

'Come to think of it, what do you reckon Lao Shou Xing will say when he meets Ronald McDonald?'

12

Land of the Sweet Bean Bun

A large red sun is slipping away from a wintry sky leaving the land to darkness. The jagged hills in the distance shift to black silhouettes and we feel like characters in a science-fiction story, being transported to the metropolis of a strange new world. Around us, a language we have no hope of comprehending codes information in complex symbols. Miniature liquid crystal television screens sparkle with astonishing clarity, selling their wares to the transit commuters. They travel well dressed, these people, in fine clothing that makes the two of us look worn and shabby. Their shoes shine, their coats are sleek, the cases they carry fashioned in stiff leather. The younger ones wear micro-headphones, black dots on wires tucked into their small brown ears. This is the early shift, going home. Many are fast asleep, exhausted. But in the Land of the Rising Sun, people live longer, on average, than anywhere else on the planet.

Each of their metro stations has its own tinkly musical identity. We guess which one is ours, tumble out and get lost trying to find an exit. Upstairs, more ambient music floats in the ether to ease the stressed nerves of those who scurry by, while a station sweeper works around a coin on the floor, leaving it for whichever of them dropped it earlier.

Outside, it is bitterly cold. The Tokyo of my imagination was a monochrome chaos of buildings and telegraph wires. For real, it appears to be all chrome and neon colours, neat and compact. Still we can't find our way. The third man we ask thinks it best to walk us right to the door of the *ryokan*, a traditional-style hotel we've booked.

We practise our bowing and it's boots off, socks sliding on polished wooden floors. With a constant supply of green tea and a murmuring stream of more tinkly music, the *ryokan* is like living in a Japanese restaurant. Our room has a futon and kimonos to wear as dressing-gowns. Vanella and I bow to each other, trying to perfect the action. We think we're going to like it here. There's only one problem. This is the cheapest available room in town and it's costing us one whole day's budget. For all the kimono comforts, life is going to have to be frugal.

A quick sortie in search of food confirms that prices are terrifying. The menus we check out require serious investment. Even the local supermarket seems expensive, its arcane delights so exquisitely presented we almost want to cry. In the end we make do, slurping hungrily at the stand-up noodle bar on the corner.

The following morning dawns bright and clear, as we venture out to explore our new world. It is the day when winter turns to spring, what the Japanese call *setsubun*. Pink plastic blossom hangs from the trees down the main streets and celebrations are taking place around the city. So we join the crowds gathering at the Hosen-ji temple to watch a ceremony involving fifty elders dressed as warrior-monks, a bizarre combination if ever there was.

They arrive in procession, each carrying a sword and a spear, wearing shirts made of leather strips tied to look like chain-mail. Their monkish other half expresses itself in hessian hoods, which are curled out and stiffened at the shoulders, like nuns' wimples frozen in a gale. Below, they wear see-through cloaks in muted colours and the baggiest trousers ever. With great solemnity, they wobble in on wooden clogs nearly a foot high. Being monks may be enlightening, but waging war must be a riot.

We watch the leaders perform a complex series of rituals while the remainder sit waiting beneath the temple's towering pagoda. There is much nasal chanting and bashing of cymbals. Someone blows a giant conch shell held in rope netting; a huge drum rather like a beer barrel resounds, booming. They set light to a mound of green branches, and wooden blocks inscribed by the spectators are thrown on to fuel the blaze.

Then the real excitement begins. The most distinguished warrior-monks climb on to a broad platform and start hurling things into the crowd. I've read that the custom is to throw beans and to ensure our health, happiness and prosperity, we have to catch as many as our age. In our case, it looks like tangerines and unshelled peanuts.

'*Oni wa soto, fuku wa uchi*,' the old men shout as they throw. 'Devils out, good fortune in.'

It's hilarious. Everyone goes completely crazy trying to catch whatever they can.

After a while, Vanella and I saunter casually back on to the street with twenty-three tangerines and a couple of handfuls of peanuts stuffed in our pockets. Not quite enough to guarantee the good luck, but it should keep us away from the noodle bar for a while longer. It can be an advantage being tall in the Land of the Rising Sun.

~

Two days later, Mount Fuji stands proud against a sharp blue sky as we ride the early-morning train. We are bound for Uzurihara, Japan's long-life village.

At Uenohara station, we are met by Kazuo, Kimberly and someone called Mr Hiraga. Everyone bows and we exchange introductions. Kazuo is vice-director of the Yamanashi Prefecture International Association. He says we are younger than he expected and we return the compliment. He's in his early forties, wears glasses and has straight black hair. Kimberly is his assistant; she's over on a work exchange from Canada and speaks excellent Japanese. Mr Hiraga, it transpires, has appeared out of nowhere. They are still a little bemused as they tell us. Only yesterday he wandered into their office unannounced and when they mentioned the expedition to Uzurihara, he said he knew all about the place. So they invited him along. Mr Hiraga is very formal, a silver-haired gentleman soberly dressed in a dark blue suit. His business card reads 'Hiraga Associates International Inc.'

As Kazuo's minibus winds its way up the wooded valleys into the hills, Mr Hiraga holds forth, reading from typed notes on a small square of fax paper. It's as if we're on a school outing.

'The distinguished Dr Toyosuke Komiki introduced Uzurihara to the world for its longevity in the 1950s,' he says. 'It had been discovered that many aged people lived there, so Dr Komiki came to research. The diet of this region is of particular interest. It is called *choju* food. In looking for the causes of the shortening of present-day lifespan in the village, Dr Komiki indicates the urbanization of eating habits and the change in the amount and quality of exercise resulting from the introduction of the motor car and the telephone.'

'That's very interesting,' I say. 'Do you know what's so special about the food?'

'Ah, the *choju* food, it includes taro root, the devil's tongue jelly, toasted barley powder and a special kind of bun.'

Vanella nudges me and raises an eyebrow. Things are looking up. It was tangerines for breakfast yet again.

We keep on climbing until we find Mr Ichimiya's house at the top end of the village, overlooking red rooftops and fir trees like giant bonsai. Once the local schoolmaster, Mr Ichimiya is an inscrutable gentleman of ninety-something, who still looks seventy-something. We all bow very low and, boots off, we are shown into a small sunlit space with *tatami* matting on the floor and paper screens for walls. A low square table occupies the centre of the room, covered with a velvet quilt and a lacquered top. Mr Ichimiya's daughter-in-law fusses around, inviting us to squat on the soft cushions and drape the thick material over our knees for warmth.

I can't help eyeing the table. Each place is arranged with a number of bowls: fresh strawberries and kiwi fruit, a selection of pickled vegetables, figs, spinach topped with crunchy fish flakes and a portion of runner beans. Mr Ichimiya's daughter-in-law brings in another larger bowl of steamed buns and pours green tea for everyone before kneeling, subservient, behind the schoolmaster.

'This is the *sakemanju*,' says Mr Hiraga, offering me a bun. 'It is one of their foods, to make them healthy and live long. Please. It is sweet inside and the dough on the outside is made by natural fermentation. According to doctors, the bacteria are very good when taken into the body.'

White and round, soft, warm, its centre filled with a sweet red bean paste, the *sakemanju* is delicious.

We learn that Mr Ichimiya was born in Uzurihara in the thirty-fourth year of the Meiji emperor. He used to be the primary-school teacher, for children between the ages of six and twelve. According to Mr Hiraga, the mayor, the policeman and the schoolmaster were the three most important people in such villages.

'Mr Ichimiya must have been quite respected,' he says.

'No!' interrupts the schoolmaster. 'I was feared.'

Everyone laughs, some of us nervously, but not Mr Ichimiya. He remains straight-faced and serious, sitting on his haunches with one hand on each knee. He dresses well: his dark two-piece suit is made from a fine cloth. It occurs to me he looks something like Gregory Peck would look if he was grey-haired and Japanese – as long as Gregory Peck didn't smile.

The status of teachers used to be more that of a principal. This was in the time before the Second World War, when Japan was an empire and everyone believed the emperor was a god. Mr Ichimiya would visit the various schoolhouses around the area and taught all subjects. The ethical code was very strict. Everything he told them, the children had to obey. So did the parents. They had no say in educational policy in those days.

Vanella always likes to know what qualities are required for certain professions, so she asks Mr Ichimiya what makes a good schoolmaster.

'The love of children,' he replies.

'What do you love about them?'

'I love the straight mind of children, especially those who do not look to be led by the teacher. Every child has a born character which cannot be changed. But through conversation, communication can be established and the child can develop. The role of the teacher is to allow the personality to grow.'

'What were your children like?' she asks. 'Were they good, or were they naughty?'

'They were very serious.'

'Serious? Why so serious?'

This prompts much discussion, which Mr Hiraga is eventually able to sum up: 'At that time it was so poor in terms of the economy, the children had to work extremely hard.'

'And why is it,' I innocently ask, 'that Japanese people seem to work so hard?'

'It is the born character of the Japanese people to work hard,' says the schoolmaster. 'This cannot be changed. They are not born lazy like foreigners.'

We laugh again. I find his remark genuinely funny, but our friends immediately launch into diplomacy. Mr Ichimiya isn't joking.

'Remember the young and the old can say whatever they like,' whispers Kimberly.

Mr Hiraga is working very hard. 'It may be unnecessary to say, but in Japan aged people do take the liberty to talk a little bit freely,' he warns. 'He does not wish to say anything bad about foreigners, because you are a guest from far away.'

'I am too honest to be polite,' confirms a poker-faced Mr Ichimiya.

My real problem is that no one is eating. Vanella and I have been holding back, so nobody else has touched a thing. We're caught in a kind of etiquette gridlock. Discreetly I pick a pickled yellow root with my chopsticks and the flavour explodes in my mouth.

Vanella, meanwhile, defuses the tension by chatting about the village. We hear it used to be very isolated. Everyone worked at home, farming or weaving. Many households kept silkworms, a full-time occupation for the women because they had to collect the silk twenty-four hours a day. The men gathered logs from the woods, some produced charcoal. There was no road in the old days, so their wagons weren't much help. They had to load up the horses or simply walk all the way down to the market in Uenohara to sell their wares, just as Mr Ichimiya walked to his schoolhouses. The furthest was an hour away, up and down many steep hills.

This lifestyle made them healthy, Mr Ichimiya believes.

'It is the clean air, mountain sunshine, pure water and exercise which make people live long,' he says. 'The food is also another factor.'

Ah, yes, the food. At last. Still no one is eating. But the schoolmaster doesn't even glance at the table.

'Aged people are also well loved and respected in Japan,' he goes on. 'When I was young, my father was not the first-born, so my grandparents did not live with us. I envied those of my friends who had a grandfather or great-grandfather living with them. I used to play and talk with them. I think this kind of emotion is good for older people. When I was about four, I remember an old man, Tsuru was his name. Maybe he took pity because I had no grandparents at home, but he loved me very much. He would bake a rice-cake for me, or sometimes he gave me a boiled taro root. We used to have an open fire in the middle of the room here. Tsuru-san always took care I did not fall in the fire when I was playing.'

'And now you are as old as Tsuru-san, what do you think of old age?' I ask.

'Not much,' he says, a little morose. 'Life is a stream. No one can stop the years and months going by. I have lived for ninety-one years and eight months and I think there were more hard things than sweet in that time.'

Mr Hiraga sees me looking puzzled. 'Actually, he is not trying to give the impression that life was hard,' he explains. 'What he is trying to say is that there have been wars.'

There we are again, being polite. We wouldn't want to mention the bombs.

It's tragic. We leave Mr Ichimiya having eaten hardly anything. Kazuo checks his watch and says it's time to move on, so we bow and are whisked away to what I take to be the next house. Boots off, we are led into a spacious room, where a long low table has been laid and five places set, each surrounded by eleven dishes. Others are arranged in the middle for sharing. Altogether I can count something like sixty bowls of food. I can hardly believe it. Kazuo, Kimberly, Vanella, me and Mr Hiraga are going *choju* for lunch.

We sit cross-legged, talking excitedly as our eyes feast.

'It's not often I get the chance to eat mountain food,' Kazuo says. 'Look at this. This is white taro root, I think.'

Mr Hiraga inspects carefully. 'I've never seen that before. And here, this is home-made tofu, which is very rare nowadays.'

Soup is served and Kimberly instructs us how the Japanese say grace.

'*Ita dakimasu*,' she says. 'This means: "I humbly partake."'

'*Ita dakimasu*,' we repeat, and I humbly partake with a vengeance.

The mushrooms entice me first, one a black variety, the other smaller and lighter. I sample the black, and sense its earthy richness at the back of my nose.

Kazuo bends over, noisily slurping his soup, a noodle broth with all kinds of hidden ingredients. I take a sip. It is savoury, salty and warming.

Mr Hiraga is holding up something light brown between his chopsticks. 'This is a bamboo heart,' he says. 'The Japanese usually eat this when it's very small, but around here they wait until it is grown to this size.'

'Oooooh . . .' Kazuo has just tried some bamboo. He catches my eye and points a chopstick.

'Mmmmm . . .' Kimberly tastes the white radish with miso on top.

'Oooh.'

'Have you had one of these?' Vanella asks me, pointing at something that looks like a pancake. 'There's some kind of pickled root inside with an orangy vinegar. It's like a mini crêpe Suzette.'

'Wow.'

The flavour is extraordinary. Next I choose mashed greens in some kind of sweet sauce.

'What's this? It tastes pickled too.'

'That is *fuki*,' says Kazuo. 'I love it.'

'It's like a thin rhubarb,' says Kimberly.

'Oh, mmmmm, yes, that's very nice.'

Vanella picks from one of the large communal bowls.

'That one is a kind of root,' explains Mr Hiraga. 'It is long, very long. The farmer has to plant it in very deep soil so it can grow straight. They have no market value if they're twisted.'

Ours are dead straight.

'And, of course, the devil's tongue.' He dangles a pale grey thing the right size and shape for a tongue. 'This is a jelly made from the starch of a variety of taro root. We call it *konnyaku*.'

I find the devil's tongue more remarkable for its clammy texture than its taste. Then, before my tastebuds forget, I take a quick bite of the only dish in any way familiar, the legendary *sakemanju*. This one tastes subtly different from the one at Mr Ichimiya's, the bean paste more fruity.

'This is the same bean here, the adzuki bean,' says Kimberly, pointing to a bowl of red beans in white rice. 'On festive occasions they make a dish with adzuki beans and rice called *sekihan*. And when they write *sekihan*, the two characters mean "red" and "rice". Here, in Japan, red and white are salutary, health-giving colours.'

Red and white . . . like the national flag, like the sun rising against a pale morning sky, the colours of the sweet bean bun.

~

It is Mr Morimoto who first mentions the twins.

Mr Morimoto used to do business with my father and I have his phone number in the book.

'But ah you must ah meet Kin-san Gin-san,' he tells me.

'I'm sorry, who?'

'Kin-san Gin-san. Very aged ah twin sisters. More than ah one hundred years old.' He pronounces Gin-san with a hard 'G', as in 'give'.

'Who are they?'

'They are very famous. They have been in ah advertising.'

'Do you know how we can find them?'

Mr Morimoto isn't sure. It seems that Kin-san Gin-san are superstars.

* * *

Then, one afternoon, Vanella and I are doing a spot of window-shopping in downtown Ginza, Tokyo's chic commercial centre, when we pass a doorway displaying the name Dentsu Inc. Remembering Dentsu's reputation as Japan's largest advertising agency, we boldly enquire within. The Dentsu empire, we discover, is housed in a multitude of offices around Ginza. We have chosen to walk into the archive department. What we need is the creative management division, a few blocks away, specifically a Mr Ina, manager of Talent Business Services Development.

A bemused Mr Ina sends someone to find a videotape. He then presses Play.

We see Kin-san Gin-san sitting on cushions in a *tatami*-matted room partitioned with wood and paper screens.

'Kin-san is one hundred,' says one of them.

'Gin-san is also one hundred,' says her sister.

Then we hear a man's voice: 'For more information about Duskin products, please dial 100 100.'

The image on the screen freezes, then flickers to black. We have been watching the commercial for Duskin household mops, which launched the careers of Japan's most celebrated twin sisters.

Mr Ina gives us a fixed smile as he points to the front page of the evening paper lying on the desk. Above a photo of a little old lady, the headline reads: 'GIN-SAN IN HOSPITAL'.

Our meeting with the twins seems doomed.

Two days later, we slide across the urban sprawl at the speed of a bullet. Pale grey in a smoky haze, the world flashes past like a movie on fast-forward. This is my imagined jumble of wires, poles, chimneys and low-rise flat rooftops. It stretches all the way to the mountains in the north and down to the very edge of a silver sea. In no time and on time, we arrive in the city of Nagoya.

I'm a bit depressed. With Gin-san in hospital, it won't be the same, meeting only one half of the twins. But when we arrive at the office of the Nagoya International Association, they say her cataract operation has gone well enough for us to pay her a visit. We will meet Kin-san at her son's house in the suburb of Minami-ku, then in the afternoon we will see Gin-san, with one of her daughters, at the Fujita Health University Hospital.

The taxi driver doesn't need directions. He knows Kin-san's house.

Everyone knows Kin-san Gin-san. Anyone we've told that we're actually going to meet them has immediately gone, 'Oooooooh,' their mouths open in wonder. They all watch the two sisters on television, when they appear on chat shows and are asked for their comments on current events. Now they are a hundred and one, they can say absolutely anything they like.

They had been identical, but in later years their faces have changed. Kin-san's head is as round as a ball, whereas Gin-san's is oblong, squarish on top. She has protruding teeth too, like a rabbit. Both sisters have short-cropped silver hair and wear smart kimonos. Very small, they reach only four feet and a few inches tall, each bent over like a question mark. And they are both very wrinkly.

Kin-san Gin-san were born in the twenty-fifth year of the Meiji emperor, in a place called Narumi, then a separate community but now a suburb of Nagoya. According to ancient custom no longer adhered to, the first-born, Gin-san, was considered the younger. Kin-san, the second-born, was the elder, because it was said that she had the responsibility of cleaning their mother's womb. Their proud parents had taken the babies to the local primary-school teacher, who in an inspired moment named them Gold and Silver.

They used to do everything together. They were born into a poor farmer's family and so helped with the agricultural work. They weren't able to travel. They never saw a town or a city, only their own village. It was a very ordinary life. They grew up and married. They raised their children and saw their grandchildren born. Until, on their hundredth birthday, they were honoured by the city of Nagoya and some bright copywriter at Dentsu Inc. saw their photo in the newspaper. Spotting their potential, he wrote them into the television commercial he was working on. Soon everyone was going around saying, '*Hyaku, hyaku.*' One hundred, one hundred. Overnight, the Japanese nation took Kin-san Gin-san to its heart.

It was not always so. At the time they were born, primitive superstition had branded them savage. The medical reasons for the birth of twins were not fully understood; only animals produced more than one offspring. People would curse them, pointing and shouting, as the little sisters walked to school.

'*Futango, futango*,' they would call out. 'You filthy twins.'

A system was devised whereby each went to school on alternate days. Then, at night, the one would tell the other what they had learnt.

Meanwhile, the other would have been helping around the house with their younger brothers and sisters. No one could tell, they had been so alike.

We are able to identify a few differences. Kin-san laughs more than her sister, a wizened cackling kind of laugh. 'Heh heh heh,' she goes, in answer to almost everything we say. Her voice is squeaky and high-pitched, while Gin-san speaks more slowly, deeper, sometimes croaking like a hinge in need of oil. But Gin-san is very sweet, the gentler of the two. Brushing aside our concern for her health, she replies by flattering us. We make such a lovely couple. I look so young, she says, and Vanella is very beautiful. So we smile, demur sufficiently and marvel at her age.

Then we play a game. We ask each sister about the other. How alike are they?

'We are very alike, very similar,' Kin-san tells us. 'If anything, Gin-san is a little talkative. In fact, she talks too much,' she confides, with a wheezy chuckle.

'Oh, yes, we are very alike,' Gin-san later agrees. Then, when we tell her what her sister said, she adds, 'Yes, that's true, I do talk more. But I am a bit stronger than Kin-san,' and so she scores her point.

Kin-san's son and Gin-san's daughter tell us that their respective mothers are just the same – incredibly stubborn. They refuse to give in over anything and have a habit of doing precisely what they want.

'So why have you lived to over a hundred?' we ask the twins.

'Destiny,' they both reply, in their separate locations. 'Everything is dictated by destiny. How long a person will live is decided at the moment of birth.'

'Is there anything that Kin-san is good at but Gin-san not so good . . . or vice versa?'

'No, nothing,' they say, with a smile and a fetching little crinkle of the nose.

'And what is the most important thing in life?'

'Your health. Regular exercise is essential.'

'What exercise do you do?'

'I go walking outside every day,' comes their identical answer.

'Is there any special diet which has helped you live to such an age?'

'Not really.' They both eat with their families, although Gin-san is particularly fond of fish and tries not to overeat.

'Are you in any way telepathic with your sister?'

'No,' they reply, shaking their heads as one.

With equal modesty, Kin-san Gin-san say they are ashamed to be so popular. Yet they are happy, living the lives of superstars.

'People are very kind. They are always coming to see us,' says Gin-san. 'I enjoy meeting people.'

Kin-san loves it too whenever they have to go into the television studio. 'I can't help it,' she says. 'I enjoy being in the spotlight. All that admiration.'

Their lives have been quite transformed since they hit the limelight. They had been living their separate ways. Kin-san has three sons, three daughters; nine grandchildren. Gin-san has four daughters and four grandchildren. And there are great-grandchildren too. But since their hundredth birthday the sisters have been reunited, together again. The stigma of being twins is no more. Now they are in demand, chased constantly by television crews, microphones jostling for an interview. They thrive on the attention and as a result have grown stronger and healthier, Gin-san's cataracts apart. During the last year and a half, they have received the adulation of the entire country and nearly three thousand letters of fan mail. In the process, Kin-san Gin-san have become a small industry. Kin-san's son now acts as their business manager. They are appearing in more advertising, posing as photographic models, doing charity work. We are shown the current Kin-san Gin-san calendar and given the Kin-san Gin-san twin doll, now available in the shops, to take away as a memento.

'Destiny,' say the twins. 'You should remember that everything in life is governed by destiny.'

As the bullet train returns us to Tokyo with a whoosh, we watch a blood red sun set behind the mountains for the last time. A kind lady sitting nearby pulls two oranges from her bag and offers them to us, smiling. We must be looking hungry. Our tangerines have run out at last.

13

Apricots and Tigers

Our journey to Shangri-La is slow. The minibus, a scraggy old blue workhorse, carries well over twenty of us squashed to a state of numbness. Grown men sit on each other's knees, shoulders hunched and heads twisted. Someone even gets in and squeezes between the driver and the driver's door. Outside, the hangers-on trade space for danger where our packs have been slung on the rack, ready to topple off down the next precipice.

Nevertheless, we are a happy crew. One man plays a kind of tambour, which works up a dance rhythm and helps to pass the time. A conductor sits at the front and controls affairs: who gets on, how much they pay and when to stop. He is skilled in pulling the back door closed with a long hairy rope, especially when on the move, except one time he's so enthusiastic a new passenger gets his arm trapped in the door. Everyone thinks this is outrageously funny. Then the man with the wonky eye, whose leg has been pressing painfully against mine, kindly falls asleep on my shoulder, breathing heavily.

We set out from Gilgit, which sits at the top end of a broad cultivated valley in the far north-east of Pakistan. A bustling trading-post fed by the river and protected by stern grey mountains, it acts like a magnet to the men of the surrounding regions. The faces milling down the main street come from Afghanistan, Peshawar and Chitral to the west, Kashmir to the east and from the hills to the north. In the centre of the town, next to the mosque, high stone walls fence in the polo ground – the popular local sport.

Our road, the Karakoram Highway, was completed as recently as the late 1970s. Before then, it was only a rough track, often no more than a mule trail, an ancient silk route linking the valleys of the Indus with the western reaches of China. In fact, the KKH, as the road is known, is strictly never complete, travelling as it does through a most unforgiving landscape. The Karakoram mountains are always on the move and conditions extreme. Nature and man fight a continual battle, destroying and repairing in turn – there are no prizes for guessing who has the upper hand. It makes for an exciting ride. Wherever the road has fallen or been washed away, it is patched with no more than a pile of stony rubble and when the bus tilts to give a brief scenic view of the valley, I catch the shrunken river far below pretending to be a stream. We drive around landslides and rocks the size of a house. But we make it. Nearly everyone does.

We arrive in the Hunza valley, famed for its apricots and the longevity of its people. Folk hereabouts are said to have lived to ages of one hundred and twenty or more. The people are also supposed to be descended from the remainders of the army of Alexander the Great, who came this far before turning for home, defeated by the mountains. And James Hilton, who in 1933 wrote *Lost Horizon*, is reputed to have named his celebrated Shangri-La after this one.

Despite the freezing temperature, spring has come. The valley is dotted around with pale pink and white apricot blossom. In tidy terraced fields, shoots of wheat sprout a new and delicate green. These cultivated patches take their shape from the contours, dry-stone walls and irrigation channels acting as dividers. Round and grey, the stone comes from the riverbed below, worn by the eternal force of the summer flood. From each bank, the terracing climbs, step by step, growing ever more slender until the slope is too steep for any more. Clusters of small, square, mud-brown houses perch where they can. And, far above, the snows fall on some of the tallest peaks in the world.

We untangle ourselves from the bus and inspect a couple of deserted hotels in the village of Aliabad. The Rakaposhi Inn, run by the obsequious Mr Ghazi, is the winner. A genial type, Mr Ghazi wears a brown Hunza hat, flat and round on top like a pancake and rolled up the sides. His brown scarf stays wrapped around his mouth, even when speaking.

'Helloo, sirr, very good sirr, yes please thank you very much, sirr,' he says and, at the slightest hint of anything mildly amusing, dissolves into an uncontrollable fit of cackling which always lasts just a little too long.

We do the deal on the room and, after a brief rest, leave Mr Ghazi huddled in a blanket in front of his electric fire. We wander up the dusty main street. The village seems very quiet, apart from three characters watching television in what looks to be some kind of café, a large white satellite dish bolted to its roof. Not far away we find the offices of AKRSP – the Aga Khan Rural Support Programme.

The people of Hunza are Ismaili Muslim, whose spiritual leader is the Aga Khan. A proud and noble tribe, they were once ruled by their kings – the Mirs – and even now don't consider themselves Pakistani. I had contacted AKRSP in Gilgit, where I was received by a succession of urbane gentlemen and given a hand-written letter which I presume is some kind of introduction.

I hand this to Mansoor Khan, local organizer for the Hunza region. He and his partner, Shah Ghazi, are young men our own age. As well as the hats and matching moustaches, they wear the traditional long-tailed shirts and pantaloon trousers. Mansoor has a khaki combat jacket on top, Shah Ghazi a tweed sports jacket.

Mansoor passes the letter across to his friend. 'Old people,' he says, without much curiosity. He seems a man of few words.

I nod. 'Is it true they still live to great ages here in Hunza?'

'Yes.'

'How old?'

He shrugs. 'Maybe a hundred, maybe more. Some are very old.'

'Can you help us meet them, some of these people?'

'Yes,' he says, so matter-of-fact I can hardly bear it. But something tells me we're going to be all right.

'Do you like China tea?' asks Mansoor. He summons the office boy, an old retainer with a full grey beard who wears what look like fluffy carpet slippers. The men speak to each other briefly and we are encouraged to warm ourselves by the dusty two-bar fire that hums at our feet. We tell them we've come all the way up from Rawalpindi. They in turn talk us through the organizational diagram of the AKRSP on the wall and their work in agriculture, health and education.

Halfway through tea, Mansoor suddenly announces that they have to go. We look surprised and Shah Ghazi quickly explains that they are expected at a meeting. 'Would you like to come?' he asks.

Not wanting to miss a thing, we climb into Mansoor's Jeep and retrace our path back down the Highway to a village in lower Hunza. Along the way, we have to cross a large ravine by a small suspension bridge, just wide enough for one vehicle. Stone archways hold the wires and supports at either end, but the rest is wood, patched at intervals with new, unweathered planks. As soon as it takes the weight of the Jeep, the bridge begins to undulate with a disconcerting wave motion that ripples across to the far side.

Mansoor grins under his impressively aquiline nose. 'Don't worry,' he says, as we're wobbling along, mid-ravine. 'This bridge was built by the British.'

Absolutely reassured, we still daren't look down and Vanella continues to grip my hand until we are well clear.

The Brits did, indeed, play their part in the history of the area. In the days of the Raj, Hunza was the northernmost and last region to be conquered, as late as 1891. Although one of the more inaccessible corners of the Empire, it was not without its strategic significance: both China and what was then the Russian Empire are not far away. Britain ruled until independence and partition in 1947, but always at arm's length, from the government agency down in Gilgit. After a few skirmishes, submission had been won, but it was easier to keep the Mirs sweet than attempt to police country like this. It was the British who had taught the locals how to build terracing and irrigate the land. In return, they had shown their masters how to play polo.

Driving up the rough track into the village, we pull up in front of the schoolhouse, a modern breeze-block construction with small windows. The meeting is already in progress, but proceedings halt while we are introduced with much standing and shaking of hands. We take our seats at the front with the main speakers, facing a room full of men, fifty or sixty of them, crammed into school desks two sizes too small. They make a robust collection of earnest, weather-worn expressions, topped with a fine display of local hats. These men are Hunzakuts, their features strong and complexions ruddy. I can see several shades of reddish-brown beard, bushy eyebrows and bristling moustache. For a small community, the variety in their faces surprises me. I'm particularly struck by their noses: we have pointed, hooked, arched, big and bulbous. Then, right at the back, the bright spots of colour on an embroidered pillbox hat catch my eye and I notice four women sitting quietly with their children.

Next to me, Vanella looks like she wants to pinch herself. We're so conspicuous, it feels like we are on stage. But there's no doubt we are the audience. The debate we witness is like watching some obscure foreign film, without the subtitles. It is conducted in Brushuski, one of three Hunza languages still spoken. The subject seems to be a matter of great importance. The proposers at the front spell out some plans, before the men of the village offer their views with a grave formality, each new speaker doing a 'Friends, Hunzakuts, countrymen . . .' and asking permission to address the assembly. Then comes a vigorous and impassioned speech or something longer and more articulate. I can see the old guard defending themselves vociferously against younger, liberal, perhaps more enlightened views. The men show little concern for us strangers; they are intent on their discussion. The women say nothing and leave halfway through.

Mansoor leans across to tap my arm. 'They talk about the building of a health centre,' he whispers. 'The question is whether or not they have a permanent doctor.'

Back and forth the argument runs until, suddenly, it's all over, the atmosphere relaxes and everyone spills out into the twilight. Apparently no final decision has been reached. Outside we shake more hands and chat with Mansoor's friends, Mustafa and Jan Alam. Mustafa seems very jovial; he wears a blue denim jacket over his traditional garb. Jan Alam is the intellectual type, with his dark bushy beard and bulky overcoat. Mansoor and Mustafa still have business to conclude, so Shah Ghazi and Jan Alam escort us on a precarious ride up the hillside, the Jeep needing at least three attempts to get round each steep corner.

They are taking us to meet Ghulam Muhammad, the old man of the village.

Our arrival causes great excitement. Children run to look at us. We smile and say hello and they run away again. More rosy cheeks appear, but the old man himself is nowhere to be seen. We are shown into a room, furnished with a patterned rug laid wall to wall, an antique sewing-machine and a few bolsters. A single dim light-bulb hangs from the ceiling. We sit cross-legged in our thick socks and the room begins to fill with curious young boys with short haircuts and a mix-and-match of Western and local dress. They gather round us chattering all at once, staring at our weird looks and sometimes touching our sleeves. We smile at their eager faces and Vanella works on her sign language. Sometimes a young girl comes to the door, peeps in and darts away.

Ghulam Muhammad makes his grand entrance, followed by a retinue of younger men. We exchange *salaams* and he takes his position leaning against the side wall. He squats on his haunches, hands resting on a battered stick with two collars of silver beaten along its length. He had once been the *trungpha*, or local chief.

Vanella counts around the room. There are nineteen of them, men and boys.

Ghulam Muhammad looks very old. One eye droops a little in his weathered face and his full beard matches the silvery white of the blossom on the trees outside. He is wrapped in a rough, cream-coloured cloak, a *shuqa*, decorated at the shoulders with two bright pink flowers. Underneath he wears a thick jacket with a fur collar, and the rest, from his hat to his socks, appears to be various shades of coarse brown cloth.

My asking the year of his birth causes great controversy. The answer eventually comes back – 1895. Almost certainly, the oldest of the Hunzakuts aren't as old as they used to be. But to our expert eye, Ghulam Muhammad is well qualified.

He can remember how, when he was a young boy, the pilgrims would use the route down the valley to make their way south on the long road to Mecca. He tells us how one time there was a great flood that came suddenly, destroying many houses. He can describe the sight of a large caravan of more than sixty horses that rode down from China. Their faces were strange, the horses wild and muscular. They came hawking silks, tea and all kinds of exotic goods too expensive to buy. And he remembers also when the English were still new lords of their land. Whenever they came to visit, they were welcomed by the Mir. A cannon would be fired and everyone would celebrate with a dance. The Englishmen would give the young boys small coins to fight or race for sport.

'We were stronger than you English,' says the old Hunzakut gruffly, a clenched fist firmly striking his knee. 'We made everything ourselves. We made our own guns, even our gunpowder. We were brave defenders. Everyone was afraid of us – the English, Chinese, Hindustanis and the Nagiris. We were only defeated by the English because of a conspiracy with the people of Nagir.'

With no form of defence, I receive his withering look. Then, with some reluctance, he is good enough to admit that the English did have bigger and better guns.

The kingdom of Nagir can be seen from central Hunza, an exact reflection a mile or so away on the opposite side of the valley. The Nagiris are Sunni Muslim by faith. Their faces are similar, but have a more gypsyish look. For as long as anyone can remember, the two clans have been arch enemies, although they seem peaceful enough nowadays.

The old man's son spreads a cloth on the floor and tea is poured, already milky, into small china cups. At least six spoonfuls of sugar then go in each one, before it is stirred methodically. We are offered ginger biscuits, and it's good to see that the Hunzakuts are still exponents in the art of dunking.

We learn that Ghulam Muhammad originally came from Karimabad, the capital of Hunza, a village to the north of where we are staying. His father had been given this land by the Mir some seventy years ago, the only drawback being that there was nothing here. It had been a barren hillside. He and his father had built the terracing and the irrigation canals themselves with basic tools and one wheelbarrow. They scraped a sparse living, dependent only on what they were able to produce. They grew wheat, apricots and tended a few goats.

'It was a hard life,' says the old chief. 'The rewards were few.'

He coughs, then again he makes three deep rasping heaves until he has the phlegm.

'When I was young,' he says, recovering his breath, 'if some family had either food to eat or good clothes to wear, people would talk about how lucky they were. But these things they would have made for themselves. Today, people say how fortunate they are because they can buy things which come from outside Hunza. And they laugh at the man who works on the land.'

He shakes his head for times gone by. For all that, when pressed, he admits he prefers the life they have now. It is more comfortable, luxurious even. They operate a communal system, whereby everything earned goes to support the family unit.

'I am happy enough,' Ghulam Muhammad tells us. 'I have good sons.'

He is head of a family of thirty-three. There is work. Making money is easy, thanks to the Highway.

Vanella points to all the youngsters and asks him what advice he gives to his great-grandchildren.

He strokes his white beard thoughtfully, then puffs out his chest and stoutly declares, 'This time demands for education. Education. I always tell them they must study and work hard with their books. This is the only thing I insist from them.'

He looks around at the sea of bright young faces, whose owners sit listening attentively. Then they all watch him as the old man coughs again loudly. 'Nrrgh . . .' he complains. 'I am not as strong as I once was.'

It is growing dark outside. The *muezzin* has long since wailed away his call to evening prayer down the hill. Only as we are saying goodbye do the women and young girls show themselves. A mother holds up her well-wrapped baby boy for us to admire. The child wears a head-dress, a flowered band with a long drape over the shoulders, decorated with the same pink flowers as Ghulam Muhammad's *shuqa*. The boy's eyes have been made up with grey kohl, a strange effect that both prettifies and makes him seem more adult. I wonder what change those eyes will witness before they are Ghulam Muhammad's age.

We find Mansoor down in the village and his friend Mustafa invites us for supper. The compromise we strike is more tea, as we've told Mr Ghazi at the Rakaposhi that we'll be back to sample his fare.

Mustafa leads us to his house, insisting we meet his grandmother. He unlatches a door in the family room, which lets into a small space with a wood-stove. There she lies, curled up in some blankets.

'She is very weak now,' says Mustafa. 'She has not been well.'

Vanella and I crouch down and smile meekly. The old lady wears a beautiful pink and lime-green embroidered pillbox, and her shoulders are draped with layers of shawls. Raising herself, she grasps first my hand, then Vanella's. Her worn face becomes briefly animated as she stammers her greetings. She kisses our hands gratefully, desperately, as if we are some feudal lord and lady. Then she sinks slowly back to her bedding, the door is closed and we are left stunned and a little embarrassed.

While tea is brewing, everyone swaps their ages and I discover that Mansoor was born in the same year as me. They try telling us some jokes, but Hunza humour doesn't translate too well and all their punchlines seem like *non sequiturs*. Next, they are intrigued to know how boys meet girls back in England. Lamely we try to describe what it's like. But how can we possibly explain that Vanella and I first kissed in a lift after an office party? It is so far removed from the system of arranged marriages they still have to abide by.

In the end, we are very late for Mr Ghazi. As Mansoor drops us off, he says he's going to Gojal, the upper Hunza region, in the morning. We are to leave at six-thirty.

'Oooh, very good, sirr, madam, great people, British people, very good, yes please thank you very much, sirr . . .'

Mr Ghazi is clearly pleased to see us, no doubt relieved that our dinner will be eaten today rather than recycled again tomorrow. We eat his rice, chapatis and vegetable slop in semi-darkness, due to the erratic electricity supply. Then we reason that it'll be warmer in bed, so retire clutching candles.

We have to go outside to reach our room in the annexe. While I search for the key, we look out into the night. It is pitch black – no moon or stars – the air thin and sharp as ice.

Just before six, I'm dancing around in my thermals desperately trying to dress before I become a brass monkey.

'Ah ooh ah ooh ooh aaah,' is something how it goes.

'God, you're a wimp, Jackson,' says a muffled voice, still wrapped in sweatshirts, sleeping-bag and bedding.

'Oooh ah . . . It's all right for you. Why don't you try getting out here?'

The highlight of Mr Ghazi's sales pitch had been the shower, but his idea of very hot water proves to be freezing cold. Having suffered more of her gibes, I find Vanella's screams from the bathroom highly entertaining.

Breakfast succeeds in warming us up, a rare comfort to look forward to: salted boiled eggs, chapatis, lashings of apricot jam and scalding hot tea. Mr Ghazi – hat, scarf, electric fire – watches while we eat and tells us how he is descended from the Mir's family. This involves producing a dog-eared sepia photo of his uncle standing with the Mir himself and several retainers, all staring gawkily at the camera. We then tell him we're going off with Mansoor for the day and that we'll be back again for dinner.

'Yes, sirr, yes, kind people, very good please thank you, sirr,' echoes Mr Ghazi, as he follows us to the door.

We wait outside where the world is quiet, bleak and overcast. Not a soul is about – only a solitary magpie which I watch scuttling among the bare branches going *chukka chukka . . . chukka chukka*. Across the valley, the kingdom of Nagir looks desolate. Rakaposhi sits shrouded in thick cloud and the lower reaches of the mountains have a new dusting of snow.

Mansoor soon turns up in the Jeep, from which blares out a tape of

Ismaili religious chants, a monotonous drone that is strangely soothing for the time of day. He seems in good spirits.

'Today is a holiday,' he says, seeing me eye the rifle tucked behind the front seats. 'We will hunt ducks. I know a good place.'

As we drive north, the road climbs high above the valley floor. Between the villages, the land is barren, brownish-grey rock interspersed with slips of bluish-grey shale. Now, at the end of winter, the river runs at a fraction of its full strength, the water an opaque slaty turquoise winding its way across a flat riverbed, foaming as it spills over shallow steps. Every now and then, we see a tiny figure wrapped in a blanket struggling across the empty expanse of what in a few months will be a raging torrent of melted snow.

First stop of the day is Shishkat, a few dwellings on a spur of land where the sleet stings our faces. Mansoor says that Shishkat means 'Land of Rock'.

Finding the house belonging to Mubarak Nazar, we are led by one of his sons through a wooden door-frame and stumble gingerly in pitch darkness through two outer chambers before we reach the main room. This is arranged on a number of rectangular split-levels with a roof structure supported by four dark wooden pillars, stained and worn waxy by the years. The different levels are spread with red bedrolls and pink cushions.

Mansoor acts like an old friend paying a call, though I'm not sure he's any more than just acquainted with the family. They greet us and we are soon made comfortable, watching the preparations that follow. The son feeds the stove with wood, the fire snapping greedily as it takes. A metal pipe funnels most of the smoke up to a square hole in the roof where polythene sheeting flaps noisily in the wind. A continuous spray blows down, sometimes a flurry of snow, and each time the outer door is opened by one more son coming to see what's happening, we feel the force of another swirling blast.

Mubarak's wife and daughters make tea in their kitchen, a space screened off behind a green curtain. They wear shawls draped over their heads and shoulders, and numerous layers of coloured wraps and pantaloons to keep them warm. Their thick plaits of dark hair are fastened with discs, topped by bright pillbox hats, each uniquely patterned with hundreds of tight, coloured stitches. Out comes a board and some dough, and one of the girls begins making parathas with a thin rolling-pin. Before long we can smell them cooking, the woodsmoke adding its own spice.

Mubarak Nazar enters. For his ninety years, he stands tall and strong. Droplets of moisture cling to his grey moustache and a few days' stubble graces his handsome brown face. He wears the hat, of course, but his is cream-coloured and set at an angle, the soft cloth moulded to the shape of his head.

'You are welcome in my house,' he says, shaking me firmly by the hand. He shakes Vanella's also, an action he seems less accustomed to.

We drink sweet milky tea and eat paratha squares, while Mubarak's daughters and granddaughters sit in corners watching us cautiously. If ever I catch their eye, they quickly look away.

Mubarak takes his place near the stove and wraps himself in a *shuqa*. I ask him what difference the Highway has made to their lives.

'Before was very different,' he says, his voice weaker than his looks suggest. 'We only had our horses. Now they come with trucks from China, up from Gilgit, sometimes from Russia.'

A calendar pinned to the wall shows a photograph of a pagoda-like structure surrounded by ornamental gardens and autumn leaves. And I notice dragons on the fluorescent pink cloth they placed on the floor before serving the tea.

'After the road was built, people began to feel unhealthy,' says Mubarak.

In the old days, they lived on apricots, wheat, pulses and occasionally some potato – no sugar, no spices or processed oils. They used raw rock salt to add flavour to their food. Meat was for special days only. When the apricot trees bore fruit, they would gorge themselves on what was shaken down, then dry and store the remainder. Nothing would be wasted, even the kernels were ground for oil or eaten as nuts, which taste like almonds. The dried fruit would never quite last the winter, so spring was always a cold and hungry time, waiting for the first crops to ripen.

It sounds like the Hunzakuts once had the components of what the Western media would call a healthy lifestyle – mainly vegetarian, natural ingredients, an abundance of fruit, a time of fasting in the spring, plus vigorous exercise and lungfuls of clear mountain air. They had a lifeplan most Californians would pay hundreds of dollars for.

'If we ever feel unwell,' Mubarak tells us, 'we eat dark bread made from *bakla* and we feel better immediately.'

His wife holds out a dented tin plate for us to inspect, three segments of wheat, barley and *bakla*, the main crops they produce. A black bean-like seed, the *bakla* is sometimes mixed with wheat; sometimes they make bread from a combination of all three. Mubarak rubs the grain between his rough fingers with satisfaction then looks at me with dark brown eyes, which are steady and warm.

'The *bakla* is good for the heart,' he says.

'Yes. It is also good for blood pressure and jaundice,' adds Mansoor. 'You know, only three Hunza people have ever died from cancer. And all three had been living for some time in Karachi.'

I ask if I can take a few grains of *bakla* and resolve to keep one in my pocket, for good health, until we reach home.

They then tell us about the *ginany* ceremony, the time when the first barley is harvested, one of the many rites involving the elders. In the old days it centred around the Mir and his household. Now each village organizes itself, but the ritual remains unchanged. A man who goes by the title Der Khan decides that the appropriate day has come, so each family makes bread and purified butter. They wash, dress in new clothes, put oil in their hair and kohl around their eyes. Each household follows the eldest men to the barley fields, where they pour the butter and flour on the crop, praying to Allah for a good harvest. One stalk of some twenty grains of barley is then cut and brought home to add to an egg soup. Every member of the family has to have three good spoonfuls. Later, they take bread and butter to Der Khan in the mosque, where the whole village assembles. Only then can the harvest begin.

We ask Mubarak Nazar about that other famous tradition, Hunza water, the illicit local grape wine they call *mell*. A man in Gilgit told me his father always swore that you have to keep drinking Hunza water until you can no longer feel your nose or until you see your companion's nose turn red. Mubarak Nazar's nose is a little bent but otherwise looks quite normal.

'I gave up drinking the *mell* about twenty years ago,' he says. 'I've had no alcohol or cigarettes since. I live in good health because I still eat *kimsh doon*, *derum phitti* and *mulideh*.'

He maintains his diet of these traditional dishes: combinations of bread, yoghurt and apricot kernel oil, prepared in various ways. Nowadays all kinds of processed foods have been introduced, so most people don't bother with these recipes any more. Rice is the novelty and tea has replaced apricot juice.

'All my life, I have never once been ill,' says Mubarak, absently stroking his stubble. 'If I sit in one place for very long, I begin to feel unhealthy. So I walk always, around the village and across the hills. You know, my eldest son sometimes seems older than me.'

The younger members of the family laugh, allowing the old man his vanity. But there may be some truth in his claim, for he does look remarkably fit.

He admits that life is easier now, but still he blames the Highway for a general decline.

'Every family has one person who is ill,' he says. 'And there is not the same brotherhood. Before, when people were in need, they would ask their neighbours or friends in other villages for help. I like the ways of the old men of Hunza. In the hearts of older men, there is brotherhood still. But not the young ones. These days, everyone is interested in his own. In the past, we all used to eat from one plate and share. Now, each has his own plate.'

Beyond Shishkat, the riverbed grows steeper, narrower and is littered with large boulders. We cross by a bridge, a replacement for the one we can see was washed away by a flood. Then we turn up the other side of the valley to discover a sinister dumping of ice and snow making the road quite impassable. We find a soldier standing in a sentry box beside some snowploughs, hugging a peach-coloured blanket. Mansoor winds down the window and establishes that the avalanche occurred only a few hours ago, that our friend is stationed here all year just to keep the road clear, but that he can't do anything because he's awaiting orders. But then we hear that an army convoy has arrived on the far side of the avalanche, on its way down to Gilgit to celebrate Independence Day.

'This is good,' says Mansoor. 'They will get through.'

He reverses back across the bridge and from a distance we watch the Army at work, while their snowploughs stand idle. The plan seems to be to find a route down under the bulk of snow, along the dry riverbed and back up the slope on the other side. But the soldiers preparing the way get so cold they decide instead to wander off collecting brushwood for small fires. These each last about seven seconds, whipped alight then extinguished by the biting wind. So they resort to jumping up and down to keep warm. Meanwhile, an impatient local driver tries to get through on the new detour, but his van becomes stuck at a strategically vital point. For two whole hours we are thus entertained, until the combined brain and brawn of the military prevails, the convoy rolls through and a dozen of us have to push another vehicle out of the snow, its wheels spinning wildly.

On our way again, the road gradually gains height as the valley sprawls down at us from the Khunjerab pass. Beyond Passu, the terrain becomes steadily more harsh, the villages more Spartan. The riverbed broadens out to form an immense flat of silt, the river itself a mere winding thread. Huge mountains hedge us in, sheer walls of brown rock topped with jagged dogs' teeth of ice and snow. This is Allah's country, for sure.

We travel in silence as the Jeep's engine strains on. After an hour or more, it slows suddenly.

'Here is a place,' says Mansoor.

At the side of the road I see what looks like a small gravel-pit, then I understand. He stops, reaches for the rifle and tiptoes, cartoon-style, to the edge.

'Poor ducks,' whispers Vanella, as we get out to watch. There are three of them. Mansoor aims carefully and then, as if prompted, they take flight. I freeze the image in my mind: the ducks rising at an angle, Mansoor's gun-barrel in pursuit, the rugged mountainside behind – it could be Allah's mantelpiece.

Mansoor holds his fire. He shrugs, starts up the Jeep and on we climb until, mid-afternoon, we reach a dismal place called Sost, the last village in Gojal and only a few miles from the Chinese border. It isn't much more than a scatter of houses and a row of shops. The customs and immigration posts for the frontier are supposed to be somewhere, but the place seems firmly closed.

'We will find you a hotel now,' Mansoor lets slip in his casual way. 'Later we can meet old people.'

'What?' we cry in unison. He's said nothing about this. Great. We haven't even a toothbrush between us. And I was really looking forward to beating up Mr Ghazi's especially virulent bedbugs, which have had me scratching red lumps all day.

Sost is Mansoor's home village. His idea is to put us up at the Khunjerab Hotel while he stays with his uncle. Our hosts, Aziz Baig and family, show us to our room, a grim cabin with dubious-looking ablutions involving a lot of buckets.

We're heading back to the Jeep when Vanella grabs my arm unusually tight.

'I need to lie down,' she says. 'Quick.'

'What's wrong?'

'I'm in pain.'

'What?'

'Hurry. I've got to lie down.'

I garble our apologies to Mansoor, saying we need to rest for ten minutes, and we retreat indoors.

Vanella is looking scared, breathing deliberately, in and out through her nose.

'Hurry,' she says, her voice quavering. 'It's bad. I know it's bad.'

The problem is her small intestine again; she has an obstruction. She lies down on the rickety old bed, pulls up her shirt and starts pressing deep into her abdomen with her fingers. She's panicking.

'Let me have a go. Come on. Try to relax. Keep breathing.'

My hands begin to work, searching for some area of tension, which normally indicates the cause of the trouble.

'Where is it? Can you tell?'

'There. There,' she says.

I roll my hands, pulling gently sideways. That often works. I can't believe this is happening. Not here. We're about as far away from civilization as we could be, let alone a half-decent hospital. I doubt we'll even be able to contact the emergency number we have on the insurance docket from here. At least we've got it with us. I suppose there's the Army. But they're on their way to Gilgit. Could a helicopter reach this far? The air ambulance? Maybe, but not till tomorrow . . .

'Any better?'

'No. Have a listen.'

I put my ear to her stomach. Normally, the odd gurgling noise indicates that things are working again. I can't hear a thing.

'Jackboot . . .'

'Yes.'

'I'm frightened.'

'Sshh . . . Relax. Let's keep trying.'

Another five minutes and I'm really beginning to worry. I can usually clear it by now. This is taking for ever. I keep massaging, working in and pulling sideways. Then suddenly I feel it go, under my fingers. It feels like a heavy rubber band releasing and we even hear the noise.

'There,' she says, breathing out. 'I think that was it.'

She sits up, pressing with her own fingers again. Her stomach makes a loud groan.

'That was it.'

We stare at each other, blinking, and deflate with the relief.

We say nothing to Mansoor and carry on as normal. Vanella manages to perk up. She seems all right, thanks be to Allah.

Mansoor finds his uncle keeping warm by the electric heater. Deram Titum is his name, a boyish-looking man in his mid-sixties. He is head of his clan and carries the quiet self-assurance his position confers. While his two grandsons prepare mutton curry and chapatis, he offers us a special delicacy, a ceremonial dish called *derum*, made for the official coming of spring, two days ago on 21 March. I am handed a small plate and a spoon. Vanella looks keen to try it, so I stall while she goes ahead. She says I always do that. In fact, I'm not adventurous at all.

My first problem is what *derum* looks like: brown and sloppy with a yellowish oil swimming around it. The brown stuff turns out to be a paste with a sweet, nutty flavour, almost bean-like. The oil is the tricky bit. It's worse than the most rancid blue cheese imaginable. We are eating a wheat paste – with liquid yak butter. And you can actually taste the yak. It's absolutely disgusting.

'Mmmm . . .' says Vanella. 'This is lovely.'

'Please, please have more,' they insist. Honoured guests can't refuse, so I take a deep breath and close my eyes.

Deram Titum tells us the village was founded in the time of Mir Nazim Khan. They had been four brothers who couldn't all work the small plot in Karimabad their father owned, so three of them came up here to a piece of wasteland, generously handed out by the Mir. For this they gave him five sheepgoats, as Mansoor calls them. It was a sixteen-day walk back down to Gilgit, if they wanted to sell some apricots.

'You had to have a good stick,' says the uncle. 'When the river was full, we would go across the mountains.'

They were hard times. They lived on apricots and wheat only, occasionally trading fruit to buy clothing.

'Everything is changing now,' he says, picking mutton from his teeth.

He claims his father's generation lived to ages of a hundred and forty or a hundred and fifty. These were the Hunzakuts of legend. I myself have seen a photo taken in the 1950s of a line of about ten of them sitting on a bench. They were the real Methuselahs.

'Yes and their fathers were even older,' says Deram Titum. 'A hundred and eighty or a hundred and ninety, they were. I tell you, they always used to say that the secret of long life is the apricot and its kernel. The fruit of the earth.'

In the fading light we drive a short distance to the north beyond Sost, then turn and cross the river by a small wobbly suspension bridge. A roadsign says Khuda-abad, which Mansoor translates as 'God's Colony'. We climb a dirt road and pull up in a paddock awash with icy puddles. Here, the apricot buds show only the faintest promise of pink.

The kids go crazy, running and shouting, as we look for Niat Shah's house. Amid the confusion we are welcomed by one of the old man's sons and taken inside, where the warm inner chamber is soon full of bodies struggling for a place, short-cropped boys with cheeky faces and young girls with looks that one day will cause some cheeky face heartache.

Niat Shah doesn't quite know what to make of us and stays seated where he is. His wife, Gul Namor, seems very suspicious. She sits in the background, rocking a wooden cradle shaped like a trough with such force that no baby could possibly sleep. But Grandma knows best and no sound can be heard from under the blankets.

Eighteen of them live in the one room. Years of woodsmoke have stained the walls to a resinous grime. In corners, dark wooden chests store wheat, barley and potatoes. One of these, they say, is over eighty years old. Once they have the fire crackling, the women move into action, boiling water for tea and making chapatis with impressive skill. The dough is rolled, then flipped on to the battered top of the stove, where it springs to life, writhing and blistering. An old stick is used to free the edges, flick the chapatis over and then off. They smell delicious.

Niat Shah sits quietly playing with his beard, hunched inside a thick Chinese military coat with a fur collar. His fingernails are black with dirt, his eyes blurred behind large spectacle frames. Gently Mansoor encourages him to talk. He says he is ninety-five and that he can remember when he was only five. It was the time the Nagiri people attacked Shimshal.

'Shimshal is a small village, two days' walk behind that mountain,' explains Mansoor, pointing to the south-east.

'There was much fighting,' says the old man. 'The people of Shimshal were taken prisoner and herded to the Mir's hunting ground. When the Hunza people heard this, a band of fifty men set out. They went there and killed sixty-eight Nagiris. Only one was left alive. He was sent back to Nagir without his tongue.'

Our eyes grow wide as we hear the tale.

'Still there is no peace,' he grumbles. 'Every country is fighting with another.'

'He is like an old lion, you know,' Mansoor leans and whispers to me.

'Another time, there was the flood in the Chipursan valley . . .'

'That is a small place fifty kilometres from here,' says Mansoor. 'Chipursan means "Who is asking?". They were a lucky people. They had tall trees, plenty of livestock and they didn't need any help from anyone. So they used to say, "Who is asking?"'

'The flood came from both sides,' says Niat Shah, 'and killed them all, except for one old woman.'

'The flood is asking, you know,' says Mansoor, with a grin.

We never find out what happened to the old lady, because Mansoor is pulling at my sleeve. 'Look, she is making thread.'

One of the old man's daughters is kneeling on a raised level by the door, patiently twisting raw wool into thread on a spindle.

'It is for this cloth,' says Mansoor, showing us the coarse brown material. 'For caps and coats.'

The children watch us watching her, staring open-mouthed. One of them has her feet planted in Vanella's giant walking boots.

Niat Shah has no doubt why he has lived to such a good age. 'It is because I am a hunter,' he declares. 'I have eaten plenty of ibex meat. I have shot seven hundred and fifty ibex in my time and more small animals than I have hairs in my beard,' he says, with a rusty laugh.

'Did you shoot with a gun?' Vanella asks, and one of his sons goes off, returning with the mother of all guns. Made in Russia, bought in China, it is well over five feet long. With it comes a leather ammunition belt, dried up now from lack of use, and a section of horn for the gunpowder. His son shows us how the gun is loaded and models the belt. It is four years since Niat Shah last used it: his eyes are growing weak now.

Next, the men parade the head of an ibex, its long horns ridged like steps. Ibex are to be found between 15,000 and 18,000 feet. At Sost, we're at 10,000. The head has a furry face and goatee beard still, and is giving off a strong gamy smell. The events of its ibex life are mapped out in the growth of its horns: how many years and when it had been injured in a fight. We work out it was twelve years old when it looked down the wrong end of Niat Shah's musket.

'The meat is very tasty, excellent protein. That's why I have lived so long,' he tells us with conviction.

He begins to warm up at last as we get him talking about his hunting days. He often used to come across bears, over in China.

'We saw tigers many times. I have killed them,' he says proudly.

'There are still tigers by the Khunjerab Pass,' says Mansoor. 'They come down to the villages and attack the sheepgoats in winter.'

'One time I had lost a lamb and spent the week looking for it,' the hunter recalls. 'When I spied it, I saw it was dead, so I put down my gun and went over to take a look. Well, two huge tigers were there. First, one jumped over me and slipped over the edge. Then when the second came at me, I was so scared I didn't know what to do. So I kicked it. It was the female. I kicked her down the mountain and she died.'

We are impressed. Niat Shah made a gift of one tiger to the Mir. Then he walked all the way to Gilgit and sold the other skin for the sum of one hundred rupees.

By the time we thank them all and take our leave, night has fallen and it is snowing heavily. Back in the chill of our hut, the register has been left for us to sign. Many of the names are Chinese, their marks left with a simple thumbprint. We work out that we are the first guests for months. No one has stayed here since the autumn.

Vanella looks in the bathroom but it's pointless thinking of having a wash. I raid the other rooms for extra bedding and we each crawl, fully clothed, into a damp bed, loaded down with two heavy quilts and yet more blankets.

I try to sleep, but my head is full of apricots and tigers.

14

In Search of a Master

The elephant giving me the eye here is Ganesh. Hand-painted on the powder-blue wall of a Brahmin's house, he has a garland of flowers encircling his neck. He is all arms, tusks and trunk. One hand goes halt, one holds an axe, another a flower, the fourth a bowl of fruit. At his feet, a rat looks up as it nibbles on a piece which has dropped from the bowl.

Inspire me, sweet Lord Ganesh! Clear the obstacles from my path. Show me wisdom and bring me to the knowledge of that which never ends.

You never know. As well as being god of new beginnings and good enterprises, Ganesh is also the Hindu god of scribes.

Turning round, cricket is the entertainment under the tree in the old courtyard. A young batsman strikes a firm on-drive for a certain four and a scrawny white cow ambles indifferently across the pitch from the well. A small boy retrieves the ball. He is bright pink – in fact, all five players have some shade of red about their faces and clothing. They are warming up for Holi, the festival when everyone goes mad covering everybody else with paint. Originally a gesture of love, this nowadays tends to involve an ambush. We are lucky to have escaped. I've seen a black and white mongrel transformed into some strange purple cross-breed, I've met bright red donkeys and I swear I even saw a pink elephant.

We are passing some time in Jaisalmer, an ancient walled town at the edge of the Thar desert, on India's north-western border. I don't know why, but I have it in my mind that we should meet a holy man. India must be the place, with a hundred and one religious sects to choose from. I see a scrawny figure in a loincloth, sitting on his *charpoi* telling tales of Krishna, leaving us with some profound thought we can take to our hearts and treasure. If not, there must be any number of wise old men living down these narrow paved streets so liberally strewn with dung. Lalit, a boy whose services he himself pressed upon us and who is also splattered pink, leads the way. He is looking for one particular house.

The old man sees us coming from the vantage of his carved stone balcony and by the time we've reached his door, he is down in the street to greet us. A tall, raggedy man with a grey moustache and roughly cropped hair, his long face twitches with excitement. He shakes our hands furiously. We follow him up a dark stone staircase, past where some women are chattering away as they work, embroidering. Then we're through an archway into his room. We pick our way around a body lying prone, sound asleep in the dust, and the old man beckons us over towards the light. He settles himself on a rug, spread over the soft sandstone paving of the raised balcony area where he lives.

Sitting perfectly upright, he smiles and opens his arms in welcome.

I ask Lalit to find out his name.

'What is your name?' he asks, in Hindi.

'Uh?'

'What is your name,' he shouts.

'My name is Kishanlal Bissa.'

Vanella laughs, in surprise. He replied in English, albeit a little shakily.

'And how old is he?'

'How old are you?' Lalit keeps up, in Hindi.

'Uh?'

'HOW OLD ARE YOU?'

He is one hundred years old, and very pleased at our reaction to this. As he rocks back and forth on his haunches, nodding eagerly, I find myself fascinated by his ear lobes, which are extraordinarily long and wobble at the slightest movement, like a turkey's wattle.

'And where was he born?'

'WHERE WERE YOU BORN?'

'Uh?' He bends his head, as if this might help.

'YOUR PLACE OF BIRTH?' bellows Lalit.

'Ah . . . Maharashtra state.'

'And what is his earliest memory?'

'WHAT IS YOUR EARLIEST MEMORY?'

'Uh?' Kishanlal smiles his apologies and tugs at an ear. His hearing really isn't what it used to be.

'AN EARLY MEMORY, SOMETHING FROM YOUR CHILDHOOD?'

'Uh?'

'WHAT CAN YOU REMEMBER FROM WHEN YOU WERE YOUNG?'

'. . . Maharani Victoria,' we hear him say, something about Queen Victoria.

'That time was much better,' relays Lalit.

'WHY WAS IT BETTER THEN?'

'Uh?'

It's no good. Poor Kishanlal can't hear us well enough, even though the noise we're making has attracted a small crowd of spectators on the rooftop opposite. So we wonder if we should try writing questions down for him.

'CAN YOU READ?'

He can. We find some paper, but it's he who picks up the pen.

'H-E-L-L-O,' he writes gingerly.

'HELLO!' shouts Vanella.

'Ha ha. Hello!' he returns, the lines crinkling on his face with pleasure.

So I write, 'Why was it better before?' then show him the page.

'Why . . . w . . . a . . . s . . . was . . . eet . . . bet . . . better, better . . . before?' Kishanlal manages, reaching the end with a sense of triumph. He looks puzzled, and then he laughs. 'I was in the fifth class reading,' he says proudly.

'YOU READ VERY GOOD ENGLISH,' I tell him.

Kishanlal smiles, but he still doesn't understand. He holds up his hands, chuckling, as if to say, 'What are we to do?'

I press my hands together in thanks and bow my head. Kishanlal mirrors my actions, once, twice, again, excitedly. Our eyes meet, and we smile.

Towards the end of the day, we follow young Lalit through the main gates of the old city, down the backstreets and the lanes that lead to a more rural neighbourhood. From this distance, the fortress walls look like a child's sandcastle about to brave the tide. Here, the houses are plain, crudely built with mud and stone, and away from the hurly-burly of the markets, life is conducted at a more easy-going pace. Birds sing in the trees; a boy is herding home some goats. Two women in bright saris walk by with large silver platters balanced on their heads – one carries mud, the other a pile of dung, fresh raw materials for a shiny new kitchen floor.

We come upon three men sitting on a rough stone wall, while their leathery camels loll nearby, feeding. Lalit hails the men and they give Vanella more than a passing glance, but they seem friendly enough. The eldest jumps down and takes us through a gate into an enclosure, with a low, square house at the back, its roof covered with branches, straw and innumerable bicycle tyres. Here we find Noor Muhammad, who is a Muslim, a dark-skinned man with eyes as black as olives.

The remaining grandsons leave the camels to join us. Their wives come out of the house and stand at a distance, bright studs in pierced noses, silver bangles strung the length of their arms. And way at the back, a small pair of eyes watches everything through a large crack in an old wooden door.

Noor Muhammad doesn't seem too happy. He sits on his *charpoi*, knees hunched up under a blanket, staring vacantly ahead.

'Are you sure this is all right?' I ask.

'Yes, go ahead. Ask him what you like,' says the grandson.

We try to introduce ourselves, but for some time the old gentleman is unmoved. He gazes on, the soft white skull-cap pulled tight on his head matching the trimmed beard beneath his hooked nose.

Finally, Noor Muhammad speaks. 'I am one hundred years old,' he says gruffly. 'I have been a herdsman. I spent my whole life working with cows.' He claims his memory is such that if ever he lost a cow, then saw it again a year later, he always knew it was his. Not only could he tell from the markings, but from its hoofprints in the sand.

Born in Umarkot, in what is now Pakistan, his family had moved to Jaisalmer when he was six or seven. At Partition, in 1947, he had decided to stay.

'Before it was much better,' he says, livening up a little. 'Now it is very bad. In that time, everyone spoke true and kind. Now everybody is telling lies. Our food was much better. Before it was pure. Now it is no good, too many things are mixed together. British time was much better.'

'Why was it better?' I ask, hoping for an answer at last.

But the old man stops, mutters something, then closes his eyes.

'He is going to sleep?'

'Angry,' says a grandson.

'Oh dear,' I say, wondering what's the matter.

'Tired.'

'We will leave him, then.'

'Don't worry. It is only the opium,' the grandson says.

'Opium?'

'Yes, he has been too long without it.'

'When did he last have some?'

'Three o'clock.'

'Does he take it every day?'

'Every morning at eight o'clock and in the afternoon, at three o'clock. He goes early to the city, to the market, with four or five friends. They sit and talk and take their opium.'

'Do they smoke it?'

'They put a little in their mouth and swallow it like a tablet, with water or tea. It is wearing off now so he is feeling tired.'

Noor Muhammad looks up from his drowse for a moment. Only then do I see that his eyes are bloodshot and the cheeks hollow under his beard. Hands clasped around his knees, slowly his eyes close.

~

Another afternoon, in Jodhpur, I walk out alone to explore the backwaters of the city and feed on the warmth and colour of the people. There is something about India that makes me feel at ease and free; something to do with this wild and wonderful, pitiable mass of humankind – life in its richest mixture. You can see things here in the space of one minute to make the jaw drop through your soul: the certainty of the ox pulling a farmer's cart; a group of teenage schoolgirls, each and every one a princess; the touch of the sunlight on a mountain of lush red chillis; the creased faces of the turbaned men who watch me go by; and then the wretched creature with no hands, who has only two ugly pink stubs for wrists, so he can neither beg, greet nor pray. Here, I am no more, no less than all of these.

I am strolling along taking in the street vendors and their stalls, when, of all people, I meet a holy man. I don't see where he comes from. I simply look up to find him standing there. He is quite a sight to behold. His high forehead is caked yellow with pigment, cracked and flaking from the heat of the day. A thick line of scarlet runs down to the point between his eyes. Four more smudges of red have been daubed, two at his temples, two where his hairline recedes most. The hair is tied back with a bright yellow band and he wears a plain length of orange cotton draped like a sash over a pinstriped waistcoat. I can't tell how old he is. His face looks young but his beard is long and grey, its curls reaching a ragged point in the middle of his chest. The man is a *sadhu*, one who has given up life's attachments and desires in search of salvation.

He stands there before me. He does nothing, but holds still and stares. His eyes seem to glower beneath his brow.

'*Namaste*,' I say, glibly, in greeting.

The *sadhu* remains silent and, for a moment, the two of us face each other. I look at him but his gaze sees right through me and I feel young, naïve and foolish. Then he turns and with a measured pace strides off, soon disappearing into the throng.

I am left wondering what has happened. I continue on my way, but I can't shake off his presence nor the look he gave me. I pass through the gateway to the old market. Amid the turmoil of carts and people and bicycles, I realize I have just met my holy man and that he told me nothing. All this time I'm searching, trying to find an answer. But I am always looking outwards, being objective. Perhaps what I'm really seeking lies within.

~

By the time we reach Delhi, we are learning to allow for all eventualities. Anything can happen. I like it that way, the exact opposite of mundane. I notice that, as a result, Vanella and I have both grown much calmer. It must have something to do with the pace of life too, its rhythm. Nothing moves terribly fast here in India. But things happen, things you can't ignore. I'm always waiting, quietly expectant, knowing that it won't be too long.

We spend most of the morning in the post office, offloading bits and pieces in a parcel home. In need of some refreshment, we find the Unity Coffee House packed with the lunch-time crowd, a mixture of local businessmen and a few Western travellers enjoying the faded plush of its décor. We are shown upstairs to a table already occupied by a plumpish Indian gentleman. He wears glasses with thick black frames. We nod in greeting and order some samosas, then chat to each other about practical matters, while the man sips tea and nibbles triangular slices of white toast.

Across the room, another man is sitting on his own. He must be in

Omari of the six works: Mfumbui, Zanzibar.

The boats: Jambiani, Zanzibar.
Ruth Muranda, midwife, mother to them all: Zimunya, Zimbabwe.

Lao Shou Xing,
Chinese god of longevity.

Mr Ichimiya,
schoolmaster of
Uzurihara, Japan,
where they eat life-
enhancing *choju* food.

Kin-san Gin-san, the oldest identical twins: Nagoya, Japan.

Ghulam Muhammad in belligerent mood: Hunza valley, Pakistan.

The Hunza valley in spring.
Niat Shah, ibex and cheeky faces: Khuda-abad, Hunza, Pakistan.

Noor Muhammad needs his opium: Jaisalmer, India.

Vanella in the pink, celebrating Holi.

Professor Deodhar, the oldest first-class cricketer: Poona, India.

his late thirties, a little older than me perhaps. His head is completely shaved, his clothes dirty and dishevelled. At first, I assume he's talking to himself, but after a while I realize he is looking straight at me, jabbering loudly in some incomprehensible language. I don't even think he's Indian. I turn away, bemused, but every time I glance back, there he is, still engaging me with another outburst.

The man at our table asks if we have the time. Twenty to three, it is. After a minute or two, with our samosas tucked away, we're making to leave when he asks what brings us to India.

'We are working on a book,' I say, and he gives an imperceptible twitch. When he hears what it's about, he is further intrigued.

'That is most interesting,' he says. 'What common factors have you found among the people you have met?'

'One of the most obvious is lifestyle,' I say. 'People seem to live longer and have a better quality life in old age if they stay active and eat a modest diet.'

'And we've noticed recently that many talk about a decline in moral values,' adds Vanella.

The man tenses. It's as if we've flicked a switch. He begins to talk, quickly and with authority.

'All that anyone wants these days is money,' he says. 'Money for this, money for that. They want things, they have to buy new things all the time or their life is no good. They are blind, dazzled, they cannot see. All over the world, and here in India especially, we have all manner of social problems which money could help to solve. But it is wasted. Our governments don't serve us well.'

He pauses briefly to recompose his train of thought and brush his tidy moustache. There is a patch he shaves at the very top of his upper lip, I notice, to prevent it becoming too bushy.

'The religions of the world are also in decline,' he goes on. 'We forget our religion, we close down our spiritual life. This is a crisis for mankind. The valleys of the Indus are the cradle of civilization, you know. People should look this way. Our ancient texts are sacred. Jesus Christ was a prophet, Muhammad a prophet also. All the tribes, still they pray to their own god. But how can there be more than one God? There is only one. We are given birth for a reason. We must strive to do well in this life so that, reincarnated, we have a better lot in the next. It is my duty to care for my ageing father. It is my daughter's duty to live in peace with her neighbour.'

The man sighs, deeply.

'India is ruined, you know,' he says. 'Much has been destroyed, through the influence of the West. We have progress, yes, but so much has been lost in the process – humility, a sense of human purpose, the belief in God, respect for our elders . . .'

Then he's pointing across the room. 'That man, you have seen him? He is lunatic, you know.'

'Yes, I know.' He's still there, though he seems to have given up eyeballing me.

'That man, he may be lunatic, but he is probably a holy man now. He has found something most men cannot find, something there in the extremes of human experience.'

'A holy man?'

'Yes, it could be most interesting. You will have read the book, of course, *In Search of the Master*.'

We haven't even heard of it, but there's no time to challenge his assumption.

'Yes, here in India you should go looking for a master,' he says firmly and so, bidding us good day, he pays his bill and leaves.

Somewhat dazed, we also prepare to go and I visit the gents. On the way out I almost bump into the lunatic, who sneers sourly at me. He carries a well-thumbed book, but the way he holds it, it's as if he won't let me see the title.

~

We find Kandli in Bombay. He comes to meet us and we all embrace, then squeeze into a quaint little taxi and rattle off through the city to the suburb where he lives. It is like meeting an old friend, though Kandli seems smaller than I remember him from Zanzibar.

'Where have you been since we met?' he says. 'You must tell me everything.' So we try as best we can. 'How was Hunza?' he asks. 'I should like to go there one day. Who else did you find on Zanzibar?' And so we tell him about Omari and his six works.

Kandli is much older than he looks, in his early fifties. We discover that he works as an officer in a bank. He appears to own one house that lies empty, while he lives in a small ground-floor flat two streets away. It is basic and sparsely furnished. There, we leave our bags and straight away Kandli suggests we go to the club. We can have a swim. He is very proud of his club, being one of the founder members.

They've built the place up from scratch and now it has all the facilities.

I learn he is an avid cricketer, a useful batsman and keen follower of the fortunes of the Indian team. I too love cricket, so we have plenty to discuss.

Later, as we're walking home, Kandli smiles dreamily and says, 'Tomorrow, we will go to Poona.'

'Poona?'

'Yes. I knew when we first met there was someone else. I will take you to see the Professor . . . Professor D. B. Deodhar. He is the oldest first-class cricketer in the world.'

We leave Kandli's house before dawn having hardly slept, due to the heat. But there is too much to see to feel tired and the air blowing through the taxi windows touches us with its cool caress. In the half-light, the streets are waking: men stretch their limbs as the pavements where they slept are swilled; others push their carts to market and an invisible cloud of coriander surprises us into inhaling lungfuls of verdant perfume. At the station, we edge our way around the sprawl of humanity still slumbering on the floor of the ticket hall and climb aboard the early train. A trusty black and yellow steam engine, with carriages made from ironwork and slats of wood, it pulls us slowly and surely away through the city. We pass by the sobering dereliction of the shanty towns and then a piece of wasteland where half the population, it seems, has come to squat for a morning constitutional. Away from the smoke, the day shines as the skies grow bright. And from our grandstand seats we watch games of cricket being played on every available scrap of ground along the way, improvised pieces of wood striking rags tied round a stone.

We reach Poona by late morning. The day is now hot and clear. As we walk from the station along a quiet lane to the Professor's house, another game of cricket is under way on the school playing-fields. It seems strange to see whites, to hear the sound of willow on leather.

We find a modest stone bungalow. We are arriving unannounced, which Kandli gives the impression is perfectly normal. Indeed, the house-boy immediately shows us into a light and airy sitting-room, littered with the shambles of academia. The walls are hung with team photos, trophies and pictures of a batsman, padded up, taking an old-fashioned stance like W. G. Grace.

Professor Deodhar has his feet up reading the morning paper.

'Oh, my friends. Good day!' he cries, rustling away the news. 'What? You have come all the way to Poona? This is excellent.'

The fact that we have come from Bombay is enough, let alone halfway around the world. The Professor sits to attention, looking mildly eccentric in a white shirt and a length of cotton wrapped around his thighs. His hair is uncombed, his feet are bare, his toes long and curled. After the briefest of introductions from Kandli, he launches abruptly into a monologue on the lasting benefits of fresh air.

'We are all creatures of nature,' he begins, speaking English in the Indian vernacular. 'Those who follow a natural course have long life, particularly fresh air, particularly on the hills. It so happened that when I was six years old, Poona suffered the ravages of the bubonic plague, because in winter we would wrap ourselves in our rugs and the lice would bite us and spread disease. And they found that if you leave the city and go outside, you would be safe. So in November and December, for ten years, my elder brother and I used to shift to a place about one mile to the north, and stay in huts specially built. We could go to the city but we were not allowed to stay.'

The Professor tips back in his chair and regards us as he inhales deep through his nose. There is certainty in his eye. Beside us, Kandli is smiling serenely.

'But some blessing came out of it, though, you see,' the Professor quickly goes on, 'because the schools and colleges were closed. We had no studies and were free throughout the day. So, naturally, in the morning we used to play games, football and cricket, then we would go for swimming, and in the evening, other games. And this hill-climbing, from an early age that particular practice became a habit with me and gave me the benefit of fresh air. When going on the hills you go slowly, you do what you can tolerate, so it has a beneficial effect on the lungs, the heart and so on. It is a gradual exercise. I used to go out on the hills, here on this side, for two hours every morning, from seven till nine. So I built up a strong heart and strong lungs.'

The Professor beats his chest with a fist to show us how.

'Then later, after my marriage,' he says, 'I stayed outside the city, because cities are covered with all kinds of dust and pollution . . . the pollution of noise, and in those days we had no drainage at all. So those who stayed in the city lost maybe twenty years of their life. My brother, he died at about eighty. But I have lived to more than a hundred, because I have excluded all sorts of pollution from my particular life.

I have made enquiries, yes. No cricketer, footballer or tennis player has lived so far to one hundred years. That is very surprising, because they must have had all the conveniences of life. But they did not live so long because they never lived in pure, uncontaminated weather . . . So that was the reason, even now, that I am nearly a hundred and two years old.'

Professor Deodhar pauses a moment in thought, catching his audience unawares. He has us so absorbed with his enthusiasm. Then, as he puts a hand to a grizzled, unshaven chin, a brief look of 'Now where was I?' passes across his face. He has come full circle from the idea of our journey to his own age, without a single question being asked.

I'm too slow off the mark. Although a sentence is half formed in my mouth, the Professor seizes the initiative. He's off again.

He never did anything unnatural in the way of lifestyle, food or drink, he says. He followed nature and believed that whatever habits, good or bad, we have by the age of ten or fifteen, they will continue. He was lucky. Whenever they went outside to play, they would take a large basket of fruit. Fruit, vegetables and milk are all that you need.

As he draws breath, it occurs to me that a lifetime of teaching must be the cause of this loquacity. He used to be professor of Sanskrit at the local college and is, no doubt, spurred on by the sight of our curious young faces. He obviously can't help but hold forth. Perhaps we should put our hands up and go, 'Sir! Sir!'

This time I don't miss my chance and I'm able to turn his attention to cricket.

From his early schooldays, he excelled in his passion for the game. He soon became a member of the Poona Young Cricketers Club. From 1911 until 1936, he was the star batsman for the Hindus in the Quadrangular Tournament, which they played each year against the Europeans, the Parsis and the Muslims. The selection of teams was made from the best players throughout India and the committee even allowed players from overseas to take part, so Englishmen like Rhodes and Hobbs would often guest for the Europeans. In those days, although India played no Test cricket, Deodhar faced all the top touring teams from England and Australia. He captained Maharashtra State from 1914, leading them to many famous victories. They won the Ranji Trophy in 1939/40 and again in 1940/41 when, approaching the age of fifty, he scored 247 against a strong Bombay team. Then in 1944, he scored a century in both innings of a crucial State match and two years later, at the age of fifty-four, he played what he considers to be his best, when he scored 83 and 60 for Bombay South Zone against the West Zone.

'I always played an attacking game,' he says, squaring his shoulder to make a flourishing stroke with the back of his hand. 'I used a direct stance. I would hold the bat much up the handle so that I could jump out, if there was a slow ball, and turn it away. I never liked playing defensively and trying to draw. I remember, in 1928, the Parsis had scored more runs than us in the first innings and we had a day and a half to save the game. So, though I usually went in number three or four, I asked my captain if I could open and my partner and I scored 132, at a rate of 18 per over. I always used to drive hard and never scored less than 50 runs in an hour. So if, in our day, there had been this one-day cricket, I would very much have appreciated it.'

I ask what he thinks is the fine art of being a batsman.

'The important thing is not to underrate the opposing bowling,' says the Professor. 'When they bowl a ball you are sure you can hit, you must watch it right from the moment it leaves the bowler's hand. Watch the situation carefully, and then if you hit the ball, you hit it as hard as possible. But never underestimate your opponent, never be over-confident, take your time, then seize your opportunity to score.'

He used to bowl too, sometimes.

'Bowling, you see, you'd be surprised,' he says, with a new glint in his eye. 'When my bowlers could not take a wicket, I used my brains. I wanted to give the batsmen particular enticement balls, so that they can hit all over. If you give a full toss on the left shoulder, he can't hit it on the off side. He has to hit it on the leg side. So I used to keep three fielders on the boundary, three near and two just close in there. On the off side I had only one fielder. I captured many wickets in that particular manner. I once took four in one match.'

The Professor grins triumphantly and we go on to discuss how the game has changed: tactics, equipment, the one-day games. He's not at all impressed by the lifestyle of today's players. In his day, they played the game for its own sake. Nowadays, the top players earn far too much money and they don't live a temperate life, so their eyesight becomes impaired. If Deodhar was coach, he'd have them all practising first thing every morning, after going to bed in good time the night before.

'A century in life is far more difficult than scoring a century on the cricket field,' he asserts, with an easy laugh. 'In cricket, if you are tired you can hit one or two boundaries to reach your century. In life, after ninety, it becomes more difficult. If you want to live long, you have to suffer the weaknesses of old age. Your digestive powers, all the powers of your body get weaker. You have to take extra care of your movements. So whatever your ambitions, you must put them into action while you are young. Whatever you want to learn, do it then. Don't wait. When you are old, you can increase the stock of your knowledge, but there is no way to turn that knowledge into action. Every moment of your youth is precious. Don't waste it. You can emancipate yourself by doing good things, by helping others, by living a clean, healthy life.'

How can we possibly disagree?

We wait for a few minutes while the Professor dons his whites one more time and prepares to pose for a photograph on the front steps.

'Tell me about this journey of yours,' he says, grasping the handle of his favourite bat. 'Where will it take you?'

'We hope to complete a circle around the world,' I begin to explain.

'Ah,' he goes, holding up a finger. '*Vishwabandhuttwa*. This is what you will learn.'

We look puzzled.

'*Vishwabandhuttwa*,' repeats the Professor. 'It is Sanskrit, this word. It combines two ideas, meaning "all the world" and "friendship". The whole world is one. We should not be against each other. We should consider everyone as our own brother and sister. All are one, in universal brotherhood.'

'I hope so.'

He nods and says, 'I know so.'

We turn to wave by the gate and I find myself shouting out, 'Goodbye, Professor,' as if my name is Tintin.

'Goodbye, Andrew. Goodbye, Vanella,' he calls. 'All the very best.' And so the good Professor returns to the routine of his day.

As we stroll back down the lane, passing a herd of goats tucking into some chopped-up water melon, Kandli catches my eye.

'A good innings, I think,' he says, beaming with delight.

Kandli refuses, point blank, to let us pay for anything. Food, drink, train tickets, not a thing. We are his guests. 'You can pay me back one day,' he says knowingly.

We have to give in, because there's no other way. But I fully expect that one morning the doorbell will ring and I'll find Kandli on the step with a bag slung over his shoulder. I'll take him to the pub, we'll go out for meals and he won't have to pay a single penny. And if I'm very lucky I'll be able to see his face as India's opening batsmen come down the steps of the pavilion at Lord's.

We decide to stay in for the evening. Vanella and I take turns in the bathroom. Standing on a duckboard, we use the jug to scoop water from a bucket and pour it over our heads. Then we emerge to find Kandli sitting cross-legged on a padded *charpoi* by the front door, meditating. He opens his eyes and smiles. 'Are you ready to eat?' he asks.

His housekeeper, a sweet lady with a crooked front tooth, is making chapatis. We gather round the kitchen table and help prepare the okra. It has to be one of the most enjoyable meals either of us has ever eaten. Chapatis, dal, curried okra and chilled lemon squash. That's all, simple flavours. Everyone eats their fill and there's still one chapati left over.

As Kandli wishes us good-night, he says that in the morning we will go looking for Morarji.

He has given up his room and made us a bed, a board balanced on two small tables covered with a sheet. We both have to climb on at the same time and put our weight in the centre to prevent the whole apparatus tipping over and crashing to the floor. We try to sleep, but again it's too hot, unbelievably humid. I set the fan to blow over us, but it's too noisy. Instead, we listen to the whine of mosquitoes dancing around our ears till dawn. But we are easily the happiest souls alive.

~

We are arriving unannounced again. Kandli remains confident, but this time I'm not so sure. We are dropping in on a man who was once prime minister of India.

The lift stops with a jolt, the concertina gates open and there, grinning, stands a pot-bellied security man. He leads us to an ante-room, from where we can hear footsteps to and fro, the squawking of a parrot and, in the kitchen, garlic and onions being fried at high velocity. After a while, a young lady comes to hear our request and says we will need to see her father-in-law, Morarji's son, Kanti. But Kanti is in the bath. We should call back later. So we make a retreat and in an hour or so, Kandli telephones. Kanti is still in the bath. He will need to call again. Finally, we are invited to return at two o'clock – to be vetted. In fact, we don't have to say much. Kanti is one of those men who fills all available space with the sound of his own voice. He sits with his back to the window so we can't see his face too well and talks at us for a good half-hour, giving us the benefit of his own opinions mostly, the upshot of which is that all questions for his father have to be approved in advance.

So we go away, compile a list and drop it by later on. After censorship has necessarily been imposed on a number of perfectly innocent topics, we are granted an audience.

Morarji Desai was born into the Anavil caste of Brahmin, the eldest son of a Gujerati schoolteacher. At the age of fifteen, two days before he was to be married, his father committed suicide, so young Morarji became head of the household before his time. He went to college in Bombay, graduated in physics, then joined the provincial civil service. During this period, he became an acolyte of Mahatma Gandhi, finally resigning his job in 1930 to join the Congress Party and become involved in Gandhi's civil disobedience movement and the campaign for independence. By 1934, Morarji had been jailed by the British on three separate occasions for such sins as persuading the peasant population to stop paying their taxes.

Progressing up the political ladder, he was elected minister for agriculture and revenue in the provisional government in Bombay. But when Congress resigned its ministries at the outbreak of the Second World War, in protest at being committed to war without prior consultation, Desai was arrested again and spent nearly three years in prison in Poona. After independence, he took up the post of home and revenue minister in Bombay, and then that of chief minister.

His politics were right-wing, to say the least. He stood against excess and corruption of any sort, prohibiting alcohol and once even attempting to close down Bombay's brothels. Such austerity cost him some popularity, but it was his move to separate the wealthy Gujerat minority from Maharashtra, which caused his most serious set-back. His response to the ensuing riots was a Gandhi-esque fast until death, but after eight days Morarji capitulated and sent in the police.

Invited by Nehru to join the government in Delhi, he became minister of commerce and industry, then of finance. At this time, he was troubled by scandals involving none other than his son, Kanti, who enjoyed considerable financial success. Morarji himself always acted with absolute integrity. Indeed, he was considered politically too conservative for the new spirit of India and perhaps a little overly righteous. It is said that Nehru decided privately that Morarji should not succeed him and so eased him out. After Nehru's death in 1964, and again in 1966, Morarji's ambition to be prime minister was thwarted as he lost out twice in the elections, the second time to Nehru's daughter, Indira Gandhi. Under her, he accepted the post of deputy prime minister and was her finance minister, until she sacked him and the Congress Party was split in two.

For much of the 1970s, Desai worked in opposition, an activity that culminated in his attack on Mrs Gandhi for electoral malpractice, whereupon she declared the infamous State of Emergency and clapped Morarji in gaol once again. After eighteen months' solitary confinement he was released, two hours before Mrs Gandhi declared a general election. Thus, at the tender age of eighty-one, Morarji became India's first non-Congress prime minister, standing for the Janata coalition.

He lasted two years and did some good work, especially in foreign policy. But the coalition of minority interests was never strong enough to provide him with any real unity and he was eventually forced to resign. Mrs Gandhi was re-elected and he retired to Bombay.

Morarji sits in an old wooden chair in the middle of the room, his house-boy cross-legged on the floor beside him. Kanti settles himself away by the door, behind his father's back. The furniture is modest, the décor a restful blue and I can see my friend Ganesh occupying a small shrine on one wall.

Morarji looks just like his photos – an uncomplicated face, the closely shaven head and glasses. For a man in his late nineties, he seems fit, very lean. His hands are strong, his skin particularly taut and clear.

Clutching my list of questions, first I ask for his impression of the differences between India when he was a boy, after Partition and now today.

'When I was a child,' he says, 'India was not a free country. It was under the British rule, and so that brings on different kinds of feelings. When one lives subordinated to another people, one is not master of oneself. After Partition, Pakistan was created and so the Hindu–Muslim feeling. It was not like that before. And, well, today India is a free country. Before it was not free. That is the whole difference.'

'And has the dream of the Indian nation been fulfilled?'

'It will be fulfilled in about ten years. That is my faith. You see, we were a very careful people during the British period, because living under a foreign rule does not make you courageous. But then the fight for independence gave us courage. I got courage that way. I am not afraid of anything.'

I find talking to Morarji a humbling experience. He thinks long and hard about his replies. Sometimes he will look away to his right and down to the floor and I'll wonder if he's heard. When he looks up, the answer is often turned round in a way you can't refute. For example, I ask what he considers his greatest achievement in politics, and he says he doesn't believe in thinking of achievement. And when quizzed on which foreign politicians he most admires, he says there is no virtue in admiring somebody more and somebody less. He admires them each for their own qualities. At every turn, his clarity and simplicity of thought show up my clumsiness, even down to the very questions set in my hand.

Looking for some romantic snapshot, I ask if he has a childhood memory he can give us, a happy moment perhaps.

'I have always lived a happy life,' he says, lightly touching the side of his glasses. 'I believe in living happily under all circumstances. You see, circumstances are not in our hands, but if you live adjusting yourself to that, then you can live happily. It is the only life you are going to live, so you have to live it.'

'What did you learn from your time spent in prison?'

'I passed nine years in gaol. I learnt the way of living happily.' Morarji smiles, and we laugh gently with him. 'I did learn also . . . because it is a hard life . . . basically either you break down or you become stronger. I became stronger.'

'How did you cope with solitary confinement during the Emergency?'

'I didn't bother about it.'

'What did you do?'

'I read some books. I used to walk and I used to do spinning.'

Spinning. This is my cue to enquire about Gandhi. Why does Morarji think he was such a great man?

'When I met him I began to worship him.'

'On one meeting?'

'The first.'

'Why was that?'

'Mahatma Gandhi believed in fearlessness, in truth, in non-violence and in humility . . . These four things I learnt from him. You see, fearlessness is a primary necessity. If one is afraid, then one is not able to do the right thing. So fearlessness comes first. Then you must always follow truth, otherwise you will live a wrong life. Then non-violence, not hurting people. And humility, remember that. One must not consider oneself superior to other people. But one should not consider oneself inferior also. All men are equal.'

In the face of such profundity, my questions still have me looking for anecdotes. I wonder if he can tell us some story about Gandhi that illustrates the kind of man he was.

'These four things which he gave us,' Morarji repeats, calmly and without emotion. 'Fearlessness, truth, non-violence and humility.'

'Mmm . . . and what is your fondest memory of him?'

'That is my fondest memory. I have never found another man equal to him, of his strength, of his nature. He is one man who is remembered in the whole world because he did not have any enemies. I tried to follow him in everything, but it is not so easy, because of one's weakness.'

'Do you think Gandhi would be pleased with India as it is today?'

'Well, it is he who has made it. It is coming up. In ten years you will see that India will rule the world . . . By rule I mean advise, not dominate,' he adds.

'What advice will India give the rest of the world?'

'These four qualities . . .' says Morarji.

This is all. There is nothing else we need to know.

Morarji is well known for his ascetic lifestyle. He gets up at four every morning. He maintains a vegetarian diet, forgoing even cereals: fruit for lunch and boiled vegetables for dinner. He retires early and only ever sleeps for six hours. He doesn't need much, because he never worries about anything.

Morarji has no fear, no anger.

'I gave up anger in fifty-two,' he declares soberly, as if it was some pleasure he'd learnt to forgo.

He also used to practise what they call urine therapy, meaning he drank his own urine first thing every morning. He originally read about this in 1948, tried it on himself and found it to be of great benefit. It cleared all disease from the skin and acted as a natural internal antiseptic.

I have to ask – one question not on the approved list. It tastes a little salty, apparently.

'Does it make you feel more healthy?'

'Yes. There is a sense of well-being.'

'Do you have some every day?'

'I stopped drinking it about three years ago.'

'Why?'

'It is not necessary now.'

'And how much?'

'As much I pass in the morning, leaving one spoonful first and one spoonful at the end. Then I would drink the rest.'

Morarji believes in regular exercise, for both body and soul. He practises yoga. He can recite the entire *Bhagavadgita* – the epic poem which is the gospel of the Hindu religion – and he prays throughout the day, remembering God in true faith.

'I used to do bodily exercises for the hands and muscles,' he tells us. 'Dumb-bells. I have strong muscles. See . . .' He rolls up the sleeve of his white *khadi* shirt to reveal a firm bicep looking like a good-sized potato.

'Very impressive!' says Vanella.

'That's bigger than mine,' I concede.

'Come, I will take hold of your hand,' says Morarji.

So I roll my sleeve, we grasp each other's hands and, locking forces, the two of us arm-wrestle.

It is Morarji who wins.

15

Life and Death on Bali

I wake to a lusty cock-a-doodle-doo. Then all is quiet and I slip back to sleep for a while. My alarm calls again and I hear neighbouring birds echo in reply. I open my eyes and for a few minutes follow the chinks of light that creep across a wall of woven palm leaf. Beside me, Vanella is breathing softly. Outside, the day is beginning. Someone bangs a wooden spoon on a pot away in the kitchen. A rustle of sarong moves past our door. Dogs bark. A young mother talks softly to her child and, from afar, comes more doodle-dooing.

A tepid shower eases me to life. I throw on a T-shirt and shorts then emerge on to a sunny verandah, secluded by bushes and sweetly scented flowers. The air feels warm and moist. Black tea is waiting in a Thermos.

As I drink from a china cup, I watch a butterfly the size of a saucer settle, blink its fluorescent wings for me then meander on its way. Across the courtyard, a young girl is carefully arranging the day's offerings. I watch as she sings to herself and practises a dance, extending her fingers, deliberately, like a lady admiring her nail varnish. She leaves some offerings on the ground, a few grains of rice on small squares of banana leaf, topped with a finely grated orange peel. These are scraps, to keep the bad spirits happy. Her mother is preparing larger baskets for the gods themselves, for the higher shrines – leaves twisted and fastened by a wooden pin, adorned with pieces of fruit, incense and bright pink petals.

There is some significance in highs and lows. If we were to make our way up through the paddy-fields and climb the densely wooded hillsides, we would eventually reach Gunung Agung and Gunung Batur, the volcanoes where the gods reside. If we went down to the sea, we might find evil spirits. The Balinese don't go down there unless they have to.

Neither do we. But we are wary of meeting drunken Australians.

Vanella still hasn't stirred, so I decide to go for a walk. Out in the dusty lane, more offerings have been created for the new day, each one exquisite: on the ground, on walls, in front of mossy stone statues. This is Ubud, a village on the southern slopes of the island of Bali. Our homestay is situated off the Monkey Forest Road, which runs north–south, while the other main street runs east–west. The crossroads where they meet is the heart of the community. On one corner stands a raised, open pavilion, the *balé bandjar*, where they're selling brightly coloured materials. To the north lies the main temple, or *pura*, with its carved stone gateway, a pagoda tower and thatched roofs showing above the outer brick walls. Along to the right I find the market, lit by the slanting rays of the morning sun. I haven't been browsing very long when I realize I am the only man there.

Balinese women are blessed with honey-coloured skin and dark brown eyes. Their hair shines with the iridescence of plumage. It is worn tied back, revealing happy smiles and rows of perfectly straight white teeth. Sitting among their generous baskets, narrow paths barely distinguishable between, the women sell a profusion of fruit and vegetables, nuts and pulses. The colours range from earthy to the most delicate. There are cloddy bricks of tobacco, root vegetables I've never seen, curly chillies, shredded herbs, bright sweets and mountains of fragrant pink and yellow flower-heads piled on woven trays. Their customers, the other wives of the village, each balance a large basket on their head, cushioned by a pad of twisted cloth, and a gentle murmur of conversation oils the commercial exchanges of the morning as they glide from stall to stall.

Dragging myself away, I return to find Vanella dressed, a selection of sliced fruit on the table and my banana pancake oozing with honey. I drink fresh tea, but instead of chewing the pancake I give a mighty chomp into my tongue, wounding it quite severely.

'Yow! How the hell did I do that?'

I Wayan Tapiep is an English teacher, a short, stocky young man with a round smiling face on square shoulders. Keen to practise, he first explains his name. The 'I' is pronounced short and means 'man'. Then, in his caste, the first four children are called Wayan, Madeh, Nyoman then Ketut. The fifth is Wayan again, and so on. Tapiep is like a Christian name.

He listens earnestly to our story. He hopes he can help us and says he'll be back tomorrow.

So we mooch around, read, snooze, until the afternoon when we decide to take a late stroll. At the crossroads we turn right, go past the market and continue to the far end of the village where we turn up a side road.

We're glad to get away. Too many travellers, we decide. The place has been ruined. The Monkey Forest Road is lined with nothing but homestays and trinket shops. We've seen tourists too, but we generally put them in the same bag as travellers anyway. A tourist has money but no time. A traveller has time but never enough money. In the end, in their numbers, they all leave a mess. A place gets popular and it's no longer what it was. Everyone is forever trying to find that unspoilt spot.

Soon we reach the ricefields, tiers of watery flats fringed with palm trees, each with a small shrine standing at its corner. We see bent figures here and there among endless rows of green shoots, every one planted by hand. Some paddies are knee-deep, with tiny sprouts just showing; some are a lush mass of green; those at the end of the cycle are ripe and golden brown, and are being cut and threshed by family groups.

We pass through a small village, where the dogs bark and the people smile. One man shows off his prize cockerel, which he keeps in a bell-shaped wicker cage at the roadside. He holds him up by the base of his petrol-blue tail, a splendid specimen with the thighs of a wrestler, sharp claws and a beady stare.

Further on, we find ourselves in a broader expanse of paddies, reflecting the grey cloud of a cooling sky and filled with the sounds of running water. A scarecrow tries to look threatening and columns of ducks scavenge in the shallows, waddling along the lines, never straying too far from their homing device, a ragged white flag placed by the farmer.

As the light is beginning to fade, we come upon a temple, an open area entered via three stone steps. The gateway is guarded by a gruesome pair, two statues discoloured by shades of mouldy grey-green lichen, wearing chequered sarongs, or *kamben*. Eyes bulging, fangs menacing, their fiery tongues hang down between pendulous breasts. Stone structures cluster around a raised central pavilion, the *paruman*, where the gods themselves sit whenever they chance by. Some offerings have been left on a yellow cloth. More faces stare out from its sides to frighten away any evil spirit bold enough to get that far. The place is quiet and empty, but in the twilight somehow charged with a presence. If the gods are passing through, it is comforting to know that they are invisible, to us mortals at least.

The whole island is scattered with temples, some ceremonial, some ancient, some tucked away like this among the ricefields. Every household has its own, for family use. The Balinese are Hindu, a discrete minority among the melting-pot of Indonesian religions. But their brand of Hinduism is unlike most belief systems. It is fused into their way of life, as essential as food or sleep. From dawn until dusk, and from the cradle to their equivalent of the grave, it is rooted in this garden paradise they inhabit.

Next morning, we realize that something's up. The *balé bandjar*, by the crossroads, seems to be serving some new purpose. It is full of men sitting cross-legged in groups, joined in some kind of communal whittling therapy. There must be seventy of them, chopping and slicing bamboo into thin, precisely measured sticks. We stand watching, puzzled.

'We are making satay,' one of them shouts.

'Ah ha. Enough satay to feed a whole village?'

'Yes.' He nods, beaming back a perfect smile.

I Wayan Tapiep first takes us to meet I Wayan Mandor. We don't have to go very far to escape from the bustle of the street. In through an ornately carved stone gateway, a walled courtyard provides peaceful seclusion. An assortment of shrines and pavilions stands among the low buildings. Birds chatter in cages, chickens peck hopefully and a scruffy puppy snuffles at our ankles.

I Wayan Mandor sits on the verandah in a bamboo armchair, blowing shallow breaths through pursed lips. They don't know exactly how old he is. In the Balinese calendar, a year is roughly two-thirds the length of ours, so when they say he is maybe a hundred and thirty-five, it is in their own timescale.

He seems a little infirm, an impression not helped by his wearing only a pair of thin cotton shorts. We can see collar-bones, ribs and all. The veins down each arm show through like lengths of twine. His nipples are black press-studs on a sagging chest. His biceps look like small fruit hanging under slack, wrinkled skin. And he has the pinched cheeks, sunken eyes, protruding mouth and cupped ears of a monkey.

Four generations live here in his son's house. One granddaughter is working in the kitchen while another prepares a score of offerings, which she places throughout the courtyard. His great-grandson races around being mischievous, grabbing incense sticks and chasing the puppy. His son, an elderly man himself, looks on benignly from his own bamboo chair.

'In Bali, life has three stages,' Tapiep explains. 'When we are a child, we play. We do whatever we want, go where we like. Sometimes we help our father, or make offerings with our mother. Then we find a girl, we marry and have our own children. We work and take care of the affairs of the village. The last step is when we are old. Then our children take care of us. This man is old enough now. He wakes up, has some coffee and sleeps again. He takes his food in the afternoon, and then relaxes.'

I Wayan Mandor was a farm worker from a small village to the north of Ubud.

'I remember tending the cows while my father worked in the rice-fields,' he says, wheezing. 'I found grass for them and led them to meet Father at the end of the day. And I can remember the time I had my teeth filed.'

'Teeth filed?' we exclaim, horrified.

'This happens to all our young people,' says Tapiep. 'Our teeth are filed when we are teenagers. It is a kind of ritual.'

The high priest comes to perform the ceremony, filing the upper teeth until there is no further sign of devilish fangs. In the old days, the teeth would sometimes be blackened as well.

Vanella is wincing and wants to know if it hurts. I Wayan Mandor sucks in more breath and says it does.

'My teeth used to stick out. So the priest filed until my tooth was thin. Then, in two or three days, it hurt very much. It had gone bad in the root.'

He shows us how the filing was done, his scrawny finger rubbing his now not-so-perfect top row.

All this explains those beautiful, regular smiles and, of course, how my own devilish fangs injured my tongue while eating my pancake.

Like most Balinese, I Wayan Mandor learnt a second craft. He used to be a musician and played in the *gamelan* orchestra accompanying shadow puppet plays. These days, he is too weak and has already passed his skills on to a younger generation. 'I can still play a little,' he says, looking accusingly at his right hand.

Then we want to know if he has ever seen a witch. Tapiep has told us that they believe in magic, good and bad. As ever, there is a balance and symmetry to their belief. Good is symbolized by anything clean, strong, or over on the right; evil is unclean, weak, or to the left. A *leyak* is a witch, who takes the shape of a demon or an animal. They are held responsible for anything bad that happens.

'I have seen *leyaks*,' says I Wayan Mandor, siphoning more air. 'I was coming from the ricefield. I had to go there at night to fill the paddies with water. It was about twelve or one o'clock. I saw a monkey, but not a real one, a monkey from someone else. More than once I have seen this. Sometimes I have seen fire walking along the road.'

He is quite matter-of-fact, as if such apparitions are perfectly normal.

'What did you do?' asks Vanella, wide-eyed.

'If the monkey tried to do anything to me, I would use my scythe to kill it and it would disappear. Otherwise, I would just keep walking.'

'Were you frightened?'

'No,' he says, surprised. 'I was happy. I liked to see them.'

Some people possess a special power called *saktí*, which protects them from the influence of black magic. I Wayan Mandor had no need to be scared. He had inherited plenty of *saktí* from his father. We, on the other hand, vow never to visit the ricefields again after dark.

On the way back, Tapiep tells us what is behind the satay-stick whittlers. We learn that it has to do with a cremation.

'Today is *purnama*,' he says, 'the full moon, the best day for washing the body. The old prince is to be cremated on Sunday, a special day because he is high caste. You can go this afternoon to watch the ceremony. At his house, over there.'

Tapiep points to a splendid gateway. He insists it will be no problem for us to go. So we dress in our *kamben*, tie an extra ceremonial sash around our waists and set out to mingle with the royal family. The princes of Bali, or *satrias*, as their caste is known, hold little political sway these days, but when it comes to the cremation of one of their elders, they still do things in style.

We are greeted at the entrance by a group of twenty *gamelan* musicians sending forth an eerie melody. They play instruments that look like xylophones, struck at speed one-handed with hammers. Hesitant, we step through the gateway to find a large crowd waiting throughout the courtyard and under the shade of richly decorated pavilions. We feel like guests at some well-to-do wedding.

The women shine like birds of the forest, in crimsons, blues and greens. They wear a bodice, tight-fitting lace jackets and *kamben* with batik designs. The men wear black: *kamben*, shirts and pointed headscarves known as *udang*. A graceful teenage girl receives us, shows us to a place where we can sit, then serves us tea. Nobody seems to mind the presence of two gatecrashers.

The high priest's platform has the look of a tree house. Some twenty feet tall, raised on four thick poles and with a thatched roof, it is surrounded by a mound of offerings: baskets of food, fruit, flowers and an impressive pile of whole roast duck. The priest, or *pedanda*, an elder with big bushy eyebrows, wears a bejewelled black hat and a black waistcoat with extravagant gold trimmings. He sits up there, on his own, because of his caste. He is higher than everyone else, quite literally.

In the main pavilion, opposite, Chokorda Raka lies in his coffin. He died over two months ago, but was embalmed so he could stay with his family. They had to wait for this auspicious time. On Sunday, his body will be burnt and his soul released. It will enter the spirit world, come full circle and be reincarnated as someone new. So this is a time for celebration, not sorrow. Even his widow looks cheerful, but then she might – once upon a time, wives were sacrificed alongside dead princes like Chokorda Raka.

Upstage, the high priest rings a bell and begins intoning prayers. He tosses some flowers and sprinkles a little holy water. The old man's body is raised from the coffin by his sons, nephews and grandsons. They roughly manhandle him overhead to a special dais, where they unwrap him and pour water all over his naked flesh. Strangely, we are both straining to get a better view.

I haven't seen many dead people. We saw a man in a subway in Beijing and knew straight away he was dead. But we didn't want to look. Now, we are transfixed by the prince and his expressionless mask. He's so lifelike, I half expect his nose to twitch and the eyes to flick open at any moment.

I remember when Granny Jackson died, they placed her in the dining-room at Cambrai on the morning of the funeral. The coffin was left open for the family to pay their last respects.

I was outside in the hall when my grandfather found me.

'Do you want to see your granny, young 'un?' he said. 'She's looking very beautiful today.'

Seeing no reason why not, I nodded. So he put his hand on my shoulder and was leading me into the room. The coffin stood over by the window. At the delicate age of fourteen, my height was such that I still needed to be up close to see inside. Then my mother emerged from the kitchen.

'No,' she called out.

Grandpa and I turned.

'No, I don't think so. You don't want to, do you?' she said.

Mum was only being protective. Another ten seconds and I would have my grandmother's face etched in my memory. In fact, I did quite want to see her again because I felt a little responsible for her death. The last time we visited her I had a terrible fluey cold. I kissed her goodbye and my father said in the car it was probably best not to spread germs. She died within the week.

Chokorda Raka is looking decidedly grey. The men are washing him down, as the women kneel to sing a wailing song. They dress him in a fresh *kamben* and place a white *udang* on his head and a yellow flower behind one ear. Then he's draped with a purple sash and a golden sheet, his hands resting on his chest where a large gold ring glints on a little finger.

Suddenly everyone crouches down, making themselves as low as possible. We quickly do the same as the high priest descends and walks over to the dais. Once he's regained his few inches of superiority, we can all stand again. He sprays holy water and petals over Chokorda Raka's head, he pours more from an earthenware bowl and more still from a brass jug, saying prayers all the while. These duties performed, we all duck down as he returns to his tower.

The men lift their prince and wrap him in palm matting. A bamboo bodice is then fitted and he's wound in a fresh white sheet. Hoisted up, they make an arch of him for the women to run through, like children in a playground game. And so he is laid to rest once more in his coffin.

We all kneel, hands held aloft in prayer, hoping for a safe passage for his soul. The priest rings a bell and delivers his final blessing. The coffin is dressed with intricate arrangements of flowers and rice-stalks: red, orange and gold. They drape banners and stack woven leaves at his feet. From the ceiling, a framed photograph of Chokorda Raka, smiling, reminds us all how he looked on better days. Now he is ready for the ultimate journey.

Friday dawns on a village gripped by industry. Down the Monkey Forest Road, a team of carpenters is sawing bamboo poles into lengths. Up by the crossroads, the *balé bandjar* has again been transformed. Two fat pigs lie prone with their trotters and snouts tied, waiting to be turned into satay. We can tell that they know. Only a few feet away, another poor piggy is already being chopped into very small pieces. The local dogs are in a state of frenzy.

Tapiep returns on Saturday. He wants us to meet I Wayan Gejer, who we find keeping cool in the shade of his verandah. He sits at an old table, upon which lies a bundle of bamboo strips. A tall basket and a tool-box full of knives rest by his feet. Smiling sagely, he nods in greeting and continues to cut the wood. His chest is bare, his skin dark brown and mottled with moles. A blue and white striped *kamben* is hitched above his stomach, a white *udang* perched on his head.

His wife appears, naked to the waist. As she loosely buttons a shirt, their grandson saunters into the courtyard with two of his mates. They wear beach shorts and flip-flops. A naked woman rises suggestively from the clutch of flames tattooed on the grandson's chest.

'Look at these bad boys,' teases Tapiep. 'This one is a playboy. He has many Australian and American girlfriends.'

The bad boys pretend to look guilty while I Wayan Gejer keeps working on the bamboo.

True to ancient custom, he kidnapped his wife in order to make her marry him. Ni Nyoman Binder tells us the story herself.

'I was still quite young,' she recalls. 'He came to our house and caught me. I cried, but there was nothing I could do. The men had their competition to see who could get the best girls. Then I remember we walked around for a long time. We couldn't go into the village in case someone else tried to kidnap me. So he picked me up in his arms and put me in an old motor car he flagged down.'

Tapiep thinks the car would have been an old *bemo* three-wheeler, one up from a motorbike, the sort that nowadays belches out a trail of dense blue smoke.

Ny Nyoman Binder laughs, stroking her long grey hair. Her mouth is stained deep red from chewing betel nut.

They went to a place fifteen kilometres away, she says, where they lived for three months, begging food from the locals. When they came home, her cousin urged her to fall in love. He said his friend would make a good husband.

'Is he?' asks Vanella.

She nods and smiles.

I Wayan Gejer is a priest. Tapiep says a man cannot become a priest until his wife has borne children. Then it will happen, by chance.

'One day we stay at home,' he says, 'the spirit enters us and we become a priest. People wanted him to become one because his father was.'

'So is it hereditary?'

'Yes, one of his relatives will also be a priest.' Tapiep points to the grandson lounging nearby. 'This one, he can be naughty now, but the bad spirit can leave him suddenly and the god will point and say, "You must become a priest."'

Our playboy seems to think this unlikely. The old man smiles calmly as his knife slices through another piece.

He is a *pemangku*, a lower-caste priest, responsible for the cemetery. Low-caste families often need to save before they can afford even a simple cremation, so the bodies of their loved ones are parked in temporary graves. The *pemangku* blesses offerings to the gods and keeps the cemetery temple clean.

'Do bad spirits ever go there?' I wonder.

'*Leyaks* are often seen,' Tapiep assures me.

'Has he seen a *leyak*?'

The old man shakes his head and smiles, displaying a betel-red mouth and blackened teeth.

'He is well protected,' says Tapiep. 'Black magic things will be afraid of him. When a witch sees him, it runs away. Sometimes it will look like a dog. A man can turn into a dog and come at night to dig up a corpse. Sometimes it will be a double-dog. But Durga, the goddess of death, guards the cemetery. We can't see Durga with our eyes, but if you go there at night or if you become a *leyak*, you hit an invisible wall and can't go in.'

I Wayan Gejer has hardly uttered a word. All the while he has been methodically shaving bamboo strips, one after another. Each measures one and a half feet long, and half an inch wide. He shaves half the length of both sides, cutting away from himself with a sharp knife.

Then he turns the strip through 180 degrees and shaves the other half, leaving it smooth and supple. His movements are precise, unhurried, the rhythm of the blade hypnotic.

Since he was a young man, he has worked as a basket-weaver. His baskets are stacked behind him, flat and round, for holding rice. Each takes him three days, but this is the crucial stage, making the bamboo thin and flexible.

A fresh pile lies on the table. Pale dust has now collected in the folds of his *kamben*, and his kindly blue eyes return the most serene of gazes.

Next morning, I find a bull with a huge pair of balls being admired by a group of young boys. He looks mean and menacing. His mouth is bared red, his pointed horns, hoofs and tail shine with gold. Standing on a criss-cross bamboo plinth, he is made of wood and covered with a skin of black felt. A mirrored golden halter hangs around his neck, tassles dangle from the ears and a starched white *udang* crowns his head. It's such a shame he'll be going up in smoke – with Chokorda Raka inside him.

On another platform stands the *badé*, an enormous tower richly decorated in gold, with nine pagoda roofs tapering to a point. These represent the different levels of the heavens. Below, a space is reserved for the coffin, where it will rest on the way to the cremation. At the base, a monstrous face stares out – Bhoma, son of the Earth – whose giant wings extend in a swirling sweep of coloured cotton-wool. His fangs, wild eyes and blood-red mouth warn off any intruding spirits.

It is the day of the cremation and people have begun to arrive from all over the island. Again we dress up and make our way through the royal gateway.

All the guests are in black today, though the mood is far from sombre. As the *gamelan* orchestra hammers out its haunting song, the men laugh and smoke, while the women chatter happily among themselves. Courteously received, we take our place in one of the pavilions. They bring us water and a small basket of jackfruit delicately wrapped in palm leaf. We try refusing, but they insist. More guests arrive laden with gifts. A young *pemangku* says prayers, sitting cross-legged at the foot of the coffin. Firecrackers explode to keep away the evil spirits. Then four German tourists, sporting checked shorts, beer bellies and video cameras, wander brazenly in from the street and are politely asked to leave.

Now we must wait – until the sun reaches its zenith and has begun to descend, appropriately, into the dying half of the day. Shortly before midday, lunch is served, a magnificent spread, which they invite us to enjoy. There are green bean salads, spicy vegetables in peanut sauce, noodles and rice perfumed with coconut. Vanella seems to be the only one who holds back at the impressive quantity of satay. Then I keep blinding myself, trying to check the position of the sun. One of the dogs can't bear to wait any longer and scampers off with a duck from a basket.

A drumbeat sounds and suddenly the object seems to be to move as fast as possible. Everything on the coffin is balanced on the heads of daughters, nieces and granddaughters. They rush through the throng of guests in the courtyard towards the crowds massed on the street outside. We hurry behind the men carrying the coffin, eager to keep up.

The *badé* is outside, its pagoda tower reaching up into a clear blue sky. We can see the bull waiting, further up the street. Both are supported on the jostling shoulders of two teams of sixty young men dressed in black, with white sweatbands. The *badé* wobbles in the confusion while Chokorda Raka is wedged halfway up, somewhere between earth and the heavens. One of the old man's sons clings to the side of the tower, riding shotgun, shaded by a fringed parasol. In his hand, he clutches an extravagantly plumed stuffed bird. A length of shot silk, red and gold, has to be draped over the end of the coffin and then, with everything in place, a signal is given to the man who sits astride the bull. And we're off.

The whole procession charges as one, shouting and screaming, towards the crossroads. The bull turns right, tilting at a crazy angle. We follow in the scrum behind the *badé*, which halts at the junction, feigns a left turn and begins to spin round as nimbly as sixty strong men are able. Having given any lurking spirits the slip, they career after the bull. Dust flies. Sweat glistens. Sunlight flashes on mirrors and gold. A throng of black shirts and shining hair chases on. Then a *whoa!* goes up and we all risk being trampled from behind. A special bamboo pole is called for to lift a telegraph wire over the very tip of the *badé* as the carriers crouch down and are hosed with water. On they run to the next wire, and then on again as fast as they can, a downhill slope, the uphill stretch, and the crowds pile into the cremation ground behind them.

Preparations now have to be made. They lug the bull up a steep grassy hillock where a splendid canopy has been erected on poles. The coffin is removed from the *badé* and the body placed inside the bull. A pyre is built, while bamboo is nailed to the canopy posts and a cradle of thick wire strung across below the bull's belly. The high priest administers his blessings with holy water. The women stand by with a colourful assortment balanced on their heads, food for Chokorda Raka to take with him on the journey and gifts to hand out along the way. Everything is loaded on to the pyre and then sloshed with gasoline from old red cans, while other relatives sit a few feet away smoking a well-earned cigarette.

After what seems an eternity, the women guide each other up the slope, carrying a tiny flame on a small woven tray.

Whoomph! The entire bulk of the bull is soon ablaze. Black felt peels away and a plume of white smoke billows into the sky. Wood burns and the heat intensifies. One of his sons comes to knock the underside with a long pole and gradually Chokorda Raka slips down on to the wire cradle. He has to burn well, in order to release his soul. They stoke the fire with more wood, they throw on bags of sugar, they pour coconut oil down bamboo pipes – anything to make him burn better.

It is a grisly sight, as the process of carbonization takes hold. The pyre burns as the afternoon wears on and the spectators begin to drift away. But the rituals are by no means over. We retreat a short distance and sit down to cool off. Soon I become aware of a man sitting on a stone next to us. He is dressed in black and smokes a white-tipped cigarette as if unused to the habit.

'Too much formalin,' he says, by way of introduction. 'He didn't burn well enough.'

'Oh, really.'

Little respect is being shown for the prince's remains. Lying now in the centre of the furnace, he is prodded and poked, his head brutally struck with a length of bamboo.

'The family needs his spirit back in the home,' the man says placidly. 'The soul lives inside the skull. It has to be freed. I know this because I am a medium. I can talk to the spirits.'

'Ah . . .'

'Will his spirit protect them?' Vanella asks.

'Yes, that is right. This evening his ashes will be taken to the sea, to the Mother Temple, Tanah Lot. There they will be cast on the water. Later, a medium will talk to his spirit to see that all is well and a shrine will be placed in the family temple.'

'His soul will then be at rest?'

'No, there is more,' says our friend. 'Another day we have to help his soul find its heaven.'

And so, for a while, we watch together as further attempts are made to reduce Chokorda Raka to ashes. In a way, I quite envy him. It's one hell of a way to go. The Balinese have everything perfectly worked out – a wonderful life in paradise and then the chance to do it all over again.

And I've always liked the idea of our ancestors' spirits being with us. I can see my grandfather cheering us on.

16

The Ancestral Spirit

My father is looking older. His hair has advanced one more shade along the spectrum from silver to white, and he's developing the same jowls Grandpa used to have under his chin. I don't suppose I would have noticed if I'd seen him every other week, but when we hugged and stood back and looked at each other the difference was there. I daresay I've changed too. I certainly feel fitter than I have for years. I've shed a few pounds, found a good balance. But Dad remembers the old me and says I look gaunt.

He has made his new home in Australia, with Felicity. I can't think of her as my stepmother, more his wife. Anyone who has ever inherited a stepmother will know what I mean. We get on well these days, but things were hard for a boy to come to terms with at first. Vanella being around has helped.

They seem happy. They live in a pretty spot an hour south of Melbourne, on the Mornington Peninsula – Port Phillip Bay on one side, the Bass Strait on the other, all the way to Tasmania. It being Australia, there's an old ute parked up in the garage, a back door with a fly-screen and koalas snoozing in the gum trees now and then. The house stands on a gentle slope. At the back, the deck looks out over a lawn down to the paddock, which contains a couple of heifers, six sheep and a dam in the bottom corner. Dad looks to be getting the garden in shape. Autumn work is going on. There are piles of earth, dead wood and a strong smell of manure about the place. I was watching him through the window the other day as he measured out his new rose-beds. He still talks to himself.

This feels like going home used to. From the age of eight until I left school, the year was always divided into three measures of home and away. Three times I'd feel a sense of euphoria that's been hard to match. Freedom. Dad would come to collect me and we'd shake hands. Then we'd load up and travel home in the car and I'd tell him my news, triumphs and acquisitions first. Back at Woodlands, Mum would have everything ready, from crisp white sheets to steak and kidney pie. And for a few precious weeks, I would be reacquainted with the boy I used to be. I could go as I pleased, invent and dream. I'd set out on secret expeditions beyond the wood or cycle up into uncharted territory past Pooh Hill tree, which Grandpa always said was the highest point between us and Russia. Then, as boredom began to creep into my days, the sour taste of regret would mix with an urge to go back into the world and see my schoolmates again.

'Come on, then, where did we get to yesterday?' Dad keeps saying every evening after dinner. There's so much to catch up on, Vanella and I take turns to spin another chapter in our tale.

But that's only part of it. What I like is hearing Dad talk. I can see he loves to tell me about his rain gauge – so many inches, where they stand compared with last month. Then he shows me how he can play with the figures on the computer. Or sometimes it's the birds.

I'm out listening to the magpies, down at the bottom of the garden. There's a chill in the air and crisp sunshine, which would be a bright November morning back home, but here it is May. They're not the most attractive birds, Antipodean magpies – black and white crows, really, with a petrol-blue sheen – but they make a curious noise, a plaintive warbling that falls away in a dive. They sing in the mornings and, for me, their sound evokes the Australian country.

Indoors, Dad is pottering about listening to some Mozart.

'Our magpies aren't brilliant,' he says, as I come in for breakfast. 'They've never been real good oggle-oggling birds. They only do it occasionally.'

'They're doing it now.'

'Have you seen the wood swallow?'

'Yes, on here,' I say, pointing to the balcony outside. 'Strange bird.'

'He has a wonderful call.'

Licking his lips, Dad lifts his head and whistles a single note, gets it wrong and tries again.

'Sometimes he'll have a trill,' he says. 'He pops along here and you see him looking up, all the time looking up.'

Dad raises his eyebrows, head and shoulders moving as one to show me the wood swallow. He tells me how he was working one day when he saw it come round to the mat and look up at the netting. 'I thought, "What the hell are you doing?" But there was a moth caught, there in the door. He hopped up, caught it, and went and had his breakfast.'

Dad brings out the bird book to find something else he's seen. He leafs through the pages muttering softly, 'Swallows, swallows . . . except it wasn't a swallow, but it's on the same page . . . 167 . . . What's that? No . . . Where's he gone?' And as he flicks back and forth, I realize I'm doing more than just watching him. It's silly. I'm savouring watching him. '. . . Here we are,' he says finally. 'Swifts, swifts, yes, that's him, a white-throated needletail.'

He shows me yellow robins, then the silver-eyes that sit in the fig tree and the fairy wrens that come to stand by his boot when he's out digging. There are the wattlebirds in summer, sometimes galahs, and the red parrots who eat the seeds off the dandelions. His fingers become the tiny little birds flitting from tree to tree when he goes out to get the paper in the morning. They move so fast, but he thinks he's pinned them down to some other kind of wren. '*Tse-tse-tse-tse*,' he goes, '. . . *tse-tse-tse-tse-tse*.'

As soon as the magpies saw someone back in the house, they were up on the rail. They were used to being fed. Dad tells me he had to keep shooing them away because they made such a mess.

'And do you know?' he says. 'They were angry. They'd go back to the tree and they'd turn and look at me like this . . .'

Dad hunches his shoulders, screws up his face and with a one-eyed scowl gives me his grumpy magpie.

~

The last time I found myself in a headmaster's study I was sixteen and holding my favourite pair of jeans. Some stupid rule said I wasn't allowed to wear them, not even on a Saturday afternoon. He had caught me himself. He made me change, then come back. I didn't like that man. He knew my name, but little else: from my humble place in the world, he seemed so petty, full of himself, and he had a high-pitched voice that was perfect to mimic. He gave me a telling-off, took my jeans and I never saw them again. The idea of letting him know what I really thought was quite out of the question. He was all powerful, and I, silent but surly obedience. I disliked him even more after that. Now, of course, I can see why he wasn't such a good headmaster. He didn't inspire.

When I'm shown into Sir James's study, I am on my own. Vanella has a suspect filling, which turned into a root emergency. Right now, she'll be sitting, as she always has in the dentist's chair, fingers hidden, tightly crossed.

A fire is crackling in the grate. Hardback books line the walls, spines of maroon and Oxford blue. Their titles cover every conceivable subject, encroaching upon the floor space in random stacks. Sir James remains seated in an armchair behind his desk, but shakes hands, mutters a gruff welcome and waves me to a chair. He is really more interested in his pipe. He's trying to get a fresh bowl going, a ritual worthy of impersonation by generations of schoolboys: the packing down with the fingers, a flick of the lighter, an empty suck, tamp, more lighter, suck, tap, pull, glow, puff . . . smoke. Then, enveloped in thick blue swirls, he looks up as if he's forgotten quite why I'm here. And I peer back at the magisterial form – side-whiskers, jowls, tweed jacket and tie – of one of the most influential men in Australia.

Sir James Darling, head of Geelong Grammar School for more than thirty years, has presided over the education of more than his share of the country's great and good. He has taught prime ministers, governors, business leaders, media moguls, writers, artists – achievers all. And he's famous for founding Timbertop, the outward-bound centre in the bush, though he modestly says that if he hadn't had the idea then someone else would.

He sounds the archetypal Englishman, gravelly and public school, but he considers himself Australian. 'I'm an Australian when I'm in England,' he declares. 'And I'm more or less an Australian out here . . . more or less.'

I find myself engaged in discourse, rather than conversation. A simple enquiry about the change he has witnessed since he first arrived from England, back in 1930, takes us from his initial response – population – to the assertion that Australia, even now, is not one country but a collection of six states . . . to the old divisions of class, the development of Anglophile and Anglophobe attitudes . . . to a final, brief reflection on the current political scene. Only then does Sir James finally run aground.

'Mmm . . . Now, then, what was your question?' he asks, looking out through a haze of smoke.

Although a natural logician, such considerations are, more often than not, peppered with sidetracks and qualifications, phrases interspersed with 'in a way' or 'very nearly' and Sir James is perfectly capable of the occasional complete U-turn. Suddenly he'll say, 'But, of course, it doesn't do that at all. When one considers how it really was . . .' and he's off on an entirely different tack.

I recognize immediately the mind of a historian in the way he lays out facts, unbiased, always probing towards a plausible truth. Not only was Australia divided into states, he argues, in the early days there were terrible, rigid divisions between Protestant and Catholic, and divisions of class he calls 'ungentlemanly' – those who had and those who had not. And with a total population of only seven million, the group to which any individual belonged actually used to be very small. So if you were in a quasi-eminent position, even as quasi-eminent as head of Geelong Grammar, you pretty well knew everybody in Victoria. And in your own social stratification, you therefore pretty well knew everyone in the whole of Australia.

'Jack Medley,' he recalls. 'He was vice-chancellor of the University of Melbourne. He liked Australia because he said that if you wanted anything you went straight to the prime minister.'

Sir James draws pensively on his pipe and looks away.

'Hasn't the role of women been a major change?' I suggest.

'Mmm,' he huffs, 'I was about to say so myself. It's probably been the most important change in my lifetime.'

His father, a preparatory-school headmaster, had taken for granted that girls needed the same education as boys. They were three girls and two boys; all went to boarding school, four of them to Oxford or Cambridge. But society at large was very different. Women didn't get the vote in Britain until after the First World War and there just weren't the opportunities. Australia had been the same, only worse.

'Extraordinary thing, isn't it,' Sir James muses, 'how the lack of domestic services changed the way of life in the class to which I belonged? We never had any money, we were *middle* middle class, but still had four maids who lived at home. They were well looked after, very much part of the family. It's an enormous change in the attitude of women that domestic service is now regarded as demeaning. Of course that's absolute rot, if service is the Christian ideal.'

Everything, he insists, hinges on the idea that life is all about service to other people. Christ was the ideal man. The Christian doctrine of service is the only real solution in the world, the only sensible way to live together.

'It's been lost, I think,' he confides. 'Now, whether it was really there I don't know . . .'

Women used not to be influenced by such idiotic concepts as competition, rivalry or greed. They used not to be concerned with ideas, more with people.

'We're in danger of losing their gift to the world,' he says, 'now that they're joining the rat race. Their gift to life . . . It's not quite common sense, it is Christian love, which very few men manage and a whole lot of women do. It's been lost, I think. Nowadays, it's regarded as mere weakness.'

How I wish Vanella was with me. She'd be saying something like, 'But don't you think everyone should have the same opportunities?'

Sir James would reply, 'I do, yes. I'm only concerned about making the very most of your talents, so we can live together in the best possible way. We wouldn't want to waste them, would we?' And so Vanella would try again, but they'd never quite agree.

I don't think I can either. I do believe I've found a true Victorian. Sir James tells me they used to consider the British Empire was God's gift to the world. They really did in those days. And, having seen what's happened since its decline, he's not sure they were wrong. All those people who won freedom for themselves were a damned sight better off without it.

He is ruminating now, I see. It's time for my history lesson.

'The keynote to all history since Christ,' he asserts, 'is that society should provide some combination of liberty and equality. All political thinking can be understood by that struggle. It's impossible, of course. If you grant liberty, you're bound to get inequality. Create egalitarianism and it can be achieved only by the suppression of liberty. The Australians and New Zealanders of the eighties and nineties of the last century got nearer achieving the idea of liberty and equality than anyone has ever done anywhere in the world.'

He doesn't include the Aboriginal people in this equation. That's a sentimental view. How many times throughout history have indigenous people been taken over? We have only to look at England, with the Normans and the Danes. Or Africa. Africa was little more than a collection of warring tribes. At least under the British Empire they were kept quiet, though they may have paid a high price for their security.

Security is the thing.

'I know this will be regarded as a heretical statement beyond acceptance,' he says, 'but I think any sensible person who's lived in Serbia or Bosnia or Macedonia would give anything for a quiet time – "I don't give a damn who rules me as long as we're not killing each other."'

Sir James believes that a moderate amount of liberty, a moderate amount of equality and a complete sense of security is more desirable to an ordinary human being than any philosophical ideas about what ought to be. What matters most is whether our families are fed and we can sleep safe in our houses at night. Societies matter, but what matters most is peace of mind.

'I suppose in a way it's a religious thing,' he ponders. 'To me, peace of mind depends on one's relationship with God, whether a God exists or not. The fact that there is something constant. That's what the Aborigines found. They got nearest to it. It's this difference between a static society and a dynamic. They didn't want to progress, they were quite happy as they were. They contrived a decent means of birth control. They worshipped the past, worshipped their ancestors. It was an acceptance of things as they are as being eternal and working within that framework.'

Just as I'm thinking how attractive this all sounds, a large clock on the mantelpiece chimes the hour and it's time to clean out the pipe and start again. Then the door opens and his daughter comes to remind him to take his pill.

'Are you going to make a cup of tea?' He waves a finger in my direction and grunts, 'Hmm . . . Better give him a cup, then he's going.'

With charred debris deposited in the marble ashtray, tea is poured and the intimacy between us rekindled. Sir James shows me his latest book. He's halfway through the manuscript and even invites me to take a look.

'Still do a piece for the *Age*,' he says, 'a reflection, they call it. Getting tired of it, though. Probably should stop. You wait till you're ninety-four. Bloody silly life.'

'Why do you say that?'

'Well, you become passive instead of active. It's extremely irritating to have an active mind and not be able to do anything about it. You get back to accepting that you can only light a candle to the glory of God. I can only do my little bit in my cabbage patch. And, really, this idea that you can still reform your world or that anything you do is going to matter . . .'

Sir James gazes away into space, his pipe glowing, its sweet aroma topping up the atmosphere. Then he turns and leans towards me. 'I'm an incurable amateur, you see. My final dictum in life is that anything that's worth doing at all is worth doing badly. If it isn't worth doing, it isn't worth doing at all. I deplore the elevation of everything into a serious business.'

'Why is that?'

'Because I'm an Englishman.'

'You just told me you were an Australian.'

'Yes, but I'm not. I'm still English in my attitude . . . and for Test Matches.'

~

When I left school, I spent six months travelling in Australia. I think the idea was that I'd set out a boy and come home a man. I worked on a sheep property in Victoria and picked grapes in the Barossa Valley. I learnt that the best way to get a sheep to go where you want is to stick a hand up its arse and push. And I found out that if you drink so much tawny port you can't remember falling off the railway platform, you'll most likely wake up with three stitches in your head.

With my bush hat well worn, I headed for the outback. I was always a little apprehensive when arriving anywhere new, but usually I'd head for the nearest bar, down a few pots and see what turned up. I'd be fine as long as I could handle my beer, speak as if fifty flies were trying to get in my mouth and always remember to let my intonation rise at the end of the sentence. No one was going to call me a *bleedin' pommie bastard*. It worked too. They thought I came from somewhere Queensland way. Then when I told them, they bought me a beer and said I was *probably all right . . . for a pom*.

My first encounter with an Aborigine was out near the Rock. He was an old fella we found sitting next to the dying embers of his fire, arms and legs scuffed silver with ash. He wore a piece of cloth tucked under his waist and a headband to tie back his white wavy hair. A bloke called Grenville was showing me round, an outback type, all knee-bones and leather. We'd drunk Carlton Draught together and talked about the Dreamtime – the spirit world beyond the physical dimension, where the Aborigines' ancestral heroes reside. The Dreamtime and its creatures once shaped the landscape they inhabit. And they passed their knowledge down the generations in the form of Dreamtime stories.

'The old fella here, see,' said Grenville, brisk and businesslike, 'there's a straight line linking him with the men who drew those paintings under the Rock thousands of years ago.'

'Does he live around here?' I asked.

'He lives with the land just like they did. He's on walkabout. Come to the Rock, a kind of pilgrimage. They call it a *bora* ground, a sort of sacred place. He'll stay a few days, maybe, then move on. Doesn't leave a trace.'

The two of them had nodded, but the Aborigine paid me scant notice, tapping his ashes with a stick as if wanting us to go. Only as we made to leave did his eyes meet mine. I remember seeing a sadness there, like an empty well, something I could never hope to understand. For the first time in my life, I'd come across a man my education told me was primitive, but whom I was now able to view with some respect.

'Shame is there aren't many left like him,' said Grenville. 'He'll be among the last.'

This time, as Vanella and I drive towards Alice Springs, dormant life is pushing up, green and hopeful, after some days of heavy rain. The desert skies are as huge and awesome as ever, but our eyes are drawn to the side of the highway. All we can see are beer cans – tinnies drained and lobbed out of the window with a belch. There must be thousands of them: some rusted over, the newest glinting blue or green in the sun.

This time, the river Todd is in full flood and packs of young Aborigines roam the puddled streets of Alice. They shamble up, offering us money with an outstretched hand and a baleful look. They want us to buy them their drink at the grog shop.

Maude Healey encountered her first Aborigine in 1906.

'Have you ever seen Cape gooseberries?' she asks us, dabbing the corner of her mouth with a napkin to catch the crumb I've been watching dance up and down for the last two minutes. 'They have furry leaves and grow in among the brush. They hang down from a kind of cloche. Oh, they make such delicious jam.'

She had been fruit-picking with her mother and two sisters, near their home on the Atherton Tableland, in northern Queensland.

'I remember as if it were yesterday,' she says brightly. 'We were down in a gully and I looked up and saw them coming along the horizon there, this Aboriginal family walking in a line.'

The man led the way. Tall, skinny and very dark, he held some spears and a few sticks in his hand. Next came the son, a young man of about nineteen. The mother brought up the rear, carrying a baby on her back in a basket woven from reeds, padded inside with soft grass like a nest. She supported its weight with a band tied around her head.

Mrs Healey lightly touches her temple and adjusts the pink headband that rests among her silvery curls.

'Mother beckoned that they should follow us to the house,' she says. 'While she went in, I stood staring. It struck me even then that they were different. They're so clever, the way they live on the land. Everything belongs to everyone, to the tribe not the individual. Then Mother came back with a silver coin, a half-crown or something, and she put it into the tiny palm of the baby in the basket. And those little brown fingers clasped so firmly around that coin.'

Mrs Healey's own hand is clenched tight.

'Now, how is your tea?' she asks. 'Do eat up the sandwiches.' Peering over, she nudges the plate towards Vanella, sliced white with the crusts removed.

'I tell you what I once tasted,' she says, with a dainty lick of the lips. 'One time, the blacks made camp just on the corner of our back yard, and they were cooking something there like a porcupine. Echidna, they call it. They put mud over them and cook them in the fire. They peel the mud and it keeps the spines, like a shell. Its insides were left in a ball. I remember putting my fingers in. I can taste it now, like chicken only richer.'

She had eaten witchetty grub with them too. They taste like brazil nuts, only they're soft and chewy.

'Of course, those tribes on the Tableland were once cannibals, you know,' she says, nodding. 'I remember there was one last survivor, a grizzled veteran named Kangaroo . . .'

Old man Kangaroo was always getting himself into trouble. His skinny shanks were scarred by the chains from the times he'd been apprehended for trespassing or stealing, when the constable would secure him to a huge log for days on end.

By the time Maude was old enough to go to school, Kangaroo used to roam the district with a handful of clubs and his blackened billy, terrorizing the maids when they were washing in the copper in the back yard. He'd lope up behind them and demand his *gibbet kia kia*, by which he meant food – a handout of tea, bread and sugar.

One afternoon, Maude's mother was sitting under the orange tree, waiting for her daughters to come home from school, when suddenly she glimpsed the figure of Kangaroo moving across the paddock towards them. The prospect of one of her little girls providing a meal for the erstwhile cannibal filled her with horror. She screamed and screamed, until the blacksmith came running from next door and went for the police. By the time a posse arrived, Kangaroo was menacing her mother with a wooden doll's chair. He wanted his *gibbet kia kia*. He was surrounded and quickly handcuffed, then locked up in the gaol until the judge came round.

At his trial, old man Kangaroo refused to take oath on the Bible. Instead he simply held up a lighted match, which he then blew out. The case ran for two weeks before the judge passed sentence. The last of the cannibals was to spend the rest of his days in prison, on Palm Island, off the coast to the south.

Mrs Healey lives in a retirement home now, with little more than the ticking of the clock for company.

~

We follow directions, making sure not to miss the turn by the Robertson Pie Shop. Then we head out across some bush country and we're speeding along a straight graded strip, scooting on over the corrugations. Kookaburras perch like sentries along the telegraph lines, seemingly unaware of the blanket of dust about to choke them. They are not going to be amused.

We reach a corner and the road dives down into the woods, which soon become dark and dense enough to be forest. Deeper and down we wind, losing the sky, twisting and turning, until at last we come to a clearing.

'This must be it.' The instructions on Vanella's piece of paper have run out, so we park and climb out.

For a moment, we both inhale. Beneath the shade of the gums, whose silvery fingers tangle high above, the air is cool. A wisp of mist still eludes the warmth of the afternoon sun shining through here and there in dappled pools. With a sudden clatter of wings, a band of rosellas breaks for the trees, flashing crimson. To our right we see some weatherboard cabins, painted white. We take the path opposite to a house with a corrugated roof, where a red-brick chimney looks as if it once grew up the outside. We hear a tunkling sound and five pale goaty faces look up, munching, to watch us struggle with the gate latch.

Rae meets us at the fly-screen, sleeves rolled, her hands held up wet and raw.

'Hello,' she says, 'I thought you weren't coming,' and her boyish features crease into a generous smile. 'I'm afraid I can't shake hands, I'm making tamarillo chutney.'

In the sun-room, her armchair is padded with cushions and a small mattress lies by the fire. Usha, a black and grey, patchy old thing, musters up a few barks before wagging us round an arthritic welcome.

While Rae cleans up, we stand admiring the view through a gap in the trees. It's as if we're looking down from an aeroplane. We can see what seems to be another land, far away – gently undulating farm country, lush and green, and in the distance, a curling shoreline with the surf just visible at the ocean's edge.

Rae has replaced her apron with an old hand-knitted sleeveless sweater. Practicality before fashion, she wears a simple crew-neck underneath, tracksuit bottoms and woolly slippers to warm her feet. She comes and points out where Bass landed when he first ventured inland with Flinders. Then there's Port Kembla, and we can just pick out a glint of metallic sun, the waters of Lake Illawarra. Settling into her chair, Rae breathes out the sigh of someone who's been on the go all day. She sits with her back straight, relaxed and easy, absently trying to tidy her short, tousled hair. I would think she cuts it herself. With this and a splendid Roman nose, her appearance is almost tomboyish.

Rae is ninety-one now and has lived on the edge of Jamberoo Mountain for more than fifty years. She came walking up this way one Easter with her husband, Pete. There were no buildings here then, just a chimney. The house had been made of cedar and the people who owned the place had sold it for the wood.

She points to a picture on the wall, an accomplished watercolour of a solitary chimney-stack.

'You bought a chimney?'

'And seventy-five acres, mostly wooded. You'd have come through it on the way down.'

Rae acquired the land on impulse while Pete was away in the war. He wrote back that it sounded lovely, but how on earth were they going to make a living?

'We used to look at each other and say we were happiest in the country,' says Rae.

'That's what we always say!' we reply in unison.

'It's the air, you know.'

'There's such a difference. The air's so filthy in cities. Trouble is, you get used to it. You don't notice till you go away.'

'Sydney's terrible these days,' Rae says.

'We think Sydney's clean, compared with London.'

Rae folds her arms and smiles. A light dances in her eye as she examines us, each in turn. 'It's hard to give up the security, isn't it? Pete and I both had accountancy jobs.'

They had worked in Sydney but always did their best to get away. They were keen bush-walkers and at weekends they'd be off exploring the Blue Mountains and the country beyond, using only a compass and a rough sketch-map. Often they'd return on Monday morning, without much sleep, to catch the first ferry across the harbour. A quick change and they could still be in time for work.

We might be kindred spirits. Vanella and I used to do the same kind of thing, away walking the hills. All this time I've lived in the city, I've never really felt at home. Some instinct keeps tugging away. I need to live where there is more space, where I can breathe some good old-fashioned air, away from the fumes and the traffic. It used to drive me mad. How many hours, I wonder, has mankind spent sitting in a traffic jam? But it's tricky, because I'm still attracted by the bright lights. And Vanella's a London girl, of course. She'll deny it, but I think her heart pulls the other way. Whenever we talk it through, we usually end up at the same question, Pete's question.

Rae had the idea of letting holiday cabins. When Pete came home, he erected some Army tents while they rebuilt the house up against the chimney. Then the cabins were finished and people came to stay – bush-walkers, artists, jaded city-dwellers who needed to escape to the tranquillity of the mountain. So they got by and lived happily until Pete died in '74, when Rae simply carried on. She couldn't possibly leave. The cabins are still booked up through next year. She's seen five generations of those first families who came to stay.

I can't believe how good she looks. The life of Jamberoo has certainly treated her well. Much of her day is spent out of doors. She grows her own vegetables. Until recently, she bred chooks for their eggs, but the foxes took them. She's kept goats since the early days and she's still up at five most mornings for the milking. Goat's milk is more beneficial than cow's, she reminds us.

Of course, the years have dealt her a few wrinkles, but Rae's healthy, tanned face has somehow never lost the freshness of youth. She remains as young as she feels. When she walks she's comfortable and easy, as if she can happily stride off through the woods whenever she pleases. Part of the land up the mountain has now been made a reserve for its rare flora and fauna. Rae used to take the children on nature trails. She knows every inch of the forest.

'To keep an interest is a great thing,' she says, by way of explanation. 'I'm still in touch with the Sydney Bush-walkers. Sometimes, you know, I sit here and walk the routes we took in my mind. You have to be as active as you can. A lot of my friends reached seventy and decided they couldn't be bothered. I work with the animals too. I talk to them a lot.'

We smile, but she's serious. Rae may live alone, but she's never lonely.

'I had three cows once,' she tells us. 'Two went down there to the milking herds and the other went to a herd over the mountain, about thirty miles away. Within a fortnight she was home. It took her two days. The man who came for her looked her in the eye and said, "Jeez, Sandy, how did you know to turn right at the Robertson Pie Shop?"'

The second time Sandy went away, Rae left the gate open just in case. Then one day she was out there mooing. She couldn't give up the enchanted life of Jamberoo and Rae had to buy her back.

'Sandy and I are together now until one of us dies,' she says contentedly.

I see Rae's nose twitch and she checks to see if we've noticed. I pretend not. It's Usha, who has eaten cake with us and is snoozing peacefully by the fire. The old girl just let go the most awful smell.

Vanella seems withdrawn as we roll away down the mountain.

'Strange fish,' she eventually says.

'What fish?'

'Didn't you find her a little distant?'

'Not especially. I liked her. Great place to live.'

'We didn't kiss her goodbye, did we? We normally would. Something made me hold back.'

'She's just very independent, that's all.'

'Bit too much, maybe.'

'I reckon she's got life pretty well sussed. Self-sufficient. At one with nature. All her animals to talk to. What else does she need?'

'Why do people make friends with animals?'

'There aren't many humans back there to make friends with.'

'Exactly.'

'You've got her down as a loner, haven't you? She did say a neighbour came to help with the milking sometimes.'

'I couldn't do without people.'

'Her people come and go. In the cabins.'

'But she doesn't seem to need anyone.'

'That's OK.'

'Is it? I find it a bit sad.'

'Maybe that's the difference between you and me.'

'Hmm . . .' she says. 'I'd like to live in the country one day. I would, really . . . But how would we make a living?'

~

We sleep in a house by the sea. In the morning, we collect spiral shells on the beach, but only the perfect ones. Their colours are Liberty-print dyes where the pattern has run. I'm absorbed, squinting to see if there's any trace of whoever used to live inside. Vanella is standing, watching three young lads in wetsuits trying to catch the next wave. I glance up and see her eyes are filled with tears.

'What's the matter?'

She looks at me, biting her lip.

'What is it?'

'I'm sorry,' she says, looking back out to sea. 'It's my mum. I can't tell you how much I miss her.'

She heaves a painful sigh and I put my arm around her and squeeze.

'Oh, Nella, I'm sorry. Was it me wittering on about my dad?'

'No . . . I don't know. It's only sometimes . . .'

I say nothing, as we watch another wave crash and foam.

'. . . I just wish I could see her again,' she whispers.

~

We cross a sparsely populated, grassy plateau where the windpumps rest idle and the farm buildings have rusted roofs. By the afternoon, we arrive in Canberra, a country town still pretending to be a capital city.

We find a quiet street and a modest bungalow. A man with a head of white hair greets us, his silver-rimmed glasses sitting conspicuously askew a pink complexion. He wears a pale blue shirt buttoned at the wrists, and a singlet underneath.

What was once his dining-room has become an overflow work space. The table is strewn with paper, shelves packed tight with books, titles such as *The Solid Earth* and *Quantum Reality*. There's a globe, a bush hat, framed pictures of Aboriginal rock paintings. It all seems deceptively normal for one who, in his time, has unleashed the hidden forces of the universe.

Mark Oliphant was born in a sleepy South Australian town. A fresh-faced youth, he won a scholarship to Cambridge, where he studied with Ernest Rutherford, the so-called father of radioactivity. Rutherford it was who discovered the nucleus. The two men worked together for ten years at the Cavendish Laboratory until Rutherford's death.

At the outbreak of war, Oliphant became one of an élite chosen to develop a technological advantage over Hitler. His first task was to design a radar system small enough to be carried by aircraft. He invented the magnetron, which used mirrors to create extremely short wavelengths. The same technology can be found today in the gadget we call the microwave oven.

'Oh for a dollar for every one of those,' says Sir Mark, with a wry smile.

'Uranium,' he's then explaining, '. . . uranium has two isotopes, one with a mass 238 times that of hydrogen, the other 235 times that of hydrogen. Now the one you want for a nuclear weapon is the 235. Unfortunately, that's only .7 per cent of natural uranium.'

I'm trying hard to concentrate. Nuclear physics was never my strong subject.

'Devising techniques to separate the isotopes was very difficult,' he recalls. 'We always hoped it would prove impossible. We hoped it just wouldn't work, this idea of fission.'

Fission. Now that, I do know, is the splitting of the atom.

Fission was first detected in Germany in 1937, by a man named Hahn who had worked with Rutherford in Montreal. When the French discovered that neutrons were released in the fission process, it became clear that a chain reaction would result and the possibility arose of a power source, and a bomb.

Oliphant had two scientists working with him in his laboratory – Rudolf Peierls and Otto Frisch. As German émigrés, they weren't allowed to have anything to do with the secret radar project. But they wanted to contribute to the war effort, so set to work calculating the feasibility of an atomic bomb. Einstein once had a go and concluded that it would be so heavy it would need to be delivered by warship. Peierls and Frisch showed that if isotopes with a mass of 235 could be separated in quantities of about ten kilograms, spontaneous fission would occur and an enormous output of energy.

With an automatic hand, Sir Mark strokes the white cat lying curled in his lap. I like him at once. I like the way he talks. He's affable, candid. His eyes are sure. They shine, a striking Scandinavian blue.

'We were dead scared,' he says, 'because we were told by the secret services that Hitler was working on the same idea. And we knew his people were scientists of the top rank.'

'So it became a race?'

'Fortunately they turned the wrong corner. The Germans went after the slow neutron reaction, whereas we concentrated on the fast reaction.'

The rest is history. When the Japanese invaded Pearl Harbor and the Americans entered the war, the Manhattan Project was set up in the wilds of New Mexico under the command of General Groves. Mark Oliphant was invited to join the team headed by Robert Oppenheimer out at Los Alamos. His job was to produce the isotopes, a boring and often frustrating process for a pure scientist. But by that time it was merely a question of building the engine.

They had all the numbers worked out. The optimum height to explode the bomb had been calculated before the first test. They knew precisely what the resulting devastation would be. After the test, the entire project passed into the hands of the military and the politicians. The scientists who had done the work had no say whatsoever. A group of them got together and sent a memorandum to President Roosevelt, expressing their fears. They urged him not to use the bomb against civilian targets. Instead they should make a demonstration of the great power that was now in the hands of the Allies. They could blast a munitions works out of existence, or blow the top off Mount Fuji. They thought that might have an interesting effect on the Japanese psyche. But it was to no avail.

When he heard the news on 6 August 1945, Mark Oliphant was sad. He realized the world would never be the same.

I think you know when you're in the company of greatness. Conversation is made easy. There's intelligence without the slightest intellectual arrogance. And the blinding good sense of what's said seems so obvious.

Science has been our theme, but we end up talking about the environment. When it comes to the mess mankind is making, I feel as powerless as anyone. I, too, wonder if our voracious consumption and its consequences won't be our eventual undoing. I ask Sir Mark if he's optimistic. Could technology yet solve our problems?

'I *know*,' he says emphatically, 'I know that technology can provide the answer, but it isn't being used by any country.'

'Why not?'

'Simply because of money. We live in an age when money is the dominant factor. The mega-corporations, centred mainly in America and Japan, really rule the world. Governments don't. They just have to say yes when these corporations want to do things. Money is everything now, in the eyes of government. Profit is the motive for doing anything. It's a crazy world we live in. I don't know where it's going to end. We've dug a deep hole for ourselves as a result of our cleverness.'

Sir Mark turns to gaze out of the window at the rain falling steadily on the patio.

'I'm very pessimistic,' he says. 'I see no sign of acceptance of what are facts by governments around the world. The world's energy resources will run out in time. Of that there is no doubt. So I've been trying to persuade our government here to develop a policy of solar energy. Australia has the lowest rainfall and the most sunshine of any continental area. You know, it's easily shown that if the Simpson Desert in South Australia were covered with solar receptors, you could provide all the electrical energy for the whole world.'

There is a brief silence while this idea sinks in.

'Wow,' says Vanella.

'That's a staggering thought.'

'You don't realize how much energy reaches us from the sun,' Sir Mark says, with a smile. 'On one square metre you can get about one kilowatt, when the sun is overhead at its highest intensity. That means that on a square kilometre, which is not a very big area, there could be 10,000 kilowatts being deposited – the equivalent of a fair-sized power station.'

'What?'

'So why doesn't the Australian government decide it's going to become an energy supplier?'

'And why haven't we all converted to solar power?'

'Because government is like industry,' Sir Mark replies. 'Unless it's going to yield a profit tomorrow, they're not interested. Any kind of long-term approach is anathema to practically all governments now. They take a political view. For instance, the environmental movement here has been trying to preserve areas of forest in southern New South Wales. But the government won't take action to stop the felling, for economic reasons. And it's not as if they are chopping them down for timber. They're sending them to Japan as woodchip.'

God, I love this man – his brain. It's the way he has everything thought through. He has a fundamental respect for the phenomenon of life that exists on earth. He sees the planet as a natural working engine and understands completely how it works. He knows how easily our precious balance can be destroyed. And he's worked out how we might go about our business more efficiently.

'Did you know that, in Australia, for every hundred people there are a hundred and forty cattle? They're grown for meat, of course. But one acre of land will produce ten pounds of protein as wool, sixty pounds of protein as meat, and six hundred pounds of protein as soya bean. It's quite clear which way we've got to go if we're to tolerate a rapidly expanding global population.'

He's also keen on the use of hydrogen as an energy source.

'The ideal way to produce hydrogen is from solar energy,' he reasons. 'The Germans have built motor cars which run on hydrogen. And the Russians managed to produce a hydrogen-powered aeroplane.'

I'm feeling quite invigorated by the Oliphant plan to save the world. We could end our dependence on fossil fuels. Imagine. Using the sun as our prime energy source, we might keep going for another millennium or two. We'd put climate change on hold, slow down global warming. We could grow soya protein instead of beef. And we might just get by.

But Sir Mark is already shaking his head. The mega-corporations, the politicians, it wouldn't suit them. Again, he's probably right. I can think of quite a few interests it wouldn't serve.

Sir Mark is agnostic. He's thought that one through too. He sees no proof that God exists, as such. It's down to us. But, ultimately, he has little faith in man.

'It's a strange world,' he says. 'It's been transformed by science into a travesty of what it ought to be. The results of our scientific endeavours have been devastating. But it is man who exterminates and destroys. Australians believe in the biblical idea of God having created man to be dominant, and, by God, they exercise that dominance. Anything that moves is shot.'

Sir Mark lifts his eyes in a small gesture of desperation and the cat, deciding it would rather be elsewhere, hops down for a stretch.

'I'm a convinced environmentalist,' he says. 'In this country, we lose at least three hundred species of animals and birds every year.'

Looking glum, he brushes the fur from his trousers.

'You know, when I was governor of South Australia, which I was only for five or six years, I used to talk to the Aboriginal elders. They used to say to me, "We know our culture is finished. All our boys and girls want are their transistor radios and televisions, just like anyone else."'

Sir Mark sighs and looks across.

'Everything, it's all being killed off.'

~

Back at Red Hill, one evening my father produces a cardboard box and starts talking about wills and which piece of furniture is which. I listen carefully but I don't really want to know and quickly forget the detail of what's said. He will be seventy this year.

Next day, we take a walk down on the beach at Shoreham, just the two of us. It being a bright Thursday morning, we are quite alone as we clamber over the rocks and leave our prints across the sand. He's always liked to walk. We used to leave Mum at home on Sunday afternoons, wander up Cuttlehurst and back down through the woods. I liked it best in winter, when the light was closing in and the rooks cawing.

We talk. Dad tells me about his work. He always talks about that first. He's still doing a bit, keeping himself busy. Then, after a pause, he asks how Mum is. They don't talk any more. Mum finds it too painful. She asked me to see if he still has the ring. She gave it back when he left. But now she's not sure she doesn't want it, just to keep.

Dad hesitates, then says he doesn't know what he's done with it. I give him a puzzled look, which he doesn't catch. I wonder. Maybe he just threw it in the sea one day. It's over now, for better or worse. He's had to start again.

So then I try to explain how we want to make a different life when we get back – more modest, more time. Vanella is beginning to talk about kids and I'm going, 'Yeah, some time,' a mixture of positive and casual. 'We shouldn't leave it too late, you know,' she says.

Dad tells me about his work on the family tree. He's been going back, tracing our ancestors. He has got as far as one John Jackson of Low Town, Ackworth, near Pontefract – my great-great-great-great-grandfather. Born in 1759, he was a tanner by trade. Dad seems to have taken the task upon himself, as if it's his duty. Like most families, we're spread all over now.

'And I think I'm going to write a book,' he suddenly says, as we turn back along the beach.

I laugh at the irony of it. 'Really? What about?'

'I'm going to tell the story, the early history of the family. About William Michael, he was the tea merchant, you know. Then the time of the mill, the different generations, and all about your grandpa. It's something I want to do. For my grandchildren. So they know their heritage.'

'That's a lovely idea.'

And so I think about the Dreamtime, and how experience is handed down, old to young. We must all pass on whatever we can to those who come after us. Somehow.

I hate flying. I enjoy the thrill of take-off, the surge of power and the lift. And it's great when a captain knows how to land a plane sweet. You still get them sometimes. But I hate being up there, thinking about the fact that I'm at 35,000 feet, supported only by metal, kerosene and a little elementary physics.

Dad once took me up in a Cessna. He still had his pilot's licence and used to fly all over Yorkshire. I was absolutely terrified, especially when he let go the controls and shouted, 'She's yours.'

We just said goodbye. I kiss him these days. Like when I was a boy.

We're headed out across the Pacific, engines throttled back to the sound of rushing air. Cabin lights are down and the video screen flickering. No turbulence tonight. I move back a few rows so I can sprawl out later to sleep. I slot a tape in the Walkman and wrap myself in the music.

I'm on my own in the dark. And I'm crying. I don't know why exactly. But I can't stop. I just have to let it out. I cry and cry.

17

New World Tales

This is some jet lag. Two mornings now, we're like dopey adolescents. Can't move. Don't want to. Just press the remote.

Boof. '. . . *Nothing relieves unwanted back pain faster . . .*' Boof. '*Okaay, here we go. Your first question, Jim. What do Americans prefer to do more than anything else? Jim, whadder you think?*' '*Um . . . Watch TV?*' '*I'm sorry. No. Janice, can you tell me?*' '*Er . . . Have sex?*' '*Woo hoo hoo. Well, she could be right, couldn't she? Woo hoo. No, the real answer is EAT! We like to eat, don't we, folks?*' Boof. '. . . *this beeeautiful new fireplace elegantly styled on an attractive curved base. And I'm going to give Stacey the first bid . . .*' Boof. '. . . *Which way'd they go? Did ya see how many?*' '*There's three of them. Round the back. Riko's got a gun. Man, he's crazy.*' '*Stay here. This ain't gonna be pretty . . . BAM . . . BAM-ADA-BAM . . . BAM BAM . . .*' Boof. '. . . *Bob, at nine forty-five this morning the gunman entered the office block behind me by the main lobby and rode the elevator to the sixteenth floor where he opened fire with a semi-automatic weapon. Eye-witnesses say he was apprehended by police after several minutes of gunfire. The death toll now stands at five . . .*' Boof.

So Wednesday afternoon, we're in a movie – hire-car, air-con, shades. We're cool. We ease into Santa Monica Boulevard and pull up at the lights. WALK – DON'T WALK. You don't walk round here, you gotta have wheels. Or Day-Glo stripes on your roller-blades. The cops pull up alongside. They serve, protect and chew gum. I don't want to be in their movie. I don't fancy the car chase.

We head for the Hills and roll up a broad avenue lined with pencil-thin palms, where red-brick houses give way to stucco-fronted mansions, sprinklers leaning back and forth across the lawns. We're looking for a low white picket fence. We park beside a small tidy bungalow. It must be the only fence in Beverly Hills without a sign that warns 'Armed Response'. In the shade of the pines, the air is sweet. Ruth, the housekeeper, lets us in, through a dining-room with a large panelled bar, into the lounge where two cats eye us from beige armchairs. To the right, an alcove, his study – it's like a bunker, dark and intimate, lined with old books. There's a swivel chair, an electric typewriter and two Anglepoise lamps cocked ready.

'Hello, hello,' calls a voice, a very English voice, and a stout figure enters with a flourish and shakes us both firmly by the hand. He's dressed gentlemen's casual in outmoded cotton. Sinking into the soft velour of his chair, he takes a lusty swig from a glass of white wine then beams from ear to ear. Mr Charles Bennett has been writing movies since Westwood really was a village.

As a young man he trod the boards, performing Shakespeare two and sometimes three times a day, in theatres all over England.

'Look there,' he says, pointing to a framed bill-poster. 'You'll see my name above John Gielgud's, playing Cassius at the Apollo. Ha ha!' He laughs with boyish glee and still enunciates like a true Thespian.

He later turned his hand to writing plays. *Blackmail*, an early piece starring Tallulah Bankhead, was seen in the West End one night by a short fat film director who loved the story so much he persuaded British International Pictures to buy it. The year was 1928, and the little fat man Alfred Hitchcock. He first shot *Blackmail* as a silent movie, but talkies were just coming in so he begged them to let him shoot the dialogue scenes again. He closed the set and, without the studio bosses knowing, reshot the whole film. *Blackmail* became the first full-length talkie made in Europe, and a huge success.

'I wrote eight pictures for Hitch,' says Bennett. '*Hit*ch' he goes, '*Hit*ch', with the emphasis up front and I note that particularly English curiosity, the *w*roll of the R.

'. . . I wrote *The Thirty-Nine Steps*, I wrote *Sabotage*, I wrote *Secret Agent*,' he says. 'Oh, there were so many, and Hitch and I became the closest of possible friends. We used to go to St Moritz together, he and his wife, Alma, and me and my wife, Maggie. We'd go for Christmas and New Year. I would ski, and Maggie would ski, and Alma would ski, and Hitch would sit at the bar in the Palace Hotel. Ha ha! Delightful!'

Bennett followed his friend to Hollywood and was signed by Universal Pictures to write screenplays for what was then a considerable salary.

'A thousand dollars a week,' he confides. 'And I can tell you how much that was. You could buy a dry martini at the Brown Derby, which was tops, for only a quarter!'

They were carefree days. He wrote picture after picture. He teamed up with Hitch again for *Foreign Correspondent* and made four films with Cecil B. de Mille.

'How do you go about writing a film?' I wonder.

'Why, you need a story,' he exclaims, as if it's obvious.

'Where do they come from?'

'Out of here.' He taps a smooth forehead. 'Imagination. I have masses of ideas. I jot them all down, though frequently never use them.'

'And then what?'

'Look, what is a film? It's a beginning, a middle and an end. And if it mounts all the way to a climax, then you've got a story. I remember one time de Mille wanted to make a picture called *Reap the Wild Wind*, with John Wayne. They'd got a sort of story but it was awful, so I shaped the whole thing into a good one and de Mille adored me from then on. The lovely thing was the ending.'

Bennett widens his eyes, holding us in his power for an instant, before continuing.

'We knew exactly where we were going,' he says, 'but we hadn't got the end. I remember de Mille in his office saying, "We haven't got the end. We've got to have a sensational end. Charles, what are you going to do?" I said I didn't know. I had a very good writer working with me called Alan le May, but he had no ideas either. So I came home and in my bath the next morning – I was actually in the bath – I thought up the underwater fight with the giant squid. The following day de Mille said, "Well, gentlemen, have we got the end?" He turned to Alan, "Got the end, Alan?" "Sorry. No, nothing." He turned to me and, to his great surprise, I said I had. So I played out the entire scene. I played both actors, I played John Wayne, I played the giant squid with its tentacles and everything. It took me twenty minutes and, having been an actor, I must say I did a pretty good job. When I'd finished, there was dead silence for about half a minute, with de Mille just sitting there, thinking. Then he said, "Yes, Charles . . . In Technicolor!"'

I'm beginning to realize Charles Bennett already has his life and times condensed to a series of well-rehearsed tales. His maxim, he reveals, is that a story has to be a good one, otherwise it flops! It also helps, I reckon, if it features a famous name or two. We hear about the time he fell in love with Gertrude Lawrence, sharing his apple with her at the age of eleven.

He regales us with more Hitchcock: the practical jokes, though none of the vicious ones. He remembers Hitch once arrived at his birthday party with a man bearing a crate, a present consisting of five hundred pairs of kippers . . . and a brush and crumb tray.

'Ha ha! That was Hitch,' he says, and for a moment we lose Charles Bennett to a bout of the giggles.

'That bar has seen more famous people than any other in the world,' he then declares. 'I've pretty well known them all. They all used to come here, particularly the English . . . Charles Laughton, you know. And I've been back and forth. Howard Hughes once rented the house and took care of my pets. One time I was away for eighteen months and I had to have a tenant . . .'

We are held again, in suspense.

'Bugsy Siegel!' he cries, and we can't help laughing at his exuberance. 'And a delightful man by the way. Charming, charming. Very good-looking. We had dinner together when I got back . . . Perfectly charming. It never crossed your mind you were with the biggest bloody murderer ever. Ha ha!'

But he hates Los Angeles. Or so he says.

'It's so dog-eat-dog. If it wasn't for the fact that I own this house and my living is here, I'd be right out of it back to England.'

He misses the bluebells in spring. But I'm not absolutely convinced, for all the faraway look in his eye. He's been missing them nearly sixty years. He'll soon be ninety-four. He could never give up this life among the stars.

'Maybe a lucky thing has happened,' he says brightly. 'Carrie Fisher – you know, Debbie Reynolds's daughter – she's become my neighbour. She has the house behind me, six acres and a gate into my garden. And she's decided I'm her close friend. She comes down here and sits on the floor. Delightful person! Her friends are people like Meryl Streep. I don't like using people but I'm going to. The best thing is to get a star saying, "I want to do that picture", and the whole thing will fall miraculously into place. Funny industry, believe me. You see, I've got a new version of *Blackmail*, completely rewritten, up to date. It takes place in Washington. *Blackmail* was one of those stories. It would still have been good if it had been told in Timbuktu.'

Bennett leans forward and points a finger at our glasses. We've been sipping mouthwash disguised as root beer, so we opt for the white wine.

'Ruth!' he shouts, then shifts himself and gets to his feet. 'She's probably asleep. I'll go.'

Vanella and I whisper while he's away. One thing still troubles me. When we outsiders come to the States, fed on a rich diet of Hollywood, we find life is just like it is on the screen. That must be why it's so alluring. Everything is familiar. Each way we turn, we're in some movie. So how is it for Americans themselves? Can they see the difference between fantasy and reality?

'When they go to the movies, most of them think what they see is for real,' says Charles Bennett, setting down the drinks. 'Take Ruth, for example. Quite recently I found out that she actually believed what she saw on screen really happens. It never crossed her mind that these things have to be written. And I should think that applies to about seventy per cent of audiences.'

'But isn't this dangerous, if they think they're looking through a window on the world? What if everyone wants to be Arnold Schwarzenegger?'

'I don't know about that. You're digging too deep for me there,' Bennett says, clearing his throat with unnecessary exaggeration. 'I'm only a writer, you know. What matters, really, is if it's entertaining.'

~

We make camp close by the canyon and spend our days on the trail of the Navajo. We travel through familiar scenery, mile after mile of scorched plain, towering buttes and red rock mesas. It's a different movie, this one, but we've seen it a hundred times. Now and again we pull over and climb out of the little bubble of air-con that conveniently shields us from harsh reality. We stand and gaze awhile, savaged by the heat, exposed to a raw silence. This sure is big country. It's a land defined by distance, cliffs tall as any mountain reduced to a ridge of purple shadow. I wouldn't walk it. This is country best travelled on horseback.

We pass communities with names like Rough Rock and Many Farms, each with a giant silver water tank on stilts. In the wide, barren spaces between, we occasionally see a few modern prefabs erected beside a circular *hogan*, the traditional Navajo dwelling made of stout timbers and thick red mud. Sometimes an old *hogan* stands alone, left to collapse and decay since its owner died.

We ask around, and every place we go we hear the same story. The

Native Americans who live in Canyon de Chelly say they're going to want money before anyone tells us anything. Maybe four hundred bucks. Elsewhere, we hear that a journalist recently paid out two thousand to get a story. They say they've been exploited one too many times. The story is the Navajo aren't talking any more.

Then we find Howard. He's waiting for his lunch at the Window Rock Senior Citizens Center, where the old timers sit around trestle-tables in their baseball caps. The women, in full skirts and sweatshirt tops, huddle gossiping in a corner. They turn to greet us with curious smiles. Lunch smells like overcooked meat and cabbage.

Howard McKinley is the oldest among them; well in his nineties, they say. He's almost blind, one eye all but closed. He hears us, squaring up with that unseeing look blind folk have.

'The Navajo way used to be to tell a story,' he says, his voice as dry as sandpaper. 'Long time ago, you'd get a storyteller and he'd talk to you all night, all day and another night, as long as you had sommin' t' eat. These days, no one stops to listen. They wanna watch television. Or they don't have time. They gotta go. They've become slaves to their watch. Time means work. Work means money.'

Howard rests, passive, like he's meditating. He looks Indian, but his face is pale. He has white man's blood in his veins. His grandfather McKinley, an Englishman, used to run a trading-post. His mother was a Navajo girl. So Howard can see both sides.

'I was born out there in the sand dunes,' he grates, vaguely pointing a crooked finger. 'My mother was herding sheep over at Church Rock, New Mexico, other side of Fort Wingate. Those days, the women used to get down from their horse, have a baby, get up and keep going.'

Howard's maternal grandfather was a medicine man. Grey Water was his name and he taught his little grandson the Navajo way.

'He taught me some philosophy,' Howard says, faltering as he collects his thoughts. 'The theme of his subject was "Fit yourself for survival", somewhat like Socrates once say. The only way you do that is get up early in the morning. He told that from the time you begin to walk, you learn survival activities. You don't run just for joggin', like they do now. The horses are way over the hill, so you take a little run, bring those horses back 'cause we're going to haul wood or we're going to haul water today. And when you haul wood, you don't look for sticks. Sharpen your axe and look for the big pieces you can pull behind the wagon. And then you learn to plough and develop the land. You learn to herd sheep and care for them so the coyotes or the wild cats don't get them. You take them every day to where there's new pasture and water. And as you grow to be a young man, you process the crops. If you take good care of the sheep, you'll earn some of 'em, and some horses, that you can use for yourself. You gotta work for it, mind. And then, when you're successful at raising crops and have a large herd, that's when you're an honourable, reputable Navajo. You're not a beggar or a hobo. And if somebody comes and they're thirsty or hungry, you are ready to serve them with water or sommin' t' eat. That's what's called a genuine Navajo.'

Genuine sounds like Clementine, the way Howard drawls it. He nods, gives his straw hat a nudge and slaps both knees a few times before resting still once more. I scrutinize his face more closely. The lines there are carved dark and deep. A muscle flickers, as if he senses I'm watching. He draws breath.

'Early on I learnt what white people call a pillar of life,' he says. Then he halts again and we have to encourage him. '. . . The philosophy of life of the Navajo is that you cannot get something for nothing. You have to work for everything, become a self-sustaining individual who can provide a livelihood for your people.'

He tells us Grey Water had the power to cure illness and provide protection from the forces of evil. He would perform lengthy ceremonies which took years to perfect, using sage brush, juniper leaves, belladonna and milkweed. He carried a pouch of corn pollen and wore turquoise and coral beads. He sang chantways and knew the Blessingway rites. Through his work he strove always to maintain *hozho*. *Hozho* means beauty, peace, happiness and harmony: the good things of life maintained in perfect balance. *Hozho* is essential to the Navajo way. They don't believe in life after death. Now is the important time, they say, the only time we know.

I ask Howard how this harmony is achieved.

'It is the whole religious background,' he says. 'There's a prayer, an old chant that begins this way.' And he raises his head, both eyes closed now, one eyelid trembling:

'I am a son of Changing Woman,
I am a son of the First Woman,
I will walk in peace with my feet,

I will walk in peace with my legs,
I will walk in peace with my healthy body,
I will walk among people that are kind and
compassionate,
I will walk in peace and health with my
surroundings.'

'That's very beautiful,' Vanella says softly.

'People call this a Blessingway,' he says. 'But I interpret it as the way of peace and tranquillity.'

He tilts his head, looking thoughtful. 'Now you can tell me something. What do you know of the story of the Navajo?'

'Only a little.'

'Well, in the Navajo tongue they call themselves *diné*, which means "the people". Way back in time, they were nomads who crossed the Bering Strait from Mongolia and came to settle in the far north-west . . .'

I quickly scan the room and see their moonish, weatherbeaten old faces. He's right. They've travelled all the way from Central Asia.

By the sixteenth century, they had migrated south and developed their agricultural skill, growing corn. Then the Spaniards came, bringing livestock. The Navajo resisted their intrusion, but eventually learnt to be shepherds, to ride horses and weave rugs. They cultivated a way of life. Then followed a time of cowboys and Indians, before other white men came whose job it was to starve and suppress them. Their crops were destroyed, their sheep stolen or killed. The people were rounded up, dispossessed of their land. They were forced to leave the tribal ground and walk three hundred miles across the hot open plains to Fort Sumner. There, they were kept for more than two years until finally they signed a piece of paper promising not to fight any more and acknowledging a few straight lines ruled on a map.

Those who survived walked all the way back home.

We find our medicine man in the end. One day, I'm thumbing through a book of portraits depicting Navajo life and I come across a photograph of an elder. His long grey hair is tied in a single plait. 'Adilthdoney Begay, Indian Wells,' it says underneath. So we sleuth around and discover he's still alive. I call his grandson, Richard, and after a couple of days he relays the news. The medicine man says he'll talk.

Richard is community service co-ordinator out at Indian Wells, a clutch of buildings in a desolate valley close by the Hopi reservation. We meet in his office, the kind of pre-fab cabin you might see on a building site. But there's a problem.

'I said to my grandpa,' says Richard, '"I don't know what kind of questions, but I'm sure they won't be asking anything 'bout religion."'

He throws me a meaningful glance and I raise an eyebrow.

'No?' I ask.

'I don't think he'll tell you anything like that.'

We can only see. His grandfather is staying with Richard's aunt. He takes us there in his pick-up, a monster dead-beat Ford with a strip of window along the back of the cab and an astonishing number of flies, crawling, buzzing, all hot and drowsy inside.

He's a good guy, Richard: in his thirties, with a round face, a broad smile and shiny black hair all the way from Mongolia. He is curious to know how people live in other countries we've been to. He says it's time the Navajo decided which direction to go, to return to more traditional ways or stand up for themselves in modern-day America.

'Everything changed in the sixties,' he tells us. 'When convenience food came in, they gave up the hard life of the past. A whole generation didn't think to pass on anything of the old ways. Now the kids are more interested in Nintendo, baseball and whatever they find at the supermarket.'

They don't even bother to learn their own language. Although Richard and others like him talk about how to keep the culture alive, there are always more pressing needs. Indian Wells, his patch, is some twenty miles by twenty. And it's poor. Ninety-five per cent of people still live out on the land; seventy per cent have no electricity. How far they can extend the power lines seems always to be the biggest debate. But the real trouble, he believes, is the lack of any sense of responsibility. They've become too dependent, living on hand outs from the federal government.

'See that cornfield?' he says. We're away on to a rocky dirt-track and he's pointing to a piece of dry scrub with an apology for a wire fence round it. 'That land belonged to my grandmother. They used to till it by hand and raise crops, but none of the young ones want to do that any more.'

I'm half expecting to see a wigwam, with horses tethered and smoke curling from an open fire; or at very least a *hogan*. But as we bump and roll up the hillside, some kind of junk-yard comes into view: a shambles of lean-tos and tumbledown shacks, rusty autos without wheels or doors, the front half only of a silver trailer caravan. Centre stage stands a one-storey house, fashioned from sections of assorted material, planks and plasterboard, some painted, some weathering with age.

Richard suggests we stay in the pick-up while he goes in. So we melt in the heat, still amazed by the number of flies. We listen to a lively exchange between various Navajo voices, wondering what it can all mean. Then the door creaks open and the medicine man emerges, clutching a red plastic fly-swat by its wire handle. He's come to take a look at us. So we jump out. The Navajo handshake, we've read, is a light touch only, but our desire to be culturally aware is scotched by his firm grip. He doesn't speak much English and stands around looking perplexed, until Richard appears with fold-down chairs to place under the canopy that makes do as a front porch.

The old man sure likes turquoise. The silver band of his broad-brimmed Stetson is inlaid, bright blue. A stone dangles from each of his ears, smooth as a bean, tied through the lobe with a thread of fresh white cotton. And a splendidly adorned necklace is set off by the boldness of his shirt, which is patterned in pink, purple and matching turquoise.

Richard grins. 'It's his Garth Brooks shirt. It was sent by my aunt, from Houston.'

It so happens that he is ninety-six today. So we wish him a happy birthday, but he says he won't be doing much to celebrate.

'How old are you?' he then asks, brusquely.

'I'll be thirty-eight in three days' time,' I say.

'You're just a kid,' he scoffs. Then he smiles and the lines crinkle softly around his eyes. They are gentle and warm, feminine eyes. 'I got grandchildren all over,' he says, gazing out across the land, pointing far and wide, over the trees to the hills beyond. He has sixty grandchildren, of whom thirty have kids themselves. In all, he has over a hundred and fifty descendants.

The first thing Adilthdoney Begay can remember is his mother's milk. He claims he never had a drop that wasn't hers. His father was a hunter, and successful in breeding livestock. He, too, was called Adilthdoney.

Richard pulls out a postcard, a photo taken in 1903 of his own great-grandfather. Proud and strong, his long dark mane reaches down to his waist. He wears a sheepskin tunic, shorn to an elaborate pattern, and a necklace of beads and bone. A finely woven rug is draped across his shoulders. 'Many Arrows, Navajo warrior', reads the title, but Richard says 'Sharpshooter' would be a more correct translation. Sharpshooter's son nods and says he remembers the day the photograph was taken, when he was a small boy.

He seems forthcoming enough, so I venture to ask if he'll tell us about his skills as a medicine man.

'And what are you going to do with that information?' he fires back, immediately suspicious. Vanella quickly reassures him that we're only interested to hear how he's lived his life and something of his work. This seems to pacify him, but he's cagey still.

'A medicine man is like a doctor,' he says. 'He administers to people. I have taught others how to perform ceremonies and offered blessings at Lake Powell and the Little Colorado river.'

But he won't say any more. He slaps the fly-swat against his palm and I notice a fly showing interest in a spot of food, which has landed some time on the dusty toe of his left boot.

'I am a real good storyteller,' he then declares, this his first unprompted remark.

'He sure is,' Richard agrees.

'What kind of stories does he tell?'

There is no reply. We look to Richard.

'Does he tell stories to his great-grandchildren?' asks Vanella.

The medicine man nods, but remains stony-faced.

So I ask him if he'll tell us a story, to pass on to the world, hoping for some tale symbolizing the importance of balance and harmony.

'Stop,' he says abruptly, and just quits talking. He looks at the ground, sulks, shuffles his feet. Poor Richard is clearly uncomfortable with such melodrama. Meanwhile, the wind blows up hot gusts of dusty air and, in the house, I can see someone with their nose pressed hard against the fly-screen, listening in.

So of course we grovel. We apologize. We didn't mean to upset him, we don't want to steal off with his stories. And, as if he's been switched back on, he starts up and of his own accord begins to tell us about his lifestyle.

'We used to live on mutton, beef, corn, water melon. That stuff they call fast food, it's no good for you. You have to grind your own corn with a stone if you want to reach my age.'

He draws in the dirt with the fly-swat, four oblique lines.

'I never took any liquor. I was a hunter,' he says gravely, 'a good marksman too, like my father. I used to catch deer and carry home the antlers. I was crazy sometimes, the way I rode. Once I even broke my horse's neck pulling the reins so hard. And I would run. In the early morning we would rise before the sun. I ran like the wind in those days.'

'How far did you go?'

He peers from under the brim of his hat and points the fly-swat. 'To those hills, way beyond there and back again. If you can't run, you're not worth a dime.'

Still he gazes out across the country, where the shadows are beginning to form and a turkey buzzard rides the thermals, wingtips outstretched.

'This place means everything to me,' he says. 'Because I was raised here. Because this is where my wife is buried. This is our land.'

He asks me how much land I own and when I describe the flat, he laughs. 'Why that's nothing,' he says.

Suddenly four young boys come tearing around the corner holding make-believe guns, pieces of wood or old bits of metal. 'Psshhew-psshhew,' they fire and dodge. They look to be all-American kids. They wear baseball caps, Levi's and trainers. 'Psshhew-psshheow.' One of them points his gun at me and I grin back down the barrel. Now are they playing cops and robbers, I wonder, or cowboys and Indians? And, if so, who are the good guys?

More firing draws them away as I ask their great-grandfather what he thinks of the white man.

'The white man?' he repeats, casting me a look of mild disbelief. He giggles, sniggering like he can't help himself. 'White men are crooked. They're always trying to trick you. But they're so obvious about it. Like there were some traders here who used to open my retirement money, then try to charge me exactly how much was in the packet.'

He gives a little grunt of disparagement.

'White men?' he says. 'They're sneaky.'

~

I look up from my book. I've recently been reading things I ought to have read but never quite got round to. I just finished some Hemingway, *The Old Man and the Sea*. Now I'm on to *The Picture of Dorian Gray*.

I look up to see Vanella cupping a breast in each hand. 'I must be pregnant,' she says. 'Don't they look bigger to you?'

She is nearly a month late with her period. She says her nipples are burning and her breasts feel unusually firm. I have to admit they do seem a little weightier than usual.

'What'll we do?'

She's been rifling through our trusty medical book. The doc firmly advises that travelling pregnant isn't such a good idea, especially in South America. So for the past few days I've been putting off thinking about it, what we might do.

'This is awful,' she says, looking pained and bewildered. 'I sort of want to be, but at the same time I don't.'

'Hmm.'

'We couldn't keep going, could we?'

'Don't suppose so. Not for long. So much for the magic of honey!'

For contraception, we use a honey cap, so called because you literally store the thing in honey. The ancient Egyptians first understood its value as a spermicide, I'm told. For years, it's served us well too. In recent months we've become quite used to the sight of a column of ants marching steadfastly up a table leg in search of the plastic pot she keeps it in.

I can't believe it. Although this might explain why Vanella's seemed so tired of late. And a bit touchy. The other night I stood accused. She tends to express her emotions. For me it isn't quite so easy. Sometimes she'll smother me in kisses and it's all too much.

I pull my head away.

'Why do you do that?' she shouts, upset.

'What? It's just . . .'

'How do you think it feels? It's like you're rejecting me.'

'I'm not, of course I'm not . . .'

'What about showing some affection?'

'I do . . . Nella, please . . .'

'No. I won't . . .'

She storms off to the bathroom and comes back in a huff. She's not talking and I'm all defensive. So much for harmony. I don't know, I know she's right. But I can't help it sometimes. I hate fighting. Then I can't handle the silence. Eventually one of us says sorry and I tell her I love her and she's all hurt still. And so it goes.

We set out for the drugstore to buy one of those kits to do the test.

Back at the motel, I sit on the bed while she's in the bathroom. I feel the world turn and wonder which way we'll be sent.

'I can't see anything, can you?'

Vanella holds the plastic tube up to the light. We're straining to find a blue dot. There's nothing.

'What does that mean?'

'Strange.'

She doesn't believe it. We wait another twenty-four hours and try again. Still nothing, but we can't be sure.

Next day, we're rolling down Highway 290 towards Houston. We're quiet, dulled by the monotony of the traffic flow and the endless repetition of fast-food signs.

'You know, I think I've got my period,' she suddenly says.

'You sure?'

'Mmm. Think so.'

She smiles. The relief I feel is something close to joy. Somehow I knew. It isn't time to turn for home. We're not ready yet. For these are the longest days of our lives.

~

We watch Angie as she moves from table to table. She clears a tray, shows a family to an empty place, bends to stroke a baby's cheek.

'Hello, I'm Granny Angie. How are y'all today?' she says cheerily, as she comes our way. Her voice is deep, a throaty Texan twang that reminds me of oilmen in ten-gallon hats.

'Why, I sure am pleased to meet you folks,' she says, and by the time I get back with coffee, she's busy chattering away. 'All my life, I've never been happy if I couldn't work,' she says. 'There's people just marvel at why in the world I am working. But I get up on a Monday morning, I feel like I'm going to heaven.'

This particular franchise of heaven is the McDonald's store by Houston's 610 Loop Freeway, where ordinarily overweight Texan folk call by to fill their faces in a controlled environment of sanitized plastic and neon. Angie is their hostess. And she is something of a celebrity. She's been in the newspapers. She's done *The Jenny Jones Show*. People come for miles just to see her.

The name Angie and a golden M are embroidered on her starched white shirt, either side of the regulation cravat. She wears her hair short, neatly combed back. There's a hint of pink lipstick. Glasses with lenses like TV screens rest on a beakish nose. Ladies and gentlemen . . . please welcome Angie Runnels, hamburger superstar, otherwise known as . . . McGranny. She doesn't look a day over seventy. In fact, she's ninety-three.

How it all happened is a story she needs no persuasion to tell. One day a new resident at the retirement home where she lives said she couldn't find the local grocery store. So Angie offered to help. They started out in the lady's car, with Angie giving directions, but the lady ignored her and went her own way.

'We got almost to Richmond, Texas, 'bout forty miles from here, before I could convince her she was goin' out of town,' recalls Angie. 'She kept sayin', "I know where I am." And the old car was jumpin' and jerkin' and stoppin', but finally I got her to turn around. And we kept jerkin' and jumpin' till we got down here. Loop 610. At this underpass, it jumped its last, five o'clock in the afternoon – people drivin' and hollerin' and blowin' their horns . . .'

The two ladies were rescued by the folks at McDonald's. While they recovered from their ordeal, the manageress was complaining how hard it was to keep staff, so Angie said that if she had two good eyes, she'd sure help. 'You're hired,' said the manageress. 'Honey, I was only jokin',' said Angie. But the application form was filled out there and then.

Angie was well qualified. Way back, she ran her own restaurant and even served her special home-made hamburgers in the days before they became so popular. It was a small place she had, out by the airport.

She leans forward, her stout elbows weighing down on the table.

'I wish I had my menu here to show you. I sold bacon and eggs for twenty-five cents, steak and potatoes for seventy-five cents, a bowl of chilli for fifteen. Right during the depression, I started out.'

Times were hard at first, but then the men came looking for oil. Those prospectors asked Angie, if they pitched their tents, would she feed them? So she did. Later they came back and started drilling.

'Well, I had all of that trade,' says Angie. 'At midnight, they'd come up there and eat after they got off the shift. I got my rest, though, in between and I had plenty of help. I had one big black cook called Lucille. One time they had been workin' down there all night and it was rainin', cold and muddy, and they couldn't get the trucks out. So Mr English, who owned the truck line, he told them, "You get me out of this jam and I'll take up at the Wings and feed you." So that's what

I Wayan Gejer, lower-caste priest and basket weaver: Ubud, Bali.

The bull blazes, as Chokorda Raka makes the ultimate journey.

I Wayan Mandor shows how his teeth were filed: Ubud, Bali.

Rae Page lives the good life on Jamberoo Mountain, New South Wales.

Adilthdoney Begay, Navajo medicine man, sure likes turquoise: Indian Wells, Arizona.

Angie Runnels, also known as 'McGranny': Houston, Texas.

Lonnie rocks: Crawfordville, Georgia.

Rosenda remembers how she danced: Puyo, Ecuador.
Señor Roa tells how he drank bear's blood from the neck: Vilcabamba, Ecuador.

Juana Mamani no longer worships the sun: Titicachi, Bolivia.

Day of the Dead: Copacabana, Bolivia.
Don Joaquín Gantier, historian, playwright and part-time wizard, calls for union: Sucre, Bolivia.

Jeanne Calment, the oldest living human being, tells how it's done: Arles, Provence.

he did. He came in there that mornin' and said, "Cilles, fix me forty-one orders of ham 'n' eggs just as quick as you can." And Lucille rolled her big eyes and said, "Now, Mr English, you know you can't eat that many ham 'n' eggs."'

Nowadays people are so particular about cholesterol, Angie complains. They're afraid to eat eggs, they throw away all the good bacon dripping and end up with bland-tasting food. 'We used to have our food cooked well and seasoned well,' she affirms with a sharp nod. 'I guess it was 'cause I grew up like that.'

Born in a log cabin, ninth in a family of ten, Angie was raised on a farm near Clayton, Alabama. The only groceries they ever bought were flour, sugar and coffee. They grew vegetables, then canned and preserved them. They ground the cornmeal, made their own grits. And they raised hogs. She remembers the cold winter mornings when they'd butcher maybe eight or ten, then string them up in the smokehouse. They'd cut and trim the meat, make lard. The scraps were always used for home-made soap.

'All I know is life was better then,' she says. 'Everything tasted so much better.'

'What about these hamburgers?' Vanella asks, with undisguised mischief. Angie plays it straight and gives her employers a tactful plug. She wouldn't want to upset them. She does have the dream job description. It's real simple – to make everyone happy.

'I meet and greet the customers when they come in,' she explains. 'They seem to appreciate it. And the children say the cutest things. They'll come and hug me and love me. My boss says I git more huggin' and lovin' than anybody. And you can't git too much of that. I have joy every day of my life because I know I'm loved. And then young men, same age as my grandson, they git up and say, "Well, you've inspired me. Now I'm ready to go to work." That does me more good than anything. You don't git too old to appreciate compliments.'

It is a virtuous circle. To make folk happy, you gotta be happy, and Angie just gets on with the job. Her energy is remarkable. She's always worked, and worked hard. It goes back to those days on the farm. Being the little one and being a girl, she was always too small to do things. She kept on being put down and she resented it. That's where her grit comes from. 'Never say can't, say can,' her mother used to tell her. She holds it true to this day. She's still ambitious.

'I'm gonna keep on workin' here until they fire me. Then I'll go some place else. I'm gonna keep workin' till I'm ninety-five or more. Then I'm gonna travel a while.'

I can't help laughing. 'Where to?'

'I'm gonna git me a car and a permanent chauffeur,' she says. 'I'm gonna go out to the country, where I can see all that beauty. I don't wanna see the sun set in the same place ever again.'

'I'll be your chauffeur any day, Angie,' I tell her.

So we give her a lift home and roll in through the gates of Holly Hall. I never thought I could get excited about an old people's home. But Holly Hall is like a five-star hotel, smart and spacious. Angie gives us the tour. She strides off down the corridor, making us work to keep up, greeting everyone she meets. She shows us her tidy room, the kitchen where she cooks her own meals and the gym where she's doing aerobics by six every morning. Then we head off back to Reception.

'Do you think this was all down to fate somehow?' Vanella asks her. 'Living here, getting that job?'

'It was nothing but a miracle,' Angie replies with conviction. 'I had asked the Lord about three days before in my prayer, if I had to live the balance of my life like I was livin' here to please make it short. I was stranded. I had been working with young folks, see. I had been doing the catering for the airlines. Then bring me and sit me down over here with nothing but two hundred old people . . .'

Angie drops her voice and looks about to check that no one's listening.

'Now, I love old people, it is a fact. But they don't look forward to tomorrow. I like to be happy. When I get up in the morning I like to say, "Good morning!" not, "This is wrong, that is wrong." When I'm on my deathbed and you ask me how I am, I'll tell you I'm fine.'

Then she leans closer and whispers, 'You know, the trouble with old people . . . they got no vision.'

~

When they named the Preservation Hall, they could only have been thinking of the music. The place itself is dead-beat, old peg-board and generations of nicotine covering the walls. It's more of a room than a hall, a square space with a stage a single step up in one corner. A few rows of seats crowd in close, then behind there's standing room raised for maybe fifty of us packed tight, dark and hot. Further back in the shadows, black faces are watching, affectionate portraits – loose, mood tones of the old jazzmen who once set this joint jumping, playing out their lives at the heart of New Orleans.

On stage, two silver-haired black gentlemen sit side by side. They're dressed like twins – short-sleeved white shirts, wide ties resting on generous stomachs. While the band is away for a smoke between sets, they stay on, heads bowed. They wait patiently, exchanging only the occasional word. They are brothers: Willie and Percy Humphrey. Willie plays clarinet; he's ninety-two. Percy, on trumpet, is three years his junior and leader of the Preservation Hall Jazz Band.

There is applause for the band. The others, they're young: trombone, double bass, drums, a white girl on banjo and a black lady at the piano, on top of which sits a whirring fan the size of a jet engine. When they're set and ready, Percy signals the number by squeezing out a half-formed, strangulated intro and from nowhere they strike up in perfect time.

The brothers are sparked to life by the beat. Percy punches out notes on the trumpet. Willie plays with his head hunched, clarinet pointing to the floor. Soon we're stompin' along to Dixieland tunes we feel we already know and the Preservation Hall swings like only it can.

They pick up the solos one by one. When their turn comes, the brothers stand to give expression to the tune. Percy goes first, his cheeks pressed out like pool balls. Willie is counting the time, his third and little fingers raised, conducting, tapping, pointing to the spaces in the music. Then he's on his feet, reed to his lips, it's his turn to blow. His voice is sure. It soars, plays and turns; it reaches higher, higher still, dances along the top of the high notes, comes round one more time, holding on right to the very end as we drown him out with wild applause.

After two sets we hit the street, where it's Saturday night and the good times are pumping. The air is leaden, hot and sticky; the crowds are trawling the French Quarter, lit its length and breadth with neon. All the world is out for the night, carrying beer in paper cups, leaving a waft of vomit to catch us unawares on the street corner. Music is spilling out of every kind of bar: blues, rhythm and blues, cajun, funk and all strains of jazz. On the sidewalk, young black kids tap-dance in trainers with silver toe-caps, attracting loose coins and whoops of appreciation. Showgirls pose and pout, beckoning from strip-club doorways. *Big Daddy's Topless Bottomless Table Top Dancing*. No one pays much attention to the evangelists who patrol up and down Bourbon

Street. They carry a weighty cross, an electronic display running along the horizontal. 'IDOLATERS . . .' it spells out, stops and flashes red against the night '. . . DRUNKARDS . . . REVELLERS . . . JESUS DIED FOR YOU . . .'

Vanella and I walk on, arm in arm, relaxed, enlivened by the music. We're nearly out of the Quarter, when right down the end by the back door to Woolworth's, we hear another tune. An old hobo in a wheelchair is blowing a mean trumpet for whoever chooses to listen.

~

Standing at the corner of Peachtree and Auburn, we look like tourists, bent over a map of the city of Atlanta. How to get to the Martin Luther King Center?

Some guy stops to show us.

'Can we walk down there? That's not too far.'

The guy, he's white, he looks at us like we're crazy.

'Walk? You don't wanna walk. You wanna be careful, man. You wanna take a cab.'

So we hail a taxi and it takes only two minutes. We spend half an hour looking around, with the words 'I have a dream . . .' ringing in our ears. Next door, we find the Ebenezer Baptist Chapel where King, his father and grandfather were all pastor. There isn't much to see: a lectern, three tiers for the gospel choir and a roundel of stained glass where Christ is kneeling. Other visitors are sitting down for a moment of quiet reflection, so we follow their example.

A black family files across, two rows in front. As they settle into the pew, their son leans round and smiles. He can't be more than fourteen. 'We'd just like to thank y'all for being here today,' he says warmly.

We smile, not knowing quite what to say. Then Vanella nudges me. 'Isn't that extraordinary?' she whispers. 'That he should want to thank us, just for coming.'

We take the bus back. We are the only white folk on board. The two elderly black ladies opposite look at us like we're crazy.

~

Lonnie Stewart sits on his front porch, gently rocking. He's consummate, effortless. The shirt is bright blue with stripes, thick cotton freshly laundered and buttoned at the neck. Khaki-coloured braces with turquoise tramlines hold his trousers high and loose. His spectacles are silver and tortoiseshell grey. Even they've got style.

We're shouting. He seems a little deaf.

'Sah?'

I'm trying to explain we'd like to hear any stories he's got. Then it dawns that it's my English. He doesn't understand the way I speak.

'Sah?'

I don't know how he's done it. He is a hundred and three, but his face is so smooth, so palpably untroubled by age. He doesn't even look old. He has hair enough, cropped close, a mere peppering of grey, and his forehead gleams like molten chocolate. Yet Lonnie's daddy was a slave.

He's grinning. 'Yessuh . . . I got some strange things I can tell yer, but yer wouldna believe em.'

He's straight in with some tale. And I'm in trouble. Vanella gives a faint smile and cocks her head, leaning forward. We have to listen real hard to catch him. He speaks black-folk speak, sometimes rushin', sometimes holdin' on.

'I went to see my sick sister one night,' he says. 'Got over yonder with the wagon . . . bout three mile from here, by the church over there. We passed the graveyard and them chillun, one o my sister's child, told me they see them lil folk come out the graveyard. Them lil folk peared in the road front of me, about that tall.'

Lonnie holds out a hand to gauge around three feet.

'I followed em a mile . . . I turned this road to come home and they was out playin before Mr Edwards'. See, I reckon there's, oh, what, fifty folk in that road. Lil bitty lil folk went like dis – "*Aaytaeytaettatah* . . ."'

It sounds like child's nonsense, rat-tat-tat.

'"*Aaynaenaneh* . . ."'

I'm struggling here. I just keep nodding.

'What were they, these people?' shouts Vanella.

'Maam?'

'Who were they?'

'Oh, it were some kinda spirit. There's folk don't believe in that. But there's some kinda spirit. About that high.'

Lonnie has a good chuckle, high-pitched, showing off two rows of creamy white teeth.

'"*Aaynendaetaettatah* . . . *daetaeytattah* . . ."' he goes again, a yapping dog.

'Were you scared?'

'Yessuh, course I scared o him. I don't want be choke to death. I hear tell some of em took it wrong . . .'

Lonnie smirks, his voice breaking with mirth.

'Heh . . . hee . . . they knock a fella's teeth out . . . hee . . . My boy used to see em. He swear that spirit used to come out play with him. When I say why he didn't tell, he say, "Papa, yer wouldna ha believed it." '

Lonnie rocks back and forth a little, like he's exercising, and I don't know what to believe. It sure is hot out here. I can feel the sweat running down inside my shirt. The porch is a real mess, floorboards rotting at the ends, rusty iron furniture, cobwebs, clutter. We're sitting on squares of white cotton we've been handed. Lonnie lives out here on his own. We're in deep country, some place near Crawfordville, Georgia, a journey south from Athens.

Now he's thinking, pulling at a patchy moustache between forefinger and thumb.

'Mmmm hmm . . . They's some strange ole things in the land,' he warns, rolling his head to one side. 'Greatest one I can tell you bout is the strange woman, used to walk dis road.' He points back beyond the dirt track we just came down. 'I use to see her by her hair.'

'A woman?'

'I guessuh . . . Tall as Thomas, she was. We start to church one night, to a celebration, some kinda sellin to do with raisin money by the school, you know. And we hear, "*Barmp . . . Barmp . . .*" '

Lonnie makes the sound hoarse, rubbing his hands together to make a rustling.

'We turn round and went on back home. But she treat us nice, she don't hurt no one. She come on behind . . . "*Barmp . . . Barmp . . . Barmp . . .*" Old Abbie's with me and he told when you look at her she'd be bout eight or ten feet tall. That was common thing, see that woman, but I ain't heard tell of her lately.'

'Who was she?'

'It won't answer, it won't answer . . .' Lonnie's laughing. His tongue shows up bright pink. His mouth is elastic. 'Sometime dem evil spirits of the dark they trouble yer. Sommin come knockin at my door. *Bamm bamm bamm* . . . Some folk can see em, some folk can't.'

'You can see them, can you?'

'I do too. But some spirits come, they didn't scare me. My wife come back here one night. She come in that room and I know she was gone. Comes in the door, I found myself on the bed and I turned, "Now don't scare me." She come in that door and kiss me. That my wife's spirit, Marie. We stay together sixty-seven odd year and we didn't fight none.'

And so he's reminded of the family reunion they just had, this last Saturday. He has so many grandchildren, great-grandchildren, he can't tell them all by name.

'What do you teach them?' Vanella asks.

'I tell em this and you tell it your folk,' he urges. 'My subject was death in the pot.' There's a gleam in Lonnie's eye.

'Death?'

'Death . . . in the pot . . . I told em, help my people, back in the old days there was a famine in the land and folk got everything they could literally scrape together to eat.'

This one's impossible to follow, some story about gourds. I can only make out snatches here and there.

'They's all right when you clean em, but they's the damnedest thing . . .'

I think he's saying they're poisonous unless you soak them to bring the bitterness out. Then we have some little fella comes to taste the food in the pot. And the man they call king, he took some meal and sprinkled it in the pot and it killed some poor boy. Something like that.

'See, them ole green gourds,' Lonnie says. 'If yer eat em raw, they's same as strychnine. It'll kill yer . . . You find it in Elijah's book . . . about death in the pot. Y'understand that?'

'Yep,' I say, nodding, lying. That wasn't any Bible story I recognize. 'Do you read the Bible?' I ask him.

'Used to read pretty good till my eyes got bad, yessuh. I stood on the wall for fifty year, teachin Sunday school. They said I was right good, I don't know. I teach em the ways of the Lord . . .' And in a preaching voice he repeats, '. . . the ways of the Lord.'

He begins to tell the story of King David, who he says was the first man to place the law of God in Jerusalem. David was about to do battle with the Philistines when God appeared and said he should wait till he heard a noise in the mulberry trees. Then God would ride into battle before him.

I have a vague recollection of this one, but nothing like Lonnie tells it. He can embellish a simple text into a work of art. He has David making speeches to his men and everyone watching, waiting for the trees. Lonnie's chuckling as he describes the fuss they hear in the branches, the sound of rustling leaves. Then he has David saddling his horse and riding to battle.

'Course his wife didn't like him, you know,' he confides to us. 'He weren't no pretty man, that David.'

This I haven't heard, but Lonnie weaves the fact of his ugliness into his next tale, an elaborate version of the story of the shepherd boy who was anointed king.

'I would have bin a preacher,' Lonnie says, as if by explanation.

'A preacher?'

'Yessuh . . . My own head was anointed, when I was less than ten years of age. Sommin happened to my head, in a dream. Sommin come down and got me by the top of my hair, just like lightnin. Before I know anything I done woke up. Well, knocked over dead, I come to reading the Bible, when Ezekiel . . . you remember Ezekiel, ain't yer? He's called out to ninety people, went down in the valley of the bones, dem dry bones. And God told him, "Hear the word of the Lord and live." He was carried down in that valley with a strand o his hair . . .'

Lonnie's laughing, rejoicing. '. . . And it held up too. Mine held me.'

He pauses, a pensive shadow passing over his noble African features.

'But I reckon it's the best thing I didn try to preach,' he says. 'I were no rich man. You know, a fella can have a hard time tryin to preach when he's poor. Christ had a hard time. You read that, ain't yer?'

We certainly have. So Lonnie's sniggering again, telling us another, this one about Jesus.

Whatever it is he's on, I'd sure like some. He's immortal, this guy. I can't imagine him ever fading. What is it? There must be some innate ability, borne across the ocean, down the generations. He's just as happy as a lark. But we can't ask him. Lonnie never even stops to think about it. He's so blissfully unaware of his nature, so wrapped up in the simple business of being. It makes me think, though. When I consider my own short lifespan, I know now that I've spent too much time in the business of achieving, not enough time spent being.

'I's just glad to be here,' Lonnie says. 'It's real good to be here.'

He hasn't a care in the world. He made a living out of growing cotton, and he did pretty well until them old boll weevils came through this way. Year after year, they all but destroyed his crop. He could hardly pick two bales to sell. Those were rough times. They lived on water melon, corn and squash. He still has some growing there in his garden.

When I do ask him, he gives me religion for an answer.

'I's here by the hand of the Lord,' he says.

He saw the light, literally.

'You can tell it when something happens, can't you?' he calls out, as if we know. Then he's almost singing, 'You can tell it. You can tell it . . .'

He's grinning again, teeth flashing.

'It happened to me, when I was sick. I prayed, I done give up to die. Now when I done give up to die, a light appeared over me and something told me, "Believe and you shall be saved . . . just believe and you shall be saved." '

A moment of silence passes between us as a gentle breeze blows across the porch. A bird trills sweetly in a nearby bush. And Lonnie sucks his lip, laughs, and rocks back and forth a little more.

~

There is a special quality to be found in people who've lived to more than a hundred years old. I could call it *centeniousness*, but I think I'll settle on *centiosity*. The adjective derived would be *centiose*, which sounds like a fine way to be.

Those who've reached the big 1–0–0, they all seem to have it, this centiosity. It's a subtle thing, but it's there for sure. It has to do with confidence, certainty – arrogance or pride have no place, of course. It's the sense you must get from sitting at the top of the tree. Like you're up there, you've made it. And you're there because you're strong. You are a survivor. Because those who don't take care or wreck themselves or get diseased, they don't usually last a hundred years. So there's a hardiness, tenacity, if not a surprising agility. And it's in the mind too, a fitness: brightness, interest, humour. Laugh? They'll laugh till the day they die. Finally, somewhere close to the heart of it, we can always sense that, inside, they live in a state of perfect calm. They're at peace. At one. Like every day is a bonus to be savoured with delight.

Mary Elliott has it. She is wonderfully centiose.

We are gathered round. Mary is by the window, where the light plays softly on her long white hair. She sits in a high-backed chair with curved wings, reminiscent of a choir-stall. Beside her lie stacks of letters and paper bags full of knitting.

Mary is pin sharp. She can remember every detail and bombards us with the names and dates of her ancestors who came to America from Cornwall and Glasgow in the late 1820s. Her voice suggests that provenance. The accent is American, East Coast, educated, but there's an old-fashioned correctness about the way she speaks. And she rounds her vowels sometimes, a faint West Country echo.

'My, there is so much to tell you,' she says, still fiddling with the fold of her collar. She dresses in fine white cotton. A sleeveless cardigan and a long blue woollen skirt are the closest she can find nowadays to the fashion of her youth.

Born in the late nineteenth century, Mary grew up in a lovely old country town, Summit, New Jersey. Her father worked in the railroad business. It was a time of inventions and progress; macadamized roads were just coming in. Until then, they had sprinklers throughout town to dampen the dust thrown up by the horses, the buggies and the carts.

Mary paints that old world with a precise touch, even down to the simple act of buying sweets. She recalls how she'd trot over to the general store, where there was a candy counter.

'Old Mr Baldwin . . .' she says, with a smile of reminiscence. 'He had a beard. He would put on his black coat to wait on people and it would have the dust of white powder on it. He would stand behind that corner counter and wait on me. And he would remark, "Candy ain't good for little girls."' Here Mary shakes her head and puts on a wavering voice some measure beyond her own to imitate the old shopkeeper. 'And yet he'd still sell it to me,' she says, 'and I wondered why he did.'

She smiles again and looks away, the sunlight from the garden reflected in her glasses. She plays with her hands, pressing her fingertips together, interlocking – here is the church, here is the steeple . . .

If anyone does, Mary deserves to have lived for a long time. She seems the very epitome of goodness and virtue. I could never imagine her doing ill in word or deed. Those seeds were sown early on. Her family were devout church-goers, Episcopalian – her father came from a strong Anglican tradition.

Even her first memory has a Christian theme. It was Christmas time, more than a hundred years ago. She was two and a half, playing with her toys in a corner of her mother's bedroom. Downstairs her mother was at the piano, singing 'O little town of Bethlehem'.

Mary tilts her head and recites the opening lines again, in the way of handling something precious.

'Dear Mother,' she says, '. . . the way she sang.'

My own earliest memory wasn't a moment but a curious sense of being. When I was a child, I used to be able to recall a particular sensation of how I once was. It would come over me without warning, something like *déjà vu*. It was always triggered by the sound of a voice, which could be anyone's, but there had to be a certain intonation. When I was old enough to think it through, I decided it had to be some memory of how I was in my pram, or even the womb. I was secure, warm, no sense of limbs, just me, dark, my being. But I was aware of sound. It was the sound that was prompted, a familiar but distant murmur, as if someone were talking in the next room. The sadness is I lost it, somewhere in my childhood. My ability to return there withered as I grew. Now, I can only remember the fact. Next up, like Mary, I'm three years old and playing with my toys in the hall at Woodlands.

'Mother and Father were an enormous influence,' she's telling us. 'They gave us a great deal. They were interested in the development of the mind, the body and the soul. They studied the Greek heroes, Scandinavian lore and deep breathing.'

Raising her head, Mary inhales instinctively, then laughs.

'We little youngsters would go into Pop's room in the morning, pound our chests and say, "See, Poppa, how big my chest is, how deeply I can breathe." I still practise on my walks, when I can pull myself up and remember. It's a life habit, you know. The girls at school used to say I walked as if I'd swallowed a ramrod, I was so straight.'

She enjoyed gymnastics, marching to music. She loved nature and walked, mile after mile, summer and winter. And she danced. They had a very fine dancing teacher come out from New York every Thursday.

'How we loved it,' she enthuses. 'I danced and danced and danced . . . Mother played the piano so beautifully.'

She talks of her mother with a trace of sadness. She died young, when Mary was only fourteen. They often spent time talking together. Once, at their country home in Sullivan County, New York state, Mary remembers them kneeling on the window-ledge, looking out across the field towards Hunter Mountain.

'Mother was a great Bible student,' she says. 'An almost sacred kind of person. She had such a beautiful character. But her health was a little delicate and I don't know if she suspected even then that she might not live very long, but she wanted in our talks to leave something that would build my character and soul. We were kneeling there that day, dreaming. And in a quiet voice, she said to me, "May, dear, everybody radiates. I want you always to radiate what is good."'

Mary has carried this thought with her ever since. Vanella always remembers a conversation she had with her mum once. Hilary pointed out that Vanella was occasionally a bit hard on people, too quick to criticize. Hilary had smiled and said, 'It's much easier to find fault than it is to be generous, you know.' And so the spirit was passed on.

Mary learnt the hard way how to cope with grief. Over the years she has lost both parents, a sister, brother, two husbands and two children. She has outlived most of her friends too. She remains positive and cheerful, always keeping them in her thoughts.

'Those dear ones who are gone are closer now spiritually than they were in life,' she says.

The longer she lives, the more her religion helps her to be resilient. She finds great comfort in her belief. It enables her to think dispassionately. She freely admits that the world is now living through those times of perplexity and turmoil, as are predicted in the Bible. These are testing times, she feels. I believe she may be right, but my response to any such revelations is usually to become a touch depressed.

Mary is optimistic.

'You know,' she says, 'we have all the ammunition we need in the Bible. "Be still and know that I am God." If only people would find time, be still, look inside themselves. We have been forgetting God for many years. Now even Congress has denied prayer in our schools. That was awfully stupid, an ignorant act, when prayer is indigenous in every clan and people throughout the whole world. It is natural for man to reach out to his creator.'

Mary smiles at us both, her kindly blue eyes sparkling with promise.

'Love,' she says simply.

'Can love help us to live longer?' I ask.

'Why, yes. Love of God and love of our fellow man, thoughtfulness of others . . .'

'How does thoughtfulness of others mean that you live longer?'

'Oh, it keeps you from thinking too much about yourself. Our Lord's life was directed at helping other people. "Suffer little children to come unto me." Jesus pointed out how the little ones love one another. It's so important to love each other, tremendously important.'

Mary pauses to deal with a wayward strand of hair.

'That's a builder, you know,' she says, with a wag of a finger. 'You grow by reaching out and helping others and their appreciation helps you.'

Then she's flustered. 'Oh, dear me,' she goes, touching a comb at the back of her head. 'Oh, I feel as if my hair . . . I used to have it high up, but it bothers me today.'

Vanella reassures her it looks lovely. She's still radiating.

'Do you get wiser as you get older?' I wonder.

'Oh, yes, definitely. Otherwise why age? The Chinese have thought for generations that the old live so they can teach the young.'

'What can you teach us?' Vanella asks. 'What advice would you give?'

There follows a long silence while Mary considers carefully, finger-tips touching, almost in prayer.

'Remember it is God who has made us and not we ourselves,' she replies. 'That's one thing. Another is to sing with a glad heart. Music, we should always have music in our lives . . . Good health habits . . . sensible eating, simple things well cooked. Outdoor exercise, outward-going, sociability . . . Hitch your wagon to a star, follow the gleam. Learn what you can . . . I think learning is thrilling. I keep learning all the while.'

Then her hand goes up.

'Oh, now my hair *is* coming down. Can you take that from me? Gracious, it's all come down. My heavens, I guess one comb is already gone.'

~

Their farmsteads lie scattered across a rich and fertile land. Their wooden buildings stand white, high and bulky, with small square peep-holes for windows on the top floors. There's a house, the barn, a curing shed and two giant cigar tubes for grain silos. Clinging together, they lord the expanse of fields all around. For crops, they grow acres of broad-leaved tobacco, dense ripening corn and low meadows of lush green alfalfa danced over by a thousand prospecting butterflies.

Through one gateway we spy a farmer and his sons gathering in the harvest by means of a sharp blade, a pitchfork, and a horse and cart.

It's an antiquated scene. They do look a bit weird, in their blue shirts, braces and straw hats.

We have been directed to the sign of the wheel-maker. Here we should find Amos Zook, who they say is very old. We pull in, down a bank to the house. A shy teenage lad points to a red-brick extension to the main building while his siblings, scruffy urchins who go barefoot, stare at our strange clothes. Maddy answers the door. She is a plain-looking woman, to our eyes quaintly dressed. Her white linen bonnet is loosely tied with a simple bow, covering a centre-parting of pale hair flattened against her forehead. Her dress is a royal blue shift, obviously hand-made, over which she wears a white apron and a pinafore that reaches all the way to a pair of extremely sensible shoes.

Maddy smiles coyly. She says Amos is taking a nap and goes in to see him. We peep into the parlour, taking in the simple wooden furniture arranged against the walls. Maddy asks if we'll come back in half an hour, after Amos has had his lunch.

The Amish are a tight-knit tribe who hail from the days of religious persecution in Europe. They were free-thinkers who believed in the separation of Church and State. They also thought we should decide for ourselves when we want to be baptized. Forced out, they left Switzerland in the late 1600s and finally sailed away to find somewhere no one would bother them. Here they still live, by strict codes of dress and behaviour, choosing to reject anything that is too much, as they say, 'of the world'. The Old Order they are called, and they keep themselves very much to themselves. They worship together, they educate their children in their own schoolhouses. They work long hours on the land and practise the virtues of thrift and self-sufficiency.

They do use machines sometimes, but not for transport. While they will never drive a motor car, let alone own one, they allow themselves to use tractors in the farmyard, and battery-powered strimmers to maintain the tidiest grass verges on God's earth. But they won't own a television, or anything so fashionable as a CD player. They shun any technology that they believe may weaken the family unit, thus most of the trappings of modern life. The rules say that telephones must be kept out of the house; sometimes they're to be found in a special wooden kiosk down by the farm gate.

It is as though we have at last travelled back in time. We stand at the roadside to watch a load of tobacco leaves roll by. The heavy cart with rumbling metal wheels needs two strong horses and an impassive farmer with a bushy red beard to drive it. Horse and carriage, pony and trap go clip-clop along the lanes, only to be overtaken by some eager outsider in a Toyota Land Cruiser. Because, of course, the tourists have to come and gawp, point their long lenses at the freak show, then buy knick-knacks or jam to take home as a souvenir.

We choose some home-made peach pie to take Amos for his dessert.

His hat is old, burnt straw, sewn where it has worn around the brim. Beneath it, Amos has a wizened, puzzled look, wild whiskery eyebrows and a pointed nose. The rest of him is typically Amish – the pudding-basin haircut, the face shaved down to the jaw-line, a beard growing below, except that Amos's beard has a bizarre arrangement of crinkly extensions dangling from it. His clothes are plain in style and colour, natural shades, greys and inky blues. Hooks and eyes fasten his waist-coat. And on his feet he wears the most ancient pair of black hobnailed boots I've ever seen.

'Ooh, I've got a headache,' he moans. 'Shame is I get headaches all the time these days . . . And my lung's still drying out.'

They don't invite us inside the house. We're sitting out by the door in picnic chairs. Maddy has a fold-down rocker, which makes a scraping sound of flimsy metal. I see she has a hole in her shoe, where it creases at the side. Amos has a conspicuous patch stitched like a window on the inside of his trouser leg.

'I don't know how long I'm gonna live,' he says. His voice is a rasping squeak, like he's holding his breath and trying to clear his throat at the same time. 'A while yet, maybe half a year.'

We try to begin at the beginning, but Amos isn't too sure. He was born in February. Now was it the seventeenth or the twenty-second? He thinks this is an absolute hoot. 'Why, fancy not being able to remember my own birthday,' he says, cackling with laughter. He has a wonderfully infectious laugh. He should do cartoon voices.

Married at the age of twenty-four, he had fourteen children. How many of each he's not sure either. 'Now, let me see . . .' Amos scratches his beard, then screws up his nose and scratches that too. 'Heh. Why, I don't know.'

Maddy frowns as she tries to work it out on her fingers. Six . . . no, five girls, nine boys, she eventually manages to count.

Amos lost his wife giving birth to the last of them so he had to bring up the kids himself.

'How did you manage?' we wonder.

'You work 'em hard, that's how. Give 'em work to do,' he says, surprised we should ask.

In time, he married again. Maddy is his stepdaughter.

He worked as a farmer, growing tobacco, tomatoes and corn, keeping horses and hogs. Then he decided to become a wheel-maker and built up a small business. He used to charge fifty dollars a wheel, depending what kind it was. A while back he sold up to his next-door neighbour. It's his sign out on the road, where a pony and trap trots by causing the pair of skittish horses in the paddock to frisk and whinny. Then a Mack truck roars past grinding its gears.

'Awful lotta change,' Amos wheezes. 'Awful lotta change. Biggest change is the traffic round here.'

He has hardly ever travelled outside Lancaster County. When he was a boy, they used to ride to Reading sometimes, to sell potatoes. They'd leave at two in the morning and come back in the day. There was always great excitement, because they knew they might catch sight of some cars. They used to count how many. At school, they would run to the windows whenever they heard a car driving by. The first he ever saw had an engine in the back and some kind of chain.

'Awful lotta change,' he's repeating when, to our left, down the grassy bank comes the most extraordinary apparition. It could have stepped straight from an eighteenth-century costume drama. All in black, head to toe, she is hobbling like an old crone, except she's maybe only sixty. Her bonnet has an extravagant peak, her waisted jacket is held together with pins; various layers of skirt are wrapped around, somehow fastened. She too wears an enormous pair of hobnailed boots. Her name is Susie.

'I've just finished working,' she natters, approaching. 'I've been digging in the garden because I wanted to get the carrots in before the fall, but I couldn't find my seeds, so I thought I'd come over here.'

'She's never been married, you know,' mumbles Amos in my ear. 'Never been married.' From her attire, I'd have assumed she is a widow. '. . . No, she's never been married.'

'I thought the earth was going to be wetter and easier to manage,' Susie says, 'but do you know it was still quite dry underneath?'

Her face is not unattractive, almost handsome in a robust countrified way, though she does have a large beady growth on one eyelid. Her clothes, we now see, are smeared with dirt from her gardening and, when she comes closer to give Maddy her copy of the *Penny Saver*, the local paper, I think I detect a whiff of something unsavoury.

Susie shuffles around, eyes ticking nervously. She wants to know what we're doing.

'That wife of his took good care of me,' Susie says, to make a contribution, and points at Amos, smiling possessively. But Amos is still more concerned about her marital status and keeps repeating the fact until I ask if he minds me taking a photo of his hat. The Amish impose a strict rule about pictures. A photograph is a graven image and thus breaks the second commandment. To pose is also an act of pride.

His hat presents no such problem. In fact, Amos thinks the whole idea quite hilarious and is more than happy to oblige. But at the sight of a camera Susie turns a bit loopy and hurries off in an agitated state, muttering. Meanwhile, the hat makes a perfect subject. And with his pinkish grey pate exposed to the world, the man himself looks thin in the face and awkwardly incomplete.

Maddy goes indoors to find the guest book, which Vanella signs.

'Why, but you don't have a zip code,' Maddy says, admiring her first ever entry from outside Lancaster County.

'Well, it's only a small place, a tiny island compared with the United States.'

'London is an island?' queries Maddy.

'No, London is the capital of England. England is part of an island.'

'Oh,' she says, and ponders awhile. 'Do you speak English in England?' she then asks, in all innocence.

Amos is back to his old self with his hat in place once more. He's grumbling again. 'Life's bad these days,' he says. 'Awful lotta stealing. Lotta killing goes on. It ain't so good.'

'Have you ever seen television?' I ask him.

Amos thinks about this. 'Mighta seen it once, but I never had one,' he says. 'There's good and bad, but I don't believe they're a good thing. Other folk, they can have 'em if they wish, but not for me.'

'Have you ever been to the cinema, seen a film?'

'Can't say I have.'

'Do you read? Books?'

'No, well, I don't know if I do read.'

'No, you're always too busy to read,' says Maddy protectively.

'Perhaps I'll retire one day and read some more,' says Amos, his weaselly old face crinkling with mirth.

~

Maybe I don't want to go back in time after all. Standing at the edge, on this the highest point, I have all Manhattan mapped out before me. And I love it.

As the day fades, the lights of the metropolis are beginning to show through. A few hundred feet below, a helicopter curls across towards the East River and disappears like a gnat in the haze. And all the way to the ground, I can just make out the yellow cabs, which push and shove like microbes under a glass. Then I get that rush of quease in my stomach and quickly step back a pace.

I love the very idea, a small island where all life is crammed, thriving, jostling ever upwards. The pulse, the energy, the air almost crackles with it down on the street. Even here I can feel the charge, the dull roar of progress carried on the breeze.

But bring my old friend Bo up here and he'll be questioning the value of all that progress.

'We can do everything so much faster, but do we have any more time?' he'll say. 'We are awash with information, but are we better armed with the truth? We have expanded our knowledge of the universe, but are we any closer to God?'

Or bring Mark Oliphant to the rail and he'll be pointing at the forest of skyscrapers, their red lights winking now, as he tells me that the mega-corporations are taking over. They control us, what we consume, even what we think.

And yes, sometimes I can picture the earth as if from space, only instead of blue ocean and swirling white cloud, I imagine an organism devouring itself, writhing in perpetual motion until everything is eaten away. But I realize now that yearning for the past won't help. The wise ones among the Navajo, they understand. Now is the only time. This is how it is. And the kind of world we hand on to our grandchildren is down to us.

A few statistics have fallen to me in the past weeks, entirely at random. Ninety-six US cities have an official pollution problem. Sixty-eight per cent of the population is overweight. Fourteen children die as a result of a gunshot each day – and that includes the suicides. In some states, they need cops to patrol in the schools.

In parts of Europe, Africa and Asia, Vanella and I have seen so often how easily they're dazzled. They want it all. They want the gloss. They want the money. The whole world wants to be like America.

But I'm not so sure they have it right. They're after the wrong piece of the action. I reckon what they need more than anything is a little vision, some of that harmony, a pioneering spirit, the ability to be without thinking, and a love of their fellow man . . . that old kind of stuff. That's how the story goes.

So hey, let's be careful out there.

Boof.

18

Los Gringos y Los Ancianos

My boot has barely left the ground when, somewhere deep down, metal engages on metal and, with a belch of evil smoke, the bus accelerates away. Hanging off the ladder, I swing myself up to the roof and find a space between the sacks of vegetables and old wooden boxes held together with twine. Apart from the risk of being garrotted by telephone wires, we reckon we're safer up top. We'll stand a better chance when the driver strays too close to the edge and we go crashing down through the trees, bound for the Río Pastaza.

Soon we're roaring along in the crisp, clean air, inhaling pungent waves of coriander from someone's basket. Beside me, Vanella holds on tight. Next to her, with his head tied poking out of a canvas bag, a wild-eyed rooster pecks neurotically at anything and nothing. And Clara, the young Quechua Indian girl who is taking us to see an old lady she knows, whoops with delight as we hunker down under our jackets to avoid being soaked by overhanging waterfalls.

We are headed east, away from the mountains and volcanoes, to Puyo, a small town on the edge of the Oriente, Ecuador's jungle region. It makes for an exhilarating ride, along lush, green, steep-sided valleys, where wisps of white cloud gently lace the hilltops. And, of course, there are those corners, which our man at the wheel does cut breath-takingly fine.

After an hour or so and a dismal village or two, we gradually lose height and the ravine spreads itself wide, bordered now by sheer cliffs of mud. In the distance a brooding darkness threatens some change in the weather, but still it catches us by surprise. We meet the first shower over a brow and within minutes we're absolutely drenched. Clara shrieks, I'm cursing and Vanella just holds on and laughs. No amount of banging will make the driver stop, even if he can hear us through the pounding salsa beat coming up through the roof. Then, at last, he slows to a halt and we clamber down and climb in among the locals, for whom the sight of gringos dripping wet and at the same time humbly grateful provides considerable amusement.

We have already grown accustomed to our new-found status in life – that of gringo. We are the object of some contempt, it seems – deeply felt too – which we don't think is at all fair. We don't consider ourselves to be gringos; surely they come from North America. But there's no escape: a white face means you have money and any effort to cheat it from you is fair game. The guy who sold us the bus tickets grinned inanely as he so blatantly tried to rip us off by charging three times too much. Even the children taunt us, mimicking their elders. And if we're out on the street, a leering *campesino* might greet us with '*Buenos días, gringitos*', putting the Hispanic fondness for diminutives to fine effect.

By early afternoon we reach Puyo and strike a deal with a local man, who takes us in his *camioneta* van to the end of a long track some distance beyond the edge of town. After he's tried short-changing us we set off, lugging the provisions Clara insisted we buy that morning at the market in Baños. We'd wanted to take some appropriate gifts, but Clara was doubly keen we should be remembered for our generosity and had assumed command of the shopping spree. So we follow her up through the sugar plantations, weighed down by ample quantities of vegetables, rice, flour, bread and salt. Clara suddenly announces that her aunt lives nearby, so we stand around smiling as they exchange their news. Then, before we know it, the aunt is gratefully accepting a good portion of the groceries. We say goodbye and on we march, the forest of vegetation growing thicker, until eventually we find a wooden shack raised on stilts, a shambles of boards loosely tied or leaning to. We look in, startling a couple of hens, but the old lady doesn't seem to be at home.

I now understand why Clara wears gumboots. It begins to rain again, only stair-rods this time, and for a full thirty minutes. We run for shelter to a neighbour's house, a woman Clara also appears to know. The old lady next door has gone to town, she says. She also tells us that she's not especially old, only about seventy. So Vanella and I watch the rain descend as only tropical rain can, thoughtfully sucking lengths of sugar cane and wondering where this goose chase will take us next. After a while the old lady herself returns, sheltering under the huge banana leaf she uses for an umbrella. She confirms that she's a mere seventy-three, but then remembers she has an aunt living nearby who is a hundred and thirty. So when the rain has eased and more groceries have been distributed, directions are given and we plod off in search of the old lady's even older aunt.

We're skidding and slipping as we pick our way in the mud, following some kind of short-cut that takes us down a steep hillside through dense undergrowth. Some steps have been dug out for the path, but they're either full of water or have collapsed into a treacherous slop. Waiting at the bottom, Clara looks uncertain. The path has disappeared. A simple wooden dwelling stands to our right, so we wander over to ask the way. Sitting on the verandah we find a bare-chested Indian with shoulder-length hair, surrounded by the rough carvings of about five hundred balsa-wood parrots. He must be the man who hacks out the shapes before a more skilled craftsman carves the detail and they're painted and sold to *los turistos*.

The Indian's eyes light up. 'Gringos!' he cries with glee, arms open wide. 'My friends! Welcome! Come, you must join me. You are most welcome in my house, gringos. Let us sit and talk. Come, we must drink.'

He climbs unsteadily down the front steps, directing his speech mainly at me. On closer inspection, I can see that all is not well in his eyes. He's completely stoned on something.

'Come, gringo. Let us drink together and you can tell me your news,' he says joyfully, grabbing a greasy bucket containing a yellow liquid with bits floating on its surface. Generously he ladles it out into a suitably greasy cup. This is *chicha*, a lethal brew made from fermented corn. Normally keen to try anything new, on this occasion we are reticent – the greasy bucket looks decidedly unsanitary and an hour of enlightened conversation isn't quite what we have in mind. So I decline as politely as I can, but this only makes our friend more insistent, and the more we decline, the more he insists and the more his enthusiastic greeting turns to anger.

'*Tranquilo*, *tranquilo*,' soothes Clara, as she herself offers to drink on our behalf. She whispers he's from a different tribe, the Shuar, who used to be head-shrinkers and among whom it is customary to accept such hospitality.

'Why won't you drink with me, gringo?' he complains, eyeing me blearily, clearly offended, even though Clara is gulping down a large mugful for us all. She then tactfully makes our excuses, we smile hopefully and squelch away across his muddy plot.

'So why do these gringos come all this way to see me if they don't want to have a drink?' we hear him calling out to our backs.

We pick our way through the trees, negotiate a branch to cross a stream, then find the route barred by a sizeable swamp. Clara is looking indecisive again, and a little tipsy. We have no choice but to turn round and go back past the Indian's house. First we tiptoe, if such is possible in six inches of mud, then we begin to scamper and, as we approach the bottom of the slippery steps, we hear shouting and swearing.

'Gringos . . . hey . . . greeengo,' he calls, as we scramble back up the slope. Halfway, I allow myself a backward glance only to see a gun being waved in our direction.

'Greeengo . . .' he screeches, and begins unsteadily to raise the rifle to his eye.

'Run, guys,' I shout. 'Run . . . Just move.'

'Greeengo . . .'

So we flee from the jaws of death, giggling helplessly, and promise never to refuse the hospitality of a head-shrinker ever again.

We seem to have been trudging about for ages, in a crushing humidity, when we stumble out on to the tarmac of a main road. Clara points cheerfully to a plain wooden house a short distance away down a grassy bank. She leads the way and calls through the door. An old, round face peeps out timidly. The little lady stands barefoot on the top step, clothed in a skirt, two shirts and a cardigan, all odd colours and none seeming to fit. She looks bemused and takes her time to check us over. Thoughtfully stroking her chin, which is ridged like a peach stone, she nods, as if to herself, and invites us in.

Wobbly stools are arranged on the bare boards of the sparse living space. The old lady sits patiently, hands folded, as we all hedge in close, trying to ignore the haze of fruit-fly emanating from a large pile of *narajillas* on the floor. Over in the corner hang colour portraits of family members in ornate gold frames. Below, a collection of faded pin-ups have been nailed to the wall – Bruce Lee, Sylvester Stallone and one or two large-breasted women. These belong presumably to the macho-looking soldier photographed in his combat gear with a giant snake wrapped around his neck.

True to form, the old lady is a little younger than a hundred and thirty. Her name is Rosenda Valentina Vargas and she says she's ninety-three.

'The government, they cheated me,' she mutters, shaking her head. 'They say I am six years younger than I really am.' The authorities, we hear, have been known to make up the dates on the ID cards of older people to reduce the amount they pay out in social security. Nothing surprises me. Truth seems a rare commodity around these parts. But if I were to count the lines etched around her mouth, there'd be at least one for each of those years.

Rosenda was born in the jungle, away to the north, in the Saparu tribe. Only a week later, her father was murdered. An errant shaman, a witch-doctor who travelled from place to place curing ills and ailments, he was cruelly put to death by some tribesmen who didn't believe in his powers. Not one to learn from her ways, Rosenda's mother then married another shaman from the Alchidona tribe, but his life was similarly threatened so the family fled to the relative safety of Indillama, not far from here. At the age of fifteen, Rosenda was given away to a local man by whom she had four children. They ran a small farm, but her husband died. He drank himself to death on *chicha*. She stayed on for a few years but now lives with her daughter.

'And is life good?' we ask.

She shrugs. 'They look after me,' she says without emotion.

'It must be very different from when you were a girl.'

'Ah, the jungle,' she says, smiling at last.

'What can you remember?' asks Vanella. 'What clothes did you wear?'

She sighs. 'I remember . . . The women used to wear a beautiful bright blue material, which they wrapped around themselves. We painted our faces and made up our eyes using pigments from plants in the forest.' So saying, she rubs imaginary fingers of colour on her wrinkled brown face. 'I still use them if I need some make-up.'

Her shoulders bob with mischief as she looks to Vanella and then laughs, showing us the only tooth she has left.

'Did you find medicines in the forest?' Vanella wonders.

'Yes, many plants have powerful properties. I know how to cure a snake bite. You need a special kind of moss, which you chew up with tobacco. Then you chew the mixture into the wound. This takes away the poison. And we used dragon's blood. That's a red sap from a tree, which cures many things. I have seen it heal wounds, even pneumonia.'

Then she points to the wall behind her. 'And these here were used during fiestas,' she says.

I have been trying to work out whatever it is hanging there. They turn out to be head-dresses, one of which is unhooked to show us.

'This one is anaconda,' she says, indicating a thick band of snakeskin with an erect plume of blue and yellow feathers. 'And that,' adds Rosenda, 'is a condor.'

'A condor?' I mouth, then twist my head around. There is, indeed, a condor converted into an extravagant hat suspended upside down on the wall. Its black and white wingspan is awesome, its vulturous head dangles menacingly.

Rosenda disappears into the back room and soon shuffles back carrying the head of a bear. 'The men used to wear these,' she says grinning, as she sets it down on a stool where it stares morosely at us.

The fiesta in question was La Diablada, where they symbolized the struggle between good and evil. 'The women would paint their bodies and wear costumes like this.' Rosenda holds up a tangle of threads and tassels, a belt and choker all-in-one, strung together with an assortment of shells, beans, beads, gold and feathers. It tinkles delicately as she lovingly displays its intricacies.

'You used to dance wearing this?' asks Vanella.

'This? This is nothing. We were covered, everywhere, from head to foot,' Rosenda replies.

'And did you dance?'

'Ah, yes,' she says, smiling warmly, 'how we loved to dance.'

She holds her arms up and does the closest she can manage to a shimmy. Then her eyes cloud. 'But now I have pains in my legs and I need my pills,' she says.

~

Armed with a breakfast of grubby cheese sandwiches bought in the bus station, we leave the colonial charm of Cuenca, its blue domes, red-tiled roofs and its pretty courtyards to be spied through dark doorways. A few days' urbanity and we are recharged, ready for an expedition into the hills. We hope to reach Vilcabamba by nightfall.

Our bus climbs, travelling a sumptuous new tarmac road. It winds all the way up to the cloud cover that shrouds bleak and desolate highlands, then winds all the way down again. By midday we reach Saraguro, a quiet town, little more than halfway to Loja. Here the men wear ponchos and long black shorts, the women have pleated black skirts, and everyone owns a black hat not unlike a trilby. Having picked up some new passengers, we seem to be threading our way out of the town when the bus suddenly grinds to a halt. There appears to be a problem. There is *un palo* on the road, they say. I'm not sure, but I wonder if *palo* means landslide. Whatever it is, the road won't be cleared until late tonight. We can either stay here in Saraguro or go back with the bus to Cuenca. Vanella and I can't work out what to do, but we're certainly not staying, so I decide to check out *el palo*. It's just up there, up the hill, they say. So I leave Vanella guarding the gear, climb some concrete steps, pass a line of urinating Ecuadorians, round a corner and find myself on the main road.

It isn't a landslide at all, but a roadblock. *El palo* means the huge log that's been dragged across the road and propped up with boulders. Some comedian has put a tyre on the bonfire, sending up a pall of thick black smoke. A banner reads 'U.N.E. SARAGURO' and a number of locals are sitting or standing around delivering banter. I sense an underlying mood of belligerence. Someone tells me it is the teachers' union, which has gone on strike. A man with a fat stomach squeezed into a thin white shirt appears to be in charge.

'*Buenos días, gringo*,' he sneers as I pass through and stride off towards a bus I can see stationed further up the hill.

'Loja, Loja,' they say when I reach it. '*Cinquo minutos. Rapido, rapido*.'

We hope to connect to Vilcabamba in Loja. So I run . . . all the way back down to the bus, collect Vanella, and the bags, and my precious brand new Panama, and the little lady from Loja who's also stranded with us. As quickly as we can, we struggle back up the hill.

'*Hola, gringos*,' some spiteful soul calls out at the roadblock, amid jeers and laughter, as we look up to see the bus has gone.

A few minutes later a Viajeros bus, the same line as the one that brought us from Cuenca, looms over the brow and joins an already lengthy queue. It's come from Loja, and the driver tells me he may go back in about three-quarters of an hour, but he won't allow us on because he's going to have a sleep. So we camp at the roadside: me, Vanella and the little lady from Loja with her bags of shopping.

Time passes, a deceptive lull. A trickle of people goes to and fro, as do the arguments at the roadblock. Two wagons belonging to one of the utility companies, stuck either side, swap passengers and cargo. A posse of Loja's taxi-drivers bowl up and all manner of negotiations continue, except any involving teachers. Then another Viajeros bus hauls in from Loja. Once the driver and his helper have urinated, sight and sound like mules, I enquire if they plan to return.

'In half an hour,' they say. They're going to eat, then head back. So we sit and wait, until some time later I myself need a pee. I wander up the hill, faithful to custom, carefully avoiding where anyone else might have been. Mid-flow, I turn to see the latest Viajeros man running up the road towards me. '*Vamos! Vamos!*' he's shouting. They're off.

Things go swiftly crazy. We thought it was just the two of us and our lady from Loja. But, in fact, it's nearly everyone sitting around the roadblock, except for the man in the white shirt. And they're coming my way, a rabble of eager faces carrying all manner of bags and luggage. As soon as I can, I set off against the tide to find Vanella. Meanwhile, the latest Viajeros bus turns round and reverses back down the incline, a milling, gabbling crowd stumbling in pursuit. The first Viajeros bus then wakes up and also decides to turn. It's mayhem, everyone pushing and shouting in a scramble for places. We choose to stick with the first bus because it's now at the back of the queue and we hope to find seats more easily. After much barging, shoving and gritting of teeth, we get the very last two, up front by the driver.

With mock punctuality we leave Saraguro on the dot of two o'clock. Soon we are out into wild country once again, patchworked in green, isolated farmhouses lit by the dappling effect of sunlight breaking through the rainclouds. Our new driver is, inevitably, a complete maniac and, somehow, after rounding most bends there happens to be a cow standing placidly in the middle of the road. Then, before our eyes, as we pile down the steepest of hills, scattering road-crews, failing to stop for an old lady with hand outstretched, the driver's helper takes a funnel and pours what's left of a can of brake fluid through a small hole above the dashboard.

From our hammocks overlooking the valley, Vanella and I watch the last of the day turn to evening. Hammocks are just the greatest invention, provided you can spare the time – the perfect antidote to a hard day. We scarcely speak, luxuriating in the stillness of the air and the unusual combination of tropical humidity with the chill of high altitude. Plumes of blue smoke curl up from farmsteads dotted around the slopes and the clouds drift by, brushing the tops of the mountains, their shapes changing blissfully slowly. First, I can make out a duck-billed platypus, swimming underwater; then it elongates and gradually becomes a woman, flying, with a hand extended beyond her upturned nose.

The sky flushes pink. The land turns from a luminous green to burnished bronze to deep charcoal. Then we feel the bastard mosquitoes, already out hunting for a taste of blood. Stars begin to prick through. Bats flit on random radar and a myriad of scratching insects work up their nightly rhythms. Soon the frogs begin to call, a sweet sound, like a wooden hammer trilling on some exotic percussion instrument. And with the coming of darkness, one by one, the fireflies reveal to us their secret phosphorescence.

Such is life, in the Sacred Valley of Longevity.

The next day we take a stroll up the Avenue of Eternal Youth. We can see the old bridge still, what's left of it. A crude stone arch now supports two rusted metal cords, a few uprights and an armful of rotten wood suspended at odd angles. Its span would once have been about forty feet and its width just enough for a mule-cart. In the way of all things, not so very long ago they built a road. Until then, the inhabitants of Vilcabamba had lived largely undisturbed by the outside world. They worked the land, drew their water from the spring and attained ripe and healthy old ages of a hundred and thirty or a hundred and forty. Or so they say. The line between truth and legend has become a little blurred by time.

Some intrepid anthropologist first stumbled this way, returning home with tales of *los ancianos*, the ancient ones. Then came the research scientists and an army of doctors, who discovered a notable absence of such civilized ailments as cancer and heart disease. They observed that the old folk didn't seem to experience what we call senility. They just kept on working until the day they died . . . presumably of old age.

As we enter the main square a snoozing dog lifts a lazy eye and a couple of *campesinos* lounging in the shade watch us make a lonely circuit, out in the midday sun. With the exception of the church, the plaza is bounded by shabby two-storey buildings, their balconies forming a covered sidewalk below. For our delectation, we have what can loosely be described as one shop, two bars and a café. We choose the latter to rest up and sample a glass of Agua d'Oro, Vilcabamba's latest export, its very own mineral water. A poster on the wall shows two wrinkled *ancianos*, a man and his wife, grinning in a long-lived fashion under the slogan 'Happiness'. They are looking especially happy, because they've clearly been given a smart new shirt, hat and shawl for the occasion of the photograph. After a gulp or two and my body has absorbed the magic fluid like a sponge, I also feel much happier, if not a little younger.

Our languorous mood is broken by the clatter of horse's hoofs and a woman with a long, tangled mane of reddish hair rides into town, bareback and barefoot. A gringo, or more correctly *una gringa*, and no longer as young as she once was, she pulls up and shouts to a fellow American who is drinking beer at the table next to us. They are locals. He's already told us everything there is to know. There aren't so many really old people any more. Outside influences have not been kind; someone brought in a flu bug and many died. He's been here since the days before the road, before the pioneering cola wagon made it through. The first gringo to call Vilcabamba his home was one Johnny Lovewisdom, a Californian hippie who came here to live out a Utopian lifestyle. Nowadays, Johnny has moved further away into the hills, three hours or so on foot. Those who followed him to settle in the Sacred Valley earn their living from the trail of young Western travellers, drawn here by tales of longevity and the San Pedro cactus, whose powerful hallucinogenic juices have been used by the shamans for as long as anyone can remember.

Abertano Roa is the oldest now, or so he says.

'On November the seventeenth I shall be one hundred and twenty,' he proudly declares.

Señor Roa cups a firm hand over his sturdy old stick, rests a thumb against his cheek and looks me in the eye. What do you reckon to that, gringo? he's thinking.

He is a hard man. His face, which betrays a Spanish ancestry, has been toughened and creased by the sun. His expression, in repose, tends to revert to that of an old man in a grump. Beneath the shade of his straw Panama, his jowls droop and his chin, stubbled with silver like his half-formed moustache, strains to meet a protruding nose.

We are sitting out in the full sun of his backyard, where a chopping-block, washing-line, straw baskets and the obligatory clucking of hens are the signs of an everyday life. His wife Sara smiles on, round and cuddly in a generous pink dress.

'I was born in Vilcabamba,' Señor Roa tells us. 'I was baptized in the old church down there on the other side of the river. I'm no outsider. I am from the land.'

'Do you know what year you were born?' I ask, trying to verify his age.

'There were no books to inscribe in those days. I remember inscribing myself, when I was thirteen years old.' He is referring to the register of births, but these books no longer exist. 'Probably they were burnt,' he says, with a shrug.

'He was already forty years old when we were married,' his wife remarks. 'I was only fifteen.'

Sara is now eighty-seven, which, by my reckoning, makes Señor Roa a hundred and twelve. Who knows? I think we'll allow him to be his own living legend.

He's given up being grumpy anyway. He is telling us all about the church. The old village was built too close to the swamp and the houses kept flooding, so they had to move to higher ground.

Señor Roa liked the place in the old days. 'Vilcabamba was quiet, very pleasant,' he says. 'We lived well. There weren't so many people then. There was plenty to go around.' And then he repeats himself at least once and maybe twice, for good measure. Everything was so cheap. Six eggs were half a peseta. A cow cost fifteen or twenty pesos. There was such an abundance of food.

'We looked after ourselves very well. Not like it is now,' he complains, wagging a finger the colour of a cooked sausage. 'Now there are more people and less food. Whatever they can, they take away from here, by the road.'

'So what did you used to eat?'

'To eat? Everything! We'd have curds, all white and tender. And when we needed, we'd kill a calf or a cow. We didn't have to buy anything. For breakfast I'd have eggs with some rice. I ate twelve fried eggs every morning.'

He's not kidding – every day, a full dozen eggs washed down with a large jug of coffee.

'I went to work well fed,' he reminds us. All his life he worked as a cowboy.

Sara smiles with faithful admiration. 'And you used to eat the animals when you went off hunting, didn't you?' she prompts.

'Bah . . . That was just for fun!' he cries.

'What did you hunt?'

'Oh, bears, lion, deer, tapirs . . . We went hunting once a month maybe.'

'You ate a bear?'

'Yes. And we used to eat mountain lions. We shot a big fat one once and roasted it dry over the fire,' he says, chuckling at the thought of it. 'And we'd trap the tapirs.'

'What about the bears?'

'The bears? First we drank their blood.'

'What?'

'The blood. We'd hunt them down and shoot them with a rifle. Then we'd cut the jugular and drink straight from the neck.'

He has to repeat himself this time because we're in need of some clarification.

'But of course. We had no cup, so we drank the blood like water from a tap. It was still warm,' says Señor Roa, smacking his lips. 'We took the life of the bear and fed on its strength.'

'And what did it taste like?'

'Oh, a bit like cow's blood. Not bad at all, really, only a little salty.'

'Do you ever eat fruit or vegetables?' Vanella enquires, hesitantly.

He nods. 'Oh, yes, plenty, plenty. Plantain, papaya, banana and sometimes an orange or two. We grew grain, maize and wheat. We grew beans. There was such abundance. The water is pure and the climate excellent. Though it is much drier now. In the old days we used to have heavy, heavy rain for days on end.'

The sound of laughter heralds the arrival of some of Señor Roa's great-grandchildren, teenagers styled in American clothes and baseball caps. Their patriarch takes to looking sullen and disinterested as they find somewhere to sit. Then he's the centre of attention once more and immediately perks up.

'So tell us, why have you lived so long?' I ask.

'I am still alive because I believe in eating well. Good nourishment,' he says, a hand tapping his belly. Then he grasps the air with both fists. 'Life comes to us through the mouth, you see.'

He tells us how the doctors came to subject the old folk to an array of medical tests. They had their blood drawn out and taken away. They were hooked up to machines and had wires stuck all over their bodies. The doctors made their diagnosis, but never told him anything other than, 'You're OK.'

'Never again,' he says solemnly. 'Why should I let them take my blood? I already know I'm OK.'

He has never smoked or drunk liquor. He used to play his guitar at weddings and make music so people could dance. If they tried to give him anything to drink, he always refused.

'He loved to play the guitar,' says Sara, smiling sweetly. 'But he's lost his hearing and cannot play now. He gets so frustrated that he can't hear as well as he did. He gets cross, and then I have to yell at him.'

We ask Señor Roa what's the secret of the longevity of his marriage. The youngsters, I see, are listening in with interest.

He thinks for a moment. 'God gave me that woman there,' he says, 'so I have to keep her until I am gone.'

Sara is more down to earth. She says he's often bad-tempered. 'But the secret of this marriage is that he has no vices,' she adds, 'so he is easy to put up with. I have patience enough. In a marriage, if the woman is angry as well as the man, they kill each other. But I am tame.'

'She married young and I married old,' pipes up Señor Roa.

'Did you have any girlfriends before then?'

'Oh, yes, I had my women,' he says, stifling a laugh. 'They couldn't resist my singing, when I played my guitar. I had to fight them off, you know.'

'Hey hey . . .' calls out one of the teenagers.

'So why did you get married?'

'Because this one,' he says, pointing to his wife, 'she just came from her house and lay beside me, so I couldn't throw her out. I said to myself, "All right, I'll keep her."'

'And why did you choose him?' we then ask Sara, and she smiles coyly.

'I had other boyfriends who were after me, but I think it was his guitar. It was probably because he used to serenade me.'

Cheers fill the backyard for the old romantic.

'Will you give him a kiss?' I ask Sara.

'No,' she says, 'he gets really upset if I do that.'

'Will you give her a kiss, then?' I tease Señor Roa. But he throws back his head in disdain, clamps his lips tight and reverts to looking glum.

* * *

Then we make Ramona cry.

Her house is but one room, with a tin roof and a weathered door on a rusty hinge. She is wary of us, but comes to sit down on a stone outside. We introduce ourselves, ask what she can tell us of her life, and it's as if we've unlocked a door to a secret chamber she always keeps closed. She replies in a plaintive little voice, her words scurrying through the tears until she breaks down weeping.

Vanella holds her hand. Ramona looks up miserably, her thin frame shaking.

Life has been hard on Ramona. Her face looks haggard and drawn, though her hair remains jet black. Some *ancianos*, it is said, never show any sign of grey.

Ramona was an orphan. Her mother died giving birth and her father wasn't the least bothered. In fact, he wanted to be rid of her, to drown her like a kitten. Instead, she was taken away and brought up by a cousin. When she was old enough she was given the housework to do, and if she did anything wrong, they used to punish and beat her. The cousin's children went to school, but Ramona never did. All she knew was housework. In the end she ran away. She went to live with her sister. Then she found out she was pregnant and gave birth to a baby daughter. The infant was immediately taken from her and raised by another family. Her daughter has died now, so Ramona only has her two sons. One lives far away in Guayaquil. The other lives here in Vilcabamba, but never even comes to see her.

So Ramona stays alone in her dark little house. And when she goes out the neighbours' children throw stones at her.

Her wrinkled hand, black with grime, grips tightly on to Vanella's.

'How come you have lived so long, when you've had such a tough life?' Vanella says, stroking to comfort her.

'I don't know,' Ramona says feebly, sniffing. 'Maybe it is because of the climate here, maybe because I have always eaten what the land gives me.'

She looks up at Vanella through a tearful smile. '*Bonita*,' she whimpers, reaching out to touch her cheek. '. . . *Bonita*.'

I sometimes wonder about the element of chance in all this – like, what happens if you turn up somewhere and ask if you can talk to their elders. Often we have little control over who we are taken to see. They aren't always dancing with health and vigour.

Someone tells us they know of some really ancient folk who live in Tumianuma, a small community in an adjacent valley. We hitch a ride in an open lorry into the back of beyond. We jump down and we're left standing in a dusty space that is neither street nor square. There is no sign of life, only a herd of goats lounging on benches in the shade of a boarded-up house. They look almost human, the way they sit.

A tiny figure appears in the distance, moving slowly towards us through the shimmering heat. As he draws close, I see he drags one foot in the sand. It is the village idiot. His face is distorted, twitching spasmodically under a filthy old hat. His speech is quite incomprehensible.

We hear a door bang and turn to see another man who has come to find out who we are. He scolds the poor idiot, shooing him away.

'There was an old lady used to live here,' he says, scratching his jaw. 'She was a hundred and forty. But she died eight years ago.'

Then he beckons, leading us to what can only be described as a hovel. There, an old man lies on the floor. His name is Juan Francisco Flores. He owns nothing but the rags he wears and a dented tin mug. Juan Francisco is dying. Of all the people we have met, he is the closest to death, I'm sure. He has only a few hours remaining. We press his hand gently and talk for a while, as best we can.

'I don't know, I'm probably seven thousand years old by now,' he says, his chest rattling as he struggles for breath.

He lived all his life in Vilcabamba, but he never married and has no children. He was born here in Tumianuma. He's come home to spend the last of his days.

'Ooooh, it was all such a long time ago,' he whispers.

I look into his haggard face. There is light in his tired eyes still. He wants to tell us more and tries to sit up.

'. . . I thought I was going to die this morning, but no. I didn't have any breakfast, then someone brought me some coffee.'

He groans a little, from the pain. 'I don't know how long I'm going to last . . .'

Vanella and I look at each other and smile meekly. Then we smile bravely for Juan Francisco. He eases out another breath and we follow it right to its end, a moment of silence . . . he grasps at more air.

There isn't much we can do. Normally we would wish him good

health and continued long life, but as we leave Juan Francisco in peace, there is little to say other than a heartfelt '*Adiós*.'

We take the road to San Pedro. The village of San Pedro de Vilcabamba perches on a hill to the north of the Sacred Valley, its houses clustered around the church as if for protection. An old cart-track leads out of the village, down through the woods and along the riverbank. Near where the track becomes a path, with gates to open and close, two footbridges span the river. One has been ingeniously fashioned from pieces of wood and fence-wire; crossing requires courage, good balance and a firm grip. The second is a stronger, more trustworthy construction. I stand in the middle, as the waters slide frothing below me. Vanella leans against a post.

We stay and let the twilight deepen. All the sharpness of the day has gone, the colours cooling now, washes of mauve and dull straw. Away down-river, the rooftops and church tower of San Pedro are looking distinctly medieval. Before us, a steep hillside is arranged in tidy strips of cultivation.

I shall remember this moment always.

Two young boys, brothers, are running the donkeys home along the levels. We can hear their sweet voices calling. Their dog barks and struts, pushing the animals on. They don't see us. We are perfectly still, following their progress as they trot the paths they know so well, towards a small dwelling perched on the slope where the light of a fire is flickering.

And we feel we have seen a glimpse of life unchanged for a hundred years.

19

Hocus-pocus

It is the Day of the Dead and everyone has gathered out at the cemetery. The weather looks set fair and, beyond the town, the waters of Lake Titicaca shine like a sapphire clasped in the barren claws of the Altiplano.

The people seem in a lively mood as they settle themselves among the graves, which often are little more than a mound of compacted earth dressed with a simple cross and some flowers in a beer bottle. Whole families of Aymara Indians are grouped together around their loved ones, as prayers are said for those lost souls who may still be suffering in purgatory. The men, modestly clothed in black, lead the children in chanting the lines they have learnt, hands pressed together in hope. And wrapped in black shawls, their bowler hats perched at all angles, the women sit together in twos and threes looking forward to a good old gossip.

Around noon, with their observances complete, they begin to spill across the hillside, resembling a flock of crows out foraging. Shopping bags are set down, cloths lifted from baskets and spread on the ground. The young ones are handed a chunk of bread, bottles are uncorked and the celebrations begin to flow, lasting until the going down of the day. As darkness falls, they join together in music – a guitar, an accordion, drums rattling out a beat and pipes whistling a fraction out of tune. Then a winding procession marches back along the dusty road and down through narrow cobbled streets. High spirits and alcohol carry them to the main square where the older men take their partners, and with a cry and a handclap, full skirts and pink-edged petticoats are soon swirling through the night.

In the morning, Vanella and I are out enjoying a little sun. From our bench in the square we watch the world go by, practising for when we're old. There's no hurry, not up here. At 12,500 feet, the air we funnel down is thin and dry. The ruddy-cheeked Aymaran ladies understand only too well. Bundles slung on their backs, they pass by at a steady plod. Their working colours are bright pinks, purples and blues, patterned in narrow stripes; their everyday bowler hats are smudged with grime. The men, drab as moles, prefer to loiter on the street corners, eyes hooded against the light. No one pays us much attention: they think we've come to see their lady of the lake. Nestled here on the Bolivian shore, the town of Copacabana's main claim to fame is its shrine to the Dark Virgin. Miracles have been known to occur, or so it is written.

A car dressed with flowers and streamers pulls up by the cathedral steps. It is an Opala saloon, which looks something like an old Ford Cortina. Off-white with a red stripe, it is extremely clapped out and belongs to an Aymaran gentleman and his family. A dozen or more adults and a progression of children, they're keyed up with anticipation and set about buying all the trinkets they can afford at the row of diminutive stalls along by the gates.

We spy a lone figure crossing the wide expanse of courtyard under the looming white walls and bell-tower of the cathedral. With his brown habit tied at the waist with a cord and tassel, he's a cheery-looking sort of priest, an elderly gentleman of European extraction who walks with a limp. Saying hello to one and all, he pinches a red carnation from inside the car and swiftly gets down to business. The bonnet is propped open, the flower dipped repeatedly in his copper pitcher to spray holy water all over the engine. Each family member now receives three whacks of wet carnation on the head, and then on their hands for steady steering. The priest looks to be saying, 'Drive carefully. Go slow and the Lord will watch over you.' Then he flicks around inside the car, a few more splashes on the roof and he's off, aiming what's left in the pitcher at a mongrel lazing on the steps. By the time it has stretched, stood up and had a sniff, the priest is gone, retreating once more to his cloister.

Corks pop. They all hug. Confetti and fresh flowers are thrown over the Opala now that it has received its holy service. The kids set off firecrackers. Crates of beer are dragged out, a dark local brew which an exuberant youth sprays liberally both inside, outside and on all four wheels of the car. Someone produces a Polaroid camera so they shuffle together to pose, stiff and serious. Then they crowd around to watch the results appear like magic, secure in the belief that everything will now be all right, and their journeys will be safe.

'Do you believe in miracles?' Vanella murmurs in my ear.

'I don't know . . . I'm not sure I do. Not this sort of thing, anyway. This is like never walking under ladders. Or the numbers.'

Room numbers, phone numbers, anything to do with seven I'll happily believe is good news. Somehow, it always is. Thirteen – that's bad news.

'And what about St Christopher?' I add. 'We wear these round our necks because maybe he offers us some kind of protection. And because Mum gave them to us. It's irrational, though. Why should a piece of pressed silver make any difference?'

'But you believe there's some force greater than us, don't you?' says Vanella.

'Yeah. My old life force.'

'So . . .'

'A miracle suggests some kind of divine intervention.'

'Extraordinary things do happen.'

'I know, but I can't believe in a God who happens to turn on a little magic just when He feels like it.'

'Hmm. Doesn't it come from us?' she says, sucking her teeth, as a coach full of pilgrims hauls in throwing up a cloud of chalky grey dust.

We find *el colegio* on the edge of the town. As we sit waiting in the schoolyard, the local children feast their curious eyes on us, but still keep a safe distance. Few gringos ever cross their threshold. A young boy dares to run up and stare at us, cheekily, full in the face. I lean forward and go, '*Hola!*' and he scampers off to hide behind his chums. The girls whisper, huddled in a group, giggling nervously.

Clementina is even more excited to meet us. She is their English teacher, an Indian girl in her late twenties, who marches us straight off to the headmaster's office, chattering all the way. She presents us to her boss with an exaggerated formality, although *el director* seems more interested in discussing the dwindling size and declining number of species of fish in the lake. Then, one at a time, shy teenagers in blue uniforms are brought in to say who is the eldest in their family. And a girl called Maritza agrees to take us to see her great-grandmother.

So, the next afternoon, we follow the old Inca road out of town towards the Island of the Sun. Near a place called Titicachi, we strike up around the hillside maintaining a respectful pace. The sun beats down, harsh and unforgiving. The air tastes sharp, it is so pure.

Over the brow, the sawing bray of a donkey in the distance heralds a tranquil scene, a belt of ancient farming land that slopes gently down to the lake. Tiny round figures in hats are bent over working the fields, irregular shapes of ploughed earth and fresh green growth. Here and there, some sheep manage to graze on bare patches of rough ground. And at the water's edge, two small boats lie moored among the reeds, from where Titicaca stretches like a sea beyond the horizon.

'Watch out for scorpions!' calls Maritza.

'What do they do?'

Clementina has already told us that the dragonflies we've watched dance by in exquisite style will steal our hair and carry it off to the witches, if we're not careful. Scorpions? They just sting you.

Clementina is still chattering away, as we follow Maritza through a dappled grove of swaying eucalyptus trees. She's now telling some story about someone's neighbour casting spells with frogs, and hair of cat and dog. Witchcraft is widely practised even today, she says, and many people in La Paz are cannibals. Of that, she is quite certain.

We reach a group of farm buildings. Those in use stand two storeys tall, walls caked with mud, cracked like crazy-paving. Immediately behind them, up the hill, we can see the old dwellings they've replaced falling silently to ruin.

'*Bisabuela! Bisabuelita!*' calls out Maritza, as she looks for her great-grandmother.

The sheep have been nibbling the grass at the front to a close-cropped lawn and, from the mildly uncomfortable smell about the place, some have recently come to a necessary end. A couple of raw skins lie drying in the heat of the afternoon.

We hear a shuffling sound and a little old lady emerges through a weatherbeaten wooden door to stand squinting into the sun. Maritza bends to kiss her and they hold hands to look at one another before turning to us.

They make a wonderful pair. Fresh-faced young Maritza sports jeans and a T-shirt, a red zipper jacket and a peaked cap with a hip design of pink and green zigzags. Her great-grandmother looks like she's been wearing the same clothes for years. Despite the weather, she is wrapped in numerous layers of skirts, woollen cardigans and shawls, flecked here and there with bits of straw. A large safety-pin secures her undershirt at the neck while another is fastened at her chest, for emergencies. Her bowler is stained and dusty, light brown with a pale band around the rim. Between them, they symbolize all that's different between old and new.

Juana Mamani de Pilco is her name. She bows her head, making a little nod as we shake hands. Her skin feels dry and tough as hide. Fussing nervously, she goes off to find a blanket, which we spread out on the flat grass. Then she squats on the low stone wall with her back to the sun and we all sit in a circle around her.

'When I was her age, we didn't wear shoes,' Juana Mamani says in a squeaky voice. 'Our skirts were made from animal skin. We lived on dried potatoes, nothing but potatoes every day. We didn't know what coffee was, or tea. There were no laws out here, no authorities, no schools like they have now. These young ones are so lucky they have the chance to study.'

She smiles at Maritza, a matriarchal pride brimming over her leathery, round face. Her features are pinched with wrinkles and her yellowed teeth number precisely two and a half.

Her son, Justino, has seen us from afar and returns from the field. He sets down his spade and small scythe, rubbing away at the dark earth on his hands. His large brown eyes come questioning; his workwear includes a pair of dark pinstripe trousers. Shaking our hands studiously, he squats down to find out what's going on.

'Great-grandma believes in the Aymara religion,' Maritza tells us.

I'm wondering what survives of the old beliefs. I've heard the Aymara still worship the earth as the source of all life. They call her Pachamama, Mother Earth. They also once bowed down to the sun, when they lived in subjugation to the Incas, their one-time neighbours.

And so we learn that Juana Mamani prays to God on Wednesdays, Thursdays and Saturdays. A native doctor had once instructed her when she was ill. She could ask things of God on those days. Mondays, Tuesdays, Fridays and Sundays weren't so convenient, because they were holy days. Wednesdays, Thursdays and Saturdays were less busy.

'There was a time,' says Juana Mamani, 'when God meant *Ama Llulla . . . Ama Quella . . . Ama Suwa*. God was these three things.'

Ama Llulla. Ama Quella. Ama Suwa. Don't be a liar. Don't be lazy. Don't be a thief.

'There was a punishment from the law of the Incas,' she recalls. 'Anyone found to be a thief would be beaten. If he stole again, he would be whipped. A third time and his hand would be cut off.'

'So who was this God?' I ask.

'We Aymara people worshipped the sun, and the moon,' Justino answers, pointing in the direction of the Island of the Sun, which the Incas believed to be the source of all creation.

'If you drink water from the ancient springs there, you will stay young for ever,' Clementina adds for us, knowledgeably.

The Island of the Moon lies close by also. Legend has it that before the sun was born, a race of people existed there. And when the sun appeared, they went to live below ground. Justino claims the archaeologists have found their bones.

Juana Mamani is whispering to Maritza. 'Through the Church,' she says. 'God exists through the Church.'

'She also believes in the Catholic religion,' confirms Maritza.

'Now we know the story of the birth of Jesus and his ascension into heaven,' says Justino.

'When did the Aymara people learn about Jesus?'

'Long ago,' says Juana Mamani, 'but there was an important meeting when the decision was made to change our belief, from Aymara to Catholic.' She remembers this happened when she was a little girl.

'They began to believe in God the Father, the Son and the Holy Spirit,' Justino explains, 'and the coming of the Lord Jesus Christ. He came to earth from heaven. And because Jesus came to earth, so the earth belonged to God. Therefore the Aymara people had to believe in Him, because they needed the earth to survive.'

I'm considering the neatness of this missionary logic, whereby Pachamama conveniently becomes the property of the Holy Trinity, when Juana Mamani is suddenly tugging at Maritza's arm.

'The sun,' she squeaks. 'It is burning.'

So we all make a fuss and ask if she wants to sit in the shade.

'No, no,' she says. She's pointing at me. It's my nose, which has apparently turned bright red.

'I'm fine,' I say, and pull down the brim of my hat, but Justino jumps up and fetches a black umbrella with two wobbly struts and no handle, which Juana Mamani uses to provide some shade. It goes rather well with her bowler, I think.

Justino then brings out another hat, brushing it with care and affection. This one used to belong to Juana Mamani's mother and is a rare, musty old thing, hand-made from wool pressed to a felt. It would make a fine prop for a portrait, but Juana Mamani is nervous. She thinks I'm going to carry off her soul in my little black box. I promise I won't and Maritza promises too, and so Juana Mamani puts her trust in the new and says she doesn't mind.

As the sun is sinking over the lake, we exchange gifts. We offer Juana Mamani biscuits and chocolate from the shop in town. She gives Maritza a bag of potatoes and bundles of herbs to take home for the family. Then she walks with us to the path, while Justino wanders away down the hill clapping his hands to scare off the birds.

'Here, take some of this,' she says, busily picking sprigs of verbena and pushing them into Maritza's bag. 'There's camomile and nettle too. You can boil them up and make tea.'

Maritza holds her great-grandmother's hands and gives them a squeeze. They smile, returning love in equal measure, and tell each other to take good care.

'Juana Mamani, why have you lived so long?' I ask her finally, as we are saying goodbye.

She looks up at me as if she's never thought about this before. 'Why, I live here,' she says, with a shrug, casting her hand out across the land. 'And God . . . God always looks after me.'

Who she means I'm not quite sure – God the Father, God the Sun, or God the Mother Earth?

When we reach the eucalyptus grove, we turn to wave. But all we can see is a small figure in a bowler hat, bent over hunting for herbs among the bushes.

~

Behind the church of San Francisco, up the hill, the steepness of which makes the unsuspecting foreigner gasp for air, we find the La Paz branch of the witches' general store. From these few stalls erected in a cobbled backstreet, we can select from the packed display of sacks, bags, jars and honeycomb boxes. We have herbs, dried flowers, leaves, roots and bark. Something for everything, a cure for any ailment.

Vanella inspects a colourful pot-pourri of ingredients laid out on tin plates: stones, minerals, seed pods from the rainforest and the bright yellow larvae of some form of grub.

'Can you tell me what this is for?' I chance, pointing at a portion of starfish.

The plump lady with plaited hair grins unnecessarily, showing us her blackened teeth. She taps her forehead. '*Murrio*,' she says. Starfish is a cure for depression.

To improve our luck, we could have a small glass phial of oil crammed with pieces of red and green vegetable matter, one floating seed and a wee copper horseshoe. Or maybe we should invest in a pocket-sized presentation of more bits: a baby shell, one red seed, one black, an embroidered heart, a crystal and a snippet of ribbon. Only two inches wide, this tiny package is protected by a plastic bag tied with golden thread. On the back, a prayer, poorly photocopied on a slip of paper, guarantees us happiness and fortune. Next, folded in used computer printout the size of a matchbox, we open a nest of red wool, containing two different seeds between two small soapstone figures, all topped with plastic tinsel and filings of pressed metal. This one is for love and fertility. And if we were then to build a house and couldn't lay hands on a fresh one, we would need a dried llama's foetus. These are piled up in a basket, like specimens of some grotesque alien form. We'd use one to make as our sacrifice to Pachamama.

We pass on the llama, but can't resist a little love and fertility.

'When shall we three meet again?' I'm forced to wonder aloud as we leave the Aymaran lady counting her bolivianos.

~

In my pocket I am carrying a piece of a pale green paper. It has lived there for some days and is now dog-eared and furry. Each time it falls out I see the name scribbled in black biro – Señor Don Joaquín Gantier. We know very little about the man, only that we must find him – at all costs. The kind lady who wrote his name was on the point of saying goodbye when she threw up her hands and cried, 'Why, of course! How could I forget? Don Joaquín! You have to see Don Joaquín. Ask for him at la Casa de la Libertad.' Then she smiled, a knowing smile in which I saw the promise of something not to be missed.

I hold my scrap of paper as if it's a talisman that will bring us safely to him. I feel as if it is meant to be, just as everything that happens to us these days is somehow meant to be.

And so, in good faith, we make our way to Sucre, the old capital, and the city welcomes us to its civilized charm. Here, in 1825, the Declaration of Independence was signed in a Jesuit chapel, which was to become Bolivia's seat of government. On the wall outside we find a plaque which reads: 'The people of Sucre pay homage to Joaquín Gantier, guardian of la Casa de la Libertad . . .'

'Don Joaquín? He is not well today,' says the man in uniform behind the desk. Begrudgingly, he lifts the receiver and dials. His conversation is brief; our man looks startled. 'Don Joaquín says you must come at once.'

Within the hour, we are perched on a creased leather sofa, whose ancient springs we can feel groaning beneath us. We are enthralled. The one and only Don Joaquín Gantier Valda – author, poet, playwright and historian – is commanding centre stage. He sits facing us in an old wooden chair with a beautifully scrolled leather back. Dressed for comfort, he wears a dark green corduroy house-coat with wide floppy collars and a woollen cardigan buttoned down the front. He's still delivering his opening speech. We haven't even had a chance to explain why we're here.

'Read the first page of Columbus,' he implores us. 'There you will see described the original encounter between Spanish culture and the savages of America . . .'

Don Joaquín plays to his audience. This is high drama. He speaks with deliberate emphasis, such feeling.

'And was there shooting? Was there killing?' he cries, turning on us with an expectant look. 'No! What happened, if you read, is that the presence of the one Supreme Being was brought to the New World.'

Don Joaquín holds up a hand, looks away, then back again, eyes questioning, before he lets himself go. 'And during fifty years at la Casa de la Libertad, all I have ever wanted is UNION!'

As the word resounds throughout the house, he shakes clenched fists to the air. Then he pauses to take stock, sufficient for us to reveal something of our purpose.

'Ah! You have seen the world,' he says, attentive. 'This is good, very good. You keep open minds.' Don Joaquín wipes his ample white moustache and nods as we tell him more. 'What an idea!' he breathes. 'But this is . . . oh . . . life! Are you married? Do you have children?' Maybe soon? Ah ha. And how long have you been married? Only four years? No matter. All you need do is pray to God and keep at it!' And so he roars, and then laughs with all his might.

Don Joaquín receives visitors in an intimate square room, which overlooks, on three of its sides, a random geometry of terracotta roofs. Its further purpose is to celebrate a life. Thus, we are surrounded by framed diplomas and awards of merit, inscribed silver plates, a bust or two of the man himself, a caricature model – all manner of personal knick-knackery.

But he's away again, telling us now about La Glorieta, an old mansion outside the town which has Arabian-style gardens. There, he says, we can see a picture of Alfonso XIII, the King of Spain, who at the turn of the century married Queen Victoria's granddaughter. We must keep up. Don Joaquín's logic is erratic. He can leap from topic to topic with only the barest of causal links. Next, he's talking about the Koran and how it prohibits the painting of the human image. Now Velázquez . . . You can tell Velázquez had some Moorish blood in him because when he painted Christ he didn't let us see his face. Dali? Dali's Christ has no face at all.

As one thought concludes with a flourish, Don Joaquín will be seized by another idea. And so he plunges into a tale about Juana Azurduy de Padilla, an historical figure he once wrote about in one of his books. A gang of her men had come to steal his family's wheat. That was long ago, in the days when their property used to extend all the way up to La Recoleta, the convent at the top of the hill.

As the story is told, I allow myself to watch, spellbound. There is urgency, such energy. His hands are never still, pointing, reinforcing, punctuating the air. The hair is white, swept back, eyebrows thick and bristling. And while the face belongs to an elderly man, it could almost be a mask. For the spirit that dances within is eager and quick, and all roles are performed with equal vitality, from the earnest commentator to the playful tease. It's all there in the eyes. They shine, dark, like precious beads. Don Joaquín, I believe, is part Spanish nobleman, part wizard.

He turns to me now, hands over his ears, accentuating the prominence of both moustache and a generous nose, which is pitted at its end like a burst sausage. He wants Vanella to cover her ears. When she has and is pretending not to listen, he returns to me and whispers gravely, 'I am ninety-three and a half, but I wouldn't want any ladies to consider me too old. Although I am this age, I wish to converse and be treated as normal.' Raising his eyebrows, with a twinkle he nods and Vanella is released.

Now he looks about, as if he's forgotten something. Abruptly, he stands and we follow him to a display case by the wall.

'There is no other man in Bolivia who has been so decorated,' he says, tapping the glass, grinning as he shows us the medals with their coloured ribbons on red brocade. 'This one here is the latest, from the King of Spain.' And he picks out the photo of him and the King standing on the steps of la Casa de la Libertad. 'Look now, this one is of the President of Germany and his wife Marianne. When I was in Bonn, I saw them married . . .'

Don Joaquín's voice trails away as he is struck by some new idea. He shepherds us back to the centre of the room, his elbows raised, fingers trilling, his brow furrowed with intent.

'Come, give me your right hand,' he says. 'Now give me yours.'

Taking both our hands he places them together and holds them grasped within the warmth of his own. He looks up into our faces, watching, waiting for his moment.

He speaks with a quiet solemnity. 'This is for eternity. This is for ever,' he says, bowing his head. 'Now, you may give her a kiss.'

We turn, smiling, and look into each other's eyes. We are man and wife. We see our soul mate, our travelling companion. Whatever we once thought we had between us, this journey is everything we have now. And so we kiss.

'Bravo!' he shouts. 'How beautiful this is to see. Come . . .' His hand beckons us nearer still and we bend our heads, listening close. I feel his breath on my cheek. The mask is alive with mischief. There is some sorcery afoot.

He addresses Vanella. 'From the look in his eyes, he loves you more than you love him,' he tells her.

Vanella considers this and Don Joaquín waits, his head cocked like a bird.

'No, he doesn't,' she protests.

'*Muy bien, muy bien*,' he cries, exultant. 'Ha haaah . . . I say that he loves her more and she says, "No, I love him more." *Muy bien!*'

And then, with a hand poised, he strikes a poetic stance and pronounces, 'The more you love, the more your eyes will weep. When a man weeps for sublime things, the stars in the sky are shining.'

He holds a rapt expression for a brief dramatic pause, then relaxes and returns us to the settee, our troth firmly pledged once more.

'Now I shall tell you how I've lived my life,' he follows quickly, and we nod, blankly, a little dazed.

'One day,' he recalls, 'I was writing in a room here overlooking the street. Suddenly, outside I heard a man shout, "Here it is." He burst right in and demanded, "You must give back all the letters my daughter has written to you." "I won't," I said. "I won't give them to you." So he beat me with his stick and I cried, "No, I will not give you those letters." So then he whipped me. I was thrown on to the sofa but managed to drag an iron across from the fire with my foot and so *thwack* . . . Then he took out his pistol.' Here Don Joaquín jams two fingers into his own neck to demonstrate. '"You coward!"' he shouts, '"Shoot me if you're a man, but I'm not giving you a single letter."'

Don Joaquín draws breath and checks our reaction.

'I still have them,' he says in triumph. 'Do you know who she was? She was my first wife, great-granddaughter of the one-time president of Argentina.'

Estelle was her name, the most intelligent and attractive of four sisters. She was so beautiful that everyone used to crowd round to stare when her presence was announced.

Don Joaquín grows quiet, his mood pursuing the memory.

'Alas, she died,' he says. 'She became ill with cancer. That was the only time I lost my faith. We were in São Paulo, Brazil. The doctor came to tell me my wife was dying. He laid his hand on my shoulder. I remember his office, a small room. On the desk was an image of Jesus Christ. At the window which gave on to the gardens was a picture of God our Father. I grew suddenly very angry. "No," I shouted. "This is fetishism. These things have no power."'

Don Joaquín heaves out a sigh and is raising his finger to conclude when he's distracted by the entrance of Maria Louisa, his second wife, a demure, silver-haired lady some years his junior. She has brought a tray of glasses and red vermouth to warm our hearts.

'So, are you happy?' Don Joaquín asks, as we sip the wine.

'Yes, we're very happy.'

'Ah, *muy bien*! Friendship and happiness, that's what life is about. For me, today is a happy day. We should all stay just as we are. You know, I shouldn't really be here at all. I was invited to the United States to attend a conference – "The Mission for a Better World". I wrote an article entitled "America"; that's why they chose me. There have been meetings.'

'And what have you concluded?'

'This is it. You have to get everyone agreed, unified, and live it out. Not just talk about it, but *live* it. The trouble with Latin America is that everyone wants to be president. Any attempt for the greater good always fails. Unity, that's my belief. That's what Bolivar wanted. "Unify! Unify!" he once wrote. "If not, anarchy will devour you." In the early days, they didn't create strong states. That is what has been missing. And that is what I have proclaimed for fifty years at la Casa de la Libertad. Union!'

Now it is time for our tour of the house. Don Joaquín takes Vanella's arm and leads us out to the gallery where, beneath columned arches, we look down on a beautiful sunlit garden and admire panoramic views across the city to the blue hills beyond. He shows us his bedroom, with its comforting smell of antique furniture, miniature portraits of Christ and a small silver cross nailed above the bed. Then we stand with him before a fine portrait of Estelle, which hangs in the next door room. Back outside, he spies the Indian maid quietly going about her duties.

'Will you please close that door?' he calls. Then to us he confides, 'We don't want to catch pneumonia. You should always keep your mouth closed and make sure to breathe through your nose. Otherwise you have no filter to keep out the germs.'

So now we follow his example, wandering about with pursed lips, two fingers clipped across our mouths like clothes-pegs.

20

Life and Death in Caracas

I suppose this was bound to happen. I wouldn't say I'm homesick. I'm full to the brim with life and the world, but I'm running on empty. I want to stop moving. For once, I just need to be still.

I mean, look at me. My T-shirt's frayed, my trousers are worn thin, darned at the knee, colour bleached out by the sun. The toe-ends of my loafers have come apart so many times now they're bonded to the soles with about three tubes of super-glue. Vanella is much the same. The swirly pattern of her skirt makes a handy disguise for the several little bunches of material where she's had to mend holes. We can just about look respectable, but in truth we're held together with a mile or two of thread and a stretch of the invaluable gaffer tape.

I've long since forgotten what it's like to be normal, grounded. I lost it, way back. I do sometimes miss the simple things. Like, when did I last make myself a sandwich? Slice some fresh bread, go look in the fridge for cheese and green pepper; a little mayonnaise and a few drops of chilli sauce. What would I give to spend the night in our own bed? And then again the next night. I can't take a shower these days without holding my mouth shut to keep the bugs out. Oh, to be dressed in a different set of clothes, to reacquaint myself with all that was once so familiar I wanted to escape from it. Enough, enough.

Caracas doesn't help. It seems we picked the scruffy end of town. Around here, the locals stare even more than they do in China. And then there are the pools of dried blood everywhere on the pavement. The taxi-driver who took us to pick up our mail told of the enormous gap between rich and poor. If you're wounded in a fight and can't afford hospital, you die.

We just hang out, waiting. The room consists of a bed, a table, the constant rattle of air-con and a crackly black-and-white TV spouting election broadcasts. If only Alejandro would call. He's our contact. The plan is to travel west up the coast to meet a venerable old gentleman who is the Bishop of Coro.

When he does call, Alejandro says we are to leave for Coro the very next day. Spurred to action, we attend to a few last-minute chores. Late afternoon, I slip out on the pretext of taking some photos to buy Vanella a present, a pair of earrings she's seen in a shop window. It'll soon be Christmas. On my way back, I call in at the local bar to stock up with mineral water. And it's very odd. The guy who serves me looks concerned and he says something about *la señora*. He's seen us together before. His Spanish is too quick for me and I nod stupidly as if I've understood. But he repeats himself, more urgently, and I catch it this time. 'You'd better go see *la señora*,' he says. Still I smile. Then, walking back, I sense there's something wrong.

I find Vanella writhing in agony. Her look tells me straight away.

'It's a bad one,' she groans, clutching her gut. 'It's serious, I know it is. Come on. Quick. Do your massage.'

I try every trick, kneading, pulling, working around her abdomen. But it's no good. I keep putting my ear to her stomach. There's nothing – no gurgles, no movement, just a dark, unyielding silence. She's obstructed. It doesn't help that she's tense, so she tries some deep breathing while I'm dispatched to buy salt. She wants to make herself sick. That doesn't work either.

'No, oh, no,' she whimpers. 'What are we going to do?'

She's beginning to panic. If it doesn't clear, we both know what we have to do. Another half-hour and I'm decided. 'We've got to go. We need help. Let's get you a bag together.'

She hobbles downstairs, bent double. I show the man at the desk the guidebook and ask which of the two hospitals listed is nearest, and best. His dirty fingernail underlines Hospital de Clínicas Caracas.

'*Emergencia! Emergencia!*' I gabble. I'm sure the taxi man thinks Vanella is about to give birth on his back seat. Steering his rusty old brown boat of an American sedan through the rush-hour traffic, he cuts down back alleys, squeezes up pavements and bounces through red lights, blowing his horn like a siren.

The doctor who sees us in casualty seems to know what he's doing. Rafael de la Fuente is his name, and he speaks English, which helps. He puts Vanella on suction to pump her out, like they used to at home.

We have to wait for a day or so, till it clears. Soon she's lying in a room with a drip hooked in her arm and a tube up her nose.

'I'm sorry,' she says mournfully. 'I'm so sorry.'

'Don't be silly. You'll be fine now. This is a serious hospital.'

I don't say anything, but the room number is 616.

Vanella's stomach swells like a balloon. Then she begins to suffer bouts of shivering. By the third night the pain is so bad, she can't sleep at all.

Dr de la Fuente keeps a close watch. It turns out he's the chief surgeon. A good-looking man in his mid-forties, he has a thick black moustache broader than his smile and an air of calm self-assurance. He doesn't normally wear the suit, more chinos and short-sleeved shirts, which reveal he also has the forearms of a stevedore.

Showing us the latest set of X-rays, he indicates where Vanella is still obstructed. He says he thinks he's going to need to operate.

'Are you sure? Can't we wait a little longer?' she pleads.

'Well, it should have cleared by now. Has it taken this long before?'

'No,' she reluctantly admits.

'From your history, I think there is something causing the constriction. If it doesn't clear itself, we shall have to do something to make it better.'

When he's gone, Vanella grips my hand. 'I'm a bit frightened, Boot. My mum never let the surgeons operate. She used to fight them off, you know. It could make things worse in the long run. She said your intestine is like snakes in a drum of oil. It isn't good to touch or even expose it to the air. What do you think he'll do?'

'He said he'd have to take a look first, didn't he? Don't worry. It'll be OK.'

She lifts her gown and looks down at her stomach, already scarred from the time they operated when she was a baby.

'Will you still love me when I have tramlines?' she says.

I have a lump in my throat as she lets go my hand and I watch them wheel her away. I follow as far as the lift, blow her a kiss, give a little wave and a smile. Back in the room, the suction pump stands ominously silent. For a while I watch the cars outside on the freeway where an intersection forms a triangle with a slip-road and a bridge. There's a Lucky Strike poster and a monster satellite dish on one of the housing-blocks that makes up the jumble of flat roofs and concrete. Away to my left, a wooded hillside climbs steeply to the ridge which runs high above the city. It could be worse, I suppose. We might have been in the middle of nowhere.

Three and a half hours later, the phone rings. It's de la Fuente, being businesslike.

'Andrew? OK. We have finished now. We made a good operation. We found a lot of adhesions, like scar tissue, inside around the intestine. The obstruction was caused by a very strong band, which was trapping part of the small bowel. So what we have done, we have freed everything, cut away the adhesions and put a tube down through the bowel so it will stay in position and avoid any kinking.'

'How is she?'

'She is in recovery now. She is doing well.'

When they wheel her back, she's all drips and tubes, one up each nostril. The nurses don't speak English, so my Spanish is on overdrive as they attempt to manoeuvre Vanella from the trolley to the bed and nearly drop her down the middle. She's very distressed and soon calling out for something to stop the pain.

'*Calmante. Calmante, por favor*,' I request, out in the corridor.

It takes far too long, but eventually the anaesthetists come to give her an extra shot and hook a needle in her spine, like an epidural, connecting her to a machine that will administer a dose of analgesic every twenty minutes.

Through the night, I lie beside her on a makeshift bed, pressing the button to activate the pain-killer whenever she cries out. In between I can only doze, listening to the occasional tapping of footsteps out in the corridor, the half-light and the stale air reminding me of my last visit to a hospital, the times we stayed with Hilary.

In the morning, Vanella looks exhausted. She's obviously uncomfortable, braving it out, but de la Fuente's quiet confidence is contagious. He tells her she's looking good and encourages her to sit up. Then she's unplugged from the drips temporarily and she teeters to the bathroom for a shower, helped by the nurse. She is dressed in a fresh gown and de la Fuente has her doing breathing exercises. She even manages a short walk up the corridor, supported by the two of us. A few hours later, she's taken downstairs for X-rays so he can check the position of the tube running through her bowel. Everything seems fine.

Back in the room, we call Vanella's father in London and she tries to sound cheerful. 'We'll be out of here in a couple of days,' she says.

That evening, her pain seems to get worse. Before very long, it's too much to bear and she becomes quite desperate. I call de la Fuente on his mobile. He's on his way home.

'On a scale of one to ten, how bad is it?' he asks.

'Eight, sometimes nine,' she says.

The drugs she's been given for the pain seem to be doing nothing, so he prescribes morphine. One of the doctors comes to give her an injection but that doesn't have much effect either. Vanella is soon distraught, in agony, begging me to get help. I try persuading the nurses, but they just shake their heads and tell me she's not allowed any more. So I call de la Fuente again and he says he's on his way back.

When he examines her, her abdomen is unusually distended, though the wound appears to be healing well. She complains of an acute pain under her ribs, and in her shoulder. Soon the room is full of doctors and anaesthetists, trying to do something to help her. They can't understand it. They give her as much as they dare, enough morphine to put all of us to sleep for a week, yet she's still awake, moaning. She must have an abnormal tolerance to drugs, they decide.

De la Fuente takes control. He holds her hand and talks her through his thoughts, one step at a time. 'Vanella, please try to relax now. Everything is OK. I'm going to give you a fresh tube for your nose and we are going to bring in another suction machine.'

When he switches on, a disconcerting quantity of dark green bile gurgles out from her stomach into the collection jar, leaving me to wonder if the original machine was ever working. At last, she grows calm and as the night creeps by, a frightened little voice keeps calling out, 'Boot . . . Boot?'

Again I don't sleep, but I do have a dream. I am in a house full of people I know intimately. But I can't see their faces. Even if I could, I know they aren't familiar any more. Still, I kiss everyone and hug them warmly.

Three days on from the operation and little has changed in the way of pain or swelling. The tubes are making Vanella's nose really sore. The veins in her arms won't take any more needles, so they've put a catheter in her jugular, tying her to a tangle of thin plastic pipes.

I get her upright, doing her breathing. Then de la Fuente calls by and decides it's time to remove the tubes. The one that comes up from her bowel is a long, gradual pull revealing something like a deflated balloon on its end. He turns off the suction and removes the one from her stomach also. Vanella immediately feels better. She becomes quite chirpy and manages a walk up the corridor. De la Fuente seems encouraged. We're optimistic. We'll be out of here in no time.

'The big question now,' he reminds us, 'is transit. We need the small bowel to begin its work again. And then there has to be transit.'

He gives her a drug to stimulate the peristaltic motion of the bowel, which makes her drowsy. While she's asleep I slip out downstairs to the cafeteria where I've found I can at least get myself a decent meal. Late afternoon, her stomach begins to swell again and she experiences severe colic pain. They try an enema to help things along, but nothing seems to work. De la Fuente keeps a concerned eye on the swelling, and takes more X-rays. He seems to think she's obstructed again, so she has to swallow painfully as he feeds the suction tube up her nose and back down her throat.

'We have to continue with suction now to keep things stable,' he says. 'I don't know what is causing this, but we should wait overnight. If you need me, you must call my home.'

More green bile bubbles out into the jar.

I can see Vanella is desperately disappointed. She refuses to believe it; she really thought she was getting better.

We pass another difficult, fitful night. The nurses keep coming to change the drips. Vanella calls out for help and I'm mopping her brow to keep her cool. In the morning, I have to work hard to raise her spirits. De la Fuente joins us at midday. He was up late, going through his textbooks and old case studies to find out what the problem might be.

'Right now, I'm still not sure,' he admits. 'I hoped that the tube would hold everything in place. Maybe when I took it out, there was some kinking at a weak point. There is also a condition called Chron's disease, which is unlikely but still possible. I think we should wait a little longer, but I may have to operate again.'

'No,' cries Vanella, half defiant, half desperate.

'We shall have to see,' he says, 'but it might be the only solution.'

'You've already operated once and it hasn't worked.'

'We needed to remove those adhesions. It was only a matter of time before something had to be done. Believe me, you are better off without them.'

'But it shouldn't be like this,' she says. 'This is the worst it's ever been.'

Seeing her fear, he sits down at her side. 'Please, you shouldn't concern yourself. We will get you better. This is my job. I'm not going to give up until I have you well again.'

'But what if you can't do anything?'

He takes her hand. 'Vanella, I won't know what to do until I see the extent of the problem. There is only so much I can tell from X-rays. But don't worry. You aren't going to die. It is good that you are fit and strong. You know, your condition is very unusual because of the problems when you were a baby. But here in Caracas we have a lot of experience with such adhesions. Because the kids . . . those who are involved in street fights, they get knife wounds in the abdomen. So by the time they are older they develop scar tissue very like yours. I have seen it like this many times. In England, this wouldn't happen so often. So maybe it is a good thing that you are here.'

Vanella smiles to show her gratitude, but I can see she's not convinced.

That evening, Rafael gives her a sleeping draught. He tells me he wants to conserve her strength. She needs rest. It has been a week now.

Next day, she feels good. Her stomach looks flatter and it's even making the occasional gurgling sound. She's very positive and is up, dressed and walking out along the corridor. It's as if she's decided she won't give de la Fuente the chance to operate again. We meet him on his rounds.

'Wow! What's this?' he says, as she gives him a kiss on the cheek.

'It's better, I'm sure it's getting better,' she says.

So he examines her and agrees there appears to be progress. He suggests more X-rays, so he can be sure. Within two hours, he's looking disappointed.

'There is some kind of kink here and some bulging or inflammation. I am sorry to tell you this, but you are still obstructed.'

Rafael sees Vanella's head drop in despair and reassures her he'll wait a little longer. Back upstairs, I hold tight as I ride the roller-coaster of her emotions.

'I just know this wouldn't be happening if we were at home,' she says.

'What else can we do? He is the expert.'

'Why should we believe he'll have any better luck second time round?'

'If he does operate, it'll be because he thinks he can sort it.'

'I don't want him to operate.'

'He might have to.'

'He could make it even worse.'

'But he's our only hope.'

'I know . . .' Her voice breaks as she blinks through the tears. 'Boot, I'm scared.'

The following morning, Rafael says he thinks he should operate. Vanella immediately resists. She asks him to try anything and everything he possibly can first. For twenty-four hours she's given more drugs to stimulate the bowel, enemas, laxatives, a colonoscope. Finally, he says he can't afford to leave it any longer. It could be dangerous. She gives in, but only after she's rapped out a deal. She wants me there the minute she comes round and enough morphine lined up to prevent a repeat of the post-operative pain she had last time.

Meanwhile, the phone keeps ringing. Back home, they want to know what's going on. So we lie. There's no point in any of them worrying. It's going to work this time anyway. But I've never seen Vanella so low. She's had enough; all she wants is to be well again.

Out in the corridor Rafael holds on to my arm. 'I think it may be a long operation tomorrow,' he says. 'Please try to keep up her strength. She needs to be mentally strong too. And you, you must eat. I know how hard this is.'

Once more she gives me her wedding ring and again I watch my wife being wheeled away on a trolley. I feel powerless and a little uneasy at not being able to be in control. For an hour, I tidy up, wash out some clothes, stare at the movie channel. Then Rafael calls and I detect a strain in his voice I haven't heard before. Her small intestine has deteriorated badly. She's developed something he calls peritoneal fibrosis, a dangerous condition that causes a kind of freezing of the bowel.

'I'm going to have to remove part of it,' he says. 'I want you to know, this may take a long time. I'm going to do everything I can. I'll call you when we finish.'

I'm left holding the phone. It must be bad. You don't say, 'I'm going to do everything I can,' unless it's bad. I don't understand this. She keeps getting worse, not better.

I pace up and down. Then I sit, try to read. But it's useless. So I pace some more, stand and gaze out at the same old view. More than four hours crawl by before he calls again. He asks me to come down so I can be there when she wakes up. I hurry to the lift, he meets me at the entrance to theatre and leads me to the surgeons' locker room, where the two doctors who've been assisting are sitting. They look exhausted. The lighting is subdued; their mood is glum.

'How's she doing?'

'You can see her now,' says Rafael. 'You will need to wear these.'

I undress and put on a grey theatre gown and trousers, complete with hospital logo. He ties a cotton mask across my mouth and hands me a cap for my head. In the recuperation suite, the anaesthetist is feeding her oxygen.

'It's Dr Jackboot,' she murmurs, as her eyes focus and she reaches out, managing a woozy smile.

Then the shivering begins, so severe her whole body shakes like she's having a fit. Rafael says it's due to hypothermia, because she has lost so much internal body heat. She's lying under two powerful lamps, loaded up with blankets.

'Hold me, hold me,' she judders. 'I'm so cold.'

I virtually pin her down until, in time, it begins to relent.

'OK, Andrew,' Rafael says finally. 'Will you come with me for two minutes, please?'

He takes me back to where the other two doctors are waiting, seated on benches beside the rows of metal lockers.

Rafael pulls up a chair and indicates I should sit down. He doesn't wait, but fixes me with a look I quickly recognize as a dangerous blend of compassion and steel.

'I have to tell you, Andrew, what we found was a disaster. The condition of Vanella's bowel was terrible. Much of it had been affected by the fibrosis. There was also some bad kinking and more strong adhesions, which were difficult to free. We had to resect two lengths of bowel. We have done everything possible, but the prognosis is not good. I have known one other case something like this. I am sorry. You should be prepared. There is a real possibility that Vanella is going to die.'

I hear myself breathe in. Then I can hear the strip-light humming above the silence. They're looking at me, trying to gauge my reaction. There's no question of being prepared. My brain is guarding the information, refusing to pass it on. I need more. I need to know what he really means.

'What are the odds?'

Rafael looks away, smooths down the end of his moustache and engages me again.

'I would say the chances of mortality are about eighty per cent. She may still recover. We will have to see how well she heals. The next twenty-four hours will be critical.'

I breathe out. I close my eyes, then open them. It's too scary in there. He doesn't give her much chance, does he? Twenty per cent? And he must be erring on the side of generous. The reality could be ten. Five. What's the difference? How can he be sure? Right now, nothing is certain.

Next Rafael is asking me if I want to see what they've removed. I find myself nodding automatically and he fetches a sealed pack from somewhere off-stage. He returns and switches on a surgical spotlight. Under the Cellophane wrap there are two lengths. I have no idea what intestine should look like, but this doesn't look at all healthy. I'm staring. Here are two pieces of Vanella – they're bright red, all mangled, kinked and swollen. And I'm struck by how aggressive, how violent the distortions are. I wish I knew what's going on.

'Come,' says Rafael. 'She needs you.'

After about an hour, we move her up to the room and, of course, she's so pleased to be back, she insists the nurse takes photos. I bend close, look at the camera and try to smile.

'This is me and Dr Jackboot,' she says dreamily, as I'm wondering what story my face will tell.

Rafael takes charge and stays until he's sure she's stable. Then he sends me away to get something to eat. I choose the back stairs and walk.

I find myself standing, halfway down. I can't believe this. She's going to die. She's going to die on me. She's not allowed to die. She can't leave me now, not now.

I'm leaning against the wall, tears staining my cheek, when two doctors come up the stairs. They ask if I'm all right. Yes, I'm all right. Come on, one step at a time.

As the anaesthetic wears off, so the pain returns. Only this time it's more like trauma. She's in a bad, delirious state. At least they're ready for her. She receives the full cocktail – epidural, jabs, intravenous, morphine neat and on drip. They still can't believe the amount she can take. Rafael says it took three times the usual level of general anaesthetic to keep her under while they operated. I've never seen so many needles. Eventually they succeed in calming her and she remains tolerably comfortable. Rafael has organized for a nurse to sit with us through the night.

But I can't sleep. My head is haunted by dread imagining. I see myself taking her home in a box. I'd be in my window seat and she'd be in the hold. It would be cold down there. Back home, I have to stand at her funeral. I have the rest of my life to live without her. I won't know what to do. She's such a part of me. And so beautiful. Lying there in the dark, I want to cry, but instead I end up praying. Please God save her, heal her, make her well.

The minutes drift into hours as she makes it through to another day. She's conscious, but very weak.

When the phone rings now I can't tell the truth because I don't want Vanella herself to hear. All I can say to her father is that she needed another operation and that she's doing fine.

Rafael attends, watchful, and together we keep the secret from her. I have to be careful. I mustn't let her catch me looking sad. Then in a lucid moment she goes and says, 'I don't know, Boot, with each new trauma I can't believe we can love each other any more. But we do, don't we? So much.' And the tears well up as she holds out a hand.

A little later on, Rafael takes me down to his office and draws anatomical sketches to explain what he's done. The way he joined the sections of bowel together looks ingenious, and tricky, using staples rather than stitches. But his mood is sober.

'So far, she is doing well, Andrew. But there is still a lot that can go wrong. If the anastomosis – in those places where we have reconnected the bowel – if it becomes disjoined, there is a risk of infection. If it heals, we don't know any more if the bowel will work. She may not be able to digest food. She may have to rely on drip-feeds for the rest of her life, or perhaps she will need some kind of colostomy. We shall have to see.'

News like this has little impact on me these days. I can only think of whatever is here and now.

Then, early evening, I'm sitting by her side as she's dozing comfortably, when I notice the colour of the liquid being pumped from her stomach change from pale brown to a dark red. Slowly it creeps out of her nose along the tube towards the collection jar. I point this out to the nurse who is passing through.

'Oh, that's normal,' she says, with hardly a glance.

But I don't like the look of it. I watch its steady progress for another minute, when Rafael happens to call by for a routine check. With him is a young female doctor. I immediately show them the tube.

'How long is it like this?' he asks.

The young doctor turns and I see the grim truth cloaked in the look she gives me. Suddenly Rafael is barking orders. They have five minutes to get Vanella down to intensive care. She has to be put on life-support. The bed, the drip-stands are wheeled hurriedly along the highly polished linoleum as she cries out, wanting to know what's happening. She's scared. They scramble into the lift and Rafael tells me to wait in the room. As the doors close, she's calling out my name. Their muffled voices submerge and I'm left to look up and down an empty corridor. I close my eyes, exhale, then turn.

They make it just in time. The problem is septicaemia, poisoning of the blood. Rafael telephones me to say he must operate again immediately, to clear the infection. I ask if I can see her first, just for one minute.

The room is dimly lit, curtains drawn around her. Vanella lies sprawled, unconscious, strapped down. She looks so undignified with a respirator tube jammed in her mouth. The lights gleam on the bank of machines massed behind her, which emit a reassuringly constant bip . . . bip . . . bip . . .

Her hand is limp. I want to hold it, keep it warm. I don't even know where the words come from.

'This is bad, Nella. I'm not sure what's going on. But I think it's bad. Just in case, I think I'd better say goodbye, my love. If there is another world beyond this one, maybe I'll see you there some day. Meanwhile, you take good care. You be strong. I love you so much. So much. Nothing can take away from us what we had.'

In the corner of my eye, I can see Rafael. He needs to do his work. I bend to kiss her forehead. It feels cool, clammy, mid-way between life and death. I inhale her musky scent for the last time, then turn and leave.

Room 616 is vacant tonight, plenty of space without a bed. I need to talk and so I call my father in Australia. I can tell him the full story now and it makes me cry. Then I wake Vanella's father up to tell him I think his daughter is probably about to die. There's some discussion of people flying out to Venezuela.

I put down the phone and the silence crowds me in. I need air. I open the window and stand looking out. The night sky is bright, with such a profusion of stars I can actually get a perspective of space. Away to my left, a strange green hue is cast by the illuminated cross, which stands on top of the ridge, overlooking the city. It seems to float, as if suspended beneath the glory of the heavens. Oh, Jesus, sweet Lord Jesus . . . She needs your help tonight.

I don't know how much later, I'm by the window, completely still. I feel as if I'm standing on a mountain top, balanced right on the edge. I'm looking out at the stars, touched by the faintest breeze. I am overwhelmed by a sense that everything is preordained. There is nothing I can do, nothing I should do, except hold true and follow my heart. Somewhere along the way I've been thinking about Bo. Dear old Bo, I want him to live for ever. 'Oh, I never die,' he said, his voice husky and slow. And he said something . . . something about a moment when the stars come out, I should remember I was not alone. Right now, I'd like to believe he's right. I'm not sure this is my kind of solitude.

Soon I realize I am cold. I close the window, face the starkness of an empty room and look for the sleeping pill Rafael gave me. Making myself comfortable on the bench-seat that is my bed, I drift easily away.

In the morning I wake, still groggy, and sleepwalk down to the cafeteria for my cheese *empanada*, fresh orange juice and coffee. In my stupor, I leave the Bag behind on the seat next to me. Vanella handed over responsibility for the Bag some days ago, a plastic zipper containing our passports, money, credit cards, travellers' cheques, air tickets – everything. Of course, when I rush back an hour later, the staff merely shrug and look to each other. I believe there is an old saying: 'When you're down, along comes a thief and steals your purse.'

So I have nothing to my name but the few dollars in my pocket. My existence is confined, my world closed down, curtained off around the bed where Vanella lies, kept alive only by the wilful intelligence of those machines. And yet I feel strangely calm. It doesn't seem right. But I'm fine. Really. What else is there to do? It couldn't be more simple. I hold her life in the balance, weighing the absolute truth that she may die . . . today, tomorrow . . . against the hope that she will live . . . that together we may live to be old and grey.

For five days the world turns. Rafael's English girl becomes the talk of the hospital and, as I go about my routine, I receive their smiles and sympathy. People I've never met come especially to find me to say they are praying for her every day at mass. Alejandro and his family come to give me their support. And, as the news spreads abroad, the phone rings and I hear that there are folk praying for her all over London, in Australia, in the little church in Gloucestershire where we were married. My mother organized that. She felt she had to do something. Sometimes a friend I haven't spoken to for two years will call and we short-cut to the present, living only in hope.

Rafael tells me it's best that Vanella feels nothing. She is fighting a serious infection of the abdomen, which has spread to the rest of her body. He keeps her on the life-support so that each day he can open her up and wash out her insides with a saline solution and antibiotics. Until they can identify the bacteria, he's also pumping her with all the antibiotics he's got. He has the wound tied with blue plastic wire as thick as washing-line, making it easier to open and close. There are eight loops, each fastened with a knot, crossing the length of the scar. It looks like a giant shoelace. He says her small bowel is now completely frozen, so inflamed there are areas he can't get to with the wash. He shouldn't really manipulate it but he has to, even though there's a risk the anastomoses might rupture.

The latest is that her white blood cell count has decreased ever so slightly. Rafael thinks he may have got the infection under control.

'I don't want to predict, Andrew,' he says. 'We still have a long way to go. She has a big illness inside.'

I nod and give him a smile. I have placed all my trust in this man, who is for now my closest friend in all the world. Even so, each time I catch sight of the cross on the hill, without thinking I whisper another prayer. I give my blood so that Vanella can have it. Sometimes I sit with her and talk. She doesn't move, but Rafael says it will help because her subconscious can hear. So I ramble on about nothing in particular, though I'm careful not to mention the Bag. She'd be furious.

Another day, and the security man at the front desk wants to see me. The Bag has been found on the pavement outside the hospital, minus cash but otherwise miraculously intact. It's like I ceased to exist. Now I'm back. And Rafael tells me, after the latest wash of her abdomen, that Vanella seems to be fighting the infection. She still carries a fever, but her blood count is continuing to improve.

Rafael wakes her up on Christmas Eve.

The nurses are still busy around the bed when I get there. I'm nervous. She sees me and I see the joy light up her eyes. It's only been five days, but I missed her. We kiss awkwardly through her tubes and I squeeze her hand. She is warm again, though her pallor tells me how ill she is.

'I'm in pain, such pain,' she whimpers, her voice blurred and feeble.

'It's OK, Vanella. You're doing well, really well,' says Rafael. 'Andrew is here now.'

'It's OK, you're all right.'

'*Calmante*,' she cries, in distress. I try to quieten her, and we go round the circle again a few more times before Rafael sends me away.

Some hours later, she is more relaxed, but she's realized where she is. And it frightens her. By stroking her forehead I find I can bring down the numbers on the machine which show her heart rate. It's as soothing for me as I imagine it is for her. I feel like I can raise her from the wreckage. But then the battle is on again. She wants more pain-killers. She's getting frustrated, and a little suspicious. She can't understand why the nurses won't give her any and starts using me to hustle for her. Then Rafael takes me to one side and explains that he's trying to reduce her dependency, cutting down the dose and giving her placebos.

'Soon. You can have some soon,' I end up having to say. I don't know what's best. Maybe I'm better off out of the way.

Next day, she still seems confused, but instead of the fear she's progressed to a wraithlike frailty. She looks so pasty pale and weak. But, God, she's alive. I tell her it's Christmas and that she's doing fine, but she's only concerned about me and wants to know how I am, how I've been without her. And in response she keeps making little cooing noises. 'Ooooh,' she goes as I open her present and show her the earrings, which I seem to have acquired half a lifetime ago.

Then I search in my pocket and slip the wedding ring back on her finger.

'With this ring, I thee wed.'

'I love you, Boot,' she says softly, smiling.

'I love you too.'

And she gives my hand a little squeeze.

Then, one by one, we introduce Stephen, her uncle, her sister Colette, and my brother Edward, who have flown in to be with us. She can't believe it. 'Ooooh,' she purrs, each time more bewildered, telling them how much she loves them. Then she notices how upset Colette is, fighting to hold back her tears, so she tugs at her hand.

'I don't like it here,' she whispers with a childlike innocence. 'Intensive *scare*, that's what I call it.'

She's so desperate to get out. Only then will she believe she's getting better. Only then will she feel she's truly stepped away from the edge. They lost the man in the bed next to her. He didn't pull through. He died two nights ago. She says the nights are unbearable, when the world grows quiet and she's too frightened to sleep. Rafael can see that moving her is the best cure and makes plans for the following day. I ask him for a new room, one that doesn't add up to thirteen.

Finally, after hours of interminable waiting, a porter comes with the wheelchair. We lift her gently in and make her comfortable. It's so sweet. She's so excited, her eyes gleaming. A pale slip of a thing, brimming with energy, she holds on to her oxygen mask and waggles the novelty balloon on a stick she's been given by the nurses. The other man, in the next bed along but one, gives her a wave as we pass. She wants to see him, so I wheel her close. He is the high-powered chairman of some bank, I gather. He's recovering from major surgery after a heart-attack.

Suddenly Vanella is standing up, leaning forward to give him a hug. They share a common bond. They've both made it back.

'I'm out of here,' she says, embracing him warmly and even planting a kiss on his cheek.

'So am I,' he replies. 'I will see you up there. Soon.'

Once we are settled in the new room, Rafael reminds us that yet again we have to wait. Transit is the crucial test. He says it could take days. Then he excuses himself and goes off to catch up on his lost holiday by playing a well-earned round of golf.

After all the exertion, Vanella decides to have a snooze and then, mid-afternoon, suddenly she calls for the bedpan. I watch in disbelief, encouraging her. She cries tears of happiness. Never has there been more delight over a single bowel movement.

One minute later, the phone rings. It's Rafael, calling in on his mobile. He's on the fairway. I tell him we have transit and he's shouting for joy. I can hear him punching the air.

'Man, that's the best news I've had all year. You know, there has just been the most fantastic rainbow. I don't know, I saw it and I thought of you guys.'

So at last we can celebrate and I tell Vanella that I really think she's going to be all right.

'I've been very ill, haven't I?' she says, giving me a quizzical look.

'We thought we were going to lose you.'

'Hmm . . . I wasn't going to die. I just kept thinking I didn't want to leave you.'

She's quiet, pensive for a moment, then she says, 'Mum was with me, you know.'

'What do you mean?'

'Wherever it is I've just been, Hilary was with me. I could feel her, her presence. She was there by the bed. It was so familiar . . . as if she'd just walked in the room.'

I have no doubt that the spirit moved among us. Quite what or how, I'm not sure. But Rafael believes so too. He says he felt something more than just him and his team at work here. 'It was amazing to see,' he tells Vanella. 'Perhaps it was the power of prayer and love. You fought so hard. I don't know, I think you were meant to live. There has to be some purpose in this. Maybe you have something important to do with your time now.'

Equally, we can't help feeling all this was somehow meant to be, that she was destined to meet this man, so that he could save her life. Still he is willing her on, bringing her back. She's having a really bad time with her lungs, which are full of liquid through disuse. She isn't strong enough to hack it out and she's drooling all the time, but he keeps building her up. And the wound is beginning to heal. We can see it closing, day by day, as she makes the long, gradual climb, each stage reflected in the rising mood of elation that pervades among us. It isn't too long before Rafael is able to remove the suction tube from her nose. She eats some soup, some jelly, then fruit, potato. Finally, he takes the catheter from her neck, and she is free.

So now I can stroll back from the hospital to the hotel, where I've moved in with Stephen, Colette and Edward. Alone, I can walk these quiet streets with an easy stride, until I reach the place where I turn to watch the city lights, beneath a sky bathed in an afterglow of vermilion. Consciously I breathe in the warm air and rejoice.

We shall be leaving soon. To see Vanella these days is an inspiration. Physically she is still weak, but a new light shines in her eyes. I believe she is blessed with the very thrill of being, with the knowledge that every moment counts. And I now realize where I've seen it before, many times. I have seen the same spirit in the eyes of the old people.

Long may it last, my love.

21

¡Viva!

Coming home isn't easy.

It's like we crash-landed in a heap, our bags spilled out across the floor of Vanella's dad's rather cramped spare room. Vanella remains confined to the bed, recuperating, while I run up and down the stairs with tea and toast. Every day the nurses come to dress her wound and gasp. They've never seen anything quite like de la Fuente's blue washing-line. And each morning when we wake, we kiss and say hello, knowing we're lucky – both of us. It's precious. There's no need to say.

Sometimes the walls seem to hedge me in and I have to get away. I leave Vanella lying there watching the daytime TV she's begun absorbing like a sponge and I venture out. Though I have nowhere to go these days, I find I'm still blessed with the eyes of an outsider. I can appreciate a certain grace in the architecture I've never seen before. I'm struck by how affluent we are, in our fashionable clothes and shiny motor cars. We seem curiously obsessed with shopping, all-consumed by the babble of the media. And for the first time I can see we have a particular look, we Anglo-Saxons, just like any other race, and I have to admit that my fellow countrymen are an unattractive, ill-looking lot. It soon fades.

Gradually, Vanella gains her strength and we begin to piece our life back together. Soon she can make it down the stairs and spends more time out of bed than in. Friends and relations call by to visit. No one knows it, but we are strangers. We don't belong, not yet. We feel isolated and clumsy. Two years is a long time to catch up. But then we realize that, in fact, nothing much has changed. Only us. There's so much we want to tell, about the people and all the things we've seen. Some want to hear, and we find we can't possibly do it justice. Others don't, they never even ask. Perhaps it's safer that way.

* * *

With some reluctance, I turn the key to the lock-up. We have been putting off this moment for days. While we were away, someone broke in through the roof and left a large hole for two months of rain to pour in before it was discovered. I heave up the metal door and it groans just like it used to till it catches with a jolt. Beside me, Vanella lets out a strangled cry. The place has been ransacked.

Bravely we pick our way through a shambles of sodden lumber. Those boxes in which we packed away our old life have all been defiled, one way or another. Things we'd so easily forgotten lie rusted or broken, turned out in random heaps around us. We unravel bags of rotten clothes, suits, shirts, sweaters, home to a host of shiny red worms and colonies of woodlice.

Not all my books came here, so I've no idea what I'll find. I pull open an old wine-box containing some Shakespeare, my sixth-form editions, reeking now of sullen must. Two loads of novels aren't even worth picking up. Then this . . . Oh, God, no. Not this one. Why did the rain choose this box to penetrate? It should have been in a safer place, but there wasn't time, I never thought . . . I'm such a fool. It's just the worst, the really important ones.

With a heavy heart, I tease open my childhood copy of *The World of Pooh*, its pages glued together with a creeping blue mould. As a boy, I would lie in bed on long summer evenings and read these stories again and again. And as I grew older the book itself became a link, my access to that sweet memory. Now, it is tainted for ever. Oh, tiddly bloody pom.

The next one I pick up is red, clothbound. I've no need to look. It is entitled *Dialect of the Huddersfield District*, a glossary of old words that first belonged to my great-grandfather. I pinched it from my dad, and when he found out he said I'd better take good care of it. I hardly dare open it, but I have to. The cover is mildewed, quite badly damaged. The damp has worked its way inside, although the words, my linguistic heritage . . . Perhaps with a little loving care they can be salvaged.

Then I slide my hand down the side of the box. I let out a wail of pain.

'What's the matter?' says Vanella.

I can't even reply. When I was that same boy, our doctor, a close family friend, once gave me his copy of *A Child's Garden of Verses* by Robert Louis Stevenson. A slim, pocket-sized edition, it had a sailing ship etched in gold on the spine. It had been a present from his mother. He had no children of his own and chose to hand it on to me. I so loved this book. I used to press my nose against its green calfskin and inhale its age. Within its pages, the poems I read took me willingly to another time, to innocence and faraway lands: 'parrot islands', 'Eastern cities', 'jungles near and far'. Stevenson's voice grew inside my head, feeding my young imagination. And even now . . .

Whenever the moon and stars are set,
  Whenever the wind is high,
All night long in the dark and wet,
  A man goes riding by . . .

But now my throat grows tight and tears fill my eyes. I had secretly vouched that, when I grew old, I would pass it on to another small child. Not any more. The spine breaks away in my hands, the paper tears and crumbles. My little ship is wrecked.

I hear Vanella crying now. I turn to see she has found a coat of Hilary's, which is quite ruined. She clasps it to her, head bowed, sobbing.

Then I find my father's flying jacket. My stomach churns. Somehow it has disintegrated, holes eaten right through the thickness of the hide. I can't even look. Why? How can I ever tell him? Silently, I wrap it in black plastic, like a secret corpse, and lay it gently on the ground.

A fine drizzle is falling from the darkening gloom of a wintry sky. With tears streaming down our faces, we stand amid the mess we've dragged out on to the concrete and hug each other, holding on, grieving our loss.

We try to make a new beginning.

Vanella is discharged by the doctors, still shaking their heads in disbelief, amazed that she could have survived. And then one of them says, 'Of course, you do know you may not be able to have children.' When she asked Rafael that question, he said he thought she'd have no problem. We seem to have agreed that we would like to have kids some time, although I'm finding the prospect slightly daunting. But now there's a seed of doubt, and Vanella is worried. She says she needs some stability. So we consider the options. Should we move away somewhere and start afresh? Or should we stay in London? In the end, it comes down to practicalities and that same dogged question: 'What do we do for a living?' Vanella decides that she'll find herself a job, back in the business. And we keep letting out the flat to bring us some income while we look for somewhere more spacious to live.

As for me, I have my work to do. I have to make something of our experience. But it's going to require time and the benefit of a little hindsight, just as Bo said. So I'm sifting through, looking for what it all means. I still need a few more of the pieces. And there remains one last part of the journey to be travelled. Our original intention was to finish up in Europe, to the west, but events in Caracas inevitably brought about a change of plan.

Come summer, I ask Vanella to join me, one more time.

'No,' she says. 'You go.'

'But it won't be the same without you.'

'I only get so many weeks' holiday. How can I?'

'You could join me for part of the way?'

'No,' she says. 'You go. This is for you to do now.' Then she gives me a knowing smile. 'Anyway, you don't really want me. You'll be better off on your own.'

I must confess I'm quite excited. I've been finding it difficult staying put, living in one place. I'd challenge anyone to travel for all that time, to get back and not suffer from a mild itching of the feet. And she may be right. I could use some time to compose my thoughts. So I set out alone to complete the circle.

~

I can see strips of blue between the broad squares of canvas stretched high like sails between the rooftops. A glance at the Arabic numerals above a doorway, or along the narrow street to the palm fronds that shimmy in the distance and, for a moment, I could be somewhere in North Africa. But then I hear the low dongling of church bells. I look up at green window-blinds, which hang down heavy as eyelids over wrought-iron balconies and a little old lady in black peeps out and gives me a smile.

Around midday, in the southern town of Seville, there is a swell along the calle Sierpes, as the people come and go. On their way to browse in a jeweller's window or hunt out a handbag for the autumn, the *señoras* leave behind a drift of heady perfume. Elderly gentlemen, innocently smelling of toilet soap, meet each other by chance and pass the time of day. In short-sleeved shirts with generous top pockets, they stand exchanging news, great clouds of tobacco smoke billowing forth. Then they continue on their way, past the hatter's darkened windows, past the peacock display of fans at the Fábrica de Paraguas, ignoring as they go the man who bellows out today's lucky lottery numbers for sale.

At midday, I duck away under an arch into Pasaje de las Delicias and come upon a quiet bar. Don Luis is here among his friends. They are seated outside today, two tables pushed together, discussing whatever there is to be discussed. The Spanish for such a gathering is *tertulia*. Another word – *aficionado* – also describes this dozen or so men who have more than a passing interest in *los toros*. Every day they meet to talk bullfighting. The youngest of them, I guess, will be in his sixties. The eldest is Don Luis Fuentes Bejarano who, at the fine age of ninety-one, is Spain's longest-living matador.

Before I know it, the two of us are sitting together at our own small table around the corner, charged with cups of strong dark coffee and a glass of *anís* for Don Luis. Then he's tapping me on the knee and holding out a leather wallet, so worn its skin is thin and flaky like the loose leaf of the half-smoked cigar he's puffing. He finds an old photo of a young man, immaculately dressed in a double-breasted suit and collarless shirt, sporting a sombrero. On his arm he escorts an attractive young woman, his wife-to-be.

'Eh, this is how a bullfighter should look when he goes out for the evening,' Don Luis tells me.

Then he's fingering more treasures, frail slips of paper worn at the edges. Here is a sepia photograph of the inaugural ceremony of Madrid's bullring, La Plaza Nueva, on 17 June 1931. 'Of the eight matadors in procession there that day, I'm the only one left alive,' he says. Then he's slapping his inner thigh, nudging me. I think he's trying to tell me how strong he still is. But I'm wrong.

'I have been gored fourteen times by the bull,' he declares instead. 'Here, in my legs.'

'Fourteen?' As I try to imagine what scars lie under such smartly pressed trousers, I'm wondering also if a matador should really be boasting about his injuries.

'I once killed six bulls all by myself in one afternoon,' says Don Luis. 'I killed them each with a single blow, all in the correct manner. I loved it so, when I could make a clean kill – not a stab but a single stroke of the sword, the bull dead in just one move. The crowd went crazy. I remember looking up at the stands. It was like a madhouse. I wouldn't change that for anything in the world.'

'Six times!' I say, mixing surprise with muted admiration.

Don Luis stirs his coffee with a pronounced clatter.

'*Hombre*, if the bull helps you, what you do is give the people a good time. Then you can enjoy yourself as well.'

Such a distinguished gentleman could only ever have been a matador, not just because he fell in love with the idea when he saw his first bullfight as a boy but simply because he looks the part. He holds himself ready, chest out, head high. The slender build, the dark hair swept back, I see him there in the ring with his braided waistcoat and tight trousers. Deftly Don Luis makes an elegant pass, swirling away the red *muleta*, as three tons of goaded, furious bull thunders past.

'So how many bulls did you kill altogether?'

'I wouldn't know, exactly,' he replies, 'but in twenty years of fighting, plus three as a novice . . .' Don Luis pauses to suck his teeth and blow a half-formed whistle. 'It must be nearly four hundred. I fought all over Spain, in Portugal, the south of France. I fought in Mexico, Peru . . . Seventy *corridas* in one year.'

In his day, there were only about ten matadors who made the grade to superstar status. Don Luis was one of them. He made his first public appearance at the age of eighteen. That day, he'd gone to watch the one and only Manuel Granero, and as the great man performed, a hot-headed young Luis leapt out of the crowd into the ring and, in a show of bravado, attempted to take on the bull himself. Promptly caught and marched off by the police, he had nevertheless tasted the admiration of his public for the first time. When he took the *alternativa* and graduated from novice, he was only twenty. Then, for six years, no one younger came through behind him. Don Luis says that today there is easily a score of matadors so young, but only because the enemy is soft. The bulls, that is. They aren't as strong any more and their horns are small. In the old days it was terrible. The enemy was so fierce.

He raps his fingers on the table, then wags one at me. 'Listen. One time, when I was throwing the *banderillas*, I was caught by the bull and the sharp tip of its horn ripped my groin. I was thrown to the ground and I looked down to see my scrotum gashed open, blood everywhere, and my two testicles hanging out. So I picked them up and went off to the infirmary, where they looked up to see me holding my balls in my hand.'

Don Luis relishes the effect his story has on me and closes his lips around the wet end of his cigar, puffing it back to life.

'You know,' he whispers, 'I was worried about only one thing. I had heard that if you lose a testicle your voice becomes like a girl's.'

That would have been a blow to the image, for sure.

When I ask Don Luis what he thinks of the top bullfighters of today, he shakes his head and pinches his lips closed. He doesn't want to stir up trouble. But then he can't resist one small swipe. In his day, they used to fight with a real sword. Now they use a wooden replica until the moment is right for the kill, when the matador receives the sword from his *moso d'estoque* at the side of the ring.

'These young men, you know, they earn five, six, sometimes ten or twelve million pesetas for an evening's work. Think about it. One million pesetas weigh exactly one kilogram, whereas a real sword weighs only six hundred grams. Now, if they can carry off five or six kilograms of pesetas after the fight, why can't they carry six hundred grams during it?'

Don Luis grins and tells me that when he retired he bought a small farm outside Seville with his earnings. Even then, he had yet to fight his last. On his seventieth birthday, he was invited by one of the bull breeders to take part in his own private *corrida*. Needless to say, Don Luis was the victor. The breeder asked if he thought he could do it again when he was eighty. Don Luis replied that if God gave him his health, he would try. So, another ten years on, he fought again and became the oldest matador in the history of bullfighting.

'Could you do it today?'

'I would like to, but it could be a little risky,' he admits, draining the last of the *anís*, his Roman nose probing deep into the glass. Then, as if to prove he is still in touch, he stands to show me the correct manner of completing the kill, the culmination of the ritual.

'The arm must be kept low. Some matadors nowadays come in with their arms up here, but they seize an advantage over the bull if they do.'

Don Luis has his elbow raised crooked, his hand pointing across his chest.

'You have to wait with your cape and then get yourself close to the bull. You put your hand on your heart and then when he comes towards you, you show him your chest and so . . .'

Don Luis makes the beginning of the lunge that would once have brought a confused and wounded enemy to a swift demise. With the crowd going wild, Don Luis parades before them, absorbing their applause. And the beast is dragged away, its blood a dull red trail across the orange sand.

~

The train north from Seville climbs up through the back hills, past sleeping *pueblos* and hot, dusty olive groves, clanking, straining, up, as high even as the hazy blue mountain tops in the far distance until at last it pulls out on to the wide open plains of Extremadura. And I'm back in the flow, happy to see the world gliding by. It's almost a state of bliss, a kind of ecstasy, as familiar to me now as these old clothes I'm wearing again.

Being on my own has made me a little philosophical of late. Two days ago I spent an hour or two in a secluded corner of the gardens of the mighty Alcázar. I sat on an old stone seat in the shade, quietly musing. I decided I had to work this out, once and for all. What's it all for? I kept on repeating myself, going through again and again, in order to get the logic right. The logic has to be irrefutable. In the end, I had to write it down to begin to make it work. It now goes something like this.

My senses tell me I am alive. I therefore must question: why? Why am I alive? I could answer that this is pure chance, or even God's will, though these don't necessarily follow. I could say it has something to do with my parents, but that's not what I'm aiming at. The best, most absolute reply I can come up with is this: I am alive *to live this life*. Simple, but indisputable. Consequently, I am forced to ask: how? How should I live this life, this outrageous gift? I am free, I have free will. So I can only conclude that I can live it how I choose. Except that, if I consider my life to be precious, which I do, I should seek by my actions to enhance and prolong it as best I can. And if I consider the lives of others to be equally precious, I must try to act in a way that also serves them. Thus, I have no option but to live solely for the experience life offers, in every sense, to seek to understand, and then pass something on.

I believe this works. It does for me, anyway. I shall leave it there a while. We shall have to see.

I've also been thinking. Having come so far, I find I no longer feel any sense of fear. When I was with Don Luis, I asked him the same question I once asked my grandfather. I wondered if he was afraid when the bull was charging down on him.

'*Hombre*, your biggest fear is for your public,' Don Luis replied. 'You worry about making them happy. You cannot feel real fear. If you were afraid, you would not be able to do it.'

Like Morarji said, we cannot act according to our true selves if we are afraid. Looking back, I now realize that almost all the old people we've met showed no sign of being frightened of death. Most were holding it at bay; a few were resigned. But they'd all had time to confront their mortality.

Something must have happened to me to accelerate the process. Perhaps something rubbed off from them. Perhaps it was Caracas. Perhaps it is because I am finding a way to live at last . . . I used to be afraid of many things – afraid of failure, afraid of what might happen, what they might think, afraid of death itself. Not any more. And I have never felt so alive.

We are passing through farming land now, in the leaden heat of the late afternoon. The men are busy loading bales on to long-suffering mules. In the *pueblos*, where each church squats beneath a Moorish tower cornered by four minarets, the old women sit out by their doors watching the children play. Then come the vineyards, mile after mile of striped, rocky terrain. Eventually we enter conquistador country, where, from a walled town, a few hundred men once went off to subdue the entire Inca civilization. And as we trundle on across this sparse, desolate interior, sectioned by fencing and quartered by birds of prey, imperceptibly the light of day bows out with an almighty crimson sunset.

~

In the small town Guadalupe, I find a widow sitting in the cool of her parlour. She smiles when she sees me. It's almost as if she's been expecting me.

A picture of old Spain, she is dressed entirely in black, with long sleeves and full skirts in chaste layers. Paula lost her husband when she was forty. Within the week, she will be ninety-nine.

'I have many good things to think about,' she tells me cheerfully. 'I always recall my memories every morning before I rise.'

Absently she plays with a strand of white hair, which she ties back from her broad forehead in a bun. She is strong, in body and spirit. She stands for most of the time, leaning gently on the table, chattering away, her face full of creases and kindness.

She can remember everything – the simple life in the village, the water that had to be carried from the fountain, the old covered wagons. When she was six, her grandmother told her how she used to wash clothes for the monks who lived in the monastery, before they were evicted and the place abandoned. That would have been in the 1830s. Paula herself can remember when the Franciscans took up residence early this century. And she recalls with affection the day King Alfonso XIII came to crown the Virgin with flowers.

'Now that was real monarchy!' she assures me.

Paula is devoted to her Blessed Lady, the Virgin of Guadalupe, a Romanesque statue miraculously found by a farmhand some seven hundred years ago. A shrine ever since, Guadalupe remains isolated, hidden away in the wooded sierras to the east of the plains of Extremadura.

Then she starts talking about a riddle. She once found it in a book. She used to love reading, whatever she could lay her hands on. Everything she read, she would learn by heart.

'Can you tell me this riddle?' I ask.

'But it's very long,' she says, hoping to put me off.

'Please,' I ask again and, lightly touching the small comb tucked in her hair, she draws breath and begins to recite:

'I am something without body; neither hands, nor feet, nor
head.
Everything that God has created surrenders itself to me.
All the four elements obey me, without me being God,
or able to be God, or anything of the sort.
I am he who made God come down from heaven to
earth; and God made use of me on many occasions.
God is such a friend of mine that when someone uses
me, I can see everything I want without resistance.
The angels in the court cannot compete with me; they
would rather withdraw than accept me there.
I calm the waves in the sea, in the worst storms;
and I cause the sun to stop in her path.

I change the winds to wherever I wish they should
come from, as many sailors will know.
I make the dry tree flower and bear fruit again; I make the green
tree dry and lose its fruit and flowers.
I am the one who tames the fire of lions and makes
them humble as sheep.
I am one who, for a man found guilty by the supreme
court, can overturn the verdict and still have it be just.
Devils cannot stand my presence; even to hear my
name they are terrified and tremble.
My name is not Jesus, nor can it be, because there is more
between us than between the sky and the earth.
He who would know my name will learn it from
experience.
My name is contained in only nine letters.'

Paula smiles with modesty as I applaud. But what is the answer? She shakes her head. She won't say.

'Neither the Father Superior nor Father Sebastian, who is very clever, have got it right,' she warns me, with a faint glow of pride. 'Only Father Mora, who was once priest here, he is the only one who has ever got it. The only one.'

Nine letters. In Spanish, remember.

~

I am now experiencing something akin to time-travel. I face two women. One is a mature, self-assured, beautiful woman of forty. She is looking down from a portrait on the wall. In front of her sits the same woman, fifty years on. The hairstyle and the cut of her short-sleeved dress are identical. The same confidence and self-belief are there. And, though time has worked its inevitable way, she is still extremely fit.

In her day, Lilí Álvarez was champion of all Spain at skiing, ice-skating and running. Best known as a tennis star, she reached the Wimbledon finals in 1926, '27 and '28. She then became a writer. She has written a dozen books. She speaks five languages. She was a *Daily Mail* correspondent during the Civil War.

'I will answer only what you ask,' she informs me, a little frostily.

It is quite clear that Lilí says what she thinks. She puts this down to being successful at such a young age. 'I think it made me rather free,' she says. 'It made me somebody before being anybody. And ever since, when I think, I think not as others do, I just think as I think it should be.'

Lilí is critical of the Catholic Church. She believes it no longer represents the true Christian way. Her next book is on that topic. She is outraged, not by the corruption in Spanish politics but by the way the public condones it, continuing to accept that the President should stay in office, while everyone knows he is implicated. She is also a feminist, and regularly makes a stand against machismo – her last book was about that.

'Machismo is the man who thinks himself superior. I'm not against man, I am against machismo. It is very difficult to explain that to a Spanish male. What we women can do, you see, is love. We are meant for love. It is difficult for men.'

'Why is that?'

'Because they are not made the same. We are prepared for it. You are not. My prediction is that, in future, women and men will be much more on the same level. It is the direction made by man which has brought us to where we are now. With women and men in equal balance, as it should be, that will change everything. Then there will be another life.'

Lilí pauses and looks across expectantly. 'Well?' she says. 'Go on . . . ask me.'

So I ask about her faith.

'I became what we call here – *una beata, una beata beatissima.*'

'What does that mean?'

'Well, *beata* . . . How does one translate? Beatitude. Does one say beatitude in English?'

'Yes . . . the Beatitudes.'

'*Beata* – those who are blessed . . . those old and very pious ladies everywhere . . . they call them *beatas*.'

'Are you still?'

'I think I am still . . . *beata beatissima*.'

'Does your age make you more religious?'

'No.'

'Less?'

'I don't think so. But I think I was more *beata* twenty years ago than I am now.'

'So what changed?'

'Oh, that I have been more thorough. I think thoroughness is really the aim of personality.'

'How have you been more thorough?'

'Altogether.'

'With your whole life?'

'Yes. I think old age brings, if you have tried to live properly . . .'

'It brings what?'

'Peace.'

Lilí smooths her skirt and looks up. She gives me an easier smile this time. I sense her guard may be lowering.

'Oh, I think we have paid too much attention to thinking,' she says, 'and not enough to living. We believe that thinking is the best thing we can do. That's wrong. The right thing is to live, inside, properly. That's what we don't know how to do.'

'What do you mean?'

'Well, for instance, we say that our Catholic religion is a religion of love. You've got to love, really love. If you don't, you are not living. We live a certain life. We can do it properly or not properly. We can do it loving or not loving. That's the real difference that exists in life – whether you love or don't love.'

'Love what . . . who?'

'You've got to love the human beings you live with. And, if you believe, then you've got to love God and He'll love you at the same time.'

'Can you prove to me that God exists?'

'No, no, you can only . . . You yourself . . . You are captured by the idea of God – then you might be able to feel Him. You might not. That's how we stand.'

'Is it chance, then, whether I do or don't?'

'No. It isn't chance. Nothing is by chance. It depends on you.'

'As to what I choose to do about it?'

'Precisely, it's up to you completely. It used to be easier when I was young.'

'Why was that?'

'Because we've become so self-conscious. We know much more *that we are here* than in the olden days.'

'More aware of our place in the universe?'

'Exactly. It was easier to believe. Now it's more difficult. Because we know so much more which can get in the way of our believing.'

'Where does that takes us? A race of disbelievers?'

'It'll take us either to triumph or to a terrible disaster – one thing or the other.'

'Do you think mankind has the sense to avoid disaster?'

'I think it hasn't the sense even to be conscious of it.'

'So are we in the hands of fate?'

'No, not exactly. Because God exists, and if He exists somehow we'll be saved . . . And if He doesn't exist, nothing will be.'

~

As I cross the border into France, I feel I am nearing the end of my pilgrimage. When I reflect on the distance we've travelled, I know now, in my heart, that everything was right. It's all beginning to fall into place, at last. All, that is, except for Paula's riddle, which has been driving me crazy. What is the answer? What does it mean? At first I guessed it might be 'faith' which, at a stretch, you could call *confianza* in Spanish – trust – to get the nine letters. Someone else I showed it to suggested *oraciones*, prayer, which fits better. But when I read the riddle through again, I know that's not right. It still puzzles me.

'God made use of me on many occasions . . . The angels in the court cannot compete with me.' What's all that about? Sometimes I'm convinced it must be talking of the Holy Spirit – *Espíritu Santo*. But the letters don't work. I don't know. It's so infuriating.

'He who would know my name will learn it from experience . . .'

As nothing is by chance in all this, I must somehow find the answer.

There is a reassuring permanence about life in Arles. I stroll the Promenades des Lices, I explore the narrow alleyways of the town and end up, to the north, watching the slate grey bulk of the river Rhône turn a slow corner. Everything here feels old. They use the Roman circus for their bullring and the cafés on the main square look out on the Place du Forum. And when the townsfolk built their houses in the surrounding maze of streets, they used generous blocks of solid sandstone. Then they allowed the paint to peel on the shutters so you couldn't be anywhere else. Canaries trill in cages; the day is unhurried and everyone knows everyone still. *C'est très gentil ici.*

I sit out at a café table with a cold beer, perfectly content. I have come to meet the oldest living human being, Madame Jeanne Calment, who is now more than one hundred and twenty years old.

Finding my way, I pass by a huge field of beaming sunflowers as I look for her home, a modern hospital on the outskirts of town, sporting radio antennae and a helicopter pad. There I ask for Madame Meuzy, the hospital administrator. She greets me and as we are talking in reception, an elderly lady is pushed past in a wheelchair. It isn't until she's out through the door that I realize. Those years have treated Madame Calment well.

'*Oui, oui, très bieng,*' she's saying to her nurse as we catch up, the accent strange and rustic to my ear.

Jeanne likes to sit outside, they tell me, where she can enjoy the air. So we cross the tarmac, up a step and over the grass to settle by the lake. The afternoon is clear and sunny, with a stiff breeze blowing from the west. Claudine, her nurse, makes Madame Calment comfortable, then I introduce myself and hold her hand, the oldest little old hand in the world.

She doesn't see too well nowadays. And she's completely deaf in one ear, her left, partially deaf in the other. They have to shout on her good side, at just the correct volume and pitch, in order to communicate. But once she understands she's fine: bright and lucid. Otherwise, she sits there looking just like anyone and everyone's granny: a floral dress, blue cardigan, silvery curls and a lovely wrinkled face.

Something is wrong. The light is too bright and she needs her sunglasses. Claudine says she's left them indoors, so I find a pair of Ray-Bans to lend her. She looks great – Jeanne Calment meets James Dean.

It's hard to come to terms with just how old she is. One day someone may come across Lao Shou Xing himself, in a remote corner of China, but until then Madame Calment is her own living proof. Cared for better than an old master in the Louvre, she is something of a national institution. *La doyenne*, they call her, with a reverence and affection tinged with pride.

Historians may argue about when our modern era is supposed to have begun, at the turn of the century or with the First World War, but Jeanne Calment is not of this age. She hails from another time. She was born in the full flood of the nineteenth century, when France was ruled by the Emperor Napoleon III and had recently lost the Franco-Prussian War, conceding Alsace and Lorraine to Bismarck's new, unified German Empire. These were the early manoeuvres which, forty years later, culminated in the outbreak of the First World War.

Jeanne remembers well that summer day in 1914, when she heard that Germany had declared war and invaded Belgium. There was *une émotion générale* in the town, she says. People were afraid. But she should remember. She was then already thirty-nine.

This little lady has lived the length of two lifetimes. She is like porcelain: hard, durable, yet fragile. She's seen it all: computers, satellites, moon rockets, television, washing-machines, the aeroplane, the motor car, the radio and even the arrival of the humble light-bulb.

'My father put the electric lights in,' she recalls. He was often first with anything new. They were a progressive family. 'Yes, before then we used paraffin lamps or candles,' she says, laughing softly.

'And did that change life greatly?'

'Yes, at that time women used to do a lot of embroidery by lamplight in the evenings.'

This is a funny old process. My questions are shouted loud in her ear. She cocks her head slightly to one side to listen, like a bird, then gives a nod when she's understood. Sometimes she pauses as she speaks, and just as I think there's nothing more, she pipes up again.

She tells me about *la vie d'orée*, her golden youth. Life was simpler in those days. They were the best of times. She would go dancing, wearing her beautiful red Arlesian dress. Her mother wore the traditional costume every day, but because Jeanne was a modern girl, she saved hers for the *fêtes*. She looked so beautiful with her long hair hung in tresses and her pretty blue eyes.

'I was such a terrible flirt,' she confesses. 'Oh, they were wonderful days.' And then she bursts into song, harking back to the aftermath of the Franco-Prussian War:

'You've taken Alsace,
You've taken Lorraine,
But you'll never take our heart . . .'

Suddenly she breaks off. 'What are you doing?' she calls out, her voice rising to a hoarse squeak.

Madame Meuzy is standing by her side enjoying the sing-song, running her fingers affectionately through Jeanne's silver curls.

'What are you up to?' she demands. 'Are you looking for lice?'

'I'm only playing with your hair, Jeanne,' Madame Meuzy shouts. So Jeanne nods, keeping a straight face. She enjoys being the comedienne.

Of course, Jeanne is well known for her encounters with the impressionist painter Vincent Van Gogh. Her father was a boat-builder but they also ran a family shop, which sold material of all kinds: lace, silk, satin, embroidery, even dresses.

'I remember there was a beautiful black satin,' she tells me. 'We used to call it the crow.' Then she startles me by delivering a brief verse, from the fable of the Fox and the Crow.

When Van Gogh was living in Arles, producing some of his greatest work, he would call in at their shop to buy his canvases. Jeanne was thirteen at the time. By all accounts, the disturbed painter did little to ingratiate himself with the locals. He was unsociable, rude and often drunk.

'Was there anything you liked about him?'

'No,' she replies, grimacing. 'He was so ugly.'

And this was when he still had both ears intact. So, next time I'm standing in a museum gazing at a vase of sunflowers or any other wild strokes of genius depicting the countryside around Arles, I will think of a pretty young girl sticking out her tongue as she watches the mad Vincent wander off one hot summer's day in 1888, with that very canvas rolled under his arm.

Some say the secret of Madame Calment's longevity is to be found in her genes. Her family tree does indeed contain a number of ancestors who reached a ripe old age. But circumstance may also have played a part. Her family was relatively well-off, bourgeois middle class. They were liberal, quite avant-garde for those days. Jeanne never really wanted for anything. She was well educated and had the opportunity to do many things the average girl could not.

'I was very happy in my marriage too,' she reveals. 'Very happy. I had a delicious husband. He was so kind.' I gather she wed her cousin, in order to protect some of the family money.

Soon after they married they travelled by train to Paris, then enjoying its *belle époque*, around the time of Toulouse-Lautrec. The Eiffel Tower was recently new to the Paris skyline and it was with great excitement that Jeanne and her husband climbed to the first level, where they ate a fine lunch in the restaurant there.

'Did you like *la vie Parisienne*?'

'Oh, yes, very much. We saw all the latest things. We went to the theatre, the opera, Sacre Coeur . . . Oh, I loved Sacre Coeur. And we saw the first film ever made.'

The year was 1896. The Lumière brothers, pioneers of the early cinema, had organized a public showing of their new invention. Jeanne was there with her husband to see those first unsteady moving pictures: a horse and cart, a bustling street scene, workers leaving a factory, a train arriving at a station.

Of all the inventions she has witnessed for the first time, I wonder which seemed the most revolutionary, the most exciting. After some thought, she announces that the winner is television.

'It brings the world closer,' she says. 'And it's always full of surprises.'

Madame Meuzy bends down to her ear. 'He's brought you some chocolates, Jeanne, did you know?'

'Ooooooh . . .' She lets out a little high-pitched squeal.

'Would you like one, Jeanne, to give you strength?'

These aren't just chocolates. They are the finest truffles Arles has to offer. I heard she had a penchant for her daily *chocolat*.

The box is duly unwrapped and a large, fresh creation popped into the oldest mouth. She is beside herself, trembling with excitement. 'Oooooh . . .' she squeals again, this time with dissolving chocolate in the way, and she munches and slurps at some length.

'Feel the box, Jeanne, it's heavy. There's plenty for several days,' Madame Meuzy reassures her, to even greater delight.

It isn't as if her diet has been exemplary. She says she always loved to eat *choux à la crème* when she was a girl.

'Eat as much as you like, when you like.' That's her motto. 'Enjoy your food,' she says. 'Eat and drink everything, but in moderation.'

She even used to smoke. In fact, she only gave up a few years ago, before it became too much of a habit.

She has always been active, though, and led an outdoor life. Madame Meuzy explains that Jeanne was something of a tomboy in her younger days and she always joined her husband on his trips into the hills to hunt partridge. Years later, at the age of a hundred, she was still to be seen riding about the town on a bicycle. I know this already because this morning I paid a visit to the Arles museum, looking for old photographs and snippets of Calment memorabilia. There I learnt that the museum is in possession of the very bicycle itself. When I asked if I could see it, I was told it was in the store-room out the back, and anyway it was only an ordinary bicycle. Not so! Just how many bicycles are there that have been ridden by a hundred-year-old?

I wonder what she thinks is the secret.

—

'Tell me why you've lived so long, Jeanne.'

'*Je suis miraculée, miraculée*,' she answers. It's as simple as that.

But I'm not sure. There is something more. Even at this extraordinary age, she is still curious, alive to what's going on around her. She was always allowed to find expression for her interests. She was artistic, she painted in watercolour and she played the piano for longer than she rode the bicycle. Even now, she keeps bursting into more snatches of song. She doesn't do this to show off or because she's soft in the head. She sings for pure enjoyment, treating me to a more than adequate rendition of the Toreador aria from *Carmen*, which Bizet completed in the year of her birth.

'My health as well,' she adds, 'I have never been ill. My health has helped me do everything. *Et la gaieté* . . . I have always been happy.'

Jeanne seems in fine form, but they're concerned she may tire soon. So I begin to wind up with a few last questions.

'What do you think of life today?' I ask her. 'Is it better or worse?'

'It's difficult to say,' Jeanne replies, growing serious. 'I'm not really qualified to judge. Some things have changed. Modern life has good and bad, but rather a lot of bad. Progress has ruined many things. Life is too quick, *trop fort*. Today everyone wants everything straight away, so they don't live well. And people are selfish now. They are more egotistical. There isn't the same charity in the world.'

Suddenly I hear the rattling whine of an engine and turn to see that *les flics* have arrived, two local policemen on one small motorbike. The senior policeman, a burly fellow, dismounts, pulling off his helmet.

'Oh, Jeanne,' shouts Madame Meuzy, 'it's the police. They've come to arrest you.'

The sergeant strides across the grass, biceps straining against the short sleeves of his blue shirt. 'Good day, Madame Calment,' he shouts, as he bends over. 'It is the Arles police here.'

'Have you come to arrest me, then?' says a hoarse little voice.

'No, Madame Calment, we have come to say hello.'

'Oh,' she says, disappointed.

'They haven't brought you any chocolates either,' says Madame Meuzy.

'No, we don't have any surprises.' But then the policeman thinks again and calls to his assistant, 'Eh! Have we a Gauloise for Madame Calment?'

We are now attracting quite a gathering. A man and his daughter who are walking by stop to pay their respects. The police stay for a smoke and everyone passes the time of day, until eventually I manage to steer her back to my questions.

'Do you believe in God, Madame Calment?'

'I believe in God because there are so many good things in life. I've had good and bad, but what has been good has been great. You forget the bad.'

She has known some sadness. Her husband died fifty years ago and she also lost her daughter. In the 1960s, her only grandson was tragically killed in a car crash. Jeanne is the last of her line. She has survived them all.

The police are on their way now. The sergeant holds her frail little hand and wishes her *bonne continuation*.

'*Merci, au revoir*,' says Jeanne.

A gust of wind blows and Claudine asks if she's cold.

'*Non, non, mais . . . un bonbon?*' she pleads, like a child, and another luscious truffle is soon devoured.

All the way around the world, we've asked nearly everyone this question. It's one of Vanella's favourites.

'What advice would you give to young people today?'

'Honesty,' Jeanne says, quick as a flash.

'Is that the most important thing in life?'

'Yes. When you are honest, you are capable of everything.'

I need no more. I squeeze her hands again and say goodbye.

'*Au revoir, Monsieur*. I am very flattered by your visit. I hope that you live to be a hundred.'

Claudine makes her ready and wheels her back indoors. And as she pushes the wheelchair down over the step on to the tarmac with a bump, we hear Jeanne call out: 'Whoa! Careful! You'll make me have an abortion.'

22

Home Sweets

I have the perfect autumn morning, crisp sunshine and a clear blue sky. The leaves that remain are vibrant with light, bright yellows and greens, while down below the dying lie scattered in russet shades across the lawn.

Here in my room, I am surrounded as usual by books and paper. Lao Shou Xing and Ganesh are with me.

Today I am wearing my special T-shirt. It has Chinese writing on it. 'A hundred ways of writing longevity,' it says, beside a block of one hundred squiggly characters which, I'm told, are gobbledegook. I have been saving it for this ultimate new beginning. The fresh white cotton feels warm and comforting next to my skin.

I've been keeping myself busy. I passed on Ruth's greeting to the Queen Mother, as promised, all the way from the African bush. Her Majesty sent back a message saying that, if I were to see Ruth again, I should return her good wishes for peace and happiness.

We have been working on the house, too. We must be mad. We bought a wreck and we're doing it up. For months we've been stripping paper, knocking down walls and walking about on bare floorboards. It's the dust that gets me. As I sit here sometimes, I can taste it. I can see it settling around me. But we're getting there, slowly. The downstairs is nearly finished.

Yesterday, I ceremonially lowered the clock into its rightful place on the mantelpiece. It's the same clock, the one from Cambrai. I opened the glass that covers its old round face and wound the key, just as my grandfather always did, once a week. Seven turns. Easing the clip till it closed, he would take hold of both sides, feel the warmth of burnished wood in his hands and tilt a fraction to set the pendulum going. And when he heard that lazy tick, he'd turn, see me and chuckle.

'Heee . . . Now then, young 'un, what have you got to tell me?'

It is a strange existence I lead these days. I spend many hours on my own, which of course I enjoy. It wouldn't really matter where we were living, here or in some remoter spot. Vanella goes off to work each morning and I stay where I am. I know people find it hard to understand. They give her strange looks. Sometimes they ask, incredulous. She must be crazy. They never say anything to me.

A few weeks ago, Vanella and I were leaving the house when I nearly knocked over an old chap who was on his way past down the street. Smartly turned out in jacket, tie and flat cap, he was bowling along at a fair pace.

'Come on, Father, do your stuff,' he called out.

I was carrying Ella, our baby daughter. The doctors had been wrong, after all.

'I were doing it in 1928,' said the man. He had a northern accent, which sounded like my native Yorkshire. 'I were working in the 1914 war . . .'

We all stopped, as his greeting extended into conversation.

'I'm ninety-two this year,' he told us. 'I'm lucky. I've been a naughty boy, I have.'

The old man pulled a guilty face, a schoolboy caught red-handed, as he pointed to the sky. 'I reckon He's given me more time to repent. Still, if you can't enjoy life, no one else is going to enjoy it for you.' And, with the biggest smile, he bade us a cheerful cheerio and continued on his way.

I see him most days now. He's up and out, early, walking down the street. He always gives us a wave or stops to pass the time. He's become a kind of totem for me.

I believe I have the riddle too.

I had to resort to books in the end. The answer is indeed the Holy Spirit, but under a different name. In English, the word is Paraclete – an old-fashioned title given to the Holy Ghost. Used in the Bible, it is often translated as 'comforter'. It means 'intercessor', and even 'advocate', which makes perfect sense of the references to a court. It is the one who is called, the one who comes to give help.

'I calm the waves in the seas in the worst storms . . . I make the dry tree flower and bear fruit again . . . I am the one who tames the fire of lions . . . Because there is more between us than between the sky and the earth.'

'He who would know my name will learn it from experience . . .'

In Spanish, *el Paracleto*.

So you see, it wasn't by chance. Nothing ever is.

I have no need to go on searching. I have it now. I am reaching the end of more than one journey that's been travelled here. I am home at last.

People sometimes ask if I am changed. Of course. I am made new. And I'm changing still. As Bo says, steadily . . . steadily.

I notice I have flecks of grey appearing at my temples. Yet I feel no older than before.

I have seen such things, such beauty, things I never dreamed.

I have been touched by the warmth of humankind.

I have been comforted by the Spirit.

And I have found a way to live, the way the elders taught us. But I know it isn't easy. It never is.

I have it here, around me. Sometimes it scares me. Sometimes it's so clear, it makes me laugh out loud.

What if I roll it all together, distil it one more time? I can make it take a new shape – the very essence of what the elders have given us.

What if I were to hurl it up in the air? Come on, Ganesh, my friend, where does the circle begin?

It is but a question of survival, survival of the fittest. Run, jump, swim, dance, skip. Walk the earth, walk the hills. Breathe deep, inhale the pure air. Eat pure food, the fruit of the earth, the peach of immortality. Drink. Good health, long life. A little of everything: moderation in all. Early to bed, early to rise. See the sun. Be inspired. Create. Work hard, never retire. Make progress every day. Be a leading model in your living. Be more thorough. Learn the correct manner. Honesty and harmony. Give up anger, learn to forgive. Be kind, welcoming, hospitable. Do not fear. Follow truth. Live without violence. Live in humility. No man or woman is superior or inferior to any other. Human nature is stronger than any government. Love your country. Never give up. Decide what you want and don't be deflected. Hitch your wagon to a star, follow the gleam. Pursue your vision. Be optimistic, adaptable, flexible. Be centiose. Be born again. Teach your children to learn. The elder is your shield. May you live in a house where there are old people to give wise advice and where there are young people to listen. Act when you are young. See the world. Be a storyteller. Laugh till you cry. Laugh till the day you die. Let there be music, always music. Sing with a glad heart. Don't worry about a thing. Live in friendship. Union. Love. Love your fellow man. Love God. You are before, You are after, You are for ever. Remember it is God who has made us and not we ourselves. Love life. God is life. God is spirit. The more you love the more your eyes will weep. When a man weeps for sublime things, the stars in the sky will be shining. And that moment when the stars come out, remember you are not alone. Believe. Believe in miracles. Believe in angels. Believe in magic, spirits, good and bad. Beware the evil eye. Look into the eyes of the lunatic. Go in search of your master. Seek beauty, peace, harmony and balance. Walk on, in peace. Don't be sneaky. Don't be a liar. Don't be lazy. Don't be a thief. Give. Be of service. Be self-sufficient. Husband your resources. *Vishwabandhuttwa*. We are one . . .

Here in my room, the day is turning to gold as I tread these last steps.

Each day now, I am learning to live as if I shall live to be a hundred. And yet, I try to live each day as if I may die tomorrow.

I have my answer. I can say that I believe. Life. My God is life. There is a force, this creative energy inside us, with us, all around. I know it now. I can feel it. Be still and feel it.

One day, what seems a very long time ago, I put my trust in life. Who would have guessed that this is where I would end up?

Now, as I hear my grandfather calling, I turn back once more to my work.

I have everything I need – the love of my beautiful wife and the music that is my daughter's laughter, her silly words.

Author's Note

None of this would have been possible without the help of a great many people all over the world.

First, I salute the old men and women who we were honoured to meet. They gave so willingly of their time and energy. Their families were more than generous with their hospitality.

We found them and were able to talk with them through the assistance of numerous friends, contacts and interpreters. I would like to extend our thanks to: Mike Hopkins, David and Elinor Johnson, Flemming Axmark, Ingrid Jungkvist, Anna Novikova, Masha Fedorova, Dr Vladislav Bezrukov, Maya Tourta, the Institute of Gerontology – Kiev, Maria Trkala, László Rusvai, Julia Kudlik, Miloš Ruppeldt, Oldo Hlavaček, Richard Moore, Hüseyin of Marmaris, Hisham Kassem, Peter Walker, the Nanyuki Cottage Hospital, Dwijendra Joshi, Hilal Suleiman, David and Veronica Zausmer, Nessie Semba, the Great Britain–China Centre, the Chinese People's Association for Friendship with Foreign Countries, Zhang Jingua, Lu Yanxia, Sam Morimoto, Yamanashi International Association, Kazuo Tsuyuki, Kimberly Hauser, Hiraga Associates International Inc., Nagoya International Association, Toshi Asawaka, Dr Hiroshi Shibata, the Tokyo Metropolitan Institute of Gerontology, John Brunton, Ameneh Azam Ali, Mansoor Khan, Shah Ghazi, the Aga Khan Rural Support Programme, Amrik Singh, Harendra Upadhyaya, Asri Ghafar, I Wayan Tapiep, Elaine McTaggart, Terry Lane, Brenda of Window Rock, Richard Begay, Colette du Toit, the University of Georgia, Leslie Lawhorn, Denise Horton, Valarie Wilson, Christopher Kennedy, Owen and Stephanie Stevens, Clara de Puyo, Maria del Carmen Ramos, Clementina Méndez, Marcia Paz Campero, Lizz Gauvreau, Ivan Moseley, Luis Calderon Calderon, Pedro Pablo de la Peña, Leonor Loyola, Maria del Carmen Manrique de Lara, Laure Meuzy and Liz O'Hara-Boyce.

I would like to thank the family of Bo Höglund for allowing me to use the extract from his letter to the Travellers' Club of Malmö.

Mrs Dipali Ghosh translated Mansang Velji's poem; Rob and Beatriz Poynton helped me with the translation of Paula's riddle, for which many thanks.

I couldn't have written the chapter on Bali without reference to Miguel Covarrubias' excellent book, *Island of Bali* (Oxford University Press, Singapore, 1987).

The insight into the *dolgozhiteli* of the Caucasus was provided by various research reports shown to us by Vladislav Bezrukov. I was unable to note fully the sources, though I do know that the story of the infamous curse is attributable to a poet called Gamzatov.

I have made every effort to verify the spelling of words, names and places, which were sometimes scribbled down for me in my notes. I can only apologize if any are wrong.

The photographs were taken on a Nikon F3, an FM2 and occasionally a Contax T2. Colour film was Fuji Velvia; black and white was Ilford FP4. I developed the latter myself in a bizarre assortment of bathrooms, often under arduous climatic conditions. Colour processing and printing was by Team, 37 Endell Street, London WC2. My thanks go to Hugh McDermott for his invaluable help.

I wish to thank Mark Lucas, my agent, for his vision, inspiration and encouragement. I wish to thank Humphrey Price at Victor Gollancz for his enthusiasm and careful guidance.

Thank you to those who were brave enough to read the first drafts for me: my mother, my father, Felicity Jackson, Philip Sherwood, Teresa Murphy, Vivien Sheldon, Nick Hopewell-Smith. Veronica Zausmer receives a special commendation for coaching me so patiently in the early days.

Our heartfelt gratitude will ever be due to Rafael de la Fuente, the doctors and staff of Hospital de Clínicas Caracas, and to Alejandro Graterol and his family.

My mother and my father have been constant in their love and with their help throughout. I can't thank them enough.

And finally, the biggest thank you of all goes to Vanella, for her eternal love and support – not only as we travelled, but especially while I have been writing. This is her book too.

Andrew Jackson
Chiswick, September 1998